Marxist
interpretation
— for a change!

UNEQUAL UNION

CANADA 1871

Greenland

Nfld.

P.E.I.

N.B. N.S.

Quebec

Ontario

North-West Territories

Manitoba

British Columbia

U.S.A.

Alaska

Unequal Union

Roots of Crisis in the Canadas, 1815-1873

Stanley B. Ryerson

Progress Books, 1975

Books by
S. B. RYERSON
1837: The Birth of Canadian Democracy (1937)
(out of print)
French Canada: A Study in Canadian Democracy (1943)
Le Canada français: sa Tradition, son Avenir (1945)
A World to Win (1946, 1950)
(out of print)
The Founding of Canada: Beginnings to 1815 (1960, 1963)
The Open Society: Paradox and Challenge (1965)
Unequal Union (1968)
Unequal Union: Confederation and the Roots of Conflict
in the Canadas 1815-1873 (First edition 1968)
Unequal Union: Roots of Crisis in the Canadas 1815-1873
(Second edition 1973)
Second edition 1973: Paperback ISBN 0-919396-17-8
Clothbound ISBN 0-919396-18-6

Third Printing

Library of Congress Catalogue Card Number: 73-76035

Ouvrage publié à l'occasion du Centenaire de la Confédération Canadienne, et rédigé grâce à une subvention de la Commission du Centenaire.

Published on the occasion of the Centennial of Canadian Confederation. The preparation of the manuscript was subsidized by the Centennial Commission.

TO MILDRED

PREFATORY NOTE TO THE SECOND EDITION

In the course of re-working the book for an up-dated French-language edition, in the midst of the Québec events of the early 1970s, I have felt the need for either some recasting of parts of the argument, or else for a sort of meditative sequel. Circumstances of work, however, compel me to defer the latter and to limit the extent of the former. Hence, apart from a few corrections in points of detail I have made only two changes of substance. One involved an error in the discussion of Reciprocity (p. 236); I am indebted to Frank W. Park for pointing it out. The other had to do with bi-national political equality, 1848 and responsible government (concluding part of chapter 8).

The main burden of the argument of *Unequal Union* I believe has been confirmed by much of what has happened since the mid-1950s when the research and writing of it began. Some of the aspects of continuity are suggested in a paper written in the summer of 1970 and presented to the International Sociology Congress of that year. A more recent, post-October 1970 treatment appears in an essay on class in the symposium-volume on *Capitalism and the National Question* (ed. G. Teeple, U. of T. Press, 1972).

It is the interweaving of two historic processes, the one proceeding from the British Conquest and its aftermath, the other from the pattern assumed by the Industrial Revolution in its penetration of colonial British America, that set the terms for today's dilemma. They have been modified by the U.S. take-over, but not removed; rather, intensified. The intersecting issues of class and national self-determination persist, and neither the existing state-structure nor the class society of which it is the political expression can indefinitely resist the pressures for change.

Département d'histoire,   S.B.R.
Université du Québec à Montréal

Preface

This book, a sequel to THE FOUNDING OF CANADA: *Beginnings to 1815*, completes an outline sketch of some of the driving forces that brought into being our present economic and political structure. As indicated in a foreword to the earlier book, what I have undertaken is not by any means a comprehensive coverage but only "a preliminary breaking of ground, suggesting a line of approach to a re-interpretation of this country's history." The period covered embraces the origins of capitalist industry, the revolutionary prelude to the ascent to power of a class of Canadian businessmen, the emergence of the class of industrial wage-earners, the relationships of French-Canadian and English-speaking Canadian national communities. In dealing with these, I present rather a series of studies than an exhaustive narrative or analysis. It is my hope that the work will incite further exploration on the part of others; as well as making some contribution to the eventual production of a full-scale, "three-dimensional" history such as can do justice to social structure and national realities. It is an exhilarating sign of our times of change, not only that work is being done on hitherto untouched or largely neglected areas of our social past and present, but that there is growing recognition of the significance of *class* and *nation* in Canadian development. These at times find astonishing expression in the discourse of our early protagonists of reaction and democracy: which is not the least of my reasons for citing them in their own words wherever possible. (Present-day authorities are cited mainly on points of controversy.)

In the sixteen years of intermittent research for this book and its predecessor I piled up a debt of assistance rendered by a very large number of co-workers and friends. Rather than attempting to catalogue it in detail, I can only acknowledge the debt with deep-felt and all-embracing thanks to all who helped. In a few cases I have been able to allude in reference or footnotes to particular acts of assistance. Special mention, however, must be made of the kindness of Professor George Rudé, of the University of Adelaide, Australia, who placed at my disposal his file of material on the *Patriotes* transported to Van Diemen's Land. I also gratefully acknowledge the assistance of the Public Archives of Canada and the National Gallery, la Bibliothèque de l'Assemblée Législative du Québec and its director, M. Charles Bonenfant, la Bibliothèque Saint-Sulpice and the Collection Gagnon de la Bibliothèque Municipale de Montréal, the Toronto Public Library and the Library of the University of Toronto. My acknowledgments are due likewise to other institutions and individuals, as credited in reference notes or in the text. For the design of the book I am deeply indebted to the late Carl Dair, who also designed THE FOUNDING OF CANADA.

I am grateful to the Centennial Commission for its grant in aid of publication, and for its patience with my slowness (the MS was submitted by September 1, 1967, but editing and work on production extended beyond the year's end).

The contemporary issues—to which, I trust, the present study offers a background of some relevance—promise to hold the anxious attention of Canadians and *Canadiens* (or *Québecois*), at least for the decade to come: may these pages make some contribution to a sense of direction as well as of urgency in both "the Canadas."

Contents

Credits: 1. Reproduced by courtesy of the National Gallery of Canada.
2. J. Bouchette: *The British Dominions in North America*
(1832). 3a. H. Y. Hind and others: *The Dominion of Canada* (1868). 3b. M. Macfie: *Vancouver Island and British
Columbia* (1865). 4a, b; 5a, b; 6b, 7, 8: *Canadian Illustrated
News*, courtesy of the Toronto Public Library. 6a. *Le Canadien*, courtesy of Gagnon Collection, Bibliothèque Municipale de Montréal.

PROLOGUE

Prologue:

Divergent Angles of Vision

In October 1806 John Black, former Quebec shipyard owner and member of the colonial Assembly, now residing in Paul St., Finsbury Square, London, penned for consideration of the King's ministers certain "Observations on the Government and Politics of Canada." Twenty years' residence in Canada had convinced him as to "the impossibility the Country can prosper under the present constitution."

This was the constitution established by Act of 1791; it provided for an elective assembly and an appointive executive, and had been accompanied by the administrative division of the old "Province of Quebec" (the former New France) into Upper and Lower Canada. In John Black's opinion, the resulting form of government was doubly flawed. Not only were the "lower orders" represented in the Assembly to an undue, disturbing degree; but the English governing and mercantile interest found themselves regularly faced in the Lower Canada Assembly with a French majority. True, the men of means were a minority, and the English were a minority (and they were largely the same minority); but why should it be made so difficult for them to rule? Black described the dilemma thus:

> The House of Assembly of Lower Canada is composed of Fifty Members, and notwithstanding the Government and Commerce of the Colony are in the hands of the Eng-

lish, still at the General Elections British influence can
never get more than *Twelve Members* returned who have
to contend with the passions and prejudices of *Thirty-
eight* French; the majority of whom are by no means the
most respectable of the King's Canadian subjects.

As a result of a lamentably broad electoral franchise
(£5 to £10 income in the towns of Quebec and Montreal,
£2 property in the counties), the elective system, he
observes, produces a socially distressing outcome: instead
of enlisting "the Sense and Education of the Country"
it "draws forth a majority of the most inflamed of the
worser order." In what way, under a system of representative government, the interests of the men of property
may be protected against encroachments by "the mob,"
is already problem enough; but here the social question
is aggravated by that of nationality. The result, Black
laments, is that in electoral contests, "the nefarious and
the Political Bankrupt, the Demagogue and the insiduous
and Ambitious title of Friend of the People are all united
in the Same Person, which makes the Country ring
throughout into the word 'don't vote for an English-Man',
don't vote for a 'Seignior', a 'Merchant', a 'Judge' or a
'Lawyer', all of whom are represented to have an interest
in Taxing and oppressing the poor . . ."

John Black's "Observations" show that within a few
years of the granting of elective institutions to the Canadas both the *national* question and the *class* question had
made their presence felt. How to maintain British ascendancy over a Canadian French majority population in the
St. Lawrence valley; how to ensure that, in the face of a
democratic opposition, the interest of the ruling mercantile-seigneurial minority should prevail in shaping policy:
these perplexing questions cried out for an answer. Mr.
Black's suggested solution was but one of many put for-

ward: not particularly memorable, perhaps, but among
the earliest, and notable rather for its spirit (which was
typical) than for its detail. If it was the case that democracy imperilled the mercantile interest, there could be no
doubt as to which would have to give ground; let the
property qualification for Members of the Assembly be
established "to the extent of at least *one hundred and
fifty pounds* per annum in landed property, or a permanent Salary to that amount." Lengthen the life-span of
the Assembly, in the hopes of reducing the opportunity
of election of undesirables: "Make the Parliament sit for
seven years in lieu of four years" — whereby "the evil of
being obliged to provide for such scrambling Demagogues
will more seldom occur."

As for the problem posed by the presence in the province of a French-Canadian majority, it could perhaps be
circumvented thus (emphasis mine) :

> *Unite the Provinces of Upper and Lower Canada* if it
> conveniently can be done, if not erect eight new Counties
> on the three Million acres of Land recently granted who
> would bring the English considerably nearer the French
> in point of Number . . .

"Unite the Provinces," as a contrivance to strengthen
the electoral position of the British element: this was
later not to be the *whole* argument for eventual union of
the scattered colonies (the British minority would moreover, in time, become a majority) — but in the eyes of
French Canadians it loomed very large indeed; and the
events of the half-century or so that followed the writing
of John Black's "Observations" were hardly such as to
dissipate the suspicion.

The colonial condition cannot have looked or felt the

same for members of the two communities. True, both British and French communities were colonies of settlement; each was in a sense a "fragment" that had broken away from an old-established European community. Each embodied a break and a continuity with the culture and tradition of its "old country." The very fact of emigration involved a rejection: because the departure either was in response to an economic coercion — dispossession of peasants or yeomen, unemployment of workers — or arose from voluntary choice in a search for betterment. Yet the emigrants preserved a continuity of attachment, a sense of identification, with the national homeland — to be transmuted in the new environment. Both groups had to contend with the rigors of North American existence, and undergo the consequences of imperial rule exercised from overseas. These points of likeness provided some basis for a common interest to emerge. But there was, as well, the difference.

As the traveller Joseph Sansom noted in 1817, "English Canada, and French Canada, are two different things." "Different" not least, inasmuch as the British presence was the consequence of conquest. The Seven Years War that ended with the cession of New France had been but the most recent clash in an ancient contest that had pitted English against French from the days of Crécy and Agincourt. Resumed in North America, the struggle bore the imprint of the different stages of socio-economic evolution of the two metropolitan societies from which the respective colonies derived. A time-lag of a century and a half between the English and the French revolutions entailed both an earlier growth of industry in Britain and a more advanced economy in its Atlantic colonies than in New France.

Thus the colonial condition of the King's "new subjects" (those acquired by the Treaty of Paris) was that of inhabitants of an occupied country: their identity and survival as a community were in suspense. On the other hand, the British settlers in the North American provinces were colonists with a difference: they were co-heirs to a conquest. Their Britishness was not only a mark of identification with a great empire; it was an assurance of superiority vis-à-vis the conquered French. This illusion (from vestiges of which English Canada has yet wholly to liberate itself) was nurtured by the very character of colonialism. The state structure brought into being by the Conquest placed political power in the hands of British military administrators; it made possible the assumption of economic supremacy by British mercantile capitalists, who within a quarter century of Wolfe's victory took possession of the fur trade, fisheries and timber trade that French entrepreneurs had built up under the old régime. The French presence in the structure of political and economic rule was limited to the assisting role of a handful of clerical-seigneurial collaborators. The community was, in fact, a subject nation.

What it felt like to be in the position of colonials subjected within their own land to national inequality, is suggested by some verses that were published in one of the earliest numbers of the first French-Canadian opposition newspaper, *Le Canadien* (December 20, 1806):

Les Moissonneurs

Faucille en main, au champ de la Fortune,
On voit courir l'Anglois, le Canadien;
Tous deux actifs et d'une ardeur commune,
Pour acquérir ce qu'on nomme du bien;

Mais en avant l'Anglois ayant sa place,
Heureux Faucheur il peut seul moissonner,
L'autre humblement le suivant à la trace,
Travaille autant et ne fait que glaner.*

If the French and English angles of vision were (and
have remained) so different, what of that of the peoples
who came to America perhaps two hundred centuries
before the European invasion—those whose ancient society
was encroached upon, disrupted and degraded by the
incursion of a vast and alien commercial piracy?

Silence. The answer is unrecorded. Only remembered
deeds of long-past defiance, the Iroquois wars of resistance, Pontiac's "conspiracy," speak of Indian refusal in
the face of fate.

What for the Europeans was the gradual growth of
settlement, economic expansion, material success, was for
the Indian peoples a slow contraction of their country,
social disintegration, a growing subjugation and the
erosion of hope.

This too is one of the dimensions of colonialism. Like
the others it asserts the stubborn, continuing past, alive
in our present experience.

The communities of which we have been speaking—
Indian, French-Canadian, British colonial settlers — are
identifiable as entities possessing certain characteristics
in common. They have in varying measure the character

---

*Le Canadien is of course the Canadian whose language is French.
The verses should be of interest to people who claim to see in
French-Canadian nationalism a recent and artificial creation of con-
temporary politics, dating from perhaps—1960. (Cf. D. G. Creighton,
"The Hoax of Bi-culturalism," Saturday Night, Sept. 1966.)

For translation of verses cf. Reference Notes.

"New York" - based Iroquois waged a war of aggression
against "Quebec" settlers and their Native friends (Hurons,

of peoples, of distinct national communities. The national factor is a reality, operative and influencing relationships: those of Indian people to the usurpers of their homeland; the relations between French Canadians and the conquering British; and those of both European groups toward the Indian. Yet important as is the fact of national identity and difference, it is not the prime mover. It cannot provide the explanation for the dynamic of social change either within the community, or on the scale of relations among peoples. Attempts at explanation solely in terms of nation or race end up in a reactionary mysticism whose unfailing (if tacit) premise is the alleged innate superiority of the exponent's own race or nation.

Why *were* these communities juxtaposed to one another in the northern half of North America at the close of the 18th century? The answer of necessity leads us to consider the character of the epoch: that of the mercantile-colonial empires built by West European powers as part of the process of establishing a new socio-economic formation, "business society," capitalism, in place of the feudal system that had prevailed in the Middle Ages. Renaissance and Reformation, age of discovery and piracy and colonial plantation, English and French Revolutions, Industrial Revolution: four centuries of upheaval and social transformation, in the course of which the village market grew into the world market, the old reigning aristocracy of landowners gave way to the new ruling class of merchants, factory-owners, bankers—businessmen.

The British colonies in North America in the period we are considering are situated historically in an age of transition: the Reform Bill of 1832 and the triumph of Free Trade in the 1840s will mark the passage in Britain from the dominance of an alliance of landowners and great merchants to that of the new industrial bourgeoisie.

xx There was a difference between the French way and the English way of treating the Nations

(Gaspuin, etc)

Colonies established under the aegis and (in part) in
the image of the former, exposed to and involved in the
upheaval attendant on the Industrial Revolution, will
emerge from frontier agrarian backwardness, give battle
for self-government and in some queer way at last par-
tially achieve it—just as the new industrial masters of the
"world's workshop" are embarking on a fresh phase of
empire-building, the prelude to the imperialism of the
century to follow.

The interaction of world context and local-colonial
experience; of changes in the means and relations of production and the position of the colonial communities; of
social, class factors and national identities: all of this
finds expression in the labor and collective effort, the
conflict and struggle and compromise that pervade the
lives of the inhabitants of British North America in the
years between the War of 1812 and the enactment of
Confederation.

The sense in which the terms "class" and "nation" are
used in this study requires a word of explanation. Both
words are bedevilled these days not only by the ambigui-
ties and multiple meanings that are the normal accompaniment of the customary evolution of language, but also
by the overtones of conflicting ideologies. My concern is
not to claim exemption from a point of view (such claims,
no matter how sincerely advanced, are a delusion) but to
be understood; and for this, there has to be consistency
in the use of terms.

By social *class*, then, is meant a definite group of persons occupying in the social order a position that is determined by their relationship (as owners or non-owners) to
the means of producing wealth. Slave-owner and slave,
feudal overlord and serf, factory-owner and hired wage-

earner, all are historical examples of such groups. Thanks to a certain form of ownership (slaveholding, feudal tenure, capitalist proprietorship) one group is able to appropriate the fruits of the labor of the other.

The growth in productivity of labor (leading to the attainment of a surplus of goods) made class society possible. A large number of working producers (slaves, serfs, wage-workers) are able to support by their labor a minority made up of owners: "Men at work" maintain the men of property. The particular historical arrangement in terms of property and servitude is what distinguishes one social system from another. The fact that in society (as in nature) there are no "pure" phenomena, that there are innumerable shadings of difference and variation, does not by any means exclude such basic cleavages and polarizations as those between capital and labor. (Latent and "unnoticed," these come forcibly to the surface when the underlying conflict of class interest erupts, as in a strike or lock-out.)

Thus classes are an objectively existing, materially-based social reality. They are not mere statistical abstractions, dwelling only in the subjective view of the observer; nor are they just a matter of "attitudes" or "behavior" or "status-consciousness" on the part of individuals.* The social, class structure exists and evolves independently of the individual consciousness. The antagonism and conflict of ruling and ruled, exploiting and exploited classes was known and recognized as a fact of history long before Marx and Engels offered for the first time a scientifically grounded explanation of it in terms of relations and forces

---

*This subjective or metaphysical-idealist conception of social class is widely held: cf. John Porter, Introduction to *The Vertical Mosaic* and E. Bjarnason's criticism of this view in *The Marxist Quarterly* (No. 16); and H. Aptheker, *The World of C. Wright Mills.*

of production, socio-economic formations or systems, and the revolutionary process of their replacement one by another. In this process, possession of *state-power* is crucial. The state ("bodies of armed men and prisons," in Engels' phrase) is the apparatus of coercion on which a socially and economically dominant class relies in the last resort in order to maintain its rule.

In dealing with social systems, property and class relationships, we disregard ethnic differences and identities. Yet interwoven with the social-economic arrangements are the equally real relationships of the tribe, people, nationality, nation. The community possesses not only social structure but ethnicity. Efforts to understand what this latter involves are made difficult by the fact that the term "nation" is used in two quite different senses, in French as well as in English. Each sense is perfectly legitimate, but failure to clarify the difference between the two, and a perpetual tendency to mix up the two usages, results in endless confusion. Here they are:

A. According to one meaning, the nation is an independent country, a sovereign state: e.g., the United States or, in the case of one country's evolution, "Canada—colony to nation." The focus is on the state, and not on the ethnic character of its population. The adjective *national* refers to things pertaining to that state, and *nationality* is the condition of citizenship or adherence to the state in question. This may be called the juridical sense of the word "nation." A recent example of this usage: ". . . the nation is a group of human beings, culturally homogeneous or otherwise, who live on a territory defined by the same borders and subject to the same political system."

B. According to the other meaning, a nation is an ethnic community with certain specific characteristics; and such a community may exist whether or not it possesses its own state structure. Thus in the 19th century the Polish nation, with its lands partitioned among three different states—Prussia, Austria, Russia—fought to achieve independent statehood.

The specific features of the nation as a socio-ethnic community include the following: a common *language* (this is its most specific trait: if all the world's peoples had spoken a single language the "national question" would hardly have arisen in the form we have known it); a common *territory* and *economic life*, which are the material bases for the cohesion and integration necessary to existence as a national community; and, arising on the foundation of all these, a common *culture* and sense of identity.

In this view, the nation is (like the class) a materially-based social entity: it is not merely a subjective phenomenon, a "will to live in common," a "national spirit." National consciousness, national sentiment, are the product and expression of the historical emergence and experience of the nation. The striving of the nation to achieve a politically independent existence, to establish its own state, appears as the "normal" accompaniment of its development. And the struggle for self-determination often leaves its imprint on the national character.

The formation of nations was both an extended historical process and one that (in the West at least) was linked with a definite era: that of the passage from feudal to capitalist society. For the scattered, isolated tribes and peoples to become fused into cohesive national communities required the role of the market, the rise of towns, the leadership of the trading and industrial bourgeoisie. It is no accident that the struggles to establish national states largely coincided with the struggle for power waged by the ascendant bourgeoisie—from the 16th century Dutch wars

of independence to the 19th century unification movements in Italy and Germany.

The nation may or may not manage to secure a state of
its own. Three main variants in the process may be distinguished:

The "classical" solution has been the achievement of a
nation-state, i.e., the independent statehood of one national community: the French, or Italian, or German
state, for instance. (Never in "pure" form, however: the
Bretons and Basques in France, the Basques and Catalans
in Spain, are examples of persisting small national communities within what are essentially nation-states.)

The alternative solution, that of a *multinational* state,
has occurred particularly where there was a marked inequality of development as between the communities involved, often with persistence of feudal relations in one
and developed capitalist relations in another of the con-
tiguous national communities. The Hapsburg and Russian Empires of the last century, Belgium, the United
Kingdom, Switzerland, Czechoslovakia, Canada, are examples of such multinational (or binational) states.

A third pattern is that of the present-day emergence of
nations in continents previously held in thrall by Western business imperialism: Africa and large parts of Asia.
Here, as Jean Chesneaux has pointed out, the process is
often far more complex than was the case in Europe; the
interaction of nation-forming and state-forming is often
different (the role of state independence as a factor in consolidating a national community); and the anti-imperialist
struggle plays an extremely important part in the emergence and character of the new nation. He refers for
example to the controversy over the date of formation of
the Vietnamese nation:

> For some, it dates from the departure of the Chinese in
> the 10th century; for others, it was formed under the Lê

dynasty (15th-18th centuries), at the latest at the time of
the great national insurrection of the Tyson (1772-1802)
which is its political expression (unifying the country hitherto divided among rival seigneuries, replacing Chinese
with Vietnamese as the language of administration, etc.)
Others emphasize the consolidation of the different constituent elements of the Vietnamese nation within the framework of the colonial regime and in the course of the actual
struggle of the Vietnamese people against it . . . Still
others, finally, consider that the Vietnamese nation is fully
constituted only with the insurrection of August 1945 and
the restoration of Vietnamese independence after eighty
years of foreign domination.

For those who are acquainted with the current debates
over the date of origin of the French-Canadian nation
(and also that of the "Canadian nation" which is English-
speaking) the foregoing will strike a familiar chord.

In this view, history is made by people acting, collec-
tively and as individuals, in three intersecting areas of
social being: that of the "metabolism" of man and nature,
with man gradually (and latterly with growing accelera-
tion) extending his mastery of natural forces, multiplying
the productivity of labor, creating new technologies; that
of class antagonism and conflict, rooted in social and economic contradictions, posing with mounting insistency
the necessity of resolving the dilemma of social labor versus private appropriation; and (partly as a function of the
foregoing yet with a certain autonomous logic of its own)
the area of relations between national communities, the
tensions and conflicts born of oppression of one people by
another, and the urge to banish inequality, to break
through to the "republic of man," the world community.
It is the action of human beings that determines the
course of history. Yet this history is more than the simple

arithmetical sum of billions of individual biographies. It
is in the context of an evolving social existence that individual decisions, initiatives, mistakes, achievements, occur
and in varying degree are meaningful. In the interaction
of the social setting and the individual, the former has
priority—but not that of an absolute power. The view that
"man's affairs are settled by ineluctable, impersonal, and
calculable forces" to the exclusion of "human beings—uncertain, personal and incalculable"— is not Marxism, but
a mechanistic determinism. Marx and Engels rejected the
idea of history as a kind of metaphysical "person apart,"
for whom "mankind is a mere *mass* bearing with it a varying degree of consciousness or unconsciousness . . . *History*
does *nothing*, it 'possesses *no* immense wealth,' it 'wages
no battles.' It is *man*, real living man, that does all that,
that possesses and fights; 'history' is not a person apart,
using man as a means for *its own* particular aims; history
is *nothing but* the activity of man pursuing his aims."

It is with this approach to the historical process that
some facets of the background of the 1867 Confederation
are explored in what follows.

PART ONE

REVOLT AGAINST COLONIALISM

1

Roots of Conflict in Lower Canada

For a quarter of a century after the War of 1812 the
British colonies in North America were the scene of
acute class and national conflicts. During the War, in
the face of invasion, the internal struggle had been thrust
into the background; now, with the danger removed, it
flared afresh. The men who had fought at Stoney Creek
and Châteauguay were less than ever inclined to put up
with an arbitrary and irresponsible government. The
settlers' grievances expressed not only vexation over
abuses, but the pressure of productive forces striving for
growth, held back by fetters of vested property and privilege. A native capitalist industry was in the making;
but landlordism and colonial rule lay athwart its path.
The settlers in the colonial provinces carried on a stubborn, many-sided struggle against the local oligarchy of
landowners, merchants and officials, and against the
oppressive rule of the British Colonial Office. This struggle
embraced practically every aspect of life in the Canadas:
the land question (land monopoly and feudalism); freedom of trade and manufacture, native industry and
capitalist development; political democracy; national self-
determination in French Canada; and Canadian independence.

As in the other colonies, the land question occupied
a central place in the social and political conflict in
Lower Canada. Over two million acres were the property

of the Catholic Church, and some six million in the hands of the seigneurs. A letter published in the newspaper of the revolutionary democrats of Lower Canada, the *Minerve*, of March 9, 1837, referred to "the frightful picture of feudal oppression." Its victims were "the farmers who can have no land without submitting to revolting conditions of servitude, corvées, arbitrary rents, rights of 'lods et ventes', new titles, banal rights, reservation (by the seigneur) of wood, waters, fishing, hunting, minerals, lime, stone, sand, etc." Another correspondent queried: "What use is there in going to court with the seigneur? he is richer than we, and will end by ruining us utterly." Wrote Durham, two years later: "There is every reason to believe that a great number of the peasants who fought at St. Denis and St. Charles, imagined that the principal result of success would be the overthrow of tithes and feudal burthens."

The "feudal burthens" in French Canada had been more firmly fastened, following the British Conquest and the Quebec Act. They had been envenomed further still by what Durham referred to as the "intrusion of the English": "By degrees, large portions of land were occupied by them; nor did they confine themselves to the unsettled and distant country of the townships. The wealthy capitalist invested his money in the purchase of seigneurial properties; and it is estimated, that at the present moment fully half of the more valuable seigneuries are actually owned by English proprietors." Simon Mc-Tavish, of the North-West Company, who got hold of the seigneury of Terrebonne, north of Montreal, was one example.

But if alien ownership of the seigneuries was a source of bitterness, the brazen handing over of huge expanses of unsettled land to companies of London speculators became one of the prime causes of revolt. A mass meeting in St. Charles parish in 1832 protested against "an attempt recently made by the ministry, to grant to a company of rich capitalists, strangers to the interests of the country, the concession of a very large portion of the uncultivated lands of the crown, without consulting the colonial legislature, which, by its constitution, ought alone to have the government of those lands . . ."

In 1833 the "attempt" became reality: some 850,000 acres in the Eastern townships were granted to the British American Land Company (one sixth of its shares being reserved for inhabitants of the colony "in the event that any of them should choose to become stockholders in it"). In the summer of 1834 the Convention of the Patriotes of the Montreal district adopted resolutions "condemnatory of the alienation of the public property of this Province to a company of foreign speculators, without the consent, and against the will of the people, whose property the lands in question were . . ."

Thus did the system of land-monopoly lie like a log-jam athwart the path of economic advance. Among what Durham spoke of as the "deep-seated impediments in the way of industrial progress," outstanding was "the possession of almost the whole soil . . . by absentee proprietors, who would neither promote nor permit its cultivation, combined with the defective government which first caused and has since perpetuated the evil."

As the Quebec *Canadien* put it: "We pay tribute yearly to the gods of Great Britain, and the Capital which, expended amongst us, could have encouraged the arts, science and industry, is wholly lost and swallowed up in the treasury of our lofty masters and overlords, the Canada Land companies."

The land monopoly and seigneurial tenure impeded

settlement, the spread of communications and the growth
of a home market, and blocked the path of capitalist
development. Not without reason did the Assembly of
Lower Canada in 1836 point to the direct connection
between the handing over of immense expanses of land
to London speculators and "the system of Metropolitan
ascendancy and Colonial Degradation."

Two things are worth noting at this point. One is the
interweaving of merchant-capitalist and landowning interests: the growing penetration of investment capital into
the seigneurial structure, with attendant pressure to trans-
form semi-feudal institutions into capitalist real-estate.
The other is the first signs of a *challenge* to the old
mercantile-seigneurial ruling group as a result of the beginnings of industrialism. Both these processes were directly related to the impact of the Industrial Revolution
in Britain. Both operated within the framework of colonialism: in the Canadas, the dominance of "the English"
was of the pattern of the Conquest; and industrialization,
far from weakening the dominance, reinforced it.

Capital—and wage labor: these were the key ingredients
in the new economic order launched by the technological
upheaval of the 1780s in Britain. Privately-owned factories using steam-driven machinery and employing hired
"hands": these were the end-product of a whole historical
epoch. What Marx spoke of as the "primitive accumulation of capital" was the dual process of piling-up money-
capital—e.g., through the robbery of native peoples in the
newly "discovered" continents (as in the exploitation of
Indian fur trappers, a transaction thinly disguised as
"trade")—and the dispossession of masses of peasants or
small producers, turning them into propertyless proletarians. "Labor," it was noted by a Select Committee on

Emigration in 1827, "is the article a poor man has to bring to market . . ." Labor-power had become a commodity.

The formidable expansion of production made possible by the Industrial Revolution brought with it a formidable expansion of profits. Accumulated as surplus capital, they sought an outlet. The capital "invested in colonial speculation," one authority argued in 1803, is that "which cannot find profitable employment at home." "Colonization," wrote John Stuart Mill somewhat later, "is the best affair of business in which the capital of an old and wealthy country can engage."

Accompanying a glut of capital was one of another kind. A writer on "The Means of Reducing the Poor Rates" argued in 1817 that with "a well-regulated system of colonization," "the glut of hands . . . (would be) removed from the labor market": such a "safety-valve" might avert "an explosion." Hopefully, he wrote, "want would cease to engender the desire of change; the ideas of relief and revolution would lose their fatal connection in the mind of the multitude . . ."

The mass export of surplus "hands" to the North American colonies provided one of the essential ingredients of a future industrialization. That it happened to coincide with a chronic crisis in the Lower Canada countryside, and agricultural over-population on the seigneuries, was to entail bitter consequences: the massive emigration of landless French Canadians south of the border, and a deepening of national resentments. The "shovelling out of paupers" from the British Isles continued throughout the 1820s and '30s.* The *Quebec Gazette* in 1831 spoke of

---

*The misery of the exported poor was compounded, in the summer of 1832, by the catastrophe of cholera. Brought in the immigrant ships from Britain, the disastrous epidemic swept the province, taking

their shipment up the St. Lawrence and journeying westward as "similar to the passage of an immense army,
much-exposed and ill-supplied, and leaving the inhabitants to take care of and provide for the sick, wounded
and disabled, and bury their dead."

For "systematic colonization" to produce industrial
growth in the colonies one major difficulty had to be overcome. *Availability of free land* stood in the way of turning poor settlers into wage-workers. Free land and wage
labor contradict each other: if one can have a farm or become a small craftsman on one's own, why work for some-
one else?

This difficulty greatly preoccupied the leading English
colonization theorist, E. C. Wakefield (author of *A View
of the Art of Colonization,* and *England and America;*
Marx examines his views in the concluding chapter of
Vol. I of *Capital*). Wakefield found that in the North
American settlements "a passion for owning land prevents
the existence of a class of laborers for hire. . . . Cheapness
of land is the cause of scarcity of labor for hire . . . Where
everyone who so pleases can obtain a piece of land for himself, not only is labor very dear, as respects the laborer's
share of the product, but the difficulty is to obtain combined labor at any price." Wakefield tells of "talking with
some capitalists of Canada and New York," who had
ready capital with which to start a business but, they lamented, "we could not begin such operations with labor,

---

in the space of a few months over 20,000 lives. A Patriote meeting
held in the Richelieu valley charged that "England will always be
held accountable for having permitted so extensive an emigration at a
time when it was under the dreadful influence of the cholera, which,
by this means, has been introduced into the colony the climate of
which was the most healthy in America, and which is now covered
with mourning and desolation."

which, we knew, would soon leave us." Even where capitalists import their own wage workers, these soon "cease ... to be laborers for hire; they become independent landowners, if not competitors with their former masters in the labor market." To which Marx appends the comment: "Think of the horror! The excellent capitalist has imported bodily from Europe, with his own good money, his own competitors! The end of the world has come!"

Somehow or other, the obstacle must be overcome. As one of Wakefield's followers put it, there must be found a way of meeting "the urgent desire for cheaper and more subservient laborers—for a class to whom the capitalist might dictate terms, instead of being dictated to by them. . . . In ancient civilized countries the laborer, though free, is by law of nature dependent on capitalists; in colonies this dependence must be created by artificial means." To extend the "Law of Nature" by artificial means to North America, all that was needed, seemingly, was to *incorporate land companies*, give them unsettled lands for speculation and profit—and thus a respectable number of immigrants would be kept in their "place"— in the ranks of the propertyless. The solution adopted was to charter the Canada Company (1825) and the British American Land Co., in Upper and Lower Canada, with some three million acres of land between them. These institutions were "aids to immigration" of a kind that lined the pockets of speculators, kept up the price of land, and ensured that a portion of the immigrant population should remain landless—and hence available for hire.

To those who objected that the artificial creation of land-monopolies would discourage settlement (and perhaps—as indeed occurred—add to the flow of migration to the United States), Lord Goderich replied in a dispatch in 1831 that he saw "no ground for such an apprehension." And he went on:

> Has it on the other hand been sufficiently considered by those who make that objection, whether it would conduce to the real prosperity of the province, to encourage every man who can labor to do so only on his own account, to obtain and cultivate his allotment of land without giving or receiving assistance from others? Without some division of labor, without a class of persons willing to work for wages, how can society be prevented from falling into a state of almost primitive rudeness, and how are the comforts and refinements of civilized life to be preserved?

"A class of persons willing to work for wages": this propertyless prerequisite of capitalism was indeed in the making; and the "comforts and refinements of civilized life" were to be preserved to those willing and able to extract profit from the employment of wage labor. The "division of labor" between owner and non-owner, between industrialist and factory hand, became possible only with the break-up of the old, self-sufficient, "natural economy" and with the spread of trade, the universalizing of commodity production to embrace labor power itself as a marketable item. This process was now under way on the St. Lawrence. It involved the gradual transformation of the way of life once general on the seigneuries, and still to prove remarkably resistant in large areas: the one described in 1827 by a French geographer, who wrote of the *habitant* farmers:

> They cultivate flax, and their sheep furnish them with the wool of which their garments are made; they tan the hides of their cattle and use them as moccasins or boots. The men knit their stockings and caps, and plait the straw hats that are worn by them in the summer season. They make, besides, their bread, butter, cheese, soap, candles,

and sugar; all of which are supplied from the produce of their lands. The farmers construct their carts, wheels, ploughs and canoes.

Trade in agricultural produce, the demands of war, and the growth of small-scale local industries, combined to break down the self-sufficient habitant-pioneer economy. The shift from fur trade to timber trade accelerated this process. Certainly, the loss to Montreal of its position as headquarters of the Northwest Company's western empire was a serious set-back to the rising Anglo-Canadian merchant bourgeoisie; but the swift expansion of the timber trade and ship-building, occasioned by the Napoleonic wars and the blockade of the Baltic, brought into being a new business élite. Although closely associated with the London and Liverpool shipping interests, the timber magnates (unlike the fur-barons, their predecessors) were operating actual industrial enterprises within the colony. The sawmills and logging camps and shipyards employed men from the farms and villages, as well as newly-landed immigrants. They enlarged the home market and at the same time stimulated further industrial beginnings. Bouchette, surveyor-general of Lower Canada, in 1830 refers to "the sawmills belonging to Mr. Papineau," which furnish "supplies of white and red pine deals and boards... for the markets of Montreal and Quebec." Between 1825 and 1840 the number of sawmills in the Canadas increased from 394 to 963. In 1821 a steam-driven sawmill had been put in operation in Saint John, N.B. A few years later, Bouchette tells us, the Queen's dockyard had "a spacious sawmill, with numerous sets of saws, worked with prodigious velocity by a steam-engine of considerable power."

Shipbuilding was an industry that had been established on a significant scale under the French régime. In addition to the yards at Quebec, others were in operation at

Sorel and, in 1806, at Montreal. On Nov. 8, 1809, this news item appeared in the *Quebec Gazette*:

"The Steam Boat, which was built at Montreal last winter, arrived here on Saturday last, being her first trip . . . 36 hours is the time which she takes from Montreal to Quebec." (The return journey took all of a week.) This was Molson's *Accommodation*, of forty tons, 85-foot length, propelled by "open double-spoked perpendicular wheels," her engine "made at the ancient works at Three Rivers . . ." "No wind or tide can stop her," marvelled the Quebec *Mercury*; the day following her arrival from Montreal "she went up against a wind and tide from Bréhaut's wharf to Lymburner's . . ." "She had berths for twenty passengers, but brought only ten to Quebec; the passage-money down was eight dollars, and up, nine dollars." Steam navigation had arrived, only two years later than in the U.S., and eight years after the first steamer on the Clyde. By the early 1830s, marine engines were being built at Montreal as well as at York, in Upper Canada.

An early factory in Montreal was the rope works, established in 1825. "Every description of cordage is manufactured here," writes the author of *Hochelaga Depicta* (1839) "on a patent method, by appropriate machinery. The quantity of hemp consumed is from 150 to 250 tons annually, employing from thirty-six to fifty hands . . . The walk is 1200 feet in length, the greater part two stories high, and another portion three stories. A new stone building has just been erected, to contain a steam-engine, giving motion to all the patent machinery for the manufacture of the different kinds of cordage, with additional apparatus for making ship blocks. The hemp used in these works is Russian, imported from England."

For industry to develop, iron was an indispensable base.

ON THE RIVER

The beginnings were painful and slow. The iron mines and forges (at) St. Maurice, above Three Rivers, had been sporadically started and stopped since the 1730s. After converting old ordnance into bar iron, just after the Conquest, and casting shot for the invading U.S. army that besieged Quebec in 1775, the works were turned to manufacturing such cast-iron products as stoves and kettles: "In 1831 the establishment consisted of every convenience, furnaces, forges, foundries, workshops, houses and other buildings. . . . Two hundred and fifty to three hundred men were employed in the works. Of these the overseers and employees in the model department were English and Scotch, and the unskilled workmen generally Canadians."

TODAY, A FEDERAL "PARK" CUM MUSEUM OPEN TO VISITORS

Capitalist industry in Lower Canada appears to have started developing in these years along three fairly distinct paths. One follows the line of growth of the timber trade: sawmills and shipyards are its focal points. A second, more directly an outgrowth of the industrial revolution in England, leads to the establishment of manufactories and machine shops. (The Molsons' making of ships' engines in Montreal is one example.) In both cases, it is English or Anglo-Canadian capitalists who are in command, while the work-force is French-Canadian, except for certain skilled tradesmen from Britain. A third line of growth, only weakly developed (and generally overlooked by present-day historians) is in the small-scale consumer-goods enterprises emerging in the towns and villages in response to the gradual extension of the domestic market. Here is the birth-place of a French-Canadian industrial bourgeoisie. The rising "middle class" in Lower Canada was not *only* made up of notaries, doctors, shopkeepers: it included a few manufacturers as well.

The village of St. Denis on the Richelieu offers an illustration of industrial beginnings under mainly French-Canadian leadership. A river port and district centre for the grain trade, Bouchette wrote of it in 1815: "Between the main street and the river are vast warehouses that serve chiefly as granaries, where a great quantity of the wheat from the adjacent seigneuries is stored for export, since the land for several leagues around is . . . the most fertile in grain in the whole Montreal district."

In addition to the usual village craftsmen (cobbler, carpenter, blacksmith, saddler) employing one or a few helpers, at St. Denis there were potteries which by 1837 had 20 kilns in operation. These still were small, individual establishments (later put out of business by competition from Montreal and St. Johns). In a different dimension was the hat manufactory established in 1825 by Charles St. Germain: employing thirty workers, it was the largest producer in this line in Canada, specializing in "beavers" (top hats). Another member of the family operated a carding mill. A distillery owned by Dr. Wolfred Nelson, Dr. Kimber and Louis Deschambault employed a dozen men. Ten or so worked at the carriage works of Francois Gadbois, whose products were sold at Quebec, in Montreal and in Upper Canada.

We have here the small beginnings of an indigenous industrial capitalism, based on the main agricultural area of Lower Canada.*

All three of these currents of incipient industrialism were subject to the restrictive conditions of a colonial-mercantile environment. Power in the colony was in the hands of a triple alliance of class forces, none of which was particularly interested in the growth of a native industry as such. Imperial advantage and imperial trade

---

*The Desjardins foundry at Rigaud is one other example among many: it enters historical record as a source of Patriote munitions.

were what concerned the British officials and the English-Canadian merchant-landowners; while their collaborators, the French-Canadian higher clergy and seigneurs, were committed to uphold the policies of the other two—the dominant—ruling groups. The forces of indigenous industrialism were thus to find themselves increasingly at odds with the imperial-mercantile framework whose chief upholders and beneficiaries were those leaders of the "commercial empire of the St. Lawrence" whom Fernand Ouellet lists as "importers, timber merchants, grain dealers, ship owners and bank shareholders . . ."* But long before an industrial capitalist class could take form, the issue of national equality and national rights had come to occupy the centre of the political stage in Lower Canada.

---

*For a comment on Professor Ouellet's somewhat Creightonesque interpretation, see "Postscript," below. He views the Montreal merchants as the bearers of capitalist progress and the Patriote movement as a reactionary obstacle to it. Hence the picture in Lower Canada is one of "conflicts between the capitalist classes and the liberal professions." The peculiarity of merchant's capital, its tendency to ally itself with feudal and colonialist forces in *opposition* to industrial capital is overlooked—with distressing results.

2

Democracy and Self-Determination

The colonial state structure brought into being by the Constitutional Act of 1791 answered the requirements of the local ruling merchant-landlord group and of the mercantile imperialists in Britain. It did not correspond to the needs of the local industrialists, or of the masses of settlers, censitaires, professionals and urban working people. The half-century of struggle for "responsible government" that ensued was the political expression of the contradiction between an expanding native capitalist industry and the restrictive bonds of merchant-colonial rule.

The Constitutional Act, reflecting the immediate influence of local pressures and, more broadly, that of the French Revolution, had granted an elective legislative assembly to Upper and to Lower Canada. It thereby did no more than concede to British subjects in North America rights acquired by Britons a century and a half earlier in the English Revolution. In the words of Lieutenant Governor Simcoe in 1792, the colonists were to enjoy "the very image and transcript of the Constitution of Great Britain." They took him at his word.

The claim that the Assembly in each province was, in effect, the counterpart of the "Commons" was raised at the second session of the Upper Canada Assembly (1793), when it successfully asserted the privilege of immunity from arrest for its members. Likewise, the Lower Canada Assembly through its speaker, J. A. Panet, claimed from the first "the freedom of speech and generally the immunities and liberties enjoyed by the Commons of Great Britain."

On the assumption that the representative institutions they had won were indeed such as they imagined them to be, the colonists expected that the decisions of the elected parliamentary majority would have the force of law, and that administrations would be formed which would be answerable to the peoples' representatives. They were in for a rude awakening. The administration, it turned out, was to be named by and answerable to the colonial Governor, without regard for the composition or desires of the Assembly; and the latter's legislation and decisions were to be wholly subject to the approval of the non-elective Legislative and Executive Councils. This, said the law officers of the Crown, was as it should be; for to endow a colonial assembly with the attributes of Parliament would be "to give subordinate bodies the mighty power of supremacy."

Durham, years later, expressed his astonishment at such an illogical mixture of "representative and irresponsible government" — "the combining of apparently popular institutions with an utter absence of all efficient control of the people over their rulers . . ." Yet from the point of view of the imperialists and their agents in the colonies, it was logical enough. The Governor ruled the colony on behalf of the imperial authorities; to exercise his rule he appointed an Executive satisfactory to himself; meanwhile, to satisfy popular pressure, there had to be an elective assembly—but the colonial government was not answerable to it, but to Downing Street.

Collision was thus inevitable between the appointed Executive and Legislative Councils on the one hand (representing the interests of the imperialist rulers and

the local merchant-landlord cliques) and the elected
Assemblies (representing the settlers and censitaires,
professionals and local industrialists). Between 1822 and
1836 the Legislative Council in Lower Canada threw out
234 bills passed by the Assembly; in Upper Canada, close
to 300 such bills were thrown out in the space of ten
years.

The demand for a "responsible" executive—responsible
for its actions to the elected representatives of the people
—was put forward in 1809 by Pierre Bédard in the Lower
Canada Assembly. Later, the "responsible government"
slogan became the rallying-cry of the Upper Canada reformers, while "an elective legislative council" became
that of their Lower Canadian and Maritime counterparts.
Both demands however in fact implied the supremacy of
the elected, representative body over appointed officials.

From the outset, the main bone of contention was control of the public purse. As early as 1793 the Lower Canada Assembly had asserted its right to initiate bills "having
as their effect the imposing of a burden upon the people."
In its turn, in 1806 the Upper Canada Assembly protested
against the expenditure of funds without its consent as a
violation of the "first . . . (and) most constitutional
of the privileges of the Commons."

Inseparable from the parliamentary contest was the
wide-ranging struggle over the innumerable economic and
political grievances that landlordism and colonial-compact
rule engendered. Gradually as the struggle sharpened, the
fundamental political issue of *Canadian independence*
was thrust to the fore. It was to be proclaimed in "declarations of independence" in both the Canadas.

In Lower Canada, the struggle involved not only

colonial self-government, as in the other provinces, but the right of national self-determination for the French-Canadian nation. From the Conquest onward, this was to become the burning issue in the valley of the St. Lawrence. The conquerors who, as a manoeuvre to head off a convergence with the rebellious colonies to the south, had granted concessions to the French Canadians in the Quebec Act of 1774, had not abandoned the idea of eventually anglicizing the whole of Lower Canada. In furthering this design the London authorities found eager helpers in the colonial merchants. As one of their organs, the *Mercury*, wrote: "After 47 years of possession it is only right that the province should finally become English." The threat to French-Canadian survival called into being a national-democratic movement of resistance, with the slogan "Our language, our institutions and our laws!"

Sir James Craig, whose regime was marked by a concerted offensive against national rights and democratic freedoms, complained bitterly of the "spirit of independence" and "insubordination" among the people of Lower Canada; in 1810 he wrote that "it seems to be a favorite object with them to be considered as a separate Nation; *la Nation canadienne* is their constant expression."

Following the War of 1812, a new drive to anglicize Lower Canada got under way. In 1822 a bill was introduced at Westminster providing for the union of Upper and Lower Canada as a means of eliminating the latter as a separate entity. The purpose of this attempt was not misunderstood. A storm of protest broke forth, and 60,000 names were affixed to petitions in Lower Canada demanding withdrawal of the bill. It was withdrawn.

The leader of this powerful national-democratic movement in French Canada was Louis-Joseph Papineau. Born on October 7, 1786, he was the son of the surveyor-notary Joseph Papineau, himself a leading democrat in the Lower Canadian Assembly. The young Papineau was elected to the Assembly in 1810, fought in the war of 1812, and in 1815 at the age of 28 was elected Speaker of the Assembly (the post customarily held at that time by the majority leader). As a student at the Seminary of Quebec, the young Papineau had read extensively the forbidden works of the French revolutionary materialists —the Encyclopedists, d'Holbach, Diderot, Voltaire and others—and of the English materialist philosophers. Growing up in the years that followed the French Revolution, he was profoundly influenced by that historic upheaval, and to the end of his life bore the imprint of its revolutionary-democratic thought, interwoven with the national-democratic spirit of French Canada's fight for survival. In his last public speech before his death, Papineau summed up in these words his life-long creed as a democrat: "The good teachings of modern times, I have found condensed, explained, and given over to the love of peoples . . . in a few lines of the Declaration of Independence of 1776 and of the Declaration of the Rights of Man and the Citizen of 1789."

The struggle in Lower Canada started with the resistance of the French Canadians to national oppression. It soon embraced the issues of legislative control of the revenue, freedom of press and assembly, and colonial self-government. It thus paralleled the struggles in Upper Canada and those (in a less acute form) in the Atlantic provinces. Soon, as the contest sharpened, there came the first beginnings of joint effort and mutual support on the part of the national-democratic, patriotic forces in all three areas.

In November 1827 Governor Dalhousie prorogued the

Assembly of Lower Canada two days after its opening, rather than recognize Louis-Joseph Papineau as Speaker of the House, though he had been elected to the post by a vote of 41 to 5. The contest between Assembly and Executive, which had been going on intermittently for twenty years, now once more approached the breaking point.

The central matter in dispute was the right of the Assembly to control the revenues of the colonial province. The Reformers demanded replacement of the irresponsible and appointive Legislative Council with an elective one. But inseparable from the question of representative government was the issue of French-Canadian national rights. To the growth of the sentiment of nationality, of the existence of a "nation canadienne," Colonial Secretary Huskisson counterposed England's "duty and interest": having "carried our language, our free institutions, and our system of laws, to the most remote corners of the globe," it was now imperative to "imbue (the colony) with English feeling, and benefit it with English laws and institutions." It is noteworthy that in the elections held earlier that year, the name of "patriote" had for the first time been attached to the party of popular opposition— the "Parti canadien."

Dalhousie's arbitrary dissolution of the Assembly, was followed by the arrest of Jocelyn Waller, reformer and editor of the *Canadian Spectator* and a friend of Papineau's. Other newspapers were prosecuted, judges removed from office, French-Canadian militia battalions dissolved. Petitions addressed to London protesting against the repression gathered the signatures of no less than eighty-seven thousand persons. Once again the Governor was replaced; his successor, Kempt, being instructed to calm the agitation but to yield nothing. Kempt in turn

was followed by Aylmer, who offered negligible concessions, hedged about with vague promises; and then had
the two leading Patriote journalists arrested—Tracey of
the *Vindicator,* Duvernay of the *Minerve.* A Patriote rally
protested "That the liberty of the press forms an essential
in the attributes of every free government. Consequently
this meeting considers that the arrest and imprisonment
of Messrs. Duvernay and Tracey, by the legislative council, has been an arbitrary act, and a violation of the rights
and liberties of the subject." The elections of 1832 witnessed a bloody fusillade by the troops on St. James Street,
Montreal. Those responsible for the deaths of three young
French Canadians faced trial, were acquitted, and received
the commendation of the Governor.

In order to resist attempts to reduce the French Canadians to what one contemporary described as "a perpetual
state of pupilage and incapacity for national independence," the Patriotes in 1834 founded the "Société Saint-
Jean Baptiste." Headed by the journalist Ludger Duvernay, it was devoted to the struggle for preservation of the
French-Canadian cultural and democratic heritage.

In 1834 the Assembly adopted the "92 Resolutions."
These, like the Seventh Report on Grievances in Upper
Canada, set forth the political program of the democratic
opposition. They comprised an exhaustive catalogue of
the multifarious grievances that cried out for redress in
all spheres of life in Lower Canada. Their burden was
plain: a demand for basic change in colonial policy, for
measures leading to a democratic national regeneration.
Among the main propositions advanced were these:

*On French-Canadian national identity, equality and
rights*: "The majority of the inhabitants of the country
are by no means disposed to repudiate any of the advantages that derive from their origin and descent from the

French nation which, in terms of contributions to the progress of civilization, science, letters and art has never lagged behind the British nation, and today in the cause of liberty and in the science of government is its worthy emulator. . . ." Lower Canada would not readily surrender "the religion, the habits and customs and usages that are those of the great majority of its inhabitants." (52nd resolution).

On structural reforms of government: The 21st resolution invoked the right of Canadian subjects to amend or revise their own Constitution—recognition of which by Britain would "preserve friendly relations with this colony, as long as the connection lasts, and those of an ally should the course of time bring new relationships." The 43rd resolution asserted that "The Constitution and form of government most suitable for this colony are not to be sought solely in analogy with the institutions of Great Britain, with a state of society entirely different from ours . . ." (In the words of Papineau, "We demand political institutions in conformity with the conditions of society in which we are living.")

Nos. 64 to 74 called for control of the provincial revenue by the Assembly; No. 79 demanded for the Assembly all the "powers, privileges and immunities" possessed by the British House of Commons. The idea of the *supremacy of Parliament* pervaded the resolutions. As early as in 1810 Pierre Bédard had persuaded the Assembly to assert the principle of its supremacy in relation to all other branches of government; the patriotes were now elaborating their conception of a popular assembly which would become the veritable directing centre of national life, with an Executive fully answerable to it and acting as a committee charged with carrying out its decisions.

About a third of all the resolutions (Nos. 9 to 40, and

84) were devoted to exposing the abusive and tyrannical workings of the irresponsible appointive Executive and Legislative Councils. Here was the hub of what Durham later referred to as the Assembly's "unremitting warfare," aimed at securing for itself the powers inherent in a representative body, in line with the "very nature of representative government." The demand which in Upper Canada was advanced in the slogan "responsible government" was put forward here in the form: "an elective Legislative Council."

In 1830, a contemporary had noted, out of twelve members of the Legislative Council holding offices, "seven are large landed proprietors . . . three are merchants and one has been absent from the province for several years." "The Legislative Council," observed *Le Canadien*, "has rightly been regarded as the cause of all our political ills. By means of this body the minority has been enabled to throw out or retard numerous measures demanded by the majority. . . . It is thanks to the identity and community of interest of this body with the Executive that the administration has always been able to evade the plaints of the people and their representatives. There must be a change in the running of colonial affairs . . ." A resolution moved in the Assembly urged a change as regards the Legislative Council "in such manner that the said council may be as free and independent of the governor as the nature of the colony will admit of, by adopting a system of election." As regards the Executive, *Le Canadien* asserted that there could be no hope of good government "until the Constitution surrounds the King's representative with men responsible for all administrative acts, and enjoying the confidence of the House, as is the case with any well-organized representative government."

The concept of *Canadian independence* was not spelled

out in the 92 Resolutions; but Nos. 50 and 86 unmistakably gave notice that unless the main demands were met, that would be the alternative. The former reminded the people of England that the population of British America would soon equal or surpass that of the thirteen colonies at the time when they had decided in favor of "the inestimable advantage of governing themselves, instead of being governed," and undertook to throw off "a colonial regime which was, generally speaking, far better than that of British America today." No. 80 warned Parliament not to act in such a way, by oppressing the people of this colony "as to cause them to regret their dependence on the British Empire and to seek elsewhere a remedy for their ills."

The framers of the resolutions stated from the outset that they sought the "peace and contentment" of their country on the basis of the common interest of its inhabitants "without distinction of origin or of belief." It was in this spirit that the Patriote movement had pressed for removal of the limitations on the civil rights of the small Jewish community in Canada, then numbering less than 200. Ever since Ezekiel Hart had been elected in 1807 by the French-Canadian constituency of Trois Rivières and had been denied the right to take his seat in the Assembly, this question had been an issue in the political struggle. In 1832 a bill introduced by John Neilson and vigorously supported by Papineau and his followers became law: it provided "That all persons professing (the) the Jewish Religion being natural born British subjects inhabiting and residing in this Province are entitled . . . to the full rights and privileges of the other subjects of His Majesty . . . and capable of taking, having or enjoying any office or place of trust whatsoever, in this Province."

The 89th to 91st resolutions contained proposals for the setting up of correspondence committees in Lower Canada to communicate with the English radicals and the opponents of colonial tyranny in Upper Canada.

Aylmer, in closing the session, charged that the grievances enumerated in the 92 Resolutions were nothing but the products of their authors' imagination. The Patriotes' rejoinder was to go to the people and secure 80,000 signatures to a petition in support of their program.

The reply of reaction was to multiply its provocations to violence. In June 1834 troops fired on a peaceful meeting in Montreal's Champ de Mars. Rumors were spread that 10,000 Patriotes were about to march on the city. Regiments were ordered to stand by and artillery was paraded in the streets. The party of reaction, impatient with what it considered the hesitating measures of the authorities, constituted armed organizations of its own, the "Carabineers," which the Governor under popular pressure was forced to declare illegal. They promptly reconstituted themselves under the name of the "British Legion" and later the "Doric Club." Incitements to assassination appeared in the guise of advertisements, such as the following:

"Canadian" shooting-match:

> Notice: A plaster figure representing a certain great agitator, to serve as bulls-eye. A prize to be awarded to the sharpshooter who at 50 yards distance hits the head of the said personage. Members of the British Legion or the Doric Club are respectfully requested to hold themselves in readiness.

As the struggle sharpened, the cleavage deepened between the "moderates" and the left wing in the democratic camp. For some time a right-wing group had been forming, centred at Quebec; it included John Neilson, Etienne Parent, E. Bédard, A. Cuvillier (a director of the Bank of Montreal) and others. In 1833 there was division over a proposal to establish elective parish councils, with the "moderates" joining with the clergy and the "Bureaucrats" to oppose it.

The Quebec group was variously known as the "petite famille" and the "lambs" (in contrast to the "wolves," or left wing, centred in Montreal). Bédard's acceptance of a judgeship at the hands of the Château clique bespoke the opportunism of the right wing, of which he was a leading spokesman. In the debate on the 92 Resolutions matters came to an open break: John Neilson, editor of the *Quebec Gazette* and long a leader of the Reform movement, flatly opposed the resolutions. "The moment the Constitution is attacked," he argued, "free rein is given to popular passions." The right wing represented in the main the Lower Canadian liberal bourgeoisie: like their counterparts in Upper Canada, as the struggle sharpened they broke with the petty-bourgeois revolutionary democrats and, despite protestations of democratic sentiments, gravitated increasingly to the side of the forces of colonial counter-revolution.

In the summer of 1834 an epidemic of typhus again swept the province, claiming over 6,000 victims. The Governor and his executive, who had refused to enact a law on quarantine at the session just ended, were widely denounced for irresponsibility.

The 92 Resolutions had dealt principally with questions of parliamentary reform and national rights. In the electoral struggle that ensued in the autumn of 1834, the Patriotes advanced a program of economic struggle as well. They campaigned for a boycott of English goods and the purchase, wherever possible, of Canadian products.

Wearing exclusively domestic fabrics and drinking Canadian beer or spirits came to be looked on as an expression
of patriotic political conviction. At the same time it was
designed to encourage Canadian manufacture and to de-
press the hated government's revenues from customs
duties. As Papineau declared later when the campaign for
a boycott reached its height:

> Some will tell us: But you are destroying commerce! I
> reply first of all, that if commerce were inseparable from
> the triumph of our oppressors and from our degradation,
> then commerce must be destroyed. But this is not the case.
> Our efforts can give it a new and better direction . . .
> Multiply our flock, so as to have more wool, our cattle for
> food, for improving the land, for tanning more leather;
> let us have more craftsmen to put out more abundant
> products; sow more hemp to have more linen and, during
> our long winters, employ usefully at the loom our indus-
> trious and comely female fellow-citizens . . . and thereby
> help us liberate the country.

Aylmer had declared that the grievances set forth in
the 92 Resolutions had no basis of support in popular
opinion. The result of the elections of October 1834
gave him his answer: out of 88 seats in the Assembly, the
Patriotes won 77.

As early as 1827, the Patriotes of Lower Canada had
begun to create a network of parish and regional committees charged with the task of organizing meetings, preparing resolutions, sending petitions. In July 1834 these
local committees, in line with the concluding recommendations of the 92 Resolutions, were brought under a unified leadership. There was established in Montreal a
"Permanent and Central Committee" composed of deputies from the parish or county committees. These in turn
were to hold annual conventions, adopt resolutions,

formulate plans of work, take organizational decisions. The committee of Two-Mountains County, north-west of Montreal Island, held conventions in 1835, '36 and '37. It is interesting to notice that the committee elected at the last convention, in addition to a majority of French Canadians, included names such as Phelan, Ryan, Purcel, Hawley, Hills and Watts. At the meeting of this committee held on Aug. 13, 1837, at St. Benoit a petition was received from a Mme. Girouard who had organized "a group of women to adopt resolutions with the aim of contributing insofar as the weakness of their sex permits, to the success of the Patriote cause." The committee endorsed the petition and authorized the formation of the "Association of Patriote Women of Two Mountains County."

A leading part in the campaign for the boycott and in the organization of smuggling was taken by those whom Duvernay referred to as "vigorous youths, determined and well organized." The youth formed the main body of the "Fils de la Liberté," whose manifesto of 1837 proclaimed their aim: "to emancipate our country from all human authority save that of the bold democracy residing in its bosom." This was the semi-military defense organization of the Patriotes. Its anthem was *"Moi, je préfère ma patrie: avant tout, je suis Canadien!"* Its members included André Ouimet, president, De Lorimier, Duquette, Daunais, and others who later were to give their lives in the struggle.

The Patriote movement, through its committees of correspondence directed by the Central Committee in Montreal, embraced a broad area of Lower Canada. A powerful instrument of agitation and leadership was its press: in Montreal *La Minerve* and *The Vindicator* (published by Dr. O'Callaghan, for whom Canada was in truth "the Ireland of America"); *l'Echo du Pays* and the *Township Reformer*; and, under right-wing influence, *Le Canadien*, published at Quebec by Etienne Parent. Outstanding as a national and democratic newspaper was *La Minerve*: its collaborators included Papineau, Morin, Lafontaine, Girod. Its first issue stated as its purpose to teach Canadians "to resist every usurpation of their rights"; it devoted space to questions of history—and at the same time conducted a vigorous agitation on all current political issues.

The repressive measures of the authorities had included the removal of French-Canadian judges or others who showed signs of radical sympathies, and dismissal of militia officers guilty of the same "crime." Already under Dalhousie's regime, separate French-Canadian regiments had been dissolved. In reply to these measures the Patriote committees proceeded in one locality after another to constitute their own judiciary, militia and administrative apparatus. In this way they not only replaced officials whom the Governor had dismissed, but began to lay the basis for municipal and local administrations which the colony had hitherto lacked.

Meeting at St. Benoit in October 1837 the Permanent Committee of Two-Mountains County decided to set up its own judicial and military organizations, "making usage of the authority confided to it by the people." The resolution to this effect states that the Governor, by removing arbitrarily "a great number of respectable citizens, who fulfilled with integrity and to the satisfaction of the people the charges of magistrates and officers of militia," had thus "put the inhabitants of the country to the necessity of taking measures for the protection of peace and order . . ." Any Reformer who refused to abide by the decision of the elected judge, jury or Permanent Committee, or who had recourse to the reactionary colonial tribunals, was liable to disciplinary measures, including loss of his right to vote or be elected at Reform meetings; and to be treated by all Reformers as an enemy of the community, everyone "strictly abstaining from any relationship whether friendly or commercial" with him. Militia officers removed by the Governor because of their patriotic stand were to be re-elected by those who in each parish had formed their own corps of militia. These latter were to be drilled in "the exercise of arms and light troop-movements." All reports of militia registration were to be forwarded to the Central Committee, which undertook to obtain arms and equipment. In thus combining the functions of political leadership and judicial and military administration, the Patriote Committees began to assume the character of organs of State power.

While the logic of the struggle was impelling the popular movement towards measures of revolutionary self-defense, it would appear that the main leadership of the movement, at this time, and indeed up to the last moment, had no clear intention and had made no plans for starting an armed struggle. Although conscious that a crisis was approaching, they were resolved to leave to their oppressors the role of the Party of Violence. At the most, the Patriotes would defend themselves if attacked: a stance that was to impose a fatal limitation on their struggle once the storm broke.

Three years before the outbreak, Papineau accused the ruling party of being the fomentor of violence: "The Reform Party has committed no violence. It was in its interest that none should be committed. The servile party from the first had an interest in violence being committed; this interest became each day more pressing, and each day the violence became greater."

Faced with the 92 Resolutions and petitions signed by over a quarter of the entire adult population, Downing Street in 1835 appointed a "commission of enquiry" headed by Lord Gosford; while allowing the impression to gain currency that liberal concessions were being contemplated, the imperial power prepared to resist all the main demands of the Canadians. How little intention there was of making any serious concession is to be seen in the fact that at the very time when the Gosford Commission was being set up, Secretary for the Colonies Glenelg declared that responsible government was "inconsistent with a due advertence to the essential distinctions between a metropolitan and a colonial government and is therefore inadmissible." Two years later, Lord John Russell was to take an identical stand on responsible government: "I hold this proposition to be entirely incompatible with the relations between the mother country and the colony."

The Assembly of Lower Canada, which had been battling for a quarter of a century for its right to control the public funds, in 1836 refused to continue its deliberations any further, until London should concede the demand for an elective Legislative Council. London's reply was not long delayed. The Gosford Commission's report (early in 1837) called for rejection of an elective legislative council and of responsible government, considering the latter the equivalent of "a veritable independence." On the basis of this report, Russell introduced into the Commons a series of resolutions designed to coerce the Canadians into submission. After reiterating the Commission's rejection of the demands of the Assembly, the resolutions went on to authorize the Governor to dispose of the revenues of the Province without the assent of its elected representatives. To accompany this brazen violation of an elementary principle of representative government, plans were made to send at once to Canada two additional regiments of troops. At the last moment, however, it was considered more prudent simply to transfer regiments from New Brunswick to the St. Lawrence.

This decision of the imperial government to force a showdown—and the Russell resolutions could mean nothing else—was taken at a time when the class and national struggles in the Canadas were being sharpened further by economic crisis. A letter in the *Minerve* of March 13, 1837, describes the effects of the crisis in Lower Canada. Referring to a report by another correspondent on conditions in Rimouski, the writer observes: "If this correspondent . . . were to travel at this moment through the least afflicted district of this Province, he would still see scenes similar to that of which he has given us so passionate a picture. He would come upon a frightful number of families, driven from their homes by hunger, out into the street, going from door to door, besieging rich and poor alike. If he were to enter the houses, he would see, in far greater number than one would imagine, pale and shivering children, asking bread of a mother who has nothing but tears left to offer them having shared her last crust with them the day previous, while her husband, weakened with hunger, is seeking somewhere to work; but often in vain, for those who formerly employed the poor fear to run short themselves. . . ."

This crisis of 1836-37 was the second in the cyclical series, embracing Western Europe and North America, that had started with the crisis of overproduction of 1825. But for Lower Canada it simply aggravated an already existing condition: the disastrous agricultural decline dating from the early 1830s. Exhaustion of soils through the

persisting use of backward techniques, compounded by
the plague of the wheat-fly, caused the collapse of wheat-
farming in the St. Lawrence and Richelieu valleys. The
effect was to start the drain of emigration to the States
(20,000 in the years 1830-37) *, and to intensify the tensions within the province.

The economic crisis and financial panic of that winter
and spring led the patriot-reformers to reflect on the
"periodical madness which afflicts the merchants," a mal-
ady with which the editor of *The Vindicator* contrasted
the "sound views" of "the farming and mechanic interests." An answer to the evils distracting the country is not
to be expected, "in these days of extraordinary delusion
among mercantile men," from business speculators:

> The traders, as a body, are a useful class, but not the most
> patriotick. The spirit of traffick is always adverse to the
> spirit of liberty. We care not whom the remark pleases nor
> whom it offends; but it is the truth, which all history cor-
> roborates, that the mercantile community, in the aggre-
> gate, is ever impelled by sordid motives of action. The im-
> mediate interests of trade, not the permanent interests of
> their country, supply their strongest impulse. They peruse
> their ledger with more devotion than the Constitution;
> they regard pecuniary independence more than political;
> and they would be content to wear ignominious chains, so
> that the links were forged of gold . . . an equal currency
> is to them a phrase of better import than equal rights, a
> uniform system of exchange a grander object than a uni-
> form system of freedom. For a sound social polity one must
> look to the classes whose labor is the real source of wealth.†

---

*Some thousands had found an alternative, which was to "go up
the Gatineau or the St. Maurice and work for the English timber
merchants."

†"This article," C. Vance justly observes, "is remarkable for the
clarity with which it expresses the class alignment in the fight for
democracy in Canada in 1837. It states what was fundamental in the

The farmer, *The Vindicator* argues, "is a member . . . of a class on which we must mainly depend for the steady and effectual defence of the institutions of liberty, amidst the violent assaults, which, it is easy to foresee, mercantile rapacity will fiercely wage against them. To the cultivators of the soil, gentle and simple, and to the hardy followers of the mechanick arts, we turn our eyes in these days of passion and prejudice, for that calm good sense and intrepidity, which are necessary to the great blessing of equal political rights."

Adoption of the "coercion resolutions" by the British parliament slammed the door shut on any possibility of a peaceful settlement. From mid-May onwards, protest rallies were held throughout the length and breadth of Lower Canada: at St. Ours and St. Laurent, at St. Denis, Yamaska, Lacadie, Vaudreuil and in the Saguenay district. In Montreal joint meetings were held by French Canadians and Irish democrats. More and more the rallies took on the character of demonstrations of strength, mobilizations of Patriote supporters. "Down with the Russell resolutions;"—"Flee, tyrants, for the People are awakening!"—"In unity is strength!"—"All honor to our Patriote women!"—"Death rather than Enslavement!"—"Defend the People's rights and liberties!"—such were the slogans displayed and proclaimed at the mass rallies in the valleys of the St. Lawrence, the Richelieu, the Rivière du Nord. Hoisted aloft was the Phrygian cap of republicanism, and the tune of the French revolutionary song "La Carma-

---

outlook of the movement—respect for labor and the common people as a whole as the source of all wealth and the natural base and source of political rule . . ." ("1837: Labor and the Democratic Tradition," in *The Marxist Quarterly*, no. 12).

gnole" rang out with new, Canadian words. Overhead flew for the first time in our history, a Canadian flag: horizontal bands of green, red and white, adorned with a beaver, a maple leaf and a maskinonge. Other banners carried, on a white field, an eagle with a maple branch in its beak; and, in another variant, a single beacon-star with the inscription, *Notre Avenir*—"Our future."

The meeting at Saint-Ours on May 7 set the tone for the summer of defiant agitation. The Twelve Resolutions it adopted, prepared by the Permanent and Central Committee, were the answer of the Patriotes to the Coercion Resolutions of Lord John Russell: "We deny the right of the Parliament of England to legislate on the internal affairs of this Colony, against our consent. . . . Holding ourselves to be bound by force alone to the English government, . . . we consider it a matter of duty, as of honor, to resist a tyrannical power by all the means at our disposal . . ." This "declaration of independence" marked a turning-point in the struggle in Lower Canada. The issue of national independence was now for the first time placed in the forefront of the Patriote program.

True, the question had been broached before. In the session of 1831-32 in the House of Assembly, Thomas Lee had expressed regret that the Canadians had not broken with Britain and struck out for independence in 1775. A much-discussed article in the revolutionary-democratic *Minerve,* in February 1832, argued that "Immediate separation from England is the sole means of preserving our nationality." "We want reforms," Papineau had written to the English radical, Roebuck, "and we want separation rather than no reforms." But, as in the 92 Resolutions, the demand for independence was held in reserve as the last resort. That point had now been reached.

The St. Ours resolutions declared null and void the

hated Acts that had given monopoly control of hundreds of thousands of acres to the British American Land Company, and called for a boycott of English manufactured goods. "We shall consider as deserving well of his country whoever establishes manufactories of silk, cloth, sugar, spirits, etc.," The rally acclaimed Papineau, designated by the country as the outstanding "leader and regenerator of his people" and instituted the "Papineau Penny" (le Tribut Papineau) as a means of building a financial war-chest for the struggle.

The resolutions, after expressing appreciation for the stand taken in Parliament by the English Radicals and working men, went on: "The working men of London who, in a spirit of liberty and justice . . . presented a petition to the House of Commons, have equally a claim to our profound gratitude." In March, the London Workingmen's Association had held a meeting to protest against the Russell Resolutions, and organized a petition to Parliament in support of the Canadians' demands. At the same time it sent an address of greeting to the Patriote Central Committee. Signed by a dozen workers of different trades—engravers, goldsmiths, carpenters, etc.—the message addressed the Canadians as "friends in the cause of liberty, oppressed brothers" and greeted the resistance offered by the Patriotes to Gosford's repressive measures. "The cause of democracy," it continued, "is everywhere triumphant. . . . Can there be rebellion in a country when the liberties of a million men are trampled underfoot by a contemptible invading minority?"

". . . Brother Canadians, do not let yourselves be deceived by fair promises. Trust in the sacredness of your cause. You have the full approval of your distant brothers. Have faith in your leaders. We augur your triumph." And, in conclusion, "May the sun of independence shine on your growing cities, your joyous hearths, your deep forests and your frozen lakes—such is the ardent wish of the Workingmen's Association."

The Address linked the issues of democracy and national rights in the colony with that of working-class power in the metropolis: "It is then today or never that the working classes must strike a decisive blow for their complete emancipation. . . . A parliament which represents only capitalist property owners of money or land, will never protect the working classes; its object is to make money dear; and work cheap; yours on the other hand is to lower the cost of money and raise the price of labor; between these opposing interests peace is impossible." It urged: Bring the "bourgeois parliament face to face with a democratic assembly, and you will soon overthrow the men of wealth. . ."

The circular calling the London rally bore the heading: "Democracy or Despotism, Meeting of the Working Men's Association in favor of Canadian Rights." In an item later reprinted by *The Vindicator,* the *London Constitutional* announced on April 3, 1837: "The working men of London meet this day to vindicate the political rights of their fellow-men in Canada. The working class of England know that if the right of the taxed to control the expenditure of the taxes is denied in Canada, it may be so in England, and the Working Men's Association has come forward to defend that common right. . . ." Over 2,000 people attending the meeting endorsed the Address. When its text was received by the Montreal Permanent and Central Committee, two thousand copies in French and 1,000 in English were printed, with county and parish committees being urged "to cause the said Address to be read to the people at the doors of their several Parish Churches."

The spirit in which the expressions of international solidarity were exchanged was summed up in this comment in the London radical newspaper: "What care we in what language our cherished principles are expressed, they are still *our* principles whether uttered in Canadian-French, or Belgian, Dutch, or Polish or modern Greek. .."

To this message from the London workers the Patriote Central Committee in Montreal sent a stirring reply whose conclusion reaffirms the solidarity shown to them: "We desire, through your Association, to proclaim, that whatever course we shall be compelled to adopt, we have no contest with the people of England. We war only against the agressions of their and our tyrannical oppressors." This exchange of messages is the first expression in the history of our country of the influence of the modern working class movement. The Chartists, the first mass political organization of the industrial proletariat, in giving active support to the struggle of the Canadians for national independence asserted the principle of internationalism that is inherent in the world working class movement.

At St. Ours and the meetings which followed it, tribute was paid likewise to the fraternal support accorded by the democrats of Upper Canada and of the Maritimes to the Patriote cause. Thus, the rally in Two Mountains County, at Ste. Scholastique, offered "thanks to the House of Assembly and people of Nova Scotia, to the Reformers of Upper Canada and of the other colonies, who have supported our demand for an elective Legislative Council and a responsible government." In reply to those who alleged this was a "racial" conflict or one inspired by a narrow nationalism, the meeting affirmed: "We have never entertained but on the contrary have ever reproved the unfortunate national distinctions which our common

enemies have sought maliciously to foment among us . . .
we are striving to assure to the whole people, without
distinction, the same rights, equal justice and a common
liberty."

In mid-June Gosford issued a proclamation banning
all further mass meetings. In reply the Patriote Central
Committee declared the ban "unconstitutional, and a
violation of the rights and privileges of the people of the
province." Three days after the proclamation, 4,000
people gathered in a meeting at Berthier: ten days later
a meeting of about the same number was held in Montreal; then all through the province the rallies resumed
with more enthusiasm than before.

In July, Bishop Lartigue of Montreal ordered the
priests to refuse absolution to any who preached resistance
to "the government under which we have the happiness
to live." In a further manifesto three months later he
denounced the "pernicious doctrines" of democracy and
the harmfulness of the concept of "the Sovereign people."
The whole of the higher clergy had aligned itself with
the authorities (to whom, indeed, they had owed their
privileged position ever since the Quebec Act). But the
lower clergy, particularly in the rural parishes, included
a number of sympathizers with the popular cause. The
declarations of Lartigue did not pass unchallenged: at a
mass meeting at Ste. Rose, north of Montreal, a resolution
was adopted protesting against them, affirming that authority derives, in part at least, from the sovereign people,
and stating bluntly that the religious authorities had no
business interfering in political matters.

As the political crisis sharpened in Lower Canada, the
division within the Patriote ranks was accentuated. In
March, 700 voters of Quebec City had signed an address
which in effect repudiated their right-wing representatives

and endorsed the policy of Papineau. But Etienne Parent in *Le Canadien* argued insistently in favor of a policy of "moderation": the Patriotes must "give thought as to whether the state of affairs is so intolerable that, to end it, we must *risk all* . . ." Outright resistance would lead, he argued, only to "anarchy." (Not for nothing was a Jesuit historian, a century later, to hold up Parent as one standing in the very forefront of "those who kept the majority of the population within the bounds of duty.") The split in the movement and the paralyzing influence of the right wing were to weigh heavily in favor of reaction in the days of the decisive struggle.

On August 18, Gosford convened the Assembly in order to convey the decisions of the British Government, based on the Russell resolutions; he let it be understood, however, that their implementation would be postponed. The Assembly, in the absence of any concessions to their main demands, once again refused to vote the subsidies and reaffirmed the stand taken in 1836. Thereupon the governor prorogued the session. There followed a new wave of dismissals of militia officers and justices of the peace, who were promptly reinstated by the people. Clashes between groups of Patriotes and such para-military organizations of reaction as the Doric Club, the Britannic Legion, etc., now became increasingly frequent.

Started by students and youthful professionals, the "Fils de la Liberté" were soon joined by hundreds of young apprentices, journeymen, unemployed. Their activities spread from Montreal to the near-by towns. The presence of a police-spy planted in their leadership enabled the Governor to follow their movements, but not to check the enthusiasm which their activities evoked.

The mass movement of protest against coercion reached its climax in the great rally of the Six Counties of the

Richelieu. On October 23rd some five thousand people gathered at the village of St. Charles. The meeting was the most powerful and militant demonstration that had yet taken place. Its organizers, Wolfred Nelson, Dr. Coté, Storrow Brown, Girod, were of the opinion that armed resistance had now become inevitable. Papineau, however, in his address continued to urge the boycott as the chief form of resistance. Nelson interjected: "As for me, I am of a different opinion from that of M. Papineau. I claim the time has come to melt down our pewter plates and spoons into bullets." When another speaker supported Papineau's position, he was booed down by the crowd. The resolutions adopted by the rally, while reaffirming in the main the stand taken at St. Ours in May, went further in calling for measures to establish a popular militia and judiciary organization in the counties, and to extend the "Fils de la Liberté" beyond Montreal; but there was no call to arms, nor indication of any plan of campaign for an uprising.

Within a matter of days after the St. Charles rally, the authorities decided the time had come to strike. Papineau having left Montreal for the Richelieu at the insistence of his friends (his house had been attacked a few days earlier), Sir John Colborne persuaded the Governor to issue warrants for the arrest of the leading Patriotes and to authorize the troops to carry out the arrests. The ill-armed Patriotes gathered in the towns and villages to defend their leaders; the troops were marched against them. In Durham's view, "The rebellion (was) precipitated by the British from an instinctive sense of the danger of allowing the Canadians full time for preparation . . ."

3

A National-Democratic Revolution

It was in the valley of the Richelieu that the people's movement had reached its highest point; here the forming of the Confederation of the Six Counties foreshadowed the coming into being of a provisional people's government, challenging the imperial power. It was here that Papineau and other leaders had come from Montreal to join the main body of the Patriote forces. So it was against the encampments on the Richelieu that Colborne launched his troops in the first phase of what he planned as a full-scale military campaign. The veteran of Waterloo had 6,000 men under his command. Opposing them were an unprepared, ill-armed Patriote militia; their leaders having foresworn the offensive, they waited, defensively, for the enemy onslaught.

The main body of the Patriote forces had gathered in the villages of St. Denis and St. Charles, situated six miles apart on the Richelieu. Colonel Gore was sent down the St. Lawrence to Sorel, whence his troops were to march south, along the right bank of the Richelieu, against the Patriote force at St. Denis. Simultaneously, Colonel Wetherall crossed over to Chambly, from which point he was to advance, from the opposite direction to Gore, on St. Charles. This converging movement was intended to allow at the same time the "mopping-up" of any Patriote forces which might be encountered en route: notably, at St. Ours, above Sorel on the Richelieu, and at Longueuil, where two arrested Patriotes had been freed by a handful of militiamen, and a detachment of regular cavalry put to flight.

At St. Denis preparations for the defense by some 800 Patriotes led by Dr. Wolfred Nelson were under way. Arriving in the outskirts of the village at about 9 a.m., Gore decided to proceed at once to the attack. Dividing his troops into three detachments, he sent one toward the wood east of the village, another along the river bank to the west, and the main column, with the cannon, along the high road into the centre of the village.

The Patriotes, of whom only about a hundred were armed—with old flint-lock rifles, the rest having nothing but scythes and pitchforks—had barricaded themselves, some in the stone house of the Saint-Germains on the highroad, the rest in neighboring buildings. Those without firearms massed behind the walls of the church, ready to participate in the engagement at the first opportunity. Papineau, meanwhile, had been prevailed upon by Nelson to retire to the safety of St. Hyacinthe.

For six hours the British troops attempted to carry the village by storm: they were met with a withering fire. After attacking in the open, the redcoats entrenched themselves behind fences and wood piles. Three times the troops charged, without success. They were then attacked by a body of Patriotes, a hundred or so in number, who had come to join Nelson from St. Ours and the neighboring villages. Gore's troops began to yield ground; at 3 p.m. he ordered the retreat. The cannon was left in the hands of the Patriotes, as well as a number of prisoners.

Like wildfire, the news spread through the countryside: the Patriotes had put British regulars to rout! Gore had lost sixty casualties, half of them killed, and his field-piece. The Patriotes lost twelve killed, four wounded.

Meanwhile, Colonel Wetherall was advancing on St. Charles with six companies of infantry, a detachment of cavalry and two pieces of artillery. Here the Patriotes were commanded by T. Storrow Brown, leader of the Fils de la Liberté, one of those for whose arrest a warrant had been issued. With his 200 men (who were as ill-armed as those at St. Denis had been) Brown took up a position in the stone manor-house of the seigneur, Debartzch.

Wetherall reached St. Charles on November 25 with a well-equipped and fresh force. At the first discharge of artillery fire, T. S. Brown fled, leaving his men leaderless and occupying an impossible position in the face of an overwhelming enemy. The first return fire of the Patriotes disconcerted the troops; but once the artillery had demolished the improvised fortifications, Wetherall launched his main force in a bayonet charge. In fierce hand-to-hand fighting the Patriotes were overpowered and butchered. A few managed to escape; about forty were killed, the rest wounded or captured. The troops reported only three killed and eighteen wounded, likely an underestimate. At Pointe-Olivier a body of Patriotes attempted to attack Wetherall's troops on their return march to Montreal, but were repulsed after a brief skirmish. On November 30 Gore returned to St. Denis and avenged his defeat of the week before: he had every house in the village except two burned to the ground.

Papineau, O'Callaghan, Duvernay and other Patriote leaders, meeting on the U.S. border, decided that so long as the North had not been put down, it was necessary to create a diversion in the South that would prevent Colborne from throwing his whole force against the Patriotes in Two-Mountains. Accordingly, a force of eighty was organized and moved in the direction of St. Césaire, whither Nelson had retreated. At Moore's Corners, close to the frontier, they were met on December 6 by a British force of four hundred and, after a brief struggle, dispersed.

As in the Richelieu Valley, the Patriotes north-west of Montreal gathered to defend their leaders threatened with arrest. These were, at St. Benoit, Girouard and Masson; at St. Eustache, Dr. Chénier and the Swiss, Amury Girod.

On November 24 Girod received word of the Patriote victory at St. Denis and a message from Robert Nelson (brother of Wolfred) about the situation in Montreal— that "the town was in a state of panic, that there were no troops there, or few at the most." On the strength of a promise that the forces south of the St. Lawrence would create a diversion, Girod decided in his own words "to move next day on Montreal and to attack it." In this he was over-ruled by Chénier, Girouard and other leaders. "They resolved to stay on the defensive," writes Girod; "I repented for the first time that I had placed my confidence in such hesitant men."

On December 5th, Gosford proclaimed martial law in the district of Montreal. Colborne was already concentrating his forces for the expedition to the north. To the beacon-fires of devastated villages set alight by the forces of Gore and Wetherall, were to be added a new chain of fires in Two-Mountains. The object was not merely to defeat the hated "rebels" but to exterminate them. Girouard, writing from Montreal Prison in April 1838 bears witness to the fact:

> It had been decreed by the authorities that the imposing forces which made up the expedition against the Canadians in the county of Two-Mountains were not intended

simply to take possession of the so-called revolt or rebellion, but actually, to root out utterly the patriotism in the country, with fire, sword and pillage, among all our brave blue-bonnets . . .

Colborne's strategy in this expedition was essentially a repetition of that employed in the earlier operation south of the St. Lawrence. As his points of concentration he chose Carillon, on the left bank of the Ottawa, and St. Martin, north of Montreal. Thus St. Benoit and St. Eustache would be caught between two fires, in the same manner as had St. Denis and St. Charles.

At St. Martin, Colborne himself took command. His two thousand men included companies of the 32nd, 83rd and Royal regiments, accompanied by seventy sleighs laden with munitions and provisions; the Royal Artillery, with seven pieces of cannon; and numerous volunteer detachments—cavalry, carabineers, etc. Another thousand remained to garrison Montreal. With those posted at other points, Colborne thus disposed of well over 6,000 men; and two additional regiments were on their way from England.

Opposing this overwhelming force were five hundred men at St. Eustache, less than half of whom had rifles; and a slightly smaller number at St. Benoit. Another five hundred, who had been with Chénier at St. Eustache, disbanded at the last minute at the urging of the parish priest, Paquin. In contrast, Canon Chartier, the *curé* of St. Benoit, was an enthusiastic Patriote. The priest at St. Charles had given the Patriotes his blessing; Chartier worked actively with the Patriote command, helping to raise barricades and fortifications and encouraging the men.

By December 10, both St. Eustache and St. Benoit were fortified, and the Patriotes proceeded to await the arrival of the enemy. On the morning of the 14th Colborne with his 2,000 men moved out of St. Martin, crossed the river above St. Rose, and advanced on St. Eustache. A small body of volunteers under Globenski, seigneur of St. Eustache, took the shorter route, across Isle Jésus to a point across the river from the village.

The first warning which the Patriotes received was a fusillade, on the morning of the 14th, from across the river. It was Globenski and his volunteers. Chénier with a hundred and fifty men had started across the ice to the attack when a cannon shot, fired from the shore which they had just left, brought them to a halt. Turning, they saw the main body of Colborne's troops, stretching for two miles along the road which skirts the river bank, their bayonets glistening in the cold December sunlight. The Patriote ranks broke in confusion. Chénier regained the village in haste and began posting his men (estimates of whose number vary from 250 to 400) in the church and the surrounding houses.

Before attempting to enter the village, Colborne subjected it to a heavy artillery bombardment, and at the same time disposed his forces of infantry in a vast semicircle, some three miles long, around the outskirts, and well out of range of Patriote bullets. For a full hour the bombardment of the helpless village continued. At one o'clock in the afternoon an artillery detachment was sent part way up the street facing the church. For another hour the cannonade continued, now concentrated chiefly on the main stronghold—the church itself.

By now, the infantry began to move forward; a part took up a position on the frozen surface of the river; other detachments were moved up towards the first houses at the edge of the village. Thus far, they had scarcely come within range of the fire of the Patriotes. It was now two o'clock, and the troops had not begun an attack.

Finally, under cover of the smoke from a house near the church set on fire by a scouting-detachment, Colborne ordered the advance. The bayonet charge took place as the fire caught three of the houses where the Patriotes were barricaded. Driven forth by the smoke and flames, they fought as they could, against many times their number, fell, or attempted to escape across the ice.

There remained only the Church, which some of Colborne's men managed to enter from the rear and put to the torch.

As the Patriotes made a rush out of the building, one of them, named Forget, was recognized by a captain of the Government volunteers. "What are you doing here, Forget?" exclaimed the officer. "Fighting for my country," came the brief, bitter answer. A few minutes later Forget and his two sons died under the fire of the Government troops. Chénier, too, fell fighting, after leaping from a window of the church.

At four o'clock, the whole village was in flames. As night came on, the disbanded troops gave themselves up to rapine and pillage. Sixty houses were reduced to ashes by the fire; those that remained were ransacked by drunken troops and volunteers. The body of Chénier was taken to the inn, and left lying on the counter for three days. Legend has it that the heart was cut out and exposed to view in the window.

The troops had lost about thirty killed; the Patriotes well over twice that number, and more than a hundred prisoners. Next day, Colborne marched to meet Townshend at St. Benoit. Caught between two armies each of two thousand men, with no hope of aid from any quarter, the handful of Patriotes there decided to surrender. The only answer to their flag of truce was a repetition of the ravaging fire and pillage with which St. Eustache had been visited. Colborne departed only when the flames reached his own headquarters in the village. St. Benoit was razed to the ground. Girouard, captured shortly afterward, while in prison wrote to a friend about Colborne's sack of St. Benoit:

> It would be impossible for me to describe to you the desolation which his march and the barbarous scenes accompanying it spread through our homes . . . A considerable number of the inhabitants were assembled in my courtyard, which, as you know, is very large; they were lined up, and two cannon placed in the gateway were aimed at them, while they were told that they would be exterminated in a few minutes. There are no insults and outrages which were not heaped upon them, no threats which were not made, to intimidate them into declaring the hiding-places of those who were called their leaders. Not one would give the least indication . . . Some officers having learned that Paul Barazeau had guided me to Eboulis, they tortured him to force him to tell my place of retreat. They put a pistol to his throat and several times placed him on a block, threatening to behead him, but the generous Patriot held his ground, and the barbarians' violence was wasted.

> Then began scenes of devastation and destruction more atrocious than any seen in a town taken by storm and given over to pillage after a long, hard siege. After completely pillaging the village, the enemy set fire to it and reduced it from one end to the other to a heap of ashes. They then went in different directions, ravaging and burning on their way, carrying their fire as far as the village of Ste. Scholastique.

Colborne earned his title of "the Firebrand" (Vieux Brûlot); when he was named Lord Seaton, there were

French Canadians, with bitter memories in their hearts, who pronounced it "Satan."

Early in 1838 the Patriotes who had sought refuge across the border set about organizing an expedition into Lower Canada. Led by Robert Nelson and Dr. Côté (Papineau had withdrawn from participation in the struggle), they received assistance and support from democratic elements in northern New York and Vermont. On February 28, a long procession of sleighs bearing several hundred Patriotes, 1500 rifles, munitions and three field pieces, crossed Lake Champlain and entered the province. In the face of the onset of heavily superior forces of British soldiery, "Loyalist" (Tory) volunteers and U.S. troops under General Wool (who kept Colborne informed of the Patriote preparations), Nelson's force withdrew across the border, Nelson and Côté being taken prisoner and handed over to the U.S. authorities. The expedition is chiefly memorable for the "Declaration of Independence" issued by Nelson, calling for the establishment in Canada of a "patriotic and responsible government." The declaration, a significant expression of the political and social aims of the Patriote movement, included the following provisions:

> That from this day forward, the people of Lower Canada are absolved from all allegiance to Great Britain, and that the political connexion between that power and Lower Canada is now dissolved.
>
> That a republican form of government is best suited to Lower Canada, which is this day declared to be a republic.
>
> That under the free government of Lower Canada all persons shall enjoy the same rights: the Indians shall no longer be under any civil disqualification, but shall enjoy the same rights as any other citizens of Lower Canada.
>
> That all union between church and state is hereby de-

clared to be dissolved, and every person shall be at liberty
freely to exercise such religion or belief as shall be dictated to him by his conscience.

That the feudal or seigneurial tenure of land is hereby
abolished as completely as if such tenure had never existed in Canada.

That sentence of death shall no longer be passed or
executed, except in cases of murder.

That the liberty and freedom of the press shall exist in
all public matters and affairs.

That trial by jury is guaranteed to the people of Lower
Canada in its most extended and liberal sense.

That as general and public education is necessary, and
due by the Government to the people, an act to provide
for the same shall be passed as soon as the circumstances
of the country will permit.

To secure the elective franchise, all elections shall be
had by ballot.

That the French and English language shall be used in
all public affairs.

Despite the failure of the February expedition, Patriote
activity went on unabated, with the secret, semi-military
organization of the "Frères Chasseurs" (Hunters' Lodges)
being built up in Canada and in northern States. It was
pledged to "fight to the death for Papineau and Canadian
independence." Colborne and the imperial authorities
had word of its activities through an informer—the owner
of the house in which some of its leaders held their
meetings.

All through the summer of 1838 preparations went
forward for a rising. "Camps" were organized, at which
the men were to gather in the night of November 3-4 at
Beauharnois, St. Clément, Chateauguay, Pointe-Olivier,
St. Constant, Terrebonne and the lower Richelieu. In the
last-named area, near St. Ours, close to a thousand had
gathered. It was planned to move on Chambly, then take

Montreal. The main camp was at Napierville, where four to five thousand gathered under the command of Robert Nelson. Here he once again issued the proclamation of Canadian independence. In addition to the old commanders, two French officers, Hindenlang and Touvrey, had joined the leadership of the Patriote force.

In Montreal Colborne (who had now replaced Durham as Governor-General, after the former's brief administration) declared martial law; and proceeded with some six to seven thousand troops and a battery of artillery to march on Napierville.

Here Nelson's two thousand men had less than three hundred rifles amongst them; arms and munitions were expected from across the border, but a "neutrality" proclamation of President Van Buren and the intervention of the American authorities cut off most of the supply. A schooner laden with a couple of hundred rifles, a cannon and ammunition, was sent down Lake Champlain, and anchored off Rouse's Point on the evening of the 5th; but a force of government volunteers having seized the mill at Lacolle, mid-way between the foot of the lake and Napierville, the supplies were intercepted and communications cut off.

At the approach of Colborne's main force, the Patriotes fell back on Odelltown, close to the frontier; but it was in the hands of Tory volunteers. Caught between them and Colborne's force, the Patriotes after a brief engagement were dispersed. The whole county of La Prairie was given over to fire and pillage, and the jails filled.

On Lord Durham's arrival in Lower Canada in May, 1838 he had found the jails packed with prisoners. Fearing the effect of public trials, he issued an "Ordinance to provide for the security of Lower Canada," whereby eight Patriot leaders (including Wolfred Nelson and B. Viger) were to be deported to Bermuda; a dozen others of those who were already in the United States (including Papineau, Duvernay, T. S. Brown, Canon Chartier, and Georges-Etienne Cartier) were declared guilty of high treason and condemned to be executed should they re-enter Canada. The rest of the prisoners were set free. On news reaching England of these sentences, passed without trial of the accused, the British Government disallowed the Ordinance; whereupon Durham resigned his post. His place was taken by Colborne who at the first opportunity resorted to court-martials in order to crush opposition.

In Montreal, following the rising of 1837, 501 were imprisoned; at Quebec, five. After the second rising, at the end of 1838, 116 were jailed on charges of treason in Montreal, 18 at Quebec, 19 at Sherbrooke and two at Three Rivers. Of 108 brought to trial by court-martial, nine were acquitted, 27 freed under bond, 58 deported to Australia (cf. *Appendix*), and 12 were executed. The 108 who were court-martialled included:

66 farmers	1 each of: teacher soldier
6 notaries	miller "bourgeois"
5 blacksmiths	clerk
5 merchants	cabinetmaker
4 innkeepers	seamen
3 bailiffs	2 shoemakers
2 doctors	2 carpenters
2 students	2 waggoners

These died on the scaffold:

> Cardinal, Joseph-Narcisse, of Châteauguay, notary
> Daunais, Amable, of St. Cyprien, farmer
> Decoigne, Pierre Théophile, of Napierville, notary
> DeLorimier, Chevalier, of Montreal, notary
> Duquette, Joseph, of Châteauguay, student
> Hamelin, François Xavier, of St. Philippe, farmer

Hindenlang, Charles, of Paris, army officer
Narbonne, Pierre-Rémi, of St. Rémi, bailiff
Nicolas, François, of St. Athanase, school teacher
Robert, Joseph, of St. Philippe, farmer
Sanguinet, Ambroise, of St. Philippe, farmer
Sanguinet, Charles, of St. Philippe, farmer.

Of those executed in Montreal one, Hamelin, was eighteen years old; Daunais and Duquette were each twenty; Narbonne, twenty-three. Cardinal, who was thirty, wrote to his wife on the eve of his execution: "Tomorrow, at the time that I am writing now, my soul will be before its Creator and Judge . . . My only regret, in dying, is that I leave you, dear one, with five unhappy orphans, of whom one is not yet born. . . ."

Another of the twelve, Delorimier, wrote before his death his "Political Testament":

> I die without remorse; all that I desired was the good of my country, in insurrection and in independence . . . For 17 to 18 years I have taken an active part in almost every popular movement, always with conviction and sincerity. My efforts have been for the independence of my compatriots; thus far we have been unfortunate . . .
>
> But the wounds of my country will heal—the peace-loving Canadian will see liberty and happiness born anew on the St. Lawrence . . .
>
> To you, my compatriots, my execution and that of my comrades on the scaffold will be of use . . .
>
> I have only a few hours to live, and I have sought to divide them between my duty to religion and that due to my compatriots; for them I die on the gallows the infamous death of a murderer, for them I leave behind my young children and my wife, alone, for them I die with the cry on my lips: *Vive la Liberté, Vive l'Indépendance!*

The national-democratic people's uprising in Lower

Canada met defeat at the hands of the British soldiery and colonial reaction. Among the main reasons for the defeat were these:

—The armed struggle was only partly organized, and largely spontaneous; despite the fairly marked development of elements of people's power and widespread organization (much more advanced than in Upper Canada), there was no clear plan for the conquest of political power, and the initiative in the struggle was left to the forces of colonial reaction;

—The policy of the defensive, as in every popular uprising, proved fatal: instead of moving on Montreal from the Richelieu and Two-Mountains (the two main bases of Patriote support) and initiating a simultaneous move from within the city, the people's forces allowed themselves to be struck down singly, one after the other, with Montreal serving as Colborne's base for a successful operation on "interior lines";

—The Patriotes failed to launch an action in either of the two urban centres, Montreal or Quebec; in the case of the former, the fact that it was the main centre of English merchant-imperial influence was a determining factor, as was in the latter, the strength of Etienne Parent and the right wing of the people's movement; undoubtedly in both centres (as at Toronto) the still embryonic character of the working class, its lack of organization and political consciousness, deprived the revolution of a major driving force;

—The leaders of the Patriote movement, mainly pettybourgeois in social composition, in their agitation and program largely evaded the issue of struggle against feudal tenure and did not organize mass struggle in the countryside for its abolition; most of these same leaders, in the military showdown, failed to stand the test—Dr.

Chénier, who perished, and Wolfred Nelson's stand at St. Denis, were among the exceptions;

—The right-wing elements—representing, in effect, the bourgeoisie—who feared the mass struggle, went over to the side of reaction, paralyzing the movement in the key Quebec area and dividing it in others;

—While some of the lower clergy sympathized with and in some instances actively helped the insurgents, the upper hierarchy of the Church rendered invaluable aid to the imperial authorities by threatening Patriote supporters with excommunication and by denouncing popular resistance;

—The hopes of substantial assistance on the part of sympathetic U.S. democrats were largely frustrated by the collusion of the American authorities with the British in bringing about the defeat of the rising in 1838.

Each of the foregoing went into the making of the defeat; yet merely to enumerate them as disparate causal factors is not enough. We are left, as Charles Gagnon has pointed out in an important study, with "quite incoherent explanations." They need to be integrated in an overall view: one that sees the risings as a bourgeois-democratic, class and national revolution, the driving forces of which were insufficiently mature to secure victory. There had been neither a development of a French-Canadian industrial bourgeoisie of any substance, nor an urban-plebeian movement strong enough to combine with the peasant rising. It is within this setting that one must situate the confusion, vacillations and in many cases cowardice of a petty-bourgeois leadership, and its deficiencies of perspective and organization. A similar inadequacy will be seen in the case of Upper Canada, whose rising in solidarity with the Patriotes was to fail both in its fraternal purpose and its local objectives.

Yet these defeated initiatives of the bourgeois and
national revolutions in the two Canadas were not the end
but rather the beginning of the process of establishing a
capitalist democracy in British North America.

4

Land, Liberty -- and Capital

Free land, and a larger liberty—these were the magnet-pull of the New World drawing millions across the Atlantic in the century after the Napoleonic wars. Yet issues involving landownership and popular liberties in the colonies of British North America were to give rise to struggles that became rebellion. The causes lay in the colonial structure of rule, the character of property relations, and national inequality and oppression.

British settlement in the Maritime colonies and in Upper Canada took place under the aegis of governments that sought to implant a society dominated by large land-owners and merchants, safeguarded from infections of republicanism. The aim of creating a colonial aristocracy was to be furthered by the practice of granting large estates to army officers, government officials, wealthy merchants. In Nova Scotia some six million acres were thus granted; and in Prince Edward Island, 1,400,000 acres were given in 20,000 acre lots to Lords Westmoreland and Selkirk, Sir James Montgomery and a handful of "members of the British aristocracy, military officers and others having claims upon the gratitude of Government."

In Upper Canada, of 16 million acres of public land surveyed by 1824, some 11 million had been granted: in most cases, given free to "privileged persons who had Deserved well of the state." A notable instance was that of Col. Thomas Talbot, owner of the largest estates in the western part of the province. A member of the Legislative Council, he had acquired 60,000 acres; "for every farm he allotted to a settler, he himself received an even larger acreage." (For each 50 acres thus assigned, he obtained 200 for himself.)

Of the eight million acres obtained by individuals, five million were in the hands of speculators who "wanted to get as much land as they could, keep it for a rise, let others settle around it, and increase the value of the vacant land monopolized; and then, of course, make their fortunes."

In addition to these private acquisitions, it had been decreed by the Act of 1791 that one seventh of all land surveyed was to be "reserved" to the crown, and another seventh to be held for the maintenance of "a Protestant clergy" (taken to refer to the Church of England, which the colonial authorities wished to establish as a state church, despite the fact that the majority of the settlers were adherents of other denominations). Three million acres in the Canadas were in this manner set aside as Clergy Reserves. "These reserved lands," it was noted in 1828, "as they are at present distributed over the country, retard more than any other circumstance the improvement of the Colony, lying as they do in the detached portions in each township, and intervening between the occupations of actual settlers, who have no means of cutting roads through the woods and morasses, which thus separate them from their neighbors."

It was the Scottish radical democrat Robert Gourlay who in 1817 initiated the first systematic public discussion of grievances in Upper Canada. Before coming to Canada he had, he later wrote, "espoused the cause of the farmers against the Lairds of Fife . . . published a specific plan for parliamentary reform . . . and all along have taken part with the poor against the rich." He had published two pamphlets on the "Tyranny of the Poor Laws" and got up a petition (it was not acted on) asking that overseers of the poor "should not have the power to call out children under 12 to work during the winter half-year." He had been present in 1816 at the huge meeting of unemployed at Spa Fields, London.

In his "Address to the Resident Landowners of Upper Canada" Gourlay set forth a series of questions to settlers with the purpose of compiling an exhaustive "Statistical Account of Upper Canada." Population, employment, resources, costs and prices, schools, mills, roads—all were included, ending with his Question 31: "What, in your opinion, retards the improvement of your township in particular, or the Province in general; and what would most contribute to the same?" In each township, the settlers were urged to gather in meetings and discuss the questions raised in it. Replies came back from some forty localities across the province. A sampling of the replies to the 31st Question includes the following:

> The reserve of two-sevenths of the lands for the crown and clergy, must for a long time keep the country a wilderness; a harbor for wolves; a hindrance to a compact and good neighborhood . . . A defect in the system of colonization, and too great a quantity of the lands in the hands of individuals, who do not reside in the province, and are not assessed for those lands . . . (*Township of Sandwich*)

> Land held in fee by distant owners in large quantities, not responsible for defraying any charges for opening roads, while the whole burden falls on actual settlers, is a hindrance to the growth of the settlement. (*Norwich*)

> . . . In many places of this province, large tracts of land have been granted to certain individuals, and these being generally men of fortune, are under no necessity of selling their lands, but hold them at so high a price, that poor people are not able to buy them. (*Trafalgar*)

> What hinders the improvement of the township, is, bad roads, want of men and money. (*Waterloo*)

> . . . the immense tracts of land held by non-residents . . . we are certain that we do not exaggerate in stating the number of acres at from 12 to 15,000, exclusive of the crown and clergy reserves which are two-seventh parts of the whole land in the township. (*Kingston*)

The prompt response to Gourlay's initiative, the widespread holding of township meetings which discussed grievances and called for reforms, was matched by the vehemence with which the colonial oligarchy reacted to the challenge. A raw nerve, clearly, had been impinged upon: the rights of property writ large and enshrined in special privilege. Gourlay had proposed the calling of a Convention of delegates from the township meetings, and was himself touring the province. Blasts of denunciation from an outraged officialdom presaged reprisal. In further Addresses to the settlers Gourlay upheld their right of petitioning the Legislature, urged them to act unitedly in their common interest:

"Every man," he wrote, "who has a spark of sincerity or patriotism in his soul has now sufficient cause to bestir himself . . . Every eye should be resolutely bent on the one thing needful—a radical change of system in the Government of Upper Canada."

At York, on July 6 to 10, 1818, there convened the "Meeting of the Upper Canadian Convention of the Friends of Enquiry." Delegates were present from the Western, Niagara, Gore, London, Midland, Newcastle and Johnstown districts. They adopted petitions addressed to the Governor and to the Prince Regent in England.

They were answered with terror and persecution. Gourlay was arrested, imprisoned, charged with sedition and banished under the provisions of the infamous Alien

Act of 1804. Bartimus Ferguson, editor of the *Niagara Spectator*, who had published Gourlay's writings and carried forward the agitation against the oligarchy, was arrested, charged with libel, and sentenced to the pillory and eighteen months imprisonment (a sentence only remitted in part on his making humble submission).

This first round in the struggle of the settlers against the landed oligarchy at York had ended in repression. But the case of Gourlay, "the banished Briton," was not soon forgotten; nor was a resumption of agitation against land-monopoly and privilege long delayed.

Meanwhile, the system of free grants of vast tracts of land to favored individuals was being supplemented by a new type of business venture. Large-scale landownership, despite its ancient lineage as a feudal institution, was by now firmly enmeshed in the cash relationships of a mercantile society; in 1820 one Joseph Pinsent had published a series of letters to Lord Liverpool urging adoption of a policy of "sale of public lands to capitalists." Acquisition of estates for speculative purposes linked with government-sponsored colonization schemes, was becoming an object of active interest on the part of "persons who, with different objects in view, were desirous of employing their capital in the settlement and cultivation of lands in Canada."

The "matter of land" was increasingly to become a matter of *capital*, and of its aggrandizement. By 1825 the Canada Land Company, headed by War Claims Commissioner John Galt, had acquired 2,300,000 acres of Crown reserves in Upper Canada (one million acres of this comprising the Huron Tract). Within fifteen years the Huron Tract was to acquire a population of some six thousand settlers, spread over 20 townships.

The mutually profitable intertwining of interests of

the colonial Family Compact and the London capitalists
was spelled out in the advice of Bishop Strachan to John
Galt, commissioner of the Canada Co.: "Now I wish to
lay it down as a principle never to be departed from,
that it is in the interest of the Canada Co. to support the
Colonial authorities and never to take a side against
them." (Sept. 25, 1826). By 1833, with the stock of the
company "only 17% paid for . . . selling at 55% premium,
the most buoyant security in the London market," Galt
observed with satisfaction: "Every day confirms the sound-
ness of my undertakings in the Upper Province, and the
Company have pocketed above £300,000 through my
instrumentality." The operations of the Canada Co. were
understandably resented by the settlers. It had sold the
lands granted to it "at a price enormously greater than
their real cash value," as A. T. Galt (son of John) admitted some years later.

According to evidence given before the Upper Canada
Assembly's committee on grievances (1835), land for
which the Company had paid "about one shilling per
acre" was selling for 12s. 6d. to 13s. 9d. per acre. Agents
of the Company in their treatment of settlers were "very
arbitrary . . . tyrannical"; settlers evicted from their farms
"are scared out of the tract and ejected without any form
of law or justice. Many persons have been driven out of
the territory; there is no other law there except what the
Company's servants make."

The witness was Col. Van Egmond, veteran of Waterloo and staunch defender of the settlers in the Huron
Tract.

In 1824 a new Reform newspaper started publication
in Queenston. Its first issue flayed the evils of colonialism

and called for independent development of a Canadian manufacturing industry:

> We earnestly desire to see established, throughout Upper and Lower Canada, New-Brunswick, and Nova Scotia, efficient societies for the improvement of arts and manufactures. We would like to see the manufacturer not quite four thousand miles from the farmer . . .
>
> Our foreign commerce, confined and shackled as it is, and it has been, is entirely in the hands of the British capitalists: our lumber trade is merely encouraged to support British wornout shipping. We are inundated, glutted with British manufactures . . .

The paper was the *Colonial Advocate;* its editor, William Lyon Mackenzie. Born in Dundee, Scotland, on March 12, 1795, the young Scot brought with him an outlook strongly marked by the influences of British radicalism and French revolutionary thought. The conditions he encountered in the colony on his arrival in 1820—first as surveyor on the Lachine canal, then as a store-keeper in York, Dundas and Queenston—led him to abandon trade for the political struggle. Of the motives which led him to take this step, he later wrote in a now famous passage:

> I had long seen the country in the hands of a few shrewd, crafty, covetous men, under whose management one of the most lovely and desirable sections of America remained a comparative desert. The most obvious public improvements were stayed; dissension was created among classes; citizens were banished and imprisoned in defiance of all law; the people had been long forbidden, under severe pains and penalties, from meeting anywhere to petition for justice; large estates were wrested from their owners in utter contempt of even the forms of the courts; the Church of England, the adherents of which were few, monopolized as much of the lands of the colony as all the

religious houses and dignitaries of the Roman Catholic Church had had the control of in Scotland at the era of the Reformation; other sects were treated with contempt and scarcely tolerated; a sordid band of land-jobbers grasped the soil as their patrimony, and with a few leading officials, who divided the public revenue among themselves, formed "the family compact" and were the avowed enemies of common schools, of civil and religious liberty, of all legislative or other checks to their own will. Other men had opposed, and been converted by them. At one-and-twenty I might have united with them, but chose rather to join the oppressed, nor have I ever regretted that choice, or wavered from the object of my early pursuit.

Control of the colony by this "family compact" had its roots in the then prevailing conditions of land-monopoly and colonial dependency. The local ruling class of land-owners, merchants and officials depended for their power on toadying to the British Colonial administrators, and for their wealth on the toil of the Canadian settlers and Indian trappers. Even before the War of 1812, Judge Thorpe had described them as "a shopkeeper aristocracy," "the vilest miscreants on earth, who have gorged themselves on the plunder of every Department, and squeezed every dollar out of the wretched inhabitants." Durham wrote of them: "The bench, the magistracy, the high offices of the Episcopal Church, and a great part of the legal profession, are filled by the adherents of this party; by grant or purchase, they have acquired nearly the whole of the waste lands of the Province; they are all-powerful in the chartered banks, and, till lately, shared among themselves almost exclusively all offices of trust and profit."

W. L. Mackenzie's description—somewhat more colorful and specific—appears in his *Sketches of Canada and the United States:*

This family connection rules Upper Canada according to its own good pleasure, and has no efficient check from this country to guard the people against its acts of tyranny and oppression. It includes the whole of the judges of the supreme civil and criminal tribunal—active Tory politicians . . . It includes half the executive council or provincial cabinet. It includes the Speaker and other eight members of the Legislative Council. It includes the persons who have the control of the Canada Land Company's monopoly. It includes the president and solicitor of the Bank, and about half the Bank Directors; . . . This family compact surround the Lieutenant Governor, and mould him, like wax, to their will; they fill every office with their relatives, dependants and partisans; by them justices of the peace and officers of the militia are made and unmade; . . . the whole of the revenues of Upper Canada are in reality at their mercy;—they are Paymasters, Receivers, Auditors, King, Lords and Commons!

Samuel Hart, radical editor of the Cobourg *Plain Speaker* denounced those who, "wallowing in luxury . . . arrogate to themselves the right of governing . . . (They) are not the Producing Class in any other sense than this— they produce discord—engender strife—create rebellions —foster disease—and fatten upon the miseries of their fellow creatures."

"The farmer toils, the merchant toils, the labourer toils, and the Family Compact reap the fruit of their exertions," wrote Mackenzie in *Patrick Swift's Almanac* for 1834.

Farmer, laborer, merchant, landowner—already the colonial economy is marked by a social division of labor that comes from the breaking down of pioneer self-sufficiency and leads to the crystallizing of distinct social classes. In Upper Canada and the Maritimes, as in the rather different setting of Lower Canada, the early 19th century presents a picture of the varied stages of this process of change, the outcome of which is industrial capitalism: the system of large-scale, factory, machine production carried on by wage-workers hired by the factory owners whose aim is to "make money" through extracting profits.

In the first stages of settlement there is an almost self-sufficient "natural economy" in which the pioneer family contends against the wilderness, and there are only tenuous links with the outside world of the market (from which, of course, the settlers themselves have come: the primitiveness of their condition is a transitory, consciously accepted hardship).

"Tedious and laborious," one settler writes, was the work of clearing with axe and whipsaw the heavily timbered lands north of the lower Great Lakes. Having put up a log dwelling, the settler and his family had to look to their own provisioning, in clothing as in most else. An early Canadian pioneer, Mrs. Amelia Harris, gives this picture of frontier housekeeping in Norfolk County:

> It was flax, the Pedlar's pack, and Buckskins that the early settlers had to depend upon for clothing when their first supply was worn out. Deerskins were carefully preserved and dressed and the men had trowsers and coats made of them . . . Chopping, Log(g)ing, and clearing wild land required strong linen for Shirts and plaid for their own dresses. Almost every thrifty farm house had a Loom, and both wife and daughters learned to weave.

The "pedlar's pack" was the link connecting the isolated settler with the distant worlds of commerce and manufacture. On it Mrs. Harris depended for some "very indifferent printed Calicos . . . a piece of check for aprons . . . ribbons with tape, needles, and pins, and horn combs."

Gradually, as the settlers cleared the land and started

farms, the largely self-sufficient family economy gave way
to a measure of division of labor, with simple commodity
exchange of farm crops for the handiwork of the artisan.
Thus, two years after Carleton Place, near Ottawa, was
settled, a blacksmith's shop and cooperage were started;
and the following year a settler of means started a tannery,
a potash works, a store and a "groggery."

Commodity exchange received a strong impetus from
the activity of the colonial merchant. An account written
in 1825 says that for farm produce the merchants will give
in exchange "broadcloth, implements of husbandry, gro-
ceries and every sort of article that is necessary . . ." The
service was hardly philanthropic: the writer hastens to
note "the exorbitant rate at which all merchandise of British manufacture is sold in Upper Canada. . . . The different articles of wearing apparel cost nearly twice as
much as they do on the other side of the Atlantic, and are
of very inferior quality." The first millionaire family in
Toronto, the Cawthras, made their fortune in dry-goods
retailing. One settler at Perth, William Miller, wrote
home that "A pot which you will get for 4 shillings will
cost £2 here." Some sizeable fortunes were made by fleec-
ing the settlers in this manner.

Together with the growth of an internal market came
that of the productive forces: from individual, petty production to the small beginnings of co-operative social
labor of several or many working together. During the
quarter century after the War of 1812 small-scale production was the rule, with few exceptions. The watermill,
which had been in use since the early middle ages, was
typical of this level of production; the petty industry
based upon it was of necessity rural, in locations, determined by available water-courses. Grist mills and sawmills

were among the first and most widespread small enterprises. Gourlay in 1817 tells of settlers on the Thames
bringing their logs to the nearest mill, the arrangement
for payment being that the millowner and the sawyer
each kept a quarter of the lumber sawn. A settler in
Lanark (Ottawa Valley) writes in 1821 complaining of
"the scarcity of corn mills and the great distance to which
he has to send his grain to be grinded"— fourteen miles,
and draught animals hard to come by.

Around the mills, or at trading posts, villages grew up.
In the second issue of his *Colonial Advocate*, May 28,
1824, William Lyon Mackenzie reports on industrial beginnings in the Niagara area: "In and near St. John's village, which is one of the most flourishing in the District,
there are four grist mills, five sawmills, Beckett's woollen
factory, dyeing and fulling works, and carding and shear-
ing machines, tannery, still houses, cast iron foundry,
cabinet makers, waggon makers and many other mechanics."

Going up Yonge Street, north of Toronto, at that time
one would pass a series of mills, tanneries, pottery works.
At Markham the "German mills" (built by settlers who
came to Upper Canada in 1794) included a sawmill, grist-
mill, distillery and brewery. At Newmarket there were
mills and tanneries. In the Don Valley east of York, on
the Mill Road, were "multifarious works" including flour
mills, sawmills, fulling and carding mills, breweries, paper
mills, and a shop with axe-grinding machinery.

At a certain stage, small-scale production carried on by
a master and one or two apprentices or journeymen grows
to the dimension of what Marx designates as *manufacture*: production by a number of craftsmen, still working
by hand, but assembled under one roof and one overseer:

the earliest form of capitalist production.* This "manu-factory" stage in many branches of industry in Canada lasted through the greater part of the 19th century. It was the prelude to large-scale, power-driven machine produc-tion—full-blown industrial capitalism. Thanks to colonial-ism and Family Compact rule, industrial growth in the Canadas as compared with the States was retarded by at least a generation. Nevertheless, the decades leading up to the Rebellion witnessed a number of attempts to get industry going on a modern footing: endeavors that reflect the coming into being and early strivings of a small native industrial bourgeoisie.

In 1824 the *Colonial Advocate* reports that "an opulent merchant of St. Davids, Niagara, is building a steam mill on a large scale." Machinery for the spinning of wool—believed to be the first to enter the province—was import-ed from the United States; it comprised one slubbing billy of 25 spindles, and a spinning jenny of 50. Of the launch-ing of this enterprise Mackenzie observes: "It is a sincere pleasure to us to record instances like this of Canadian enterprise and public spirit." A few weeks later he reports the establishment of a woollen factory in Flamboro West, near Burlington. The owner gets the whole of the ma-chinery made on the spot, or in the neighborhood; cast-ings are "very neatly executed" at a foundry in nearby Ancaster, an English mechanic making all the spindles and steel machinery. Had the iron been gotten from Mar-mora, "the whole concern would have been purely Upper Canadian, from the material of the building up to the coat." In the same village a flour mill is worked with cast-

---

*This definition of "manufacture," as used by Marx, in relation to a definite stage in the development of capitalist production, preceding machine-production, must be distinguished from the later usage of the term, as covering secondary or processing industry.

iron machinery made in Montreal—a further argument in support of "native manufactures."

Mackenzie not only advocated industrialization with his pen; in 1825 he participated in efforts to found a paper manufactory near York. The effort failing "in consequence of the difficulty of obtaining shareholders," he looked (without result) to the Legislature, "by bounty or otherwise, [to] set the mill agoing." Observing that a steam-driven paper mill in Pittsburgh employs 190 workers, Mackenzie comments: "We suppose that there are not nineteen persons employed in the manufacture of paper throughout British North America."

Distilling, however, made more headway. The steps leading to the erection of one of the oldest distilleries, near the foot of Parliament Street, Toronto, are recorded in Dr. Scadding's *Toronto of Old*: "Down by the Bay, a windmill built for Mr. Worts had been followed by large brick and wood buildings sheltering elaborate machinery driven by steam power." Shortly thereafter, a further change took place: "gigantic structures of massive, dark-colored stone tower up before the eye, vying . . . in ponderous strength with the works of the castle builders of feudal times." DARK SATANIC MILLS ?

Trade and shipping became a still greater stimulus to industrial growth once the steam engine had made its appearance. By 1817 there were two steamers plying Lake Ontario (one of over 700 tons), the year after, one on Lake Erie; and in 1819 a steamer was built and launched on the Ottawa, powered by a Canadian-made engine—one of the first produced in the Canadas. In the early 1830s the York Foundry and Steam Engine Manufactory was building marine engines, as described by a contemporary:

> The works comprise seven turning lathes, a boring mill, drilling machine, blowing apparatus, etc., all of which are

put into operation by one ten-horse-power high-pressure engine. There are also ten or a dozen apartments in which are carried on the various businesses of moulding, pattern making, blacksmithing, Copper and Tin working, finishing, Plough making, wheelwrighting, etc. etc. The quantity of iron melting averages at near a ton a day, and the number of workmen employed amounts to about eighty.

These were "Dutcher's Foundrymen," to whom Mackenzie was to refer in 1837 as being (along with "Armstrong's axemakers" who worked in a shop by the Don) the men "who can be depended on."

The creation of a capitalist industry required not only capital, plant, machinery; above all, it called for the presence of large numbers of workingmen, "free" of all encumbrances of property, available to be hired by owners of capital. As early as 1793 a merchant landowner in the township of Whitby advertised for "Carpenters, Smiths, Husbandrymen, Laborers and Women of Good Character" to settle on his estate and work for him. Such workers were provided, in the first place, by the British Isles, whose people were experiencing the horrors of the early years of triumph of the factory system. Industrialization in Britain was ruining masses of small handicraftsmen, while a new wave of forcible enclosures was driving peasants off the land. Recurring crises of over-production, from 1815 on, were creating masses of unemployed. "If trade does not increase," remarked one reverend gentleman, "there will be a war of the rich against the poor."

Failing redress of their demands for work and decent wages, more and more workers and dispossessed small farmers turned their gaze westward. Soldiers back from the war in Canada told of the fertile farms and vast expanses of land waiting in the colony. In 1820 the mechanics of

Paisley sent a petition to Parliament; stating that "it was dreadful to see 400 persons in every square mile without the means of subsistence," they asked for aid to emigrate, preferably to Canada. In 1813 Bathurst, the Colonial Secretary, had written to Governor-General Prevost at Quebec that "there are at this moment a considerable number of the natives of Sutherland and Caithness who are only waiting for an opportunity to leave their native country"; he suggested that "the male part of this population be rendered in some degree valuable both for the present defence and the future protection of Upper Canada by offering to them grants of land in that province and a free passage for themselves and their families." By 1816 the project began to materialize. Departure was delayed for some time due to a demand of £16 deposit (from penniless emigrants!), but finally about 500 persons sailed from Greenock, leaving Ben Lomond behind them and heading through the Firth for the open sea. They were settled in Glengarry County. In 1819 three more shiploads came; and in 1820 twelve hundred of "the laboring population of the County of Lanark," who had organized an "emigration society," took the same route westward. ("This is not a Radical cargo," was the hopeful comment of Governor Dalhousie.) They settled in the Bathurst district, above Perth.

Meanwhile, the Hunger was in Ireland: in 1821-2 it greatly worsened with failure of the potato crop. Under the rule of English landlords Ireland produced meat and vegetables in fine profusion, but for export, not for Irish eating. The Lord Bishop of Limerick wrote: "The existing state of things is truly frightful . . ." The tenantry of one estate could not pay their rent and were promptly evicted: "They were in the most deplorable state, without houses, without food, without clothing or money—starving and almost dying in the ditches." In 1823 a shipment of destitute Irish was brought out under the direction of Peter Robinson and settled northwest of Bytown (Ottawa). Two years later another group was brought from County Cork (two thousand were asked for: 50,000 applied). They were taken north of Cobourg, given 100 acres per family and rations to get started on. The settlement they founded was named Peterborough. In the same year "the MacNab" set up a semi-feudal colony on the Ottawa; and another landowner-autocrat, Thomas Talbot, "planted" settlers on his 65,000 acres north of Lake Erie.

But the great mass of the half-million who got passage to Canada in the 1820s and 30s came, not under organized land-settlement schemes, but as unorganized "ballast" in returning lumber ships—foul, leaky hulks, often scarce fit for cattle. Durham in his Report cited the evidence of Dr. Morrin, Inspecting Physician of the Port of Quebec:

> I am almost at a loss for words to describe the state in which the emigrants frequently arrived; with a few exceptions, the state of the ships was quite abominable; so much so, that the harbor-master's boatmen had no difficulty, at the distance of gun-shot, either when the wind was favorable or in a dead calm, in distinguishing by the odor alone a crowded emigrant ship. I have known as many as from 30 to 40 deaths to have taken place, in the course of a voyage, from typhus fever on board of a ship containing from 500 to 600 passengers . . . As to those who were not sick on arriving, I have to say that they were generally forcibly landed by the masters of vessels, without a shilling in their pockets to procure them a night's lodging, and very few of them with the means of subsistence for more than a very short period. They commonly established themselves along the wharfs and at the different landing-places, crowding into any place of shelter they could obtain, where they subsisted principally upon the charity of the inhabitants. For six weeks at a time, from the commencement of

the emigrant-ship season, I have known the shores of the
river along Quebec, for about a mile and a half, crowded
with these unfortunate people, the places of those who
might have moved off being constantly supplied by fresh
arrivals, and there being daily drafts of from 10 to 30
taken to the hospital with infectious disease.

Between 1824 and 1841 the population of the Canadas
was roughly doubled. In 1824 about 8,000 emigrants came
to Canada from Britain; between that year and 1829,
about 10-11,000 came each year; in 1830, the number rose
to 25,000; the year after, 50,000 (of whom 34,000 were
from Ireland), and a like number the next year.

Of the newcomers, many became settlers on the land;
some grew prosperous, but some suffered insurmountable
difficulties, like those of the Lanark weavers who were
set down in what Sir John Colborne conceded was "a very
inferior tract of country . . . a continuous succession of
rocky knolls with scraps or bits, seldom exceeding an acre
in extent, of good land between." In 1825 a petition was
signed by three hundred settlers from this district (Bathurst); having experienced "crosses, losses and disappoint-
ments," they were utterly unable to make repayment of
sums advanced to them when they were brought out from
Scotland.

But for many it was not even possible to obtain a patch
of land. These joined the ranks of the class of wage-
workers that was just beginning to take shape. Laborers
employed on canal-building; loggers and sawmill workers; building and metal-trades and shipyard workers;
mariners, waggoners, service trades—such were the first re-
cruits to the working class.

The working people who came to Canada from the
British Isles brought with them memories not only of bitter hardship and hunger, but of militant resistance to

oppression. Their spirit of independence was to form a vital part of the tradition of democratic struggle of the Canadian people.

Out of the nightmare-horrors of the factory-hells of industrial England there had grown up movements of protest and theories of far-reaching reform and, in some instances, of fundamental social change. Such was the vision of Robert Owen, industrialist-reformer and Utopian Socialist, who visited North America in 1824. Owen conceived of a reconstruction of society on socialist lines, carried through by philanthropic effort, education, and the force of example of small, ideal co-operative communities. In the late 1820s one of his followers, a retired British Navy purser, Capt. Henry Jones, established an egalitarian Socialist settlement on the shore of Lake Huron, in Lambton County, 12 miles east of present-day Sarnia. He named it "Toon O'Maxwell," after Owen's home in New Lanark. For a time the settlers ran their community on the basis of common ownership and collective living; they built a one-storey community log-house, each family having an apartment, and a common kitchen and dining room. The men worked together, clearing the land, using in part equipment discarded from military stores of the 1812 war. But the communitarian experiment did not last long. An Indian Methodist missionary, Peter Jones (no relative of the Captain) records in his diary for Saturday, August 1, 1829: "Started for St. Clair this morning. In the afternoon we passed a new settlement of white people eight or ten miles east of the mouth of the lake. This settlement was formed by a Mr. Jones, who tried to carry out what is called the Owen system of having all things common, but I was informed the thing did not work well here . . ."

The Owenite settlement vanished, leaving scarcely a

trace; its members took up individual tracts. The inspiration for "Toon O'Maxwell" was utopian, and neither the material nor the theoretical basis for a Socialist reshaping of society as yet existed. But the spirit of striving for betterment, the determination to alter conditions in the interests of those who toil, asserted themselves in other, more immediately practical ways.

In 1827, printing-trades workers at Quebec had organized the first trade union in Canada; it "took part in the regulation of wages, cared for its sick and held musical and dramatic entertainments." There are indications that other groups of workers —"labor circles"— were in existence also in Lower Canada before 1830. During the '30s there was a shoe-makers' union in existence in Montreal.

In 1832, the printers at York organized a local (a first start had been made in 1824)—the first trade union in Upper Canada. Shortly thereafter, unions of shoemakers, coopers and stonemasons were established. Between the interests of masters who were in business to make a profit for themselves, and workingmen who sold their labor-power for subsistence, such records as there are show that the early struggles were over matters of wages and hours of work. The Cobourg *Star and Reformer* of July 13, 1836, carried a report of a workers' protest meeting against long hours and "domestic slavery"; the paper recorded it thus:

> Pursuant to notice a meeting of Mechanics and Laborers of the village of Cobourg and vicinity assembled at the Common School House on Monday the 11th instant to take into consideration the present unsettled conditions and existing usages practised by most Mechanics and Laborers in this place as respects the quantity of time required of most of the Mechanics and Laborers in daily labor, and to adopt a specific time for a day's labor.

Then, under the sub-heading "No More Slavery!"—"it was resolved that the number of hours which we now work is nothing better than domestic Slavery, is altogether derogatory to the improvement of our moral and intellectual powers and progress in the arts and sciences, and is one of the chief causes of vice and ignorance." It was therefore resolved that "we hold ourselves under a sacred obligation that we will not labor more than 10 hours for a day's work." A committee of nine was struck off to carry these decisions into effect. A further meeting on July 15 decided on a working schedule for the summer months: from 6 a.m. to 6 p.m., with a one-hour break at 7:30 for breakfast, and 12 to 1 for lunch; and in winter, from 7 a.m. to 6 p.m., with breakfast eaten before work, and 12 to 1 off for lunch. All workers signing their names to this agreement were called upon to abide by its conditions, and work no more than 10 hours daily.

The historic struggle for the shorter work-day was thus under way in Upper Canada even before the 1837 Rising. Here as elsewhere, capitalism from its earliest beginnings carried within itself the seeds of a fundamental challenge in the form of a social force that embodied co-operative, social labor: the industrial working class. The struggle between the conflicting interests of Labor and Capital would in time become dominant in the social life of industrial communities; but in the period we are considering, the eventual possibility and particular form of an industrial capitalist development hinged on the outcome of a series of struggles around such issues as those of colonial independence, freedom of trade, the attainment of a "market democracy."

In each of the colonies the ruling class was wholeheartedly committed to the preservation of colonial status.

The English Tory merchants' "Constitutional Association" at Quebec stood pledged "to use every effort to maintain the connection of this colony with the parent state, and a just subordination to its authority."

The demands of the rising native bourgeoisie for "freedom to trade" challenged the rigid imperial system of colonial "Restriction, Regulation and Restraint." The Navigation Acts, forbidding transport of goods to or from a colony in any but British ships, were one part of the policy. Opposition to the development of local manufactures and industry in the colonies, was another. A ban on clothing manufacture in the Canadas had been imposed in 1768; in 1784, restrictions were placed on commerce with the United States and the West Indies.

Even the conservative *Quebec Gazette*, on Aug. 9, 1821, complained of these restrictions: "These Statutes restrain us from trying to obtain a market, and making purchases all over the world; they restrain foreigners from coming here to purchase or sell, should they be so inclined; they oblige us to have our goods carried solely in British ships —in short, they oblige us to buy and sell there, and then. by the operation of the Corn Laws, they enact, in effect, that we shall not buy or sell at all." This paper then drew the conclusion: "The power of regulating the trade of the Colonies, which belongs to the British Parliament, is in fact a power over the fortunes, the industry, and the prosperity of every individual in the Colonies. It is a Magic Wand at whose motions our limbs may be dried up, and our prosperity vanish like a shadow . . ."

In the first number of the *Colonial Advocate*, Mackenzie denounced what he described as "a system revolting to the feelings of every independent thinking colonist;"

> Our foreign commerce, confined and shackled as it is, and it has been, is entirely in the hands of the British

manufacturers . . . Our farmers are indebted to our country merchants, our country merchants are deeply bound down in the same manner, and by the same causes, to the Montreal wholesale dealers. Few of these Montreal commission merchants are men of capital; they are generally merely the factors or agents of British houses, and thus a chain of debt, dependence and degradation is begun and kept up, the links of which are fast bound round the souls and bodies of our yeomanry; and that with few exceptions from the richest to the poorest, while the tether stake is fast in British factories.

Representatives of the local bourgeoisie called for *freedom of the market.* The Upper Canada Reformers proclaimed: "That the right of obtaining articles of luxury, or necessity, in the cheapest market, is inherent in the people . . ." and issued the slogan: "Freedom of trade —every man to be allowed to buy at the cheapest market and sell at the dearest." They denounced the land-monopoly as an obstacle to industrial development: writing from St. Catharines in Upper Canada the mill-owner W. H. Merritt complained that "the proceeds of all those lands are vested in Great Britain when the Province is literally beggared for want of capital."

The glaring contrast between economic progress in the U.S. and economic stagnation in the colonies spurred the Canadians to protest. "While our neighbours on the other side of the river are rapidly going ahead," the *Sandwich Western Herald* lamented, "we . . . seem to be nearly at a standstill." "Some change in our circumstances is absolutely necessary to prevent ruin," wrote an Upper Canadian correspondent of the Montreal *Gazette* in 1833.

The key issue for economic development of the nation was to be clearly stated in Mackenzie's Navy Island proclamation (Dec. 13, 1837):

"Until Independence is won, trade and industry will

be dormant, houses and lands will be unsaleable, merchants will be embarrassed, and farmers and mechanics harassed and troubled; that point once gained, the prospect is fair and cheering, a long day of prosperity may be ours."

5

"Some Change in Our Circumstances"

Upper Canadian insistence on the urgent need of "some change in our circumstances" resulted in a broad coalition of interests opposed to the Family Compact. The opposition embraced local industrialists and small merchants, professionals, large sections of the poorer settlers, urban working people. A "moderate" wing, headed by Marshall S. Bidwell and Dr. Warren Baldwin, put major emphasis on the demand for cabinet responsibility (the theory of which Dr. Baldwin expounded in a letter to the imperial authorities in 1828). A radical-democratic wing, headed by Dr. John Rolph and W. L. Mackenzie, moved as the struggle sharpened to outright advocacy of independence.

But the struggle was not limited to the demand of political democracy. The abuses of colonial-compact rule called forth widely varying forms of protest agitation. Reforms were sought in the realms of public health and education and civil liberties; while religious equality, opposition to the establishment of an Anglican state church, and demands for abolition of the clergy reserves system came from the dissenters, the largest group of whom were the Methodists. Nor was the Reform movement indifferent to the question of peace and war; large numbers of its supporters had known the horrors of the long-drawn wars against France in Europe, and of bloodshed and invasion on Canadian soil in 1812-15. Thus, in 1826 there were no less than a dozen organized "peace societies" in the province; the year following, a book urging universal peace was published by one John Casey, a resident of Upper Canada. "Patrick Swift's Almanac" for 1834 (published by Mackenzie) told of the organization of a group known as the "Children of Peace," in Sharon (or Hope): "This society numbers about 280 members in Hope, east of Newmarket. They have also started places of preaching at the Old Court House, York, on Yonge St., and at Markham . . ."

Anti-slavery agitation, and active help to the Abolitionist movement in the U.S., found a place in the work of the Canadian Reformers. The seventh clause of the Patriots' draft of a Constitution for Upper Canada stated: "There shall neither be slavery or involuntary servitude in this State, . . . People of colour, who have come into this State, with the design of becoming permanent inhabitants thereof, and are now resident therein, shall be entitled to all the rights of native Canadians, upon taking an oath or affirmation to support the constitution."

Public health became a pressing issue with the repeated incursions of cholera in the '30s. In Lower Canada the first board of health was established in 1832 as a result of public outcry over the inadequacy of measures taken to combat the scourge of cholera. During one of these outbreaks in Upper Canada, "at Dumfries thirty died in thirty hours": small villages were afflicted as well as the larger towns. Some years earlier the *Colonial Advocate* reported the opening of a medical school at St. Thomas —founded jointly by two leading Reformers, Drs. Duncombe and Rolph. The former campaigned actively for many years for a change in the treatment of the mentally ill, for whom at that time there was no other public provision than imprisonment. He moved in the Assembly in 1836 for the setting up of a commission on asylums.

(The Toronto asylum was established only fourteen years afterwards).

Educational facilities, other than those provided privately for children of the rich, were obtained only by slow degrees, as a result of widespread public pressure. In many instances the settlers themselves joined forces to establish and support a local school.

As Margaret Fairley has strongly emphasized, William Lyon Mackenzie's humanist "vision of a happy people" was at the heart of his philosophy of politics and education. His *Catechism of Education* (1830) defined education as "the best employment of all the means which can be made use of by man, for rendering the *human* mind to the greatest possible degree the *cause* of human happiness." The role of health, of creative labor and leisure, all are stressed. "Without the bodily labor of the great bulk of mankind the well-being of the species cannot be maintained; but if that bodily labor is carried beyond a certain extent, neither intellect, virtue nor happiness can flourish upon the earth." Those who fear popular sovereignty are disposed to deny education to the people, lest knowledge lead them to power:

> Such is an unavoidable opinion in the breasts of those who think that the human race ought to consist of two classes— one that of the oppressors, another that of the oppressed. But if education be to communicate the art of happiness; and if intelligence consists of knowledge and sagacity, the question whether the people should be educated is the same with the question whether they should be happy or miserable.

Mackenzie rejects the stand of Milton, who "seems to have had in view no education but that of the gentleman."

The Reformers campaigned vigorously on the related issues of civil and religious freedom. The church of

England, in possession of the vast clergy reserve lands, was well on the way to becoming the state church. Nonconformists, (though they comprised the majority), were denied the right to solemnize marriages or receive a title to lands for chapels or cemeteries. Of the Anglicans Durham observed, "The Church . . . for which alone it is proposed that the state should provide, is the Church which, being that of the wealthy, can best provide for itself, and has the fewest poor to supply with gratuitous religious instruction."

Eight thousand people in 1828 signed a petition circulated by the "Friends of Religious Liberty," a committee of twenty-three which included Mackenzie, Robert Baldwin, Jesse Ketchum and Egerton Ryerson. The last two were the authors of the petition; it asked the British parliament "to leave the ministers of all denominations of Christians to be supported by the people among whom they labour . . . to do away with all political distinctions on account of religious faith . . . to remove all ministers of religion from seats and places of power in the Provincial Government—to grant to the Clergy of all denominations of Christians the enjoyment of equal rights and privileges in everything that appertains to them as subjects . . . and as ministers of the Gospel, particularly the right of solemnizing Matrimony . . . to modify the Charter of King's College established at York in Upper Canada, so as to exclude all sectarian tests and preferences—and to appropriate the proceeds of the sale of lands heretofore set apart for the support of a Protestant Clergy, to the purposes of general education and various internal improvements."

Settlers in the Huron tract who after toiling to clear a patch of land found themselves in the clutches of the Canada Company; workers on the Welland Canal, living in miserable shanties and laboring from sun-up to night-fall; pioneers in the district of Bathurst, on the Ottawa, trying to scrape a living from barren soil; yeomen and mechanics of countryside and town and village—these were the readers of Mackenzie's *Colonial Advocate.* In its pages they found a forthright, hard-hitting expression of their grievances and aspirations.

Reaction, fearful of the awakening popular movement, organized a gang of young upper-class hoodlums (sons of the Jarvises, Ridouts and others) to raid Mackenzie's print-shop, smash its equipment, dump the presses into the Bay. This outburst of ruling-class violence only kindled fresh hatred of the Compact and stirred the opposition to renewed effort. Two years after the attack, in 1828, the people of York elected Mackenzie to the Assembly of Upper Canada. In this election the Reform forces for the first time won a majority of seats. But under the existing system of colonial rule the election of a Reform majority in the Assembly did not entail a change in government. The Executive, faced in the Assembly with a vote of non-confidence of 37 to 1, calmly ignored it.

From his seat in the Assembly Mackenzie pressed the attack on the Compact with unrelenting vigor, combining his work as a people's representative with that of editor of the *Advocate,* conducting agitation and organizational activity among the people. When reactionaries charged him with "disloyalty," his rejoinder was:

> I have said that I despise and hold in utter detestation the venal tribe, who . . . are now fattening on the spoils of this country—is this sedition? Then I am seditious. I have pointed out the neglect which successive governors, more or less ignorant of our wants, have been guilty of in regard to domestic improvements, and have delivered my opinion with the freedom of a Briton in Britain. Is this treason? Then I am also a rebellious subject.

With the help of the "loyalty" issue—the pretense that the Reformers were "foreign agents," and that what they sought was "annexation to the States" — the Tory Compact carried the 1830 elections. Mackenzie having held his seat, they trumped-up charges of "gross, scandalous and malicious libel" and expelled him from the House. His constituents in York re-elected him—and again he was expelled. No less than five times did the Compact engineer his expulsion, but his constituents invariably sent him back. At one time, a delegation of over 900 went to the Governor to protest: to no avail. Another time, hundreds of irate citizens invaded the precincts of the Assembly, bringing the business of the House to a standstill. In 1832 in Hamilton an attempt was made on Mackenzie's life.

The resolutions adopted at Reform meetings began to take on a tone of exasperation: one, at Whitby, uttered the warning: "Loyal as the inhabitants of this country unquestionably are, your petitioners will not disguise from your Excellency that they consider longer endurance, under their present oppression, neither a virtue nor a duty."

As the struggle sharpened and the masses of the people began to challenge the rule of the oligarchy there appeared in the Reform ranks (in the words of J. C. Dent, the 19th century chronicler) "symptoms of want of cohesion." A cleavage made itself felt between "the men of moderate views," like the Baldwins and Bidwells, on the one hand, and on the other, the "ultra-Radicals, composed for the most part of unlettered farmers and recently arrived immigrants, who showed an inclination to rally themselves under the banner of Mackenzie." "The worst symptom of all," in the eyes of the moderates, was "the ascendancy of Mackenzie and his satellites among the rural and uneducated part of the community"; Dent emphasizes Mackenzie's influence on "the farmers and mechanics."

As against the radical democrats, headed by Mackenzie, Samuel Lount and others, who stood their ground in the contest with reaction, the representatives of the local bourgeoisie were wavering. When the time of testing should come, they would go over to the side of the oligarchy. For the business elements, a "deal" with the Compact and the Colonial Office, such as would allow them some share in political power while maintaining the colonial status, was decidedly preferable to the prospect of a revolutionary struggle. In Dent's words, the right wing "saw the Radical element assuming an importance which as they believed was fraught with far greater danger to the commonwealth than was likely to arise from the continued ascendancy of the Compact."

The split in the Reform coalition began to develop in 1833, over the issue of independence versus colonialism. The English radical Joseph Hume had referred, in a letter published by Mackenzie, to a "crisis which is fast approaching in the affairs of the Canadas and which will terminate in independence and freedom from the baneful domination of the Mother Country . . ." This (since known as the "baneful domination" letter) was the occasion of a break between the Methodist leadership and Mackenzie. *Now Independence,"* wrote Ryerson in righteous horror, "is recommended as the motto and watchword of Reformers . . ." And in the name of the arch-tory founders of his own church, he went on: ". . . If a Wesley and a Fletcher wrote to *suppress* a revolution in America, never will I hesitate, with a zealous and devoted band of labourers, to aid zealously though feebly to *prevent* the revolution in Canada." It is to be noted that this break with the radical wing coincided with a new arrangement conceded by London, whereby the Methodists were to obtain a share in the Clergy Reserve grants.

In 1834 the radical-democratic left wing formed the Canadian Alliance Society, as a separate political organization. In the words of Mackenzie's biographer: "The Alliance was to exercise the duties of a political vigilance committee, by watching the proceedings of the Legislature . . ." The members were to devote themselves to the political education of the people, by "diffusing of sound political information by pamphlets and tracts." They were to look beyond Upper Canada by entering into close alliance with any similar association that may be formed in Lower Canada or the other colonies."

With the incorporation of York as a city in 1834 Mackenzie was elected the first Mayor of Toronto: a blow to the Compact in what they regarded as their own stronghold. In a general election held in the same year, the Reform forces once again secured a majority in the Assembly. A "committee on grievances" (the seventh to be set up) held hearings under Mackenzie's chairmanship. Its Report presented a summary of the popular demands and a program of popular struggle.

The chief demand put forward was one for which Mackenzie had long been agitating: in his own words, "An administration or executive government responsible to the province for its conduct." With a pointed reference to the English revolution the report recalled that "aristocratic encroachments" had been checked on that occasion by the winning of control by Parliament over the expenditure of funds. "No such system . . . to protect from Executive usurpation of popular rights can be found in Upper Canada."

The reply of the Colonial Office was contained in its instructions to a new lieutenant-governor, Sir Francis

Bond Head. It was in effect a refusal of the Assembly's demands. Yet the authorities showed an awareness of the need to temporize. Bond Head appointed to the Executive Council three of the "moderate" Reform leaders (Baldwin, Rolph and Dunn). Since he henceforth disregarded their advice, their position was clearly untenable and they soon resigned.

A delegation from a Reform meeting in Toronto reiterated the demand for "cheap, honest and responsible government." They concluded their representations in these terms: "If your Excellency will not govern us upon these principles you will exercise arbitrary sway, you will violate our Charter, virtually abrogate our law, and justly forfeit our submission to your authority." Mackenzie commented later that this was "the first low murmur of insurrection."

In 1836 Bond Head arbitrarily dissolved the Assembly and in the election which ensued threw himself and all the forces at his command into the campaign. Demagogy, threats, intimidation at the polls, gangsterism, all combined to give Sir Francis his desired majority. The demagogy harped on the theme of "loyalty": the Reformers pictured as "foreign agents," busily preparing to impose republican institutions via a Yankee invasion of the province. The atmosphere is suggested by Mackenzie's description of polling-day in Samuel Lount's constituency: "The whole space around the hustings was filled by an infuriated drunken mob, armed by dirks and knives and urged to shed blood, by conduct of the Queen's Lieutenant-Governor." Later, Durham wrote of the members then elected to the Assembly that "The circumstances under which they were elected, were such as to render them peculiarly objects of suspicion and reproach to a large number of their countrymen."

A commission of inquiry, headed by Lord Gosford, made its report on the situation in the Canadas in the spring of 1837. It contained the usual apparent concessions combined with actual refusal of the demands of the Reformers. Lord John Russell, categorically rejecting the idea of responsible government, had Parliament authorize the seizure of revenues by the Executive in Lower Canada.

At the news of Russell's resolutions a storm of indignation broke loose in the Lower province; meeting after meeting was held to protest against Colonial tyranny. Mackenzie and the Upper Canada Reformers pledged their support to the Patriotes in their struggle. At a meeting of the Toronto Alliance Society, on April 17th 1837, the "coercion" resolutions of the Imperial Government were strongly denounced and the sympathy of the Upper Canadian Reformers was extended to their brethren in Lower Canada.

The tide was rising. Both in Lower and Upper Canada, the authorities and the Compact calculatingly envisaged the possibility of a resort to civil war as the sole means of suppressing opposition once and for all.

Even the conservative *Christian Guardian* pointed to the opponents of reform as the originators of violence: "The disorder which disgraces those meetings of late has in no instance originated with the yeomanry or mechanics of the country, but with a few poor ignorant men of turbulent dispositions . . . prepared for, and *led on to the work by interested individuals who seem to be much alarmed at any attempt to correct abuses . . .*"

The flagrant intervention of Bond Head in the 1836 elections engendered conviction that only through decisive action by the people themselves could a solution be found for their ills. A "Declaration of the Toronto Reformers," drafted at the end of July, 1837, called for a

Convention of the people "to take into consideration the political condition of Upper Canada, with authority to its members to appoint commissioners, to meet others to be named on behalf of Lower Canada and any other colonies, armed with suitable powers as a congress to seek an effectual remedy for the grievances of the colonists," This document later became known as the "Declaration of Independence of Upper Canada."

The meeting placed great emphasis on support for the Lower Canada Patriotes, resolving:

> 1. That the warmest thanks and admiration are due from the Reformers of Upper Canada to the Honorable Louis Papineau, Speaker of the House of Assembly of Lower Canada, and his compatriots in and out of the legislature, for their past uniform, manly and noble independence, in favour of civil and religious liberty; and for their present devoted, honorable and patriotic opposition to the attempt of the British Government to violate their Constitution without their consent, subvert the powers and privileges of their local Parliament, and overawe them by coercive measures into a disgraceful abandonment of their just and reasonable wishes.
>
> 2. That the Reformers of Upper Canada are called upon by every tie of feeling, interest and duty, to make common cause with their fellow-citizens of Lower Canada, whose successful coercion would doubtless be in time visited upon us, and the redress of whose grievances would be the best guarantee for the redress of our own.

The same meeting adopted a plan "for uniting, organizing and registering the Reformers of Upper Canada as a political union." "The machinery of agitation," wrote Lindsey, "of which the motive power was in Toronto, was to have four separate centres of action outside the city." The democratic, but centralized organization envisaged by Mackenzie, he outlined in detail thus:

1. In order to avoid the mixture of persons unknown
to each other, no Society is to consist of less than 12 or
more than 40 persons, and those to be resident as nearly
as possible in the same neighborhood.

2. Each of these Societies shall choose one of their number to be their secretary.

3. The secretaries of five of these Societies shall form a
Committee, to be called the Township Committee . . .

On the same principle of delegate representation, County
and District Committees were to be set up. Upper Canada
as a whole was divided into four Divisions—Western, Toronto, Midland (including Kingston) and Eastern. The
division Committees were to elect an overall Executive, to
"consist of three persons . . . to be invested with the
necessary powers to promote the objects for which the
Union is to be constituted."

The first public meeting after the Declaration was
adopted took place in Newmarket on August 3rd. The
Toronto Declaration was approved and delegates were
appointed to the Convention to be held in that city. Two
days later, a second public meeting took place in Lloyd-
town, addressed by Mackenzie, Lount and other leaders.
"Separation from England was advocated," writes Lindsey,
"but the emblems, devices, and mottoes displayed at this
meeting, were even more significant than the resolutions.
One flag was a large star, surrounded by six minor lustres;
in the centre a Death's head, with the inscription: 'Liberty or Death'."

6

The Rising in Upper Canada

In their Declaration of July 31, 1837, the Upper Canada Reformers had pledged their support to the movement of the Lower Canada Patriotes. At the same time, under Mackenzie's leadership, they proceeded with preparations for a people's convention that was to assume power with the backing of a mass demonstration at Toronto. The local committees in the months that followed enrolled some fifteen hundred men who were to be ready in the event of a resort to arms.

Meanwhile, it became known that four thousand stand of arms were left virtually unguarded at City Hall, the troops having been sent off by Bond Head to Lower Canada. That this was actually a manoeuvre designed to invite a premature effort at a rising was later claimed by the Lieutenant-Governor himself: "I considered," said he, "that if an attack by the rebels was inevitable, the more I encouraged them to consider me defenceless, the better."

Early in November a messenger from Lower Canada reached Toronto with a report on the mounting crisis there which seemed to indicate the prospect of an armed collision. The leading committee of Reformers thereupon met to discuss the concerting of efforts in solidarity with the Patriotes.

Writing six weeks later from the encampment at Navy Island, Mackenzie described the decision reached by the Reformers, and the steps taken to carry it out:

About the third week in November it was determined
that on Thursday the 7th of December, our forces should
secretly assemble at Montgomery's Hotel, 3 miles back of
Toronto, between 6 and 10 at night, and proceeding from
thence to the city, join our friends there, seize 4,000 stand
of arms, which had been placed by Sir Francis in the City
Hall, take him into custody, with his chief advisers, place
the garrison in the hands of the liberals, declare the Province free, call a convention together, to frame a suitable
constitution, and meantime appoint our friend Dr. Rolph
provisional administrator of the government. We expected
to do all this without shedding blood, well knowing that
the vice-regal government was too unpopular to have
many real adherents.

Only in one instance did we forward a notice of the
intended movement beyond the limits of the county of
York, and to Whitby and some other towns in it no cir-
culars were sent. We never doubted the feeling of the
Province . . .

Mackenzie was in charge of the march on Toronto.
Within the city, Rolph was the responsible executive
member, charged with maintaining contact with Papineau
and the Patriotes of Lower Canada. He was to co-ordinate
efforts within the city with the force that was to gather
at Montgomery's. Writes Mackenzie: "The country was
rife for a change, and I employed a fortnight previous to
Sunday the 3rd December, in attending meetings, assisting in organizing towns and places, and otherwise preparing for the revolution."

That Sunday evening Mackenzie got word that the date
for the gathering at Montgomery's had been advanced
from Thursday, December 7 to Monday the 4th—without
consultation and without his knowledge. Rolph, either
out of sudden panic or for some reason never explained,
had "ordered out the men beyond the ridges"; he sent a
message to Lount to begin the move on Montgomery's. By

doing so he utterly disorganized the arrangements for the march on the city. Mackenzie attempted to get word to Lount, in order to have the original plan maintained; but it was by then too late, as in Lount's section the march had already begun. Only a small number, however, had been informed of the change; so the rest were going ahead with preparations for the 7th. Among these latter was the leader of the Reform movement in the Huron Tract, Van Egmond, a veteran of Napoleon's wars, who had been named commander-in-chief of the popular forces, with Samuel Lount and Anthony Anderson as his lieutenants. When Lount got word of the change in the date he expressed the fear that Rolph would "be the ruin of us." Nevertheless, he and Anderson with about 100 men set out for Montgomery's Tavern. Thus a force was gathering on the outskirts of Toronto in the absence of the man designated to command it; and Mackenzie, Lount and Anderson were faced with the task of seizing the capital with a few hundred men, for whom not even a minimum of preparation, in arms, provisions, etc., had been made. Lount and his force arrived Monday evening, the men "exhausted after a march of between 30 and 40 miles through deep mud, and dispirited by the news of the reverse in Lower Canada."

To make matters worse, Anderson, the one man at Montgomery's with some military experience, was shot and killed on Monday night, while on a reconnoitering expedition with Mackenzie. This blow was the more serious, as Mackenzie himself was entirely without military knowledge or training.

Mackenzie was in favor of advancing on the city during the night, but was over-ruled. His narrative records that "Next day (Tuesday) we increased in number to 800, of whom very many had no arms, others had rifles, old

fowling pieces, Indian guns, pikes, etc. Vast numbers
came and went off again, when they found we had neither
muskets or bayonets."

After considerable dissension among the leaders as to the
course to be pursued, they agreed that Lount would lead
one detachment down Yonge Street, and Mackenzie the
remainder, down what is now Avenue Road, the two to
meet near Lawyers' (Osgoode) Hall. But at Gallows' Hill
(on Yonge, south of what is now St. Clair Avenue) the
combined force was met by a delegation bearing a flag of
truce from Bond Head: the messengers being none other
than Dr. Rolph and Robert Baldwin. Mackenzie's reply to
the Lieutenant-Governor's overture was the demand: "Independence, and a Convention to arrange details!" No
truce occurred, but the presence of leading Reformers as
emissaries of the Family Compact had a demoralizing
effect on the insurgents.

On Tuesday at about six o'clock, a skirmish between
a detachment of Mackenzie's men and Government volunteers ended in both parties beating a retreat. Despite the
arrival of reinforcements during the night, Wednesday
morning found the insurgent camp reduced to about five
hundred and fifty men. It was decided to remain on the
defensive, while awaiting the arrival of Van Egmond with
what was hoped to comprise the main force, expected
next day, Thursday the 7th, as originally planned. A message to Rolph, asking for information as to when Bond
Head might be expected to make an attack, went un-
answered: the doctor was already in full flight.

"Gentlemen of influence," observes Mackenzie, "who
were pledged to join us, and even the executive who commanded us to make the premature and unfortunate movement, neither corresponded with us nor joined us. To

explain their conduct was beyond my power. It discouraged many and thinned our ranks."

On Thursday morning Mackenzie despatched a group of about sixty "to go down and burn the Don Bridge, the eastern approach to Toronto, and the house at its end, to take the Montreal mail stage and mails, and to draw out the (Government) forces in that quarter if possible." The operation was carried out, but too late to effect its purpose of diverting Bond Head's force from undertaking an offensive. Van Egmond had arrived at Montgomery's and a council of war was in progress when word came that a numerous and well-armed force was advancing up Yonge Street. In answer to Mackenzie's appeal, those of his men who had arms went out to meet the oncoming military. But the odds were too heavily against them. The few hundred poorly-armed patriots stood their ground as best they could, then gave way before the fire of superior numbers. With this defeat, the rising received its death-blow.

Mackenzie and other leaders, after a hasty consultation near Hogg's Hollow, concluded that further resistance, for the time being at least, was out of the question; and flight became general. With a reward on his head, and a widespread manhunt under way, Mackenzie managed, with the help of sympathizers, to make his way to the border and pass over to Buffalo. Of the other leaders, Peter Matthews was taken prisoner near Pickering, and Samuel Lount, after a number of hair-breadth escapes, had almost reached safety in an attempt to cross Lake Erie, when a storm blew his boat back to the northern shore, and capture.

While the march on Toronto was getting under way, the Reformers in the London district had been organizing under the leadership of Dr. Duncombe. From St. Thomas,

Norwich and other settlements they gathered on December 10 at the Village of Scotland, with a view to marching via Brantford to join Mackenzie. Here they received word of Mackenzie's rout. Handicapped by lack of arms, and disheartened by the news of the defeat at Toronto, Duncombe's force dispersed at the approach of a contingent of Government troops under Colonel MacNab.

On December 13, scarcely a week after the defeat at Montgomery's, Mackenzie and a small patriot force took possession of Navy Island in the Niagara River just above the Falls. From here it was hoped to give leadership to a renewed movement of struggle in Upper Canada, and win organized support among sympathizers in the northern States. In the months that followed, public meetings in support of the Canadians were held in towns and cities from Detroit and Cleveland to New York. Money was raised and arms and munitions purchased, and volunteers joined Mackenzie's camp. However, the administration of President Van Buren, in accord with the demands of the southern slave-owners (who feared for their cotton market in England) and northern financial interests linked with English capital, effectively intervened to prevent large-scale assistance being rendered to the Canadians.

For a short time tension on the border was acute, following the seizure and spectacular burning, by Bond Head's men, of the U.S. steamer "Caroline," which the patriots had been using; but after an exchange of protests, the furore died down. There were some sporadic actions in scattered localities of the province, but a general movement failed to materialize; and the Navy Island expedition was finally abandoned a month after its launching. During January, an attempt was made to take Windsor and Sandwich, with an expedition from Detroit; but lack of leadership here also led to failure; a similar fate befell an attack in the neighborhood of Kingston, in the month following.

Meanwhile, two leaders of the rising were lodged in Toronto jail, and it soon became apparent that the Family Compact was resolved to take their lives as a lesson and warning to other patriots.

Samuel Lount had come to Canada from Pennsylvania in 1811, in his early twenties. A skilled blacksmith and farmer, he became adept as a surveyor. To this day, legends still persist in the Holland Landing area regarding his generosity and kindness to fellow-settlers. He was at first reluctant to participate in political life, but his neighbors prevailed upon him to run for parliament in the election of 1834 for Simcoe County, and he was successful. In the election of 1836, a combination of violence, intimidation and bribery by land-grants to many voters brought about his defeat. A prominent role was played by Lount both in the preparation for the rising and in leading his men in the face of the enemy. While not possessing Mackenzie's audacity, he displayed outstanding courage and fortitude.

Of Matthews, Mackenzie later wrote:

> Captain Peter Matthews was a jolly, hale, cheerful, cherry-cheeked farmer of Pickering, who lived on his own land, cultivated his own estate, and was the father of fifteen children, who beseeched the Sullivans, the Drapers, and the Robinsons in vain for that mercy to their father . . . Captain Matthews had fought bravely for the King of England in the war of 1813, was a man of unstained reputation, well beloved by his neighbours, unassuming, modest in his deportment, a Baptist unfriendly to high church ascendancy, a true patriot, and indignant at the treacherous, fraudulent conduct of the detestable junto who, in 1837, governed Canada.

On behalf of the imprisoned Lount and Matthews a

campaign for clemency was got under way, which soon embraced the length and breadth of Upper Canada. The new Lieutenant-Governor, Sir George Arthur, received petitions bearing thousands of signatures, asking for a mitigation of punishment; five thousand persons signed them in the Newmarket district, four thousand more in the Dundas area, in addition to those in Toronto itself. It is estimated that over 30,000 people of all walks of life affixed their names to the petitions. However, Arthur, who had come to Canada after serving as governor of the penal colony of Van Diemen's Land, was wholly committed to the Compact. He not only refused to consider the mass demand for clemency; he used the plight of his captives to perpetrate a heartless infamy. Lount was offered his life—provided he would turn informer and reveal the names of his associates in the organization of the march on Toronto.

Lount's wife, Elizabeth, in a moving letter penned after his death, described her interview with Arthur on the eve of her husband's execution: the Lieutenant-Governor "said 'there were others concerned in the rebellion,' and intimated that if my husband would expose them he might yet go clear; but my husband always said he would never expose others or bring them into difficulty—the cause they enlisted in was a good one, and before he would expose Mackenzie's Council he would himself be sacrificed."

On the morning of April 12, 1838, Samuel Lount and Peter Matthews were executed in Toronto, at the corner of King and Toronto Streets, on the charge of high treason.

In the words of a contemporary*: "at their execution

---

*Dr. John Beatty, who acted as chaplain to Matthews, was a founder of Victoria College; the present writer is his great-grandson.

they manifested very good composure. Sheriff Jarvis burst into tears when he entered the room to prepare them for execution. They said to him very calmly, 'Mr. Jarvis, do your duty. We are prepared to meet death and our judge.' They then, both of them, put their arms around his neck and kissed him. They were then prepared for the execution, they walked to the gallows with entire composure and firmness of step."

Men of the working people, blacksmith and farmer, Lount and Matthews thus paid the price for their devotion to the cause of popular liberty and an independent Canada. When their families asked that the bodies be given into their care, the Governor refused the request. They were buried in Potters' Field (now the corner of Bloor and Yonge Streets) whence their bodies were later transferred to the Necropolis.

In the summer of 1838, a network of "Hunters' Lodges" sprang up, at first in Vermont and later with headquarters in Cleveland, having as their object the liberation of the Canadas. This movement was composed in part of Canadians, refugees in the States, and in part of American sympathizers—most of them, according to a chronicle of the time, "men of poor fortunes." Under its leadership an attempt was made at a concerted series of invasions at Windsor, Prescott and in Lower Canada.

This was the third attempt in the direction of Windsor, others made in January and July having both failed. This time, four hundred men crossed over, and penetrated into the heart of the town before being driven back. Twenty-five of them were killed, four of these being shot in cold blood after being taken prisoner. In the Niagara Peninsula (Welland County), a partisan force of over 500 conducted sporadic operations all during 1838.

In November, an expedition was set on foot with the

aim of capturing Prescott, rallying patriot support along the St. Lawrence, and then striking at Kingston, the seat of British military power in Upper Canada. Leading the expedition was an exiled Polish revolutionary democrat, Nils Gustav Szoltewcki, known as Von Schultz. A participant in the abortive Polish uprising of 1831 against tsarist rule, Von Schultz gave up his work as a researcher and chemist in Syracuse, New York, to go to the aid of the Canadian democrats in their struggle against despotism. He recruited (and paid the expenses of) other Polish revolutionaries who joined the expedition, among them Jan Okonski, Ernest Berenc and others.

Owing to mismanagement by an American commander, the element of surprise in the move on Prescott was lost, most of the force of 700 remained out of the action, and Von Schultz was left to carry out the raid with only 170 men. They occupied a stone windmill below Prescott, and held it for four days against British troops, while vainly hoping to receive reinforcement. On November 16, after the mill had been shelled by two cannon and a howitzer, Schultz and his men were forced to surrender. Brought to trial, the Polish democrat was defended—unsuccessfully—by a young Kingston lawyer, John A. Macdonald. On December 5, 1839, Schultz-Szoltewcki was hanged at Kingston; ten others met the same fate.

Colonial reaction answered the renewed patriotic resistance with a reign of terror. In January 1839, six revolutionary democrats were hanged in Windsor Court House square. In the same month Joshua Doan, a leader of the struggle at Windsor, was hanged at London after trial by court martial. James Moreau was executed, and sixteen other participants in border raids were transported to Van Diemen's Land.

Of 885 combatants in the democratic cause who were

officially listed as arrested or escaped, 422 came from the Home (Toronto) district, 103 from the London district and 90 from the district of Gore (Hamilton area). Of the total, 375 were farmers ("yeomen"), 345 laborers, 80 carpenters, foundrymen and other tradesmen, and 85 professionals, innkeepers, merchants.

Workers thus made up nearly half, and farmers over 40 per cent of the victims of repression: a significant indication of the social forces that were engaged in action.

It has been fashionable for historians to play down or denigrate the "rebels": on occasion their struggle is even presented as a poor comic-opera effort. One rare and creditable exception to this approach is Professor Fred Landon's treatment. Of the participants in the London district he has written: "Several hundred men, poorly equipped and poorly led, took the chances of death or imprisonment, loss of reputation and property, with all the accompanying risks for their families or relatives, and marched out in semi-military order at the call of Dr. Charles Duncombe." And again:

> Considering the risks of life, reputation and property involved in rebellion, it is surprising how many did actually take up arms . . . how many more must have weighed the matter and decided that the risks were too great.

What were the main immediate causes of the defeat of the people's rising in Upper Canada?

First, the defection and splitting of the people's movement—in effect, the betrayal of the revolution—by the right wing of the colonial bourgeoisie.

Second, the absence of a cohesive, united, consistently revolutionary leadership (exemplified in Mackenzie's instability and in the dubious role of Rolph during the march on Toronto).

Third, failure of the movement to counteract the "loyalty" cry so effectively used by reaction in neutralizing sections of Reform supporters.

Fourth, the failure to pursue the offensive consistently in the struggle for political power: after initiating the march on Toronto, the patriot leaders—nearly all of whom lacked military experience—failed to carry it through to a successful conclusion, even though objective conditions were favorable.*

Fifth, the lack of effectively co-ordinated action on the part of the patriots of Upper and Lower Canada.

Sixth, the collusion of U.S. and British imperial authorities in the putting down of the people's struggle.

While the foregoing were immediate causes of the defeat, a broader underlying reason is to be found in the immature level of industrial capitalism in the colony, and the absence, accordingly, of a developed working class. The workers were an important factor in the struggle, as witness Mackenzie's statement on the eve of the rising that "Dutcher's foundry-men and Armstrong's axe-makers" were the ones, above all, "who could be depended on." But the workers, who had begun to organize into unions (the York Typographical Society, in 1832) and fight for the shorter work-day (Cobourg, in 1836, for example) had yet to achieve political consciousness and organization as a distinct class force. They were not in a position to act in their own name or give independent leadership to the struggle.

---

*Dent is of the opinion that had Mackenzie been successful, the Provisional Government would have had the support of the Reformers throughout the province; he concedes that "had the entire body of Upper Canadian Reformers taken part in the movement, there can be little doubt that the Government would have been at least temporarily overthrown . . ."

Thus, the forces for a successful bourgeois-democratic revolution had not matured sufficiently; and the path to the achievement of a state structure in the hands of the colonials was to be tortuous and long.

PART TWO

CAPITALIST INDUSTRIALISM

7

Self-Government and National Rights

The trans-Atlantic civil war, known as the American Revolution, provided a forceful demonstration that British settlers were peculiarly unsuitable material for the practice of the traditional form of imperium based on obedience and subordination. Thereafter British statesmen gradually came to accept the fact that democratic institutions, once exported, acquire a characteristic momentum which cannot be stopped at any point short of complete self-government. That crucial lesson was learned in connection with the Canadian colonies between 1839 and 1850 under the inspired leadership of Durham and Elgin working in co-operation with Canadian leaders such as Robert Baldwin.

—Professor Vincent Harlow, of Oxford, at the XI International Congress of Historical Sciences, Stockholm, 1960.

Though by now a trifle subdued, the long-hallowed myth still lingers on: the one to the effect that colonial self-government was the spontaneous gift of a generous imperial power. Professor Harlow's version at least offers a slight amendment, with the suggestion that at our "receiving end" there was some sort of dynamic at work: namely, what he refers to as the "characteristic momentum" acquired by democratic institutions that have been exported to colonies of settlement. But what was the *source* of this "momentum"? Whence came the "crucial

lesson" that London learned "between 1839 and 1850"?
Surely it was from the struggles of the colonists themselves, culminating in the insurrections of 1837-38 (how
eloquent is Harlow's silence on this date!). As for the
"inspired leadership" of the two noble lords, it was surely
nudged (to put it mildly) by the series of insurrections
and the ensuing decade of colonial agitation for autonomy.*

Having by force of arms successfully maintained its
grip on Canada, the imperial power proceeded in 1840 to
provide the colony with a new constitutional and political
framework. The Act of Union (proclaimed in February
1841) was designed to ensure the ascendancy of the "British element" within the Canadas; at the same time, direc-
tives from the Colonial Office firmly rejected the concept
of "responsible government," whose adoption Durham
had urged in his Report. Two closely interrelated issues
thus confronted the colonists: the character and terms of
the Union, and the still elusive responsible government,
or "Home Rule." Dominant throughout the decade of the
forties, these issues reflected the double contradiction that

---

*Professor Harlow, the author of *The Founding of the Second
British Empire,* offered the interpretation cited here in a paper on
"The Historiography of the British Empire and Commonwealth
since 1945"; in the discussion I advanced the criticism indicated
above, and the Congress Proceedings (p. 202) thus summarize his
concluding remarks: "V. Harlow (Oxford) in his reply to Mr. Ryerson agreed that there was a push and pull in the constitutional relationship between the metropolitan state and Canada. . . . There was
tension and (in 1837) violence between Great Britain and the Canadians, but after Britain had accepted the principle of ministerial
responsibility for Canada (in 1847) a constitutional device had been
adopted which enabled Canadian nationhood to develop to full
maturity and independence." Had it? One wonders. To this we shall
return; for the moment, suffice it to say that Professor Harlow's "but,"
in the foregoing sentence, carries a rather heavy load—if it does not,
indeed, beg the whole question.

had been left unresolved with the defeat of the rebellions: the uncertain status of the French Canadians as a distinct national community within the British colony; and the conflict between a constricting imperial framework and the mounting pressures for social, economic and political reform. The question of nationality (French Canada) and that of constitutional freedom and Canadian autonomy were closely interwoven; the cry of "Responsible Government" in some measure at least embraced them both.

Not only did the framers of the Act of Union make no provision for the introduction of responsible government; ministerial admonitions expressly forbade its adoption. True, one heard occasional reassuring references to the desirability of the Executive governing "in harmony" with the electors' aspirations—so long as these latter were suitably in accord with imperial interests. But this was not to be taken to mean "responsible government," as Lord John Russell made entirely plain in the debate at Westminster on the Union Bill. The colonial advisors of the Governor, he pointed out, cannot possibly enjoy the status of cabinet ministers: the Queen's sole advisors are the British cabinet, in whom a higher authority resides. Suppose the Governor were to act on recommendations from his colonial advisors that conflicted with his instructions from the Queen: he would then no longer be acting as a subordinate officer but as an independent sovereign. In *An Essay on the Government of Dependencies* (1841) Sir George C. Lewis argued that "A self-governing dependency (supposing the dependency not to be virtually independent) is a contradiction in terms." Like Russell, he held that "If the government of the dominant country substantially govern the dependency, the representative body cannot substantially govern it; and conversely if the dependency be substantially governed by the representative body, it cannot substantially be governed by the government of the dominant country." The youthful Gladstone declared in the Union Bill debate: "If I am asked for a definition of responsible government, I reply that it is nothing else but an independent legislature." Lord Stanley, for his part, asserted that colonial self-government "would be incompatible with the existence of monarchical institutions and with the relations that must obtain between colony and mother-country."

The Responsible Government slogan, because it called into question the "due and proper subordination" of a colonial province, was in fact a challenge to the established imperial order. Not only did it imply relinquishment by the Colonial Office of its power to intervene in the internal affairs of the colony; but the securing by the Canadians of a substantial measure of independence could open the way to a broad democratization of the whole of colonial society: a process whose first victims would likely be the staunchly pro-imperial Family Compact and Montreal mercantile élite, and whose main beneficiaries would be the local middle-class men of business and the professions. But that was not all. With Lower Canada possessing a majority of the overall population, self-government would almost certainly entail the political ascension of the subject, "conquered race." Yet Lord Durham had argued quite clearly that responsible government must be contingent on the establishment of a British majority within the province and on "putting down the French"— by contriving their exclusion from the exercise of power and ultimately their complete assimilation.

London's refusal of responsible government expressed therefore not only unreadiness to grant autonomy to a colony of British settlement, but a determination to check the national demands of the French Canadians. Downing Street put it bluntly: "It is laid down as a fundamental principle that the French must not be reinstated in power in Lower Canada."

The imperial response to rebellion in the two Canadas was to *unite* them. (It had been tried before, in relation to Ireland after the Rising of '98; Union might work this time, too.) The reasoning in this instance seems to have been: Imperial dominance requires the ascendancy of the British element in the Canadas; this can be secured only by means of a union that effects the complete erasure of Lower Canada as a separate entity. The limited recognition of French-Canadian identity that had been implicit in the separation of Lower and Upper Canada in 1791 was now to be "rectified." Lower Canada, after surviving repeated Anglo-Canadian mercantile attempts to impose a merger (in 1810, 1822), was now to be effaced; and this, at the very time when thanks to suspension of its Constitution it was bereft of voice or vote.

But if Union was to assert "British ascendancy," the new state structure must be so constructed as to ensure it. Hence Section XLI of the Act of Union, with its ruling that all official documents of the Legislative Council and Assembly "shall be in the English language only." (How better solve the problem of "equality" than by suppressing one half of the equation!)

Further, the Assembly of the new united province was to be so composed as to ensure a majority of seats to the English-speaking minority.* Canada West, though possessing a much smaller population than Canada East, was accorded an equal number of seats in the Assembly; the English-speaking section of Montreal and the Eastern Townships had their full quota of representatives; and a colossal gerrymander disfranchised tens of thousands of

---

*"The agricultural and commercial enterprise of the British settlers demanded that they should not be placed in a position of inferiority." (R. W. Langstone, *Responsible Government in Canada*, p. 103)

French Canadians in the working-class districts of Quebec and Montreal.

The architect and initiator of the Union—the new Governor, Charles Poulett Thomson (soon to become Lord Sydenham)—wrote that "From the French I expect nothing but trouble—the fact is they are unfit for representative Government. . . ." He would have preferred a continued suspension of the Constitution in Lower Canada: "If it were possible, the best thing for Lower Canada would be a despotism for ten years more, for in truth the people are not yet fit for the higher class of self-government." But this kind of thing, it was felt, might be going too far (next door to a republican democracy!). So there was a return to the unworkable mixture of an elected Assembly and an appointive Executive, responsible not to it, but to the Governor and Downing Street: the selfsame colonialist constitutional pattern that had driven the frustrated Canadas to rebellion.

The man chosen to install and start operating the new order, Sydenham "was the businessman in politics," incarnating "the new spirit in business and industry . . . the aggressive business ideals of his age." Unlike the preceding military-aristocratic governors, Poulett Thomson came from the upper ranks of the bourgeoisie: his family's firm one of the oldest in the Russian-Baltic trade, himself an entrepreneur, director of mining companies in South and Central America, member of Parliament for the industrial and Free Trade centre of Manchester. He viewed his mission to Canada as having the twofold purpose of restoring the stability of British imperial rule, and modernizing the administrative structure in line with the requirements of British investors.

Sydenham was not long in Canada before making his position on the main issue clear; as he reported to London, "I am not a bit afraid of the responsible government

cry; I have already done much to put it down in its inadmissible sense, namely, the demand that the executive
council shall be responsible to the assembly, and that the
Governor shall take their advice and be bound by it. . . .
I have told the people plainly that . . . I will place no
responsibility on the council; that they are a council for
the Governor to consult, but no more." For him to shift
the burden of responsibility to the shoulders of others
would, he felt, be tantamount to "endangering the connection of the colony with the Empire." There, indeed,
was the nub of the matter.

Colonial subjection of French Canada was to be maintained by whatever means might prove necessary. So far
as "English Canada" was concerned (or at least, "Canada
West"), it was to be "compensated" for the denial of responsible government by having the capital of the united
province located at Kingston and by transferring an enormous Upper Canadian debt to the new Union—in effect,
saddling half the burden of it on what had been a largely
debt-free Lower Canada. A contemporary French-Canadian chronicler summed up thus the balance-sheet of
union: "The Upper Canadians had become the masters
. . . they had secured a strong representation, their fin-
ances prospered, they had been accorded the seat of government and a large part of the public revenues."

Sydenham in his first Throne Speech assured the members of the new Assembly that, thanks to the Union, they
could count on "the confidence of British capitalists in
credit you may require of them." He knew whereof he
spoke: the great financial house of Baring were the holders of the $6 million debt of Upper Canada, with which
the new united Province of Canada was now mortgaged;
and one of the heads of Baring's held office as Her Majesty's Chancellor of the Exchequer. "A mercantile in-
trigue": Gosford's characterization of the proposed Union,

during the debate on it in the Lords, was hardly an exaggeration.

Two alternatives were open to the Reform forces in the Canadas. One was to work for outright repeal of the Union; the other, to accept the new set-up (albeit under protest) and strive so to alter its mode of operation as to secure "responsible government." The leading French-Canadian democrats inclined at first toward the former alternative. After all, the Union, in the words of Louis-Hyppolite LaFontaine, had been "imposed by force"; it was "an act of injustice and despotism in that it is imposed on us without our consent." Even the moderate *Le Canadien* warned of "the danger there is in effecting the union of two provinces, the representatives of one of which display so much contempt for the natural rights and privileges of the other." And, in a later issue Etienne Parent wrote:

> The government may keep us in a state of political inferiority, it may rob us, it may oppress us. It has the support of an army and of the whole power of the empire to enable it to do so. But never will we ourselves give it our support in its attempt to enslave and degrade us.

In both sections of the Province popular opposition to the new regime found widespread expression. Some forty thousand persons in the districts of Three Rivers and Quebec City signed petitions calling for repeal of the Union. Meanwhile in Upper Canada the rejection of responsible government had evoked vigorous protest: so-called "Durham meetings" were held at Guelph, Galt, Hamilton, Cooksville, Whitby, Beaverton, Cobourg and Belleville, as well as Toronto (where Sheriff Jarvis's Family Compact hangers-on broke up a meeting at Davis's Tavern on upper Yonge Street).

Clearly, a convergence of the Reform forces in English and French Canada was a possibility; yet its achievement presented serious difficulties. Most of the Reform members in the old Upper Canada Assembly had supported the proposals for Union: a stand not easily forgiven in the Lower province, where resentment over "annexation through Union" lent support to proposals for boycotting the new Assembly.

Not only were there differences in appraisal of the Union; but the popular protest movements had themselves undergone a drastic change. While their motive power, as in the 1830s, still lay in the mass actions of the "yeomen and mechanics," the leadership was now in the hands of "moderates." The place of the revolutionary democrats, removed from the scene by banishment or execution, had been taken by men of the right wing of the old Reform movements—men more directly representative of the growing class of Canadian businessmen.

Establishment of joint action on the part of the moderate reformers required the working-out of a new common program. That it would indeed be "moderate" in character is shown by the fact that at no time did the new leaders so much as breathe the watch-word of "Canadian independence." Robert Baldwin, the well-to-do liberal lawyer, fully accepted the colonial status; he strove only to assert the claim of the local manufacturing and business interests to a degree of political autonomy that would meet their needs. Indeed, as his biographer testifies, "There is hardly a speech made by Robert Baldwin at this period in which he does not assert his devotion to the unity of the Empire and his firm belief that responsible government in the colonies was the true means of its maintenance." Baldwin, moreover (unlike the Lower Canada Reformers) considered even the demand for an elective upper house "distasteful."

A major part in bringing together the Reform elements
in English and French Canada was played by the journalist and financial promoter, Francis Hincks; other businessmen associated with the movement were William H. Merritt, member of the first Union Parliament, who "kept a
general store, manufactured salt, ran a cooperage establishment, operated a sawmill and a flour-mill, was the
prime mover in the Grand River navigation scheme . . .
(he) took a leading part in railway building and was the
driving force behind the construction of the Welland
Canal"; W. P. Howland, a prominent Toronto dealer in
flour and grain; and Isaac Buchanan, the Hamilton merchant, industrialist and railway promoter.

Like Baldwin, Louis-Hyppolite LaFontaine had opposed the resort to arms in 1837 (although as a Patriote sup-
porter he was imprisoned briefly in 1839). In a private letter he assured Baldwin that he was "far from thinking of
separation," holding it "to be the material interest both
of England and Canada that the connection should subsist as long as possible"; and stating his belief that responsible government would, in fact, "secure the connection."
Of LaFontaine one authority writes: "His desire for Reform was very moderate, and as he grew older he became
more and more conservative."

What concerned these spokesmen of the emergent capitalist class was political control of the home market and
of local resources. Unprepared to challenge imperial rule,
they saw in "responsible government" the constitutional
reform that would give them authority in domestic matters. Inasmuch as the demand for self-government expressed at the same time the broader interest of the mass of
the colonists, the moderate Reform leaders were enabled
to play the part of tribunes of the people, spokesmen of
the general democratic will. Only at a later stage did a

challenge from the radical-democratic left call in question their historic mandate.

In 1841-42 joint action by the Reform leaders in both sections of the Province of Canada was debated and ultimately achieved. LaFontaine in the course of the 1841 elections for the Assembly put the case for united action thus: "The Reformers in the two provinces form an immense majority . . . Our cause is common. It is to the interest of the Reformers of the two provinces to meet on the legislative ground in a spirit of peace, union, friendship and fraternity. Unity of action is more than ever necessary."

It was in the logic of such a striving for democratic unity of action that there should emerge a common denominator of general-Canadian joint interest. The national, French-English cleavage was to be transcended. Hincks urged that "we act as Canadians, for the good of Canada"; and he promised LaFontaine that "your brother Reformers in Upper Canada will meet you and your compatriots as Canadians . . . no national animosities will be entertained." Baldwin, for his part, declared: "There is, and must be, no question of races. It were madness on one side, and guilt, deep guilt on both, to make such a question."

LaFontaine, in his manifesto to the electors of Terrebonne, set forth a sweeping program of Canadian development, to be secured through "regular and constitutional legislation"; it included "opening up our vast resources in the interior," and "providing easy navigation from the sea to the lakes" by completing the St. Lawrence waterway, "the natural channel for a great part of the produce of the west"; it demanded abolition of seigneurial tenure and measures to provide education, "the first benefit which a government can confer on its people."

For it to become effective, the emerging sense of an all-

Canadian democratic interest would have to extend to a
full recognition of the principle of equality of the two
national communities. Practical adherence to this principle found dramatic expression when LaFontaine, defeated by electoral gangsterism in Terrebonne, was offered
the support of the Reformers in the 4th Riding of York,
and elected by them to the Assembly; and later when
Baldwin, having lost his seat in Hastings, Canada West,
was elected to represent the French-Canadian constituency
of Rimouski on the lower St. Lawrence.

   In the course of the elections to the new Assembly in
the spring of 1841 Sydenham himself had campaigned un-
abashedly to rout the partisans of the "pernicious doctrine" of responsible government and to further the design of making Canada "an essentially English province."
Feeling himself duty-bound "to carry out the views of the
British Parliament" (which in the debate on the Union
Bill had "laid great stress on the necessity of securing
ample representation to the mercantile interests of Canada"), the Governor re-drew the boundaries of the cities
of Quebec and Montreal so as to exclude therefrom large
numbers of French-Canadian electors, transferring them
to the adjoining rural counties. As he explained, in justi-
fying this action to Russell: "There were attached to the
cities . . . very extensive suburbs, inhabited generally by
a poor population, unconnected with the mercantile interests to which these cities owe their importance. Had these
. . . been brought within the electoral limits, the number
of their population would have enabled them to return
one, if not both, of the members for each city." Cutting
off the French-Canadian working-class districts of Montreal and Quebec, Sydenham conceded, "will cause a great
clatter with the French and their allies, but you might
just as well have given no representation at all to either
city as far as the Trade and the British Mercantile Inter-

est is concerned, as not to do so." Thanks to the gerrymander, Sydenham secured for his own candidates "four
seats in the very heart of the enemy's country."

The Governor's intervention did not stop there: it
ranged from demagogic appeals to "loyalty" (to support
him was, after all, to support the Crown) to widespread
intimidation of electors through the use of troops and
organized mob violence. Montreal citizens, in a petition
of protest, cited instances of public squares manned by
artillery detachments, troops stationed at polling-places,
voters subjected to threats and violence at the hands of
hired ruffians armed with "bludgeons, bowie-knives, pis-
tols and other murderous weapons."

With all his strenuous effort, the self-combined Governor-General, prime minister and party campaign manager
came up with an Assembly that he could only just manage to control. His proclaimed purpose had been to avert
a crystallization of "parties"— unmanageable, dangerously
democratic "factions"— but in order to achieve this he
had in fact put together an ill-assorted party of his own;
while by his own open intervention in the electoral process he had furthered the formation of a party of opposition, united in support of responsible government.

By September, 1841, the Assembly was debating resolutions in support of that "pernicious doctrine." Moved
by Baldwin, they urged that while the Governor, "being
. . . the representative of the Sovereign, is not constitutionally responsible to any other than the authorities of
the Empire," nevertheless the advisors of the representatives of the Sovereign . . . constituting as such the Provincial administration under him . . . ought always to be men
possessed of the public confidence, (their) opinions and
policy harmonizing with those of the representatives of
the people . . ." Further, that "this House has the constitutional right of holding such advisors politically re-

sponsible for every act of the Provincial Government of a local character . . ."

If this was more than Sydenham could stomach, he was able to counter it by no stronger antidote than a watered-down dilution of the original physic. "The government," writes Baldwin's biographer, "succeeded in voting down the resolutions in the form in which they were presented, but only at the price of substituting for them a set of resolutions almost equivalent. These resolutions, hereafter associated with the name of Robert Baldwin, stand as the definite achievement of the United Reformers in their first constitutional struggle under the Union."

Within a year of the passage of these resolutions, the Reform alignment that LaFontaine described as "a thorough union in parliament between the members who represent the majority of both peoples" had won its first victory. Sir Charles Bagot, Sydenham's successor, found himself faced with an Assembly which the Executive Council could no longer control. He decided (after much heartsearching, and in direct contravention of his instructions) to offer LaFontaine and Baldwin the leading posts in a government reconstructed in accordance with their demands. This first administration to be formed in accord with the principle of "responsible government" took office at Kingston in September 1842.

This surrender to popular pressure evoked angry protests from the ultra-right. The move, declared one Tory journal, contained "the germ of colonial separation from the Mother Country"; according to the Montreal *Gazette*, "the British party has been deliberately handed over to the vindictive disposition of a French mob." In London, the ruling Tory party was "indignant . . . they have no taste for the independence and supremacy of a Canadian Parliament." Some Britishers, however, like the editor of the newspaper *John Bull*, saw clearly enough the parallel with their own struggles for the Reform Bill of 1832, and

acknowledged the presence in Canada of "a necessity...
which Sir Charles Bagot could not overrule. . . . Sir
Robert Peel must bend to the Reform Bill here and
govern in its spirit. Sir Charles Bagot has the same office
to perform in Canada."

Well might the reactionaries rage. A bi-national Reform
coalition, the very development the Union was designed
to avert, had attained office. The principle of Executive
responsibility to the majority in the Assembly was being
asserted at last; and the very fact of a joint Anglo-French-
Canadian administration suggested the prospect of further democratic advance in resolving the vital issues of
national equality and colonial autonomy.

But this first democratic triumph was to be shortlived:
London was not prepared to countenance its possible consequences. By the following summer Metcalfe, Bagot's
successor, had once more restored autocratic rule. Yet a
first breach had been effected in the old imperial system;
the forces of Reform and national rights had gained a new
confidence in their powers. Furthermore, a fresh source
of radical challenge to the old order was taking shape. It
is worthy of note that the first political triumph of the
colonial bourgeoisie in Canada was followed closely by
the entry onto the public stage of a new class force. The
strike of 1,300 construction workers on the Lachine canal
in the winter of 1843 was not only one of the earliest mass
struggles of the Canadian proletariat. It was an augury of
new alignments in the contest for self-government and
democracy in the Canadas. The hundreds of canal workers who marched into Montreal to present their grievances, the Reform elements who organized public meetings to support the strikers, the solidarity between Irish
and French-Canadian canal workers, all were portents of
a broadening coalition and of a new militant force within
it, that Downing Street would yet have to reckon with.

8

Achievement in 1848

Among the issues and forces involved in the struggle over the Act of Union were these:

—*"Responsible government": colonial autonomy:* the Reform forces in all the British North American provinces pressed for it; resistance came from the colonial conservatives (Family Compact and counterparts) and the imperial authorities (until 1846-48).

—*Defense of French-Canadian national rights:* a similar alignment as on the foregoing (but with the pressure centred of course in Lower Canada).

—*Modernization of colonial structures* (administrative and financial) in the interest, first, of British investors of capital, then of local colonial (especially Anglo-Canadian) industrialists: promoted by these, resisted by some British mercantile groups opposed to both responsible government and French-Canadian rights, and by the clerical-seigneurial forces in Lower Canada.

The immediate aim of the Union had been to restore imperial ascendancy and thus frustrate the challenge of the popular-democratic movements. But the Union was enacted just at a time when the influence of the Free Trade, manufacturing interest in Britain was growing. This meant that imperial-conservative immobilism would be challenged by the "modernization" program required by business. Some of the antiquated structures which the Colonial Office sought to preserve, the "modernizing" businessmen would be prepared to jettison. Hence the self-contradictory, zig-zag course of imperial policy in this decade. After Sydenham, the conservative "modernizer," Bagot's concessions to the colonists scandalized and appalled his superiors, who concurred in them momentarily only to seek then to annul them through the instrumentality of his successor.

Before coming to Canada in 1843, Sir Charles Metcalfe had served as an imperial administrator in India and then in Jamaica. His mission now was to reverse the distressing trend toward colonial autonomy to which Bagot had surrendered. Reporting on the occasion when he received his appointment from the Colonial Secretary, Metcalfe wrote his sister: "I have just returned from Lord Stanley, and have accepted the Government of Canada." The turn of phrase expressed perfectly his conception of the post. It would involve a contest to determine (as he put it later) "Whether the Governor is to be in some degree what his title imports, or a mere tool in the hands of the party that can obtain a majority in the representative body." The "pretensions" of the Reformers were wholly inacceptable to him: "I cannot consent to be the tool of a party." The Colonial Office instructions stipulated that "in your capacity as the Executive, you are the supreme power and responsible to no one, except to the Home Government." As Metcalfe saw it, the movement for responsible government challenged the very structure of Empire: "The tendency and object of this movement is to throw off the government of the mother country in internal affairs entirely . . . *Now comes the tug of war . . .*" The Reform leaders during Bagot's governorship, in "carrying out unrestricted their own ideas of responsible government had run a course of unchecked usurpation." To submit now to their unconscionable demands "would be to surrender the Queen's government into the hands

of rebels, and become myself their ignominious tool."
Metcalfe's argument hinged on the concept of the "royal
prerogative" in a situation where effective sovereignty re-
sided not in Canada but in the British government, whose
instrument was the colonial governor.

As the "supreme power," Metcalfe had no qualms
about making official appointments without so much as
notifying his ministers. When LaFontaine and Baldwin
remonstrated with him over what they viewed as an arbitrary pre-emption of the right to dispose of patronage,
the Governor rejected their protest. Their stipulations,
he explained, "would have reduced me to a nonentity."

In an atmosphere of intense political excitement, the
LaFontaine-Baldwin ministry resigned. The Assembly
promptly reaffirmed its confidence in them. Metcalfe called upon the leading Tory, William Draper, one of the
"men of business in the colony," who succeeded neither
in constituting a new government nor in overcoming the
resistance of the Assembly. The deadlock continued
through most of 1844, while the contest broadened to
embrace the whole colonial community. The "tug of war"
had come indeed.

Throughout the Province of Canada, Reform Associations organized great public meetings and demonstrations.
A flood of pamphlets, newspaper polemics and "tracts for
the people" debated the points at issue. At a general meeting of the Toronto Reformers Robert Baldwin declared:
"This is not a mere party struggle. It is Canada against
her oppressors. The people of Canada claiming the British
constitution against those who withhold it: the might of
public opinion against faction and corruption." The
national-democratic struggle was fostering a stronger sense
of Canadian identity, and the Reform leaders became increasingly its exponents. Speaking in Middlesex, Baldwin
returned to the theme, urging his hearers "to act as if they

remembered only that they were Canadians, since as Canadians we have a country and are a people."

Finally in the autumn of 1844 Metcalfe, having failed to put together a workable Executive, called an election. Like Sydenham before him, he conducted the campaign in person. His office as governor-general was made to serve as a rallying point for a three-pronged political offensive. First, he identified himself with the colonial conservatives: it was only among them, his biographer testified, "that loyalty, as signifying attachment to the mother country, existed in any force. It was only with that party that Metcalfe, as the representative of the Imperial Government, could properly sympathize." Second, with his watchword of "loyalty," he secured the support of a large section of the "moderates"— an enterprise in the success of which Egerton Ryerson as the leading Methodist played a considerable part. Third, Metcalfe emulated (and outdid) Sydenham in his recourse to gangs of hired hoodlums, violence, intimidation through deployment of troops, as instruments in the "electoral process."

The outcome gave the Governor a slight over-all edge in the Assembly: in Canada West his own direct intervention and the "loyalty" cry secured him a strong majority, while in Canada East his supporters were in the main rejected. He reported to the Colonial Office that "loyalty and British feeling prevail in Upper Canada and the eastern townships of Lower Canada; and . . . disaffection is predominant among the French-Canadian constituencies. By disaffection I mean an anti-British feeling, by whatever name it ought to be called, or whatever its foundation, which induces habitually a readiness to oppose Her Majesty's Government." "A feeling of disaffection," he emphasized, "is the bane of the colony."

Following the election, pressure for the granting of self-government did not abate. The fact that it had been

practically within their grasp when Bagot had conceded
the principle and the Baldwin-LaFontaine ministry had
set about implementing it, only added to the Reformers'
sense of frustration at Metcalfe's reimposition of autocratic rule. In the words of an Address from sixteen councillors of the County of Gore (Canada West): "Public
opinion in this district and, we believe, throughout the
length and breadth of Canada, will fully sustain the late
Executive in the stand they have taken, and the views
they have expressed, in relation to colonial administration
under the principle of Responsible Government . . ." To
which Metcalfe replied: "If you mean that the Governor
is to have no exercise of his own judgment in the administration of the government, and is to be a mere tool in
the hands of the Council, then I totally disagree with you
. . . Such a surrender of the prerogative of the Crown is,
in our opinion, incompatible with the existence of a
British Colony."

Considering himself "the chief ruler of the province,"
standing firm "in defense of constitutional government
and British connection," the embattled Governor saw "the
entire colony . . . as one vast party opposed to the government of Her Majesty." Let any question arise involving a
conflict between imperial and Canadian interests, and
"the great mass of the people of the colony will array
themselves against the mother-country."

The reason was not far to seek. It lay in the persistent
refusal of the overriding demand voiced in the words of
LaFontaine: "The colonies should have the management
of their own affairs. They should direct all their efforts to
this end; and to succeed, the colonial administration must
be formed and directed by and with the majority of the
representatives of the people."

Stoutly rallied in resistance to the pressures for self-
government were the Governor (backed by the coercive

power of imperial troops stationed under his command) and the local forces of colonial conservatism: such surviving Family Compact protagonists as Sir Allan MacNab, laird of Dundurn Castle in Hamilton, and the oligarch of the vast Talbot estates to the West; the clerical hierarchs, Anglican and Catholic, in both Canadas; and the Montreal merchant conservatives headed by the Moffatts, Molsons and McGills.

The forces of Reform, for their part, were by no means homogeneous. There was, firstly, the rift between the two national communities, which set its imprint on the movement. The Tories made the most they could of this, identifying the Reformers as the "French Party" and claiming (as did Metcalfe and the Montreal *Herald*) that the Reform majority in Lower Canada were "exclusively French." These assertions were rebutted by the contemporary chronicler, Gérin-Lajoie, who pointed out that "in fact almost the entire Irish population, and a good part of those of English and Scottish origin, who sincerely desired the establishment of responsible government, marched also under the banner of M. LaFontaine." The latter claimed, in 1848: "At least half, if not more, of the population of British origin in the city of Montreal belong to our party."

If ethnic diversity was one problem the Reformers faced, another was the social heterogeneity of their movement: it numbered in its ranks businessmen and professionals, farmers and workmen. The class differences were to make themselves felt in time, and find expression in division as between moderates and radicals. As yet, the cleavage was only latent. But testimony to its presence was not wanting. Metcalfe himself, after noting that the mass of Irish Catholics as well as many of the Scots "are generally arrayed on the side of the malcontents," made the further observation that "it is not among the upper

classes that the malcontents among them are to be found."
Thus early did the criterion of property and class intrude
upon debate over constitutional prerogatives. Its presence
received further emphasis when in the course of the by-
election of 1845 some hundred Irish canal workers marched into Montreal from Lachine to help Reform candidate
Drummond defeat the wealthy William Molson.

While such rumblings were a reminder of the class
realities, the unresolved issues of self-government and
national equality continued to dominate politics. In the
debates of the Legislature of the Province of Canada they
remained the focal points, so long as the pressures for
Reform continued to meet with resistance and obstruction.

The Assembly elected in 1844 mirrored not only the
opposing alignments on the responsible government issue,
but also the continued existence of those "two Canadas"
that the Union was supposed to have welded into one.
From Canada West came a "loyalist" and conservative
contingent committed to support of the Governor, while
the opposition Reform party dominated the representation from Canada East. Neither the opponents of reform
nor the advocates of responsible government were in a
position to make their will prevail.

Yet processes were at work that were to overcome the
deadlock. The very growth of modern industry and of the
power of the factory-owners that gave impetus in Britain
to the pressures for Free Trade and parliamentary reform, stimulated the demand in British North America
for modernization of the antiquated colonial structures.
For Sydenham, and Metcalfe also, stubborn resistance to
colonial self-government did not preclude a readiness to
implement some of the more limited measures of reform
that Durham had urged and Downing Street was prepared to countenance. Thus in 1845, the long-standing re-

form demand for elective municipal councils was conceded. The following year saw the establishment of a system of local school boards.

The effect of these concessions was not (as the authorities had hoped) to blunt the edge of the popular campaign
for constitutional reform but to sharpen it. At the same
time, the aim of responsible government remained in-
separably interwoven with the issue of the internal "national question." The mounting outcry for colonial autonomy reinforced the pressure for national equality: in 1846
the Assembly adopted an address to the imperial government requesting repeal of the ban on French as an official
language of the legislature. The attempt (which the Act
of Union had been designed to expedite) at effacing the
national duality was proving to be unworkable. As La-
Fontaine was to argue later, "the Act of Union had not
made of the two Canadas one single province, but had
merely joined, under one single legislature, two hitherto
distinct and separate provinces which were to continue to
be such for all other purposes . . . a confederation of two
provinces, two states . . ."

What underlay the persistence of these "two provinces,
two states" was of course the existence side by side of the
two distinct national communities. Whether separately or
in union, they could only hope to achieve self-government
(or "nationhood") through a concerted effort; and this in
turn presupposed a recognition of the principle of equality of national rights, and rejection of inferior, subject
status for French Canada. Like the united Reform coalition that had brought it to power, the Baldwin-LaFontaine
administration had represented a first attempt at establishing a democratic, bi-national government. It had rested, implicitly, on the principle that later came to be
called the "double majority." In a letter of September
1845 LaFontaine resumed the argument in support of the

principle that "the majority in each province respectively should govern . . . The present administration, as regards Upper Canada, is formed on this principle, but in Lower Canada it is formed on an opposite principle. Why this distinction between the two sections of the Province? Is there not in this fact alone a thought of injustice, nay, of oppression?"

". . . In the matter of administration Lower Canada should have what is accorded Upper Canada: nothing more, but also nothing less."

The situation thus outlined by LaFontaine was defined in sharper terms by Louis-Joseph Papineau, just returned from exile: "This Union," he declared, "places us, in relation to Upper Canada, in the same position as Ireland in relation to England."

The struggle of the French Canadians, as a nation annexed, for what we would now call the right of self-determination, was a major driving force in the Reform movement of the Canadas. Metcalfe acknowledged its weight and effectiveness in the colonial contest when he wrote: "The French party is the strongest from being thoroughly united, and acting together almost as one man."

A striking statement of the position of the Reform forces in Lower Canada is contained in the November 8, 1847 Manifesto of the Quebec City "Association Constitutionnelle de la Réforme et du Progrès." Its authors characterize in these terms the unrepresentative set-up engineered by Metcalfe: "A minority governs, just as it did under the old régime, with this difference that by means of *electoral frauds* it has become an *electoral majority*." They then take issue with the annexation of Lower Canada as the basic feature of the state structure established by the Act of Union:

A regularly constituted and politically long-established society, whether colonial or other, cannot be joined to another society against its will, without this constituting a wholly unjustifiable abuse of power . . .
Not only did they violently alter the political condition of more than half a million people, all British subjects . . . but subjected this population to the domination of a population less in numbers and in no way superior in intelligence or industry.

The root cause of what threatened to become a deep and enduring cleavage between the two peoples is declared to be the "political degradation of the majority of the inhabitants of Lower Canada"— an institutionalized national oppression:

At the very moment that they proclaimed a legislative union, they sowed the seeds of a long political division . . . The entire mass of the population of British origin in Upper Canada is declared to be superior to the population of French origin in Lower Canada; and is accorded a greater proportion of power, a larger share of independence and liberty. The new Constitution decreed in law and established in fact the oppression of Lower Canada as a locality, the oppression of the French Canadians as a race.

The tendency, widespread then as now, to see in an assertion of rights a threat of domination ("What Do They Want?") is here traced to its real source; also, the fairly common Anglo-Saxon inclination to brush aside the historically legitimate demand of an oppressed people with a slighting reference to "narrow nationalism" (or "national jealousy"), is shown to be tainted with more than a little of the dominant group's own nationalism:

Partisan spirit has often attributed the complaints of the oppressed to a desire for domination on their part; and the leaders of an oligarchy, by imbuing their own supporters

with a fear of being tyrannized in turn by those they
oppress, frighten and overawe their partisans. . . . Because
the French Canadians, maltreated as such, had to complain
and make reference to their origin which was being made
a mark of inferiority, their plaints were blamed on national
jealousy; exclusivist views were attributed to them, which
their whole history refutes; and every national prejudice
was excited in opposition to them.

The only way to overcome national hostility is to establish national equality; and the democrats of Quebec here
urge common action to achieve it, reminding the "British
minority" in Lower Canada of the existence of a genuine
common interest: "that of the moral and material prosperity of the country, an object that can only be attained
through the sacrifice of all prejudice, of all national anti-
pathy: through a common effort for the development of
the vast resources that this country offers all its inhabitants. They must also be convinced that political equality
is an indispensable condition of that harmony and common effort on which the happiness of all depends."

Lord Elgin, the son-in-law of Durham, came out to
Canada as Governor-General early in 1847. Unlike Metcalfe, he was fully prepared to accept the principle and
practice of responsible government—provided his Canadian ministers would "in return . . . carry out my views
for the maintenance of the connection with Great Britain . . ."

In the elections called at the close of 1847 as a result
of the final disintegration of the shaky ministerial majority originally engineered by Metcalfe, the new governor
in no way intervened to influence the outcome. When the
Reformers won two-thirds of the seats in the Assembly,
with a majority in both sections of the province, Elgin

was prepared to call upon their leaders to form an administration.

This reversal of the previous imperial policy was in part the outcome of the decade of popular struggles waged by the Reform forces in Canada and the Maritimes; it also sprang from deep-going changes taking place in the British Isles. There the years 1846-48 witnessed the victory of the manufacturing bourgeoisie: "Free Trade" triumphed with the repeal of the Corn Laws in 1846. The new ascendancy of the industrial capitalist interest over the merchant-landowner oligarchy not only opened the way for a drive to capture world markets, it brought changes in colonial policy as well. The old system of cramping mercantilist constraints had now become an impediment to "free competition," to freedom of expansion (and export) of capital. As Frederick Engels noted, replacement of mercantilist restriction by free trade "meant the readjustment of the whole home and foreign, commercial and financial policy of England in accordance with the interests of the manufacturing capitalists—the class which now represented the nation."

The new type of colonial relationship portended far-reaching readjustments for British North America. They did not come about automatically, but necessitated a struggle of the colonists against ultra-conservative resistance: Metcalfe's reactionary policy had enjoyed the full backing of the British Government. As late as August 1846 the Queen was urging "the continuance and consistent application" of that policy: as she saw it, "The only thing that has hitherto proved beneficial was the prudent, consistent and impartial administration of Lord Metcalfe."

The old regime died hard.

Three further factors, however, had combined with internal pressures for reform to compel a radical change:

the Irish famine, the outbreak of an economic crisis, and the European revolutionary wave that culminated in the upheavals of 1848.

The "Great Hunger" in Ireland (1845-47) set in motion a "tide of misery" (as Elgin called it) that deposited on these shores over 100,000 impoverished immigrants. Vast numbers of them were fever-stricken: some 10,000 died at Quebec and Montreal. The massive addition which immigration contributed to the labor-force multiplied the ranks of lumberworkers and canal and railway construction laborers. This reinforcement aggravated the employment problem in the economic crisis that broke out in 1847; it also added fresh sinew to the working-class component in the reform movement.

In Britain the Chartist movement, spurred by economic crisis, experienced a new upsurge. In 1847 mass pressure secured the passage of the Ten Hours Act, limiting the worktime of women and children in factories; the movement for the People's Charter aroused workingmen to give militant support to democratic social measures in Parliament "by pressure from without"— through mass meetings, petitioning and agitation in the localities. The English Chartists' pressure for reform helped create the political climate in which self-government for the Canadas became a reality. It was a season of great storms: the national and democratic revolutions that broke out one after another in February and March 1848, in France, Germany, Austria-Hungary and Italy, imparted a mighty impulse to movements for radical change far beyond their own borders.

It was in March, 1848, that Elgin called upon LaFontaine and Baldwin as the leaders of the majority in the Assembly to form a ministry. The day of "responsible government" had come at last. Its achievement was part and parcel of the general revolutionary-democratic process that was convulsing the Old World, and to which imperial Britain and its colonies were not immune. It is worthy of note that Elgin was told by the Colonial Office it was just as well that a Canadian government enjoying the support of the Assembly had been formed *before* the news of the February Revolution in Paris became known in the colony. "They are not wanting here," Elgin wrote, "persons who might under different circumstances have attempted by seditious harangues, if not by overt acts, to turn the examples of France and the sympathies of the United States to account."

Elgin had been particularly concerned lest the French-Canadian national movement join forces with the turbulent Irish proletarians employed at building the canals. The militant laborers on the Lachine canal (whose struggles over pay and conditions of work were chronic at this period) combined the revolutionary spirit of Irish patriots with working-class combativity. The Governor "feared a union between the followers of Papineau and the Irish canal workers." Back of such an ominous prospect loomed the spectre of revolution across the Atlantic: ". . . France and Ireland are in flames," wrote Elgin, "and nearly half the people of this colony are French—nearly half of the remainder Irish!"

To situate the winning of "responsible government" in the Canadas in the historic context of the revolutionary era of 1848 is not to deny that the measure itself was "granted from above," as a concession to mass pressure. This was no conquest of independence gained through revolution: the colonial bourgeoisie was edging its way toward autonomy, a step at a time. Yet, as in the case of the English Reform Bill of 1832 and the subsequent accession to power of the manufacturing interest, the achievement of a momentous advance in British North America required the propelling power of the mass movement. Thanks to it the colony (and in the first instance, of course, its ruling classes) had gained at last a large measure of autonomy with respect to domestic affairs.

Assuredly, a condition of the granting of local ministerial responsibility was the maintenance of British connection, the continued authority of the imperial metropolis in matters of defense, external relations and trade. The Royal prerogative and the role of the governor as "the link which connects the Mother Country and the colony" expressed in tangible form the continuing integration with the Empire: that "powerful instrument, under Providence," as Earl Grey described it, "of maintaining peace and order in many extensive regions of the earth and, thereby, assisting in diffusing, among millions of the human race, the blessings of Christianity and civilization."

But within this imperial framework the relation of the metropolis with the "white" colonies of settlement was henceforth to be modified. In Grey's words, "This country has no interest whatever in exercising any greater influence in the internal affairs of the colonies, than is indispensable either for the purpose of preventing any one colony from adopting measures injurious to another, or to the Empire at large."

As early as November 1846 the colonial secretary had instructed Sir John Harvey, Lieutenant-Governor of Nova Scotia, to make it plain "that any transfer which may take place of political power from the hands of one party in the province to those of another, is the result, not of an act of yours but of the wishes of the people themselves . . . It cannot be too distinctly acknowledged that it is neither possible nor desirable to carry on the government of any of the British Provinces in North America in opposition to the opinion of the inhabitants."

Gone was the policy of Sydenham and Metcalfe, of viceroys seeking to act as combined governor and prime minister and open leader of the party of colonial reaction. Grey's instructions to Elgin read: "You and the Home Government belong to neither party and have nothing to do with their contests . . . This principle must be completely established in order long to preserve our connection with the colony."

If the granting of responsible government was seen as one concession that was necessary to preservation of the British connection, the lifting of the ban on the French language was another. In August 1847 Westminster repealed the clause in the Act of Union that had made English the sole official language of the Province of Canada. Recognition of French, taken together with LaFontaine's joint accession to power with Baldwin, indicated at least a modicum of recognition of the principle of national equality for French Canada. Conceivably, this might lead in the direction of a genuinely democratic relationship of the two "nations," on a complete footing of equality— political, social, economic—a radical restructuring of Canadian society on principles of consistent political democracy and full independence. (This was to be the orientation of the radical democracy of the *Parti rouge*.) Or, alternatively, the concession to pressures for national equality might yet stop short at a point fixed by the common interest of Anglo-Canadian business, the Church in Lower Canada, and the imperial metropolis. Which orientation would prevail was not yet clear. For the moment, two points are worthy of note:

First, in imposing the abrogation of the anti-French-language clause of the Act of Union, a real victory had been gained by the bi-national reform coalition. Elgin "deliberately turned his back on the policy of denationalization advocated by Lord Durham," being, as he himself put it, "deeply convinced of the impolicy of all such attempts to denationalize the French." Impolitic attempts, because "Generally speaking they produce the opposite effects from that intended, causing the flame of national prejudice and animosity to burn more fiercely. . . . You may perhaps Americanize, but depend upon it, by methods of this description you will never Anglicize the French inhabitants of the province."

Second, Elgin's long-range approach looked to the overcoming of what has been called "the peculiar position of the French solidarity in Canadian political life." To this end he outlined a more devious and subtle method than the discredited Sydenham-Metcalfe policy of "putting down the French" through forcible denationalization. He explained to Grey at the Colonial Office:

> I believe that the problem of how to govern United Canada would be solved if the French would split into a Liberal and a Conservative Party and join in Upper Canadian parties which bear corresponding names. The great difficulty hitherto has been that a Conservative Government has meant a Government of Upper Canadians which is intolerable to the French, and a Radical Government a Government of French which is not less hateful to the British. No doubt the party titles are misnomers, for the Radical Party comprises the political section most averse to progress of any in the country. Nevertheless so it has been hitherto. The national element must merge in the political if the split to which I refer were accomplished.

By seeking to have "the national element . . . merge in the political," Elgin's policy for French Canada "aimed at wiping out the consciousness of a distinct origin in a general scheme of national development": an approach which even today has a not unfamiliar ring . . .

In the political ferment of the 1840s in the dual-national colonial Canadas, following the defeats of 1837-38, not one but two processes had been at work: one working towards a bourgeois revolution in the Canadas as against imperial restriction and control, the drive of the colonial business class for self-government; the other, a French-Canadian radical bourgeois-democratic movement for national self-determination. A common denominator of the two was to be found in a common colonial interest, expressed in a dual-national ("pan-Canadian") form; its thrust was in the direction of an autonomous, industrial-capitalist development. Yet capitalist dominance was so ill-attuned to national equality that denial of the latter appeared as a precondition of the former. Concession of self-government to the Anglo-Canadian colonial bourgeoisie was conditional on assurance of a "proper subordination of the French"— to whose numerical minority status was superimposed a political mechanism with built-in guarantees of British-imperial stability. Conceded "from above", the Canadian bourgeois revolution was, in its limited way, successful; the French-Canadian one was not.

True, the governing bi-national partnership of LaFontaine and Baldwin, reflecting the presence and collaboration of the small French-Canadian business element and (to a degree) of the powerful Church, gave an air of political equality. But this very arrangement served at the same time to mask the effective denial of any provision for self-government of the French-Canadian nation. Hence, the idyllic picture of an "all-Canadian" victory of responsible government (a sort of simultaneous success of two bourgeois revolutions) is an optical illusion. The reality was that of a limited colonial self-government with Anglo-Canadian capitalist ascendancy, buttressed by British imperial power.

9

Masters and Men

"Hurrah for Munn! Munn for ever! Long live the builders!
Trade and Commerce. Hurrah for the ships! Pif! Paf!
Ouch, my eye! my arm! I'm killed! Hey, let's run!"—
anyone with two cents' worth of memory surely remembers
these shouts of the ships' carpenters who at election time
supported Mr. Munn, carried him in triumph, called him
the father and mainstay of the working class of St. Roch.
His supporters didn't count their bruises, certain as they
then were of counting on him for steady work and reasonable pay.

At the start of the season and in summer-time, when the
shipbuilders were in need of hands, they readily offered
the ' worker higher pay than usual, to lure him from a
neighboring shipyard. . . . But now with winter setting in,
with the upkeep of a family costing more than twice as
much, the gentlemen-builders feel that if they can make
among themselves a sort of treaty of alliance, a pact of
famine against the laboring class, to whom they'll give the
lowest wage their generosity will allow, then the profits
they amass will be the sweeter for it. Why shouldn't the
worthy builders pocket the two or three shillings difference
from each worker's pay? True, the workers' families will
suffer more cold, be worse clothed, eat much more frugally;
but what does that matter to these gentlemen of substance?
. . . *They make money,* which these days is all that matters.

So now at the beginning of winter they are trying to get
labor at the cheapest price, offering the carpenter *three*
shillings a day and the laborer proportionately less. The
workers ask for *four* shillings, a moderate enough amount
and admittedly scarcely enough to maintain a family. So

there is a combination of the Ship-builders against the worker. . . .

Thus wrote Napoléon Aubin, editor of the Quebec City newspaper, *Le Fantasque*, in the issue of December 10, 1840. Not content merely to record the labor dispute he editorialized:

> It is said generally that it is Mr. Munn who started or advised this combination of the builders against the workers! He who has made a fortune out of the labor of the Canadian workers! . . .
>
> We are glad to see that for their part the workers have rallied to act unitedly in the common interest . . . Let us hope that if need be the citizenry at large will help them in their struggle against this outright, egotistical tyranny of the ship-builders . . . The workers in other trades, even the small shopkeepers, should join in to assist the carpenters. The more they are helped, the shorter will be their struggle, as the builders will finally accept the terms of their employees, which still leave them enough profit to make reasonable fortunes.
>
> The benefits of this momentary leaguing together should prove to the carpenters the need to form a permanent association . . .

Following the 1839-40 boom in shipbuilding, during which prices and profits had outstripped gains in wages, the ships' carpenters had organized a "Friendly and Benevolent Society," led by Francois Gifford and Joseph Laurin. Fernand Ouellet considers this "Société amicale et bienveillante des charpentiers de vaisseaux de Québec" to have been one of the earliest real trade unions of French-Canadian workers.* He points out that ship-

---

*". . . Rien, excepté la première association des typographes en 1828, qui permette de parler de réalité syndicale . . . ce syndicat est proprement canadien-francais" (*Histoire* . . . p. 501.) See, however, our earlier reference to labor in Montreal in the 1830s.

building at Quebec was, like the timber trade, "dominated by the Anglo-Saxons: Sharples, Gilmour, Black, Lampson, Munn, Jeffery, Oliver, Bell, Nesbitt, Lee, Nicholson and Russell . . . The most notable participation of French Canadians is at the level of the work force: ships' carpenters and day laborers."

The Quebec shipyard workers' "lively and constant opposition to the odious monopoly of the master shipbuilders," as one of their leaders described it in addressing a union meeting, expressed the irreducible antagonism that is rooted in the relationship of wage labor and capital. Operating their yards with the aim of extracting (as *Le Fantasque* put it) "enough profit to make reasonable fortunes," the masters (for whom "to make money . . . is all that matters") banded together to force "the lowest wage" upon their workers. The latter are thereby compelled to organize in their own defense. At Quebec, this opposition of class interests is compounded by the difference in nationality: the owners are "les Anglais," the workers "les Canadiens." This is the pattern being established first and foremost in the few sectors of large-scale production that as yet exist in the colony. The strategic control of the dominant heights of the capitalist economy by "les Anglais" (whether British, Anglo-Canadian or—as was even then beginning to be the case in lumber and paper-making—American) is to remain an essential feature of the new industrialism in the Canadas.

Industrialization in the mid-decades of the century was accelerated drastically by the railway-building boom which reached a peak in the early 1850s. But even before the "railway mania" took hold, an industrial capitalist economy was in the making in the colonial provinces of British North America. Two primary components in the

process were the growth of local manufactures and the
mass influx of a supply of immigrant laborers. (A third
was to be the subsequent large-scale investment of capital
in railway construction and equipment.)

It was Canada West that first witnessed the emergence
of a fairly broad base of small-scale, local manufacturing,
linked with an expanding agriculture. With the influx of
population and spread of settlement, people's ways of
living and working were changing: the old self-sufficient
pioneer economy of the country districts was retreating
to the backwoods. Taking its place were division of labor,
specialization, production for the market. The early local
industries—the "infant manufactures" whose praises had
been sung by the Reformers in the pre-Rebellion days—
either expanded to meet the new needs, or succumbed to
the new competition. With the growth of towns, whose
vital centre was the market-place, there came new industries. And these in turn, together with the introduction
of machinery and steam-power, changed the pattern of
manufactures. The experience of growing diversification
was illustrated in the case of the village of Dundas, rival
of near-by Hamilton as a centre of industrial activity. In
1837, with a population of less than 800, Dundas had an
axe-maker's shop, a foundry, a hat-maker, two carriage-
works, three cabinet-makers, three breweries and four
distilleries, four flour and grist mills,* four cooperages,
five saw and planing mills, and a stone quarry. Ten years
later, with a population of about 2,000 there were: another distillery, two more each of foundries, sawmills and
cooperages, six more cabinet or furniture "factories";
and in addition, these newly-started enterprises: an agricultural implements factory, a last factory, shoe factory,

---

*One of these, Hatt's grist mill, was started around 1800: the oldest
operating enterprise in Ontario, it now bears the name of "Top
Notch Feeds Ltd."

roller factory, lime kiln, pottery, brickyard, pump works, woollen mill, whip factory, two tanneries and two soap and candle shops.

What all of these had in common was modesty of dimension. They were small plants, with a small number of "hands" working for (and often alongside) the proprietor. The transition to large-scale factory industry was just beginning to become possible with the introduction of the steam engine and steam-driven machinery. In a very different geographic and historical context, the emergent colonial manufactures were approaching the watershed between production by hand and production by machine, of which Marx wrote in 1847: "The hand-mill gives you society with the feudal lord; the steam-mill, society with the industrial capitalist." It was industrial capitalists that were in the making in mid-century British North America. The masters who owned the early mills and workshops, in both French and English Canada, were an embryonic industrial bourgeoisie.

The 1851-52 census figures while far from complete give an approximate idea both of the overall industrial activity and of the disparity in certain respects between the two sections of the Province of Canada.

Occupational distribution in the two sections reveals both the unevenness and parallelism of their economic development. (In the classification employed, "commercial class" includes not only shopkeepers but carters, bargemen, stevedores and others; "industrial class" includes artisans following a trade or craft.)

While the percentage distribution is very close for most categories, there is a notable margin of difference in "Industrial":

Occupational Distribution

	Occupied persons (000)		Percentage distribution	
	U.C.	L.C.	U.C.	L.C.
Agricultural	86.6	78.4	35.1	38.6
Commercial	9.3	8.8	3.8	4.3
Domestic	18.0	17.1	7.3	8.4
Industrial	45.0	26.3	18.2	12.0
Professional	6.8	4.9	2.8	2.4
Not classified	80.8	67.7	32.8	33.3
(Includes laborers)				

This break-down by occupations indicates something of the general similarity in the processes of early industrial development in the two Canadas; what it does not show is the relatively greater dispersal of those engaged in industry in "Upper Canada" as compared with concentration at Montreal and Quebec City in "Lower Canada."*

The 1851 Census data on the use of steam power in grist and sawmills, and on the number of foundries, emphasize a rather striking difference in the situation in the two sections of the province:

	Grist Mills		Sawmills	
	U.C.	L.C.	U.C.	L.C.
No. of mills	612	541	1567	1065
Steam-driven	37	8	154	4
No. of hands employed	1150	807	3670	3634

	Foundries	
	U.C.	L.C.
No.	94	38
Hands employed	925	197

---

*Cf. André Raynauld's figures for 1956, showing 21 per cent of Ontario's manufacturing labor force concentrated in Toronto, whereas 40.8 per cent of Quebec's is in Montreal. The trend goes back to the mid-19th century. (*Croissance et Structures économiques . . .*, p. 242)

It would be interesting to know what proportion of the total output of the grist and sawmills was accounted for by those employing steam-power. (Later indications —to which we shall return—point to a marked tendency to concentration of production in the larger, power-driven mills.) Something else that the above figures of course do not cover is the *pattern of ownership,* in Lower Canada, as between English and French-Canadian owners of steam-driven mills and of foundries. The contrast in industrial development between the two areas that is shown, in all likelihood understates the discrepancy: the category "Lower Canada" contains within itself a French-English imbalance in distribution of ownership, of which there are plentiful scattered indications, but no detailed statistical account.

English-Canadian dominance in the industrialization process is evident in the case of the launching of textile manufactures in Lower Canada. The newspaper *Le Canadien* of April 3, 1844, carried the following news-item:

DOMESTIC MANUFACTURES

At a meeting of the inhabitants of the town of Sherbrooke it was resolved that it would be of advantage to this part of the province to establish a cotton manufactory at Sherbrooke, that such an establishment would be profitable to those who undertake it, and that if local resources did not suffice, capitalists from outside the area would be invited to take part. A committee was charged with making the preliminary arrangements and corresponding with the capitalists. The committee is composed of Messrs. E. Hale, M.P., John Fraser, Samuel Brookes, J. Pennoyer, L. C. Ball and Jos. Robertson.

A few months later it was announced that "the amount of capital required is $25,000, which is to be raised in shares of $100 each"; and the name of A. T. Galt appeared as a member of the committee appointed to "organize the company, procure machinery, and arrangements have been entered into with a gentleman from Massachusetts, who proposes to invest $2,000 in the undertaking, to purchase the machinery, and to act as general Superintendent."*

Not long after the start in Sherbrooke, the *Montreal Transcript* announced the establishment of a manufactory "at St. Athanase, on the Richelieu, opposite St. Johns," by the British North American Cotton Company, owned by A. H. Willis & Co. The editor was jubilant, having just received from the new enterprise, "with peculiar gratification, a specimen of what we believe is the very earliest essay of Canadian Manufacture of Cotton." . . . "We hail the appearance of domestic manufactures among us with great satisfaction, as they will be the means of giving employment to the dense population of our rural districts, and of keeping the money spent in such articles in the Province—a serious matter when the balance of trade is most generally against us." (August 20, 1844)

The situation obtaining in the embryonic textile industry is suggested by these figures of the 1851 Census:

	Carding & Fulling		Woollens	
	U.C.	L.C.	U.C.	L.C.
No. of Mills	147	193	74	18
No. of Hands	213	282	632	154

In a survey of manufactures published in 1846 the *Canadian Economist* mentions "a Woollen Factory recently established in the Upper Province . . . In Cobourg, Canada West, a woollen manufactory has been put into

---

*Innis and Lower, commenting on this item, express the opinion that "Many, perhaps most, Canadian industries have received their initial requirements of technical skill from the United States." (*Select Economic Documents in Canadian History*, 1783-1885, p. 301.)

operation this season, which, when in full employ is calculated to work off near 5000 yards of cloth a week."
(Some 175 hands were employed: it was thus one of the
first "large" plants, employing over one-fourth of the
total number of workers in woollen mills in Upper
Canada.)

In Canada East, while a woollen knitting mill had been
in operation at Sherbrooke for some years, the editor
notes that there had been no general development of factory production of woollens in the province, despite certain favorable factors:

> As to the woollen manufacture, the Lower Province has
> been partially devoted to it from its earliest settlement.
> Every *habitant,* male or female, is clad to this day more
> or less in the rude fabrics of their own manufacture, — the
> man in his "étoffe du pays," and the woman in her
> "jupon." Why then is this manufacture, after thirty or
> fifty years' duration, not in a more advanced state of excel-
> lence? The answer to the question is the same as has been
> given respecting agriculture—the want of education. Had
> the rural population been enlightened, they would have
> seen long ere this that their labour should be organized and
> directed; that, instead of each family in a district having
> its loom, which could furnish the family only with apparel
> of the rudest kind, each district should have had its factory,
> where the population could have been employed, and cloth-
> ed at less expense and with superior fabrics. Had this been
> done years ago, the factory or factories in every district of
> Canada would now be powerful and flourishing; and the
> men, women, and children, who are now wasting half their
> life in idleness in the rural districts, would be skilled opera-
> tives, earning good wages and promoting the welfare of
> society at large.

The explanation offered—"want of education" on the
part of rural working people, their slowness to realize
that instead of staying on the farm they should bestir

themselves and work as factory operatives, whereby their work would be "organized and directed"—is surely a choice blend of historical-idealist thinking and Victorian middle-class complacency. Actually, factory industry would be launched by those possessing the capital required to build factories, buy machinery and materials and hire "hands"; and the driving motive was to be capitalists' profit, not workers' self-improvement. To turn farm people into factory hands involved dispossessing them, "freeing" them from ties to property. Once thus freed, and made available to bring their labor-power to the labor market, they would be hired and "organized and directed" in applying themselves to the self-improvement of capital, the maximizing of the master's profit.

The presence of a work-force of propertyless wage-laborers was indeed a precondition of capitalist industry. The main source of such workers in the 1840s was the mass influx of immigrants from the British Isles, many of them already dispossessed (and hence "free"), having been either uprooted and driven off the land or ruined (in the case of small independent craftsmen) by the introduction of machine industry.

Within the Canadas, the role of the land monopoly as an impediment to settlement contributed to the creation of a force of laborers for hire; this was true of Lower Canada to a drastic extent, where the perpetuation of the seigneurial system, a chronic agrarian crisis, and a sustained high birth rate combined to give rise to mass unemployment. In the absence of an industrial development adequate to absorb the surplus, tens of thousands of young French Canadians migrated to the manufacturing towns of the United States.* This "blood-letting" of

*Cf. pp. 60, 286-90.

French Canada's potential labor-force reached its peak in the very years of mass immigration to Canada from England, Scotland and Ireland. The sense of national resentment in Lower Canada was hardly lessened by this juxtaposition of emigration of *Canadiens* and immigration of *Anglais*.

Arrivals of immigrants at Quebec in the period 1840-1857 averaged close to 35,000 annually. Laborers, farmers and farm servants formed by far the greatest part of these; of other categories, building-trades workers, smiths, shoemakers, tailors, miners and mill-wrights were numerous. The combined impact of capitalist industrialization, modernization of agriculture, and the Irish potato famine enabled the London *Economist* to observe complacently: "The departure of the redundant part of the population of Ireland and the Highlands of Scotland is an indispensable preliminary to every kind of improvement."

The three hundred petitioners of the North-Quarter Glasgow Emigration Society, seeking financial help to freight a vessel for Canada, viewed the situation from a somewhat different vantage-point. They were, they stated,

> chiefly hand-loom weavers, whose genius and industry, for many years, constituted a principal part of the splendour and opulence of this once happy land, and diffused wealth through every rank of society; but owing to their trade coming in contact with the machinery of the power-loom, and the consequent reduction of their wages, they have now to deplore the want of the commonest necessaries of life, being able to lengthen out a miserable existence; their children without education, obliged to work at their own employment in comparative infancy, and by that means perpetuate their miserable trade. Want, absolute want, with all its baneful appendages, has long been familiar in their dwellings, so as to place them in the degrading position of becoming a useless weight on the wealthier part of the

community, with every vestige of hope destroyed in their native land, and their unfortunate situation acknowledged by all.

Their fellow-countryman, the poet and former Chartist, Thomas Macqueen, then editing the Ottawa valley newspaper the *Bathurst Courier,* inveighed against the state of affairs in the Old Country —"the avaricious jostling of manufacturing enterprise," which drew its profits from "the revolting condition of the five-farthing per-yard weaver or the penny-half-penny shirt maker": a state of affairs that compelled the emigration of "such of the British workmen as want of employment or reduction of wages have driven within the precincts of a lingering starvation." On first reaching Kingston in 1842 he observed among the emigrants "misery and destitution equal to that which had induced them to leave their native land. The great annual influx of laboring men to Kingston, and the other towns along the lake shore, as far up as Toronto, has rendered labor* scarce and wages low."

As the mounting tide of misery in Ireland in the early forties drove new, still more numerous contingents across the water, these provided a large part of the "reserve army" of available "hands" for canal-building contractors and railway promoters. The conditions of the laborers employed on the construction of the Lachine and Beauharnois canals early in the winter of 1843 were such as to kindle resistance and a series of strikes. H. C. Pentland's study of the Lachine strikes tells the story of this early episode in working-class resistance to exploitation.

Housed in wretched shanties, dependent on company stores for high-priced provisions, the men "wrought from dark to dark" for two shillings a day (a rate reduced by

*i.e.: employment.

a shilling since the year before). The men's sense of awareness of exploitation is expressed in the words of Martin Donnelly, spokesman of the striking Beauharnois Canal workers: "The general impression amongst the laborers is, that the daily work of each man on the Canal is worth from six to seven shillings to the contractors." His own winter take-home pay averaged less than two shillings a week. When the magistrate at Beauharnois addressed the men, and "sought to influence them to abstain from striking, they answered that they could not, for it was out of their power to maintain themselves on the wages they received."

On February 6 the Government sent in troops. Three days later the men went back to work, with a promise of a 6d increase by March 24. As this day approached, instead of the pay increase there were layoffs—and again the men struck. Five hundred of them marched to Montreal to present their grievances. Public meetings were organized in support of the strike. Despite attempts to break the men's resistance by setting at odds the two chief groups of Irish immigrants—Connaughtmen and Munstermen— and later by bringing French-Canadian farm lads on to the job, the strikers stood firm, with solidarity finally winning them their demand of three shillings a day.

In May, French Canadians working on the Beauharnois Canal "struck for higher wages and shorter hours, but they were dismissed to the number of 19." A further strike of canal workers in June was answered by the bringing in of troops; violence and shooting ensued, and six strikers were killed. At this point the authorities felt compelled to institute an official inquiry.

The investigators included such leading representatives of banking and merchant capital as John Molson and Pierre Beaubien; they soon "discovered" that responsibility for the trouble lay with "agitators." "It is too clear," they reported, "that on this as on all similar occasions the mass was peaceably disposed but they were deceived and irritated by a few. Entering into details of former real or imaginary wrongs, the self-constituted chiefs impelled their followers to breaches of the peace." The keeper of the company store blamed the men: "They are a turbulent and discontented people that nothing can satisfy for any length of time, and who will never be kept to work peaceably unless overawed by some force for which they have respect. . . ." The commander of the troops in Canada East was of the opinion that "the Evil arises from there not being an adequate civil power maintained on the line of Works of a proper description." According to the superintendent of engineers, the danger lay in the fact that among "men, homeless and poverty-stricken . . . a Unity of Action is effected, capable of disturbing the ordinary rules which subsist *individually* between the Laborer and his Employer . . ." He would see to it that "such masses of destitute Men should not be induced or allowed to congregate in one locality."

Thus did the alarmed representatives of the ruling class respond to the emergence of a new power in society: the organized strength of working men. One thing, at least, was clear to the colonial gentry: the need of "some force" to overawe the exploited working class. "Bodies of armed men and prisons": Frederick Engels' succinct definition of the essence of the State, as the emanation of a society riven by class conflict and as the instrument of rule of the propertied classes, thus found its illustration in early colonial Canada. (Strikes by laborers building the Rideau Canal in 1827 had been met by the dispatch of troops; the contractor reporting then that the latter were "most usefully employed; their presence on the ground enables me to check the disorderly conduct of the laborers.")

In the case of the Lachine and Beauharnois strikes of

1843, the Board of Works made application to have a small force of troops stationed at the worksite. They arranged as well for a supplementary safeguard: "the special services of a Clergyman . . . to prevent disturbances there." The secular function of the religious institution was perfectly well understood, and quite specifically spelled out in a Report of the Executive Council (July 31, 1844) on "the request of a Rev. M. Brethour for payment for spiritual services rendered to canal laborers." The Report stated that "the employment of a Roman Catholic clergyman (at Beauharnois) took place . . . as a measure of Police and for the preservation through his influence of peace and order on the line of the Canal, not for the purpose of furnishing religious instruction to the laborers. It having been deemed inexpedient to station troops along the line of the Canal and the large expense which would have attended the establishment of an effective Police force, combined to render the course adopted desirable as economical and effective for the object designed."

Such employment of the clergy in labor disputes as police auxiliaries (or substitutes) was not always acceptable to them, as is evident from the case of Rev. J. C. Clark (the predecessor of Father Brethour at Beauharnois), who balked at the assignment and as a result apparently was shipped back to Ireland.

Thus was Colonial-Victorian Canada jolted by rumblings of class struggle: reminders of the presence, beneath the widely debated political-constitutional and national issues, of a different, more deep-rooted, "social question."

A characteristic feature of the emergent working class was its diversity of national origins. The Montreal area offered a microcosm of the larger picture: in 1843 Irish working people comprised as much as 69% of the West (or Queen's) Ward; in the east, 62% of Ste. Marie Ward was made up of French-Canadian *habitant* families who had moved in to the city. In between, the St. Lawrence Ward already contained the mixed population that was to remain its hallmark to the present.

One result of the numerical growth of the working class, and of confrontations with the employers such as those referred to in the shipyards and on the canals, was the emergence within the Reform movements of a current of *social criticism* that traditional histories have almost wholly ignored. Thomas Macqueen, the militant, crusading editor of the Bathurst *Courier* and the Huron *Signal,* is one who struck a note of radicalism in the agitation against abuses in the areas of settlement, for popular education and democratic reform. Napoléon Aubin was another. An original and rebellious spirit, he inscribed on the masthead of *Le Fantasque* the motto: "I neither obey nor command anybody, I go where I will, do as I please, live as I can and die when I must." His readers were notified that "The editorial office . . . is established on all public walks, streets and squares. You will find the editor when he is there." A year or two later—in 1842—Aubin was busy publishing (in English, this time) *The People's Magazine and Workingman's Guardian:* perhaps the earliest newspaper in Canada to be devoted explicitly to working-class interests. The authorities viewed it with alarm and undisguised hostility. A letter now in the Public Archives, in the handwriting of the Inspector of the Quebec City Police, addressed to Commissioner W. Ermatinger at Montreal, describes the paper as "a most infamous publication" and denounces the publisher as "an idle, drunken fellow." A couple of items from one surviving issue may convey something of its flavor; the first of these denounces a new restriction placed on use of the Quebec city market, accompanied by the introduction of a punitive tax. The Corporation of Quebec, Aubin asserts, have "formed in their minds the notion of trying the depths of the people's pockets, in a manner not agreeable to the Constitution"; the decree is a "barbarous attempt of the packed corporate legislators who have dared to deny to workingmen and others, the privilege of an open market, for the purpose of providing their families with the sustenance of life, from the means they have obtained by the sweat of their brow, on six hardworking days out of the seven days of the week."

The other item reads as follows:

IMPRISONED SEAMEN

A report read at one of the meetings at the City Hall, states the number of mariners committed to the Jail of this City, in the navigation seasons of 1840 and 1841 to be two thousand four hundred only!

This is a greater number of sailors than was ever committed to all the prisons in England in any one year, and it is said that many of these unfortunate men died of diseases contracted while in prison. The Governor-General or Parliament should inquire into this.

A thread of such radical social criticism runs through the Reform agitation; although the central public concern was with the issue of colonial self-government, the "social question" nonetheless asserted its presence. One sign of it was Lord Elgin's anxiety (referred to earlier) over the possibility of an alliance between the canal workers and the French-Canadian national democrats. The 1848 Revolution in France, in which the industrial proletariat battled in the June days as an independent force under its own banners, strengthened awareness of the potential challenge represented by the existence in a colony of an increasingly numerous working class. Characteristic was Etienne Parent's plea for class peace and respect for established order, set forth in his "Considerations on the Condition of the Laboring Classes." This was a lecture delivered at Quebec in 1852 in the working-class district of St. Roch (the area where many of the shipyard workers lived, whose strike a decade earlier had been heartily supported by Aubin's *Le Fantasque*). The words, "Condition of the Laboring Classes," Parent observed, constituted "in Europe the wherewithal to overturn ten empires." Discussing "some points that interest the class of workers," he explained, "by workers I mean not only tradesmen but all who live by manual labor ...":

> One can imagine a political society without men of learning, artists, big industrialists, but without workers—impossible; for they are the very base of the social structure.

Yet "where are our protective laws, our institutions of welfare for the poor worker who is unemployed? Seek as you will, you will see only prisons for the protection of the rich . . . The Providence of the poor is the State, which must not leave them at the mercy of the masters, who are too often pitiless."

Parent's conclusions were limited, however, to educational reform and the creation of an "élite of intelligence": "I do not propose the overthrow of the existing social and political arrangements." He rejected the ideas of "Thomas More and the whole family of utopians"— of those who would "put society back in the crucible . . . and recast it in one piece according to a new model." After all, "The law of subordination of lower to superior beings is a universal law of creation"; rejecting Louis Blanc's dream of a "universal association," Parent urged that in the face of poverty "only religion can, not radically cure or prevent the evil, but mitigate it sufficiently so that it ceases to be a danger to the state."

By the late 1840s the combined impact of industrialization in the Canadas and revolutionary upheavals in Europe appears to have aroused interest in the new theories of radical social change. The 1848 Revolution in France and the debates and controversies that attended it received extensive coverage in the press of Lower Canada; there were indications also of interest in questions of socialism and communism: not that these then posed an issue in Canadian affairs, but more likely because of upper-class disquiet at a time of unrest, and perhaps because of a certain measure of popular curiosity. Illustrative of this interest is the lengthy reporting of speeches of P. J. Proudhon in the French Assembly (his *Philosophy of Poverty* had appeared in 1846, being answered the year following by Karl Marx with *The Poverty of Philosophy*); and an article, "Sur le Communisme" which overflowed the front page of *Le Canadien* of Sept. 1, 1848. This is probably the first instance of publication in Canada of an extended argumentation (in this case, from a clerical-conservative standpoint) about communism.

The author—the Bishop of Langres, a deputy in the French National Assembly—seeks to explain the emergence of Communism as a movement and to propose a remedy. He is less worried by it as a theory (which he oversimplifies) than as a mass movement of popular protest:

> Communism is an opinion like republicanism . . . and many others . . . As a permanent social condition it is an unrealizable utopia. The equal distribution of goods, even if it could be achieved, would not last a day . . . But another matter altogether is the communism manifested in the impatient desires of masses who possess little or nothing and who ask that the goods of those who have too much be shared in common.

While on the upper surface of society a few are making fortunes in railroads and factories, in the "social depths" a different process is at work:

> There, innumerable multitudes are asking daily . . . Why are we poor and wretched while others are happy and well-to-do? Why are we and our families not sure of having even the necessary minimum, while others have a surplus of abundance?

The official world "by its very example must become an irresistible agent of communism": monopoly, monstrous and crushing taxes, plunder of the public treasury, huge scandals at the highest levels of the administrative hierarchy . . . "The immediate cause of the popular movement toward communism is that people are disgusted, not just with this or that government, but with their own position, with its stamp of inferiority . . . (they are led to) blame the present organization of society . . . Organization of labor is the slogan, of which Fourierism is the utopia, but communism in relation to property is the real, practical objective."

Struggle between classes is not something new, as the Bishop sees it; but since the French Revolution the concepts of popular sovereignty and equality of individuals before the law have opened the way to a radical subversion of the social order itself:

> At all times there have been more or less serious conflicts between the popular classes and the upper classes; but however violent, these struggles almost always aimed only at the defense of the people's rights . . . they did not provoke, nor even suggest so much as the thought of an abolition of classes (*déclassement*).

But with modern constitutions, which with their elections and equality before the law "situate the principle of power no longer at the upper levels but in the lower ranks of society"— the age-old barriers separating nobility from commoners have broken down, and "the people no longer accept being looked on as a lower class." Worse yet, "they are inclined to think that this constitutional equality is a dead letter in the absence of equality of wealth."

Where lies the remedy for this menace, which is "fermenting, growing, in the great cities"? The spreading of human reason among all classes? "But it is precisely unfettered reason that engenders, feeds and fires the ideas of communism." Brute force, then? It may work in autocratic Russia, not in France, "with its freedom of thought and public opposition." No, only "Christian education, teaching the 10th commandment ("thou shalt not covet . . .") can overcome the "vague covetousness that is communism," purge men's hearts of unbridled desire for others' property, teach them resignation, "accustom them to reject as a crime the mere thought of defying Providence . . ."

Thus did *Le Canadien* in 1848 purvey the "latest answers" to a new heresy.

That same summer a reader raised with the editor the question of *working-class representation* in the Canadian Assembly. His letter is assuredly one of the earliest expressions of this idea in Canada—put forward with diffidence, in no way suggesting radical "extremism," yet eloquent of the new processes at work. It appeared in *Le Canadien* of June 30, 1848:

> Mr. Editor:
> If the workers at Quebec raised their voice in the late election, it was not with the desire of supplanting the educated classes; but from the motive that, like them, they too have rights to exercise. Moreover, who is to say that

it is any more ridiculous for the industrial class, than it is
for the mercantile branch, to seek to have itself represented
in the Legislature. . . .

And with the suggestion that the emblem of the "ham-
mer and trowel" be widely displayed, the correspondent
signs himself: "A Worker." He was writing from the shipyard workers' district of St. Roch; was he one of those
who years before had supported Mr. Munn, the shipyard
owner, as a candidate—and now was beginning to turn
his thoughts in a new direction . . .?

10

Maritime Identity and Democracy

Like the Canadas, the colonial provinces on the Atlantic passed through successive phases of struggle for responsible government and deliberation over forms of a wider inter-colonial relationship: political processes that were the outgrowth of industrial beginnings, of an urge to autonomy and expansion on the part of a rising capitalist class. Unlike the case of the Canadas, no revolutionary outbreak marked the 1830s in the Maritimes: mass popular-democratic movements and Reform agitation sufficed to secure responsible government. Yet it can hardly be doubted that the intense pressure exerted on Downing Street by the Canadian Rebellions had not a little to do with the winning of Reform objectives at Halifax and Fredericton.

One of the strands in the vigorous regional patriotism that emerged in each of the Atlantic colonies was a strong tradition of popular-democratic militancy. The Nova Scotia colonists who in 1758 compelled the granting of a representative assembly shared the independent spirit of their neighbors in the colonies to the south. Governor Lawrence observed with some anxiety that in the new Assembly, "too many of the members chosen are such as have not been the most remarkable for promoting unity or obedience to His Majesty's government here." Radical sentiment was not lacking in the days of the American Revolution, with Rev. Secombe, that "fiery preacher of the rights of man," as one of its exponents; in two areas (on the St. John River and the Chignecto peninsula) there had been open rebellion.* In 1805 Cottman Tongue, championing popular liberties, was earning the name of "first tribune of Nova Scotia." A report to the Colonial Office in 1808 stated that

> the Lower House is as usual composed principally of farmers who have a little leaven of American democracy amongst them. They are consequently as a body suspicious of government, jealous of their rights and strongly retentive of the public purse. . . . The Council, consisting principally of His Majesty's officers, is always disposed to second the views of the Governor.

From very early times Nova Scotia witnessed expressions of militancy on the part of construction and shipyard workers. Among dockers and shipwrights there were beginnings of trade-union organization, and strikes took place in Halifax before the close of the eighteenth century. By 1816 legislation was being enacted to outlaw working-class organization, with the Nova Scotia Assembly passing "An Act to prevent unlawful Combination of Master Tradesmen, and also of their Workmen and Journeymen." The Act, clearly reflecting ruling-class concern over labor militancy and organization, refers to "great numbers of Master Tradesmen, Journeymen and Workmen, in the Town of Halifax, and other parts of the Province" who had "by unlawful Meetings and Combinations, endeavoured to regulate the rate of wages, and to effectuate other illegal purposes." Jail sentences at hard labor were provided for any "journeyman, workman or other person who shall enter into any combination, to obtain an advance of wages, or to lessen or alter the hours or duration of the time of working"; or likewise, any who

---

*Cf. the writer's *The Founding of Canada*, ch. 25.

should "directly or indirectly, decoy, persuade, solicit, intimidate, influence or prevail, or attempt or endeavour to prevail, on any journeyman or workman . . . to quit or leave his work, service or employment . . ." Even at that date, the conflict of capital and labor had so far become a fact of life in Nova Scotia as to be reflected in the legislation of the master-class.

The ruling faction in Nova Scotia was an amalgam of colonial-military officialdom with a closely-knit group of merchant-bankers possessing strong ties with London commercial houses. The Executive and Legislative Councils were made up of the same twelve men, not one of whom owed his position to election. "Five of the twelve were partners in the Halifax Banking Company . . ." An Assembly resolution of 1837 stated "that two family connections embrace five members of the Council; that, until very recently, when two of them retired from the firm, five others were copartners in one mercantile concern . . ." The rule of this colonial oligarchy was challenged by movements of protest that found their voice in a democratic press. Printers and publishers who bearded the "Committee of Twelve" were on not a few occasions the targets of official repression. In 1818 Anthony Holland, the printer of the *Acadian Recorder*, was sent to prison for criticizing a member of the ruling coterie. Two years later William Wilkie was sentenced to two years' hard labor—a "most tyrannical and cruel proceeding" as one contemporary put it—for publishing a pamphlet exposing peculation and corrupt practices by the magistrates. Subsequent instances of a like persecution in the Atlantic provinces were those of James Hazard, editor of the *P.E.I. Register*, accused of "malicious intent" but acquitted (1829); John Hooper of the *British Colonist* in Saint John (1831); Parsons, editor of the *Newfoundland Patriot*, and

Joseph Howe of the *Novascotian* (both in 1835). Among other Reform papers that played a part in the struggle of the 1830s were: the *Cape Bretonian* (est. 1832), the *Colonial Patriot*, the *Pictou Bee* (1835), and the *St. John Courier*, which thanks to an article on reform published in 1832 became the most popular paper in New Brunswick.

These embattled Maritime printers and journalists not only were spokesmen of the people's aspiration for reform, but gave expression to a growing sense of identity with the province or region as the *homeland*. "This is my own, my native land" was the motto Thomas Chandler Haliburton placed on the title-page of his *Historical and Statistical Account of Nova Scotia* (1829). Two years earlier his friend and political opponent, the printer-Reformer Joseph Howe, seeing his task as one of "rousing the provincial people from their state of despondency into faith in themselves and their country's resources," had urged Nova Scotians to undertake "improvements commensurate with our national capabilities"— and to make this the "policy of those who love Nova Scotia." In an address to the Mechanics' Institute in Halifax (Nov. 5, 1834) Howe argued that a true love of country must tend toward humane and progressive solutions in public affairs; and pointed to the emergence, among people of diverse origins, of a common national spirit:

> Love of country . . . although sometimes abused by ignorance or criminal ambition, has a constant direction favourable to the growth, knowledge, and the amelioration and improvement of human affairs. . . . Has Nova Scotia received the power to attach her children to her bosom and make them prouder and fonder of her bleak hills and sylvan valleys, than even of the fairer and more cultivated lands from which their parents came? I pause for no reply.

> The unerring law of nature is my answer; and though addressing an audience composed of all countries, it is with the conviction that their children are already natives of Nova Scotia, and that their judgments will approve of the direction I wish to give to those feelings of patriotism which that circumstance will inevitably inspire. . . .
>
> Providence has given us a separate country and the elements of a distinct character.

This "separate country" and these "elements of a distinct character" of course had their being within the domain of Empire; the "country" was a British colonial province, and the "character" had its roots in British history and cultural tradition. What is involved here is the genesis of a Maritime, Nova Scotian regional patriotism, whose components are at once British-imperial and intensely localized; Howe summed them up in the *Novascotian* of Jan. 31, 1839:

> To me . . . the dignity and integrity of the Empire are dear, and I feel, I trust, as a British subject should feel, proud of the History and Literature and Science of the Mother Country, of belonging to that Empire, which presents to the world, in all its phases, an example of greatness and glory. But, Sir, here is the country of my birth—this little spot, between Cape North and Cape Sable, is dear to me, as a Nova Scotian, above every other place—and while priding myself in the glories of the Empire, I respect, as a native should do, the soil on which I tread. . . .

Inescapably, the need of the colony for what Howe spoke of as "improvements commensurate with our national capabilities" came into conflict with the imperial-mercantile regime. Colonialism as the source of retardation is almost hinted at in an early editorial in the *Acadian* (March 16, 1827), where Howe muses: "with our manifold and positive advantages our improvement should be rapid and brilliant, our civilization should be more active in its victory over the wilderness . . . but owing to causes that ought to be revealed, the progress of our prosperity is comparatively slow. . . . To speak truth, much of the capital which has been accumulated in the province fills the coffers of foreign money establishments." In the Mechanics' Institute lecture, Howe projected a vision of commercial expansion and potential greatness: "There is no reason why Nova Scotia should not be eminently commercial." Witness the Genoese, or the Phoenicians who "produced neither the gold of Ophir nor the corn of Egypt . . . yet they made more by the interchange of these commodities than the people by whom they were prepared . . . What national connection is there between Glasgow and the North American forests? and yet one house in that city, composed of a few enterprising, intelligent, and frugal men, have established stores and mills in every part of Canada and New Brunswick, buy and sell nearly half of all the timber cut, and out of the profits of their trade have created a fleet of ships, the finest ornaments of the Clyde, and which would furnish a navy for a third rate European power."

The burgeoning provincial-patriotic spirit of the Nova Scotian middle-class reformers was clearly akin to that "bourgeois nationalism" whose "school is the marketplace." Yet that characterization does not exhaust the matter. There were other and deeper roots to national feeling, in the people's collective experience of pioneering toil. A business élite might (and would) exploit that sentiment for its own ends; but to recognize this fact is not to equate the two.

In each of the Atlantic provinces, in the course of long-drawn struggles for self-government and industrial development, a similar strong regional sense of identity took form. It smacked of the sea, their common frontier; it bespoke the individualism and enterprise of the fishery, as well as the close community of the outports; it combined as well the small farmers' will to independence, the lumber and shipyard workers' sturdy militancy; the nostalgia of the "old-comers" and the ambition of the "new-comers," and the urge to industrial progress and expansion of the rising businessmen.

As in the Canadas, the contest for démocracy, self-government and power for the local bourgeoisie assumed the form of a struggle for the supremacy of the colonial Assembly. As one Nova Scotia reformer argued: "It can hardly be questioned that the House of Representatives ought to possess powers similar to those exercised by the House of Commons." That it did not was underlined by the "brandy dispute" of 1830, which flared up over the Executive's arbitrary rejection of a bill dealing with provincial revenue. In 1832 the Nova Scotian democratic forces won a majority of seats in the elections; this however brought no change in the position of the entrenched Executive Council. In the Assembly the reformer Murdoch expressed sympathy with the struggle being waged at Quebec and Montreal: "It is not merely the interests of this one province that are involved in the present dispute, but those of a million and a half British subjects who are scattered over these North American colonies."

In 1835 Howe's vigorous reform agitation in the columns of the *Novascotian* led to his being indicted on charges of "wickedly, maliciously and seditiously contriving, devising and intending to stir up and excite discontent and dissatisfaction among His Majesty's subjects." The trial, with Howe's powerful address to the jury and subsequent acquittal, took on the character of a political demonstration.

The 1836 elections lent new strength to the campaign for what Howe (now elected for the first time to the Assembly) termed "a system of responsibility to the people, extending through all the departments supported at the public expense." The demand for constitutional reform was spelled out in the Twelve Resolutions drafted by Howe and his associates in the winter of 1837. Of these, the 12th urged the British government "to take such steps, either by granting an Elective Legislative Council, or by such other re-construction of the local Government as will ensure responsibility to the Commons, and confer upon the People of this Province, what they value above all other possessions, the blessings of the British Constitution." Howe saw as "the root of all our evils . . . that gross and palpable defect in our local Government, I mean the total absence of all responsibility to the Commons. Compared with the British Parliament this House has absolutely no power."

As a concession, the Colonial Office agreed to the re-construction of the Council into a larger legislative and smaller executive section—a "solution" which Howe had earlier dismissed as "only cutting a rotten orange into two, in order to improve its flavor." The concession was indeed a negligible one; but inasmuch as it provided for the inclusion in the Executive Council of a few members of the elective Assembly, it seemed to presage possible further moves toward cabinet government. The fact of granting the Assembly greater control over revenues pointed in the same direction. In 1840 Sydenham persuaded Howe to accept office under Lieutenant-Governor Falkland, on a vague understanding of eventual "responsible government." To Lord John Russell, Sydenham mentioned, "I have had Mr. Howe here—the Nova Scotian ex-agitator whom I converted into an Executive

Councillor . . ." Petty concessions, a semblance of gestures promising self-government, rejection of it in substance— such was the formula here as in Canada. Not for another six years would the decision be taken to grant responsible government in the colonies.

Meanwhile, the storm of rebellion had swept the Canadas. An appeal to Howe from the Patriotes of Lower Canada in 1835 for joint action had confronted him with a "delicate matter" of political conscience. The message, conveyed in a letter from Henry Chapman, urged "the advantage of co-operation between the several Colonies . . . If a simultaneous demand could be made for an elective council from all the Colonies, great indeed would be the effect upon the public mind, and on the House of Commons." Howe's reply (published by him two years later to counter Tory charges that he had maintained covert connections with revolutionists*) rejected co-operation and invoked loyalty to Britain: "Though cordially opposed to the little knots of councillors, lawyers and placemen, who stand in the way of improvement, the people of Nova Scotia and New Brunswick are sincerely attached to the mother country." Seven-eighths of the population of the Lower Provinces were "opposed in sentiment" to any such movement as that of the Patriotes, who appeared "determined to precipitate a contest with the mother country." As Howe saw it, "We can be no parties to the contest."

In contrast with the stand of Jotham Blanchard, whose *Colonial Patriot* in Pictou consistently upheld the cause of the Patriotes, Howe ranged himself with the "moder-

---

*In November, 1837, the *Novascotian* published the resolutions adopted at the great Patriote rally at St. Charles, and on December 7 printed the Address of the London Workingmen's Association to the Patriote Central Committee.

ate" right-wing reformers who broke with the revolutionary left in the Canadas. His conception of colonial evolution was akin to that of Baldwin and LaFontaine; like theirs, it pointed to a limited self-government within the British imperial framework. He argued, in his letter to Chapman:

> We cannot shut our eyes to the fact that, surrounded as we are by great and growing States, many of them now possessed of almost national resources, we must be more or less subject to influences beyond our immediate control; and that the time may not be very distant when the question of independence, or of a federative union with the adjoining colonies, may be considered, not as one forced on us by any neglect or oppression of the mother country, but as a natural consequence of our position. . . .

More clearly still, Howe set forth his conservative-reform position in the October 1846 letters to Lord John Russell on responsible government: "Canning boasted that by recognizing the independence of South America, he had called a new world into existence: may it be your Lordship's boast, that by admitting the just claims, developing the resources, and anticipating the national and honorable aspirations of North Americans, you have woven links of love between them and the mother country and indefinitely postponed all desire for independence."

Such indeed were the considerations that finally prevailed at the Colonial Office: they inspired Earl Grey's famous dispatch of Nov. 3, 1846, instructing Lieutenant Governor Sir John Harvey of Nova Scotia that "it is neither possible nor desirable to carry on the government of any of the British Provinces in North America in opposition to the opinion of the inhabitants." The defeat of the Conservative Johnston administration on a vote of

confidence in the Assembly, in January 1848, and the
ensuing formation of the Uniacke-Howe government
marked the introduction of the system of responsible government in British North America. It was a few weeks
later that the Baldwin-LaFontaine accession to power
took place in Canada.

   Despite marked differences in the circumstances in each
of the Atlantic provinces they had this in common (as
Professor W. S. MacNutt has emphasized in his recent
study) that "all were to share in some degree the conviction that government should be taken from the control
of the privileged and delivered into the hands of 'the
people'." This was indeed and in a dual sense the issue
in the winning of responsible government. Democracy
underwent enlargement, both by the executive's being
made answerable to the elected representatives of the
people and by the transfer of the centre of decision (in
domestic matters, at least) from the metropolis to the
colony.
   Unaltered, however, was the fact that "the people"
(whose political liberties were thus enlarged) included
not only the mass of farmers, fishermen, lumbermen, seamen and small townspeople, but the wealthy merchant-
capitalist élite. While government was "taken from the
control of the privileged" in the sense that the formerly
self-perpetuating executive officialdom (such as the notorious Halifax compact of the "Committee of Twelve")
had to give way to responsible cabinet government, and
that the political centre of gravity was transferred increasingly from the Colonial Office to the province—yet "the
privileged," the colonial ruling class, remained in power.
Merchant-bankers, shipowners, shipyard owners, fishery-
merchants, timber magnates, great landed proprietors, at

Halifax and Saint John, at St. John's and Charlottetown, continued to hold sway, as previously, in public affairs. Democracy in a business society was perforce a class democracy; and political issues and contests bore in more or less evident measure the imprint of class interests and class struggle.

In each of the Atlantic colonies the social structure and its built-in conflicts presented aspects that lent them a distinct identity.

For over a century the settlers on Prince Edward Island had to contend with the scourge of absentee landownership. Practically the entire island had been granted by the imperial government on one July day in 1767 to some three-score favored individuals. Resident in England, the proprietors generally neither carried out their obligation to develop and settle their estates nor even paid the quit-rent owing to the Crown. They saw to it, however, that their agents extracted rent from the tenantry. According to W. S. MacNutt, "Two great consolidated estates, the Worrell and Selkirk, comprised hundreds of thousands of acres and Sir Samuel Cunard was gradually building up an estate of 212,000 acres. All were regarded as tyrants." Their representatives and subordinates in Charlottetown formed a petty oligarchy of inter-married well-to-do families, "easily the best edition of a family compact the Atlantic Provinces could offer."

This oppressive system called into being a long succession of movements of popular protest. Led first by William Cooper, and later by George Coles, brewer and agriculturist, the popular reform movement petitioned London, held meetings, pressed for redress of grievances. During the 1830s there were cases such as that of a dispossessed tenant being reinstated in possession of his farm by the mass action of his fellow tenants; and of the burn-

ing down of the home of the landlord's agent, and the
putting down of resistance by troops sent from Charlottetown. William Cooper, "tribune for the tenantry," organized a great protest meeting of tenants in King's County
"to resist the payment of rents and the exercise of pro-
prietorial authority." With the movement spreading
throughout the province, Dr. MacNutt observes: "Prince
Edward Island was divided by a class war of virulence
almost equal to that of Newfoundland."

When in 1838 the radical Escheat (confiscation) party
won a majority at the polls, the colonial oligarchy "feared revolution." But the appointive executive backed by
the Colonial Office was able to overrule or annul any
remedial measures passed by the Assembly. Durham observed to Lord Glenelg in 1838 that "some influence . . .
has steadily counteracted the measures of the Colonial
Legislature. I cannot imagine that it is any other influence
than that of the absentee proprietors, resident in England."

In 1853 a provincial Land Purchase Act authorized
acquisition of estates by the colonial government: four
were bought, for resale to the tenants. A further move,
following a commission of inquiry, proposed to give the
tenant the right to purchase the land he occupied, and
called for an imperial loan to facilitate the taking-over by
the province of the estates. London vetoed the Act. A
Tenant League was formed in 1863; its members, according to Rev. F. W. P. Bolger's account, "comprising the
vast majority of the tenants, resolved that they would
withhold the payment of rents until the proprietors
agreed to sell their lands. Public meetings, noisy demonstrations, and the use of force were the order of the day
in the mid 1860s . . . The flames of political discontent
were dangerously high on Prince Edward Island . . ."

In 1869, when Premier Haythorne stated that "The land question is the chief public question in Prince Edward Island," some 400,000 acres were still in the hands of the absentee proprietors, among the leading half-dozen of whom were Viscount Melville and other members of English "society."

For more than a century this "property question" of the land monopoly operated to retard progress on the Island. When the matter of union with Canada came to be considered, the buying-off of the absentee proprietors was the main concern of the islanders; and their insistence on its solution was interwoven with strong feeling "in favor of the construction of a railroad, the want of which is now much felt in consequence of the increasing productions of the Colony, and the extreme badness of the roads . . ."

Productive pressures contending with the fetters of property-relations; and the local striving for political power to overcome the obstacles to growth: these ingredients of social change were present and at work, here as in the adjoining Colonies.

Not landed proprietorship, but the prohibition of it was Newfoundland's problem. As a "great English ship moored by the Banks" the island was to be preserved to the Admiralty as a "nursery of seamen," and to the English West Country merchants as a profitable monopoly. Lest agricultural settlement offer an avenue of escape from the condition of dependence on the Company of Western Adventurers (chartered in 1634), there was imposed "a false policy (which) prevented the settlement of the fairest half of the island, superior to parts of the opposite continent . . . it was originally the open and undisguised policy of a few rich merchants, to keep the trade limited to the Bank fishery, thereby ensuring wealth to them at home, and to those they employed in the island as their chief factors." Hence the "unmatchable obstacles" that Sir Richard Bonnycastle described as being thrown in the way of industrious colonists, whose dwellings were actually thrown down or burnt, and themselves and families forcibly removed, wherever they attempted to settle . . ."

Dr. William Carson, a Scottish surgeon and pamphleteer whose agitation for civil government caused no small concern to the authorities, in 1812 denounced the official policy that sought "to keep the Island of Newfoundland a barren waste, to exterminate the inhabitants, to annihilate property, and to make sailors by preventing population."

Settlement of course took place anyway, despite all manner of harassment. At one point no less than five thousand would-be settlers drawn from the fishing fleets were forcibly shipped back to England. Yet the "squatting system" continued, and population reached 20,000 by 1803.

Rigid mercantilist restrictions, severity of naval rule, and exploitation of fishermen combined to breed violent outbreaks of resistance. A mutinous conspiracy in 1800 at St. John's involved men of the Royal Newfoundland regiment and settlers over a considerable area. Irish revolutionary influence (following on the rising of '98) was a potent factor: "defection was very extensive, not only through the regiment, but through the inhabitants of this and all the out harbours, particularly to the southward," where the oath of the United Irishmen was taken "almost to a man." (Letter from St. John's, July 2, 1800.) The movement was put down savagely, with a number of executions.

Deep poverty in St. John's as in the outports stirred intermittent angry protest. On one occasion the Chief Justice was "evidently terrified" at finding a letter affixed to the Court House gate, headed "the humble petition of the distress'd of St. John's." As reproduced by Prowse, in his *History of Newfoundland*, it ran thus:

> That the poor of St. John's are very much oppressed by different orders from the Court House, which they imagine is unknown to your Lordship, Concerning the killing and shooting their doggs, without the least sine of the being sick or mad. Wee do hope that your Lordship will check the Justices that was the means of this evil Proclamation against the Interest of the poor Families, that their dependence for their Winter's Fewel is on their Doggs, and likewise several single men that is bringing out Wood for the use of the Fishery, if in case this business is not put back it will be the means of an indeferent business as ever the killing the Doggs in Ireland was before the rebellion the first Instance will be given by killing Cows and Horses, and all other disorderly Vice that can be comprehended by the Art of Man.
>
> Wee are sorry for giveing your Lordship any uneasines for directing any like business to your Honour, but Timely notice is better than use any voilance. What may be the cause of what we not wish to men't at present, by puting a stop to this great evil. Wee hope that our Prayrs will be mains of obtaining Life Everlasting for your Lordship in the world to come.
>
> Mercy wee will take, and Mercy wee will give.

In the "Hard Winter" of 1817-18, the established misery was compounded as "famine, frost, and fire combined, like three avenging furies, to scourge the unfortunate Island. A frost that sealed up the whole coast commenced early in November, and continued almost without intermission through the entire season, and on the nights of the 7th and 21st of November 1817, three hun-

dred houses were burnt, rendering two thousand individuals, in depth of that cruel winter, homeless." That
same winter, "A vessel with provisions put into Bay Bulls
in distress; the people flocked down en masse to board
her, and they would not let the ship leave the harbour
until half her cargo had been unloaded by the authorities
and distributed."

The fishery, as the great common industry of the Atlantic provinces, offers some illustration of the basic, class
structure of the colonial society. Thus a petition of merchants of St. John's in 1839 explained that the Newfoundland population, "with the exception of the learned professions, consists entirely of the merchants, possessing capital and the means of giving employment to the
fishermen, and (of) the fisherman whose wealth consists in
his labour . . ." Another, slightly earlier petition argued
that "the merchant and fishermen have but one common
interest and are bound together by one tie of mutual dependence." (Both petitions were directed against an electoral franchise the merchants considered much too broad:
"We do not desire nor can we patiently endure that persons who have no property in the country, and who can
contribute nothing to the revenues, shall exercise unlimited power and rule with a rod of iron, those who do
possess property . . .")

The nature of the "mutual dependence" between employer and employee is described in Sir Richard Bonnycastle's account of the set-up in the Newfoundland fishery.
He remarks that "as in the management of absentee
property in Ireland," three categories of persons are "employed upon one mode of obtaining the wherewithal.

"First, the British merchant, or owner, residing most
commonly in Britain, but in some cases remaining in the
country till he had amassed a fortune . . .

"Next, the middle-man or planter, as he is most absurd-
ly called" (i.e., the owner's agent or superintendent)...

"Thirdly, the working-bee, or fisherman."

The "mutual dependence" here assumes the form of an
agreement on the part of the fisherman: "I give you the
labour of my hands, for the food and clothing I require;
that is the real bargain between the merchant and the
fisherman." And Bonnycastle recalls an instance of the
"mutuality" being breached by intrusion of the real opposition of interests; it should be borne in mind here
that the men were "rewarded in kind, and not in money,
the system (being) one of truck or barter":

> No later than a few days ago, (10th March, 1842,) a fresh
> instance of the demands of the labourers, of the working-
> bees, took place, which formerly neither would have been
> attempted, nor would have ended in serious riot. The
> fishermen collected in the latter end of February, from all
> the surrounding settlements, to prepare for the annual visit
> to the ice in quest of seals. The bargain here was on the
> same principle—one-half the profit to the merchant, or
> owner, who found and fitted the ship, the other half
> to the crew. The merchant by long custom, besides the
> benefits derived from extra stores or clothing, had always
> deducted a certain varying sum for berth-money to the
> hands, excepting one or two able marksmen, who were
> charged less or went free, for the privilege of embarking
> on the most hazardous and uncertain adventure which the
> spirit of commerce leads men to undertake.
>
> The sealers had long been dissatisfied with this charge,
> and therefore met together in St. John's with banners and
> a drum, and held a consultation, which ended in a refusal
> to embark unless the merchant-owners lowered the berth-
> money, which they had this year raised to three pounds
> and three pounds ten shillings, currency, for the different
> classes, with one pound for the bow or chief gunner, who
> had hitherto gone free. Some of them committed a breach
> of the peace, which fortunately was trivial, and they were

> sentenced to a short imprisonment; but the body holding
> out a long time, a sort of compromise was affected, and
> the berth-money was lowered to two pounds, and one
> pound ten shillings, and the bow gunner, as before, free.
>
> These combinations and assemblages of any classes for
> such purposes are always unlawful and dangerous, and
> should be carefully avoided, by substituting a scale of wages
> and contracts, about which there could be little doubt or
> reasoning.
>
> But to pay the sealers, or the same men as cod-fishers,
> regular wages, would at present be impracticable, and
> would doubtless be a losing speculation, as they would
> not have the same interest to work. . . .

While the master-servant, employer-employee relationship remained as a constant (and ever-more firmly consolidated) component in the Island society, political agitation for the settlers' right to occupy the land and for
representative government rose and fell in a succession
of turbulent movements, not infrequently marked by violent outbreaks.

As against "the Gothic system of pulling down fences,
stages, and houses," Dr. Carson argued for a new policy:
"The only remedy against the evils flowing from the
present system, will be formed in giving to the people,
what they most ardently wish, and what is unquestionably their right, a civil Government; consisting of a resident Governor, a Senate House and House of Assembly."
This, together with appropriation and cultivation of the
lands, was the imperative need. In 1813 the governor was
authorized "to grant leases of small portions of land to
industrious individuals for the purpose of cultivation."
Already, squatters were installed around the outskirts of
St. John's, which "with a population of nearly 10,000,
seems to have grown out of its original situation, and to
be changing its character from a fishery to a large commercial town."

Agitation for an Assembly and self-government reached a new pitch of intensity in the late 1820s. Led now by John Kent, the movement showed signs of erupting into violence, and the social cleavage at St. John's hardened in consequence: in Dr. MacNutt's words,

> threatened with a complete loss of power the official and mercantile classes drew more closely together. . . . To a very great degree the legislative struggle that began was one of Catholic versus Protestant, but it was a class war as well.

Then at long last the years of pressure bore fruit: the winning of the English Reform Bill in 1832 was accompanied by the grant of a representative assembly to Newfoundland. It had been long delayed; in Prowse's judgment, "There can be no doubt that it was the influence of (the) West Country merchants that retarded the grant of a local legislature."

Now at least the rudiment of Home Rule was within reach; yet the usual pattern of executive irresponsibility necessitated over two decades of further struggle to win cabinet government. "Free institutions" did not come easily: "The upper and mercantile classes were on the whole bitterly opposed to them": a stand in which they were enthusiastically seconded by the Chief Justice, Henry Boulton—the Upper Canada Family Compact's involuntary gift (his removal from York having resulted from protests there) to reaction in the island colony. Only after riots, suspension of the 1832 constitution and its re-casting to limit popular representation, did the reform forces once again register a victory: in 1846, writes Prowse, "an agitation was set on foot to obtain responsible government: it was not entirely successful, but in 1848, when the world was agitated with revolution, and crowns were falling in a very promiscuous manner all over Europe, our original constitution . . . was restored to us." Responsible government went into effect in 1855.

Reflecting on "the long and painful character of Newfoundland's evolution," Harold Innis related it to the difficulty of establishing strong urban centres in areas dominated by the fishery, a condition which facilitated long-continued English mercantile control over the colony. "The scattered character of the fishing grounds, the importance of individual initiative, the relatively short seasons, and dependence on a foreign market were factors leading to the growth of a strong sense of local importance in scattered communities." The rigid political structure imposed by the mercantile interests (who "had sufficient influence to mould legislation in their favour") was long-lasting, but broke down under the combined pressure of local economic growth (centred in St. John's) and of the people's movements for reform. This Innis has described as a triumph of "individualism": "The strongly-rooted individualism which led, through New England, to the break-up of the old Empire, and which contributed to the French Revolution, finally provoked the passage of the reform bills in England and the growth of responsible government." It was actually a victory of bourgeois, or *business*, democracy. Individualism was its spiritual hallmark, but a social and political class struggle was the motor of its ascent to power.

In the years following the achievement of responsible government the Maritimes economy experienced the peak of wooden sailing-ship construction, decline in the square-timber but expansion of the sawn-lumber trade, a slow growth of manufactures, and the first phase of railway building.

In New Brunswick the timber trade and shipbuilding provided the base for an economic development that was closely tied in with the Imperial interest and which was administered by a " 'compact' . . . composed of merchants and lawyers of historic Loyalist families."

A survey of 1865 listed some twenty shipyards in Saint John, N.B., employing 1,267 men at an average wage of $1 a day. The preceding year marked the highest point in shipbuilding production in the province. In tonnage of ships owned, Saint John for a time (in the 1870s) held fourth place among British Empire ports; but with the growth of steam-power and the use of iron for ships' hulls revolutionizing the industry, the days of the wooden sailing-ship were numbered.

There was little industry in New Brunswick that was not connected with the forest. The pillage of its resources was powered by the drive for merchants' profit with no thought of conservation. Dr. MacNutt speaks of "The continued fierce assault on New Brunswick's forests, tolerated and even encouraged by a legislature that was really under the control of the timber merchants. . . ." J. F. W. Johnston, the agricultural scientist with whose *Notes on North America, Agricultural, Economical and Social* (London 1851) Marx was familiar, remarked on the situation in New Brunswick forest industry:

> Land cleared of timber does not soon cover itself again with a new growth of merchantable trees. Every year carried the scene of the woodmen's labours farther up the main rivers, and into more remote creeks and tributaries, adding to the labour of procuring and to the cost of the logs when brought to the place of shipment. Hence, prices must rise at home, or profits must decline in the colony, and the trade gradually lessen. All these had already taken place to a certain extent, when the further increase of home prices was rendered almost impossible by the equali-

zation of the timber duties. In this alteration of our British laws, a large number of those engaged in the timber trade have been inclined to see the sole caues of the comparatively unprosperous circumstances in which they have recently been placed.

In so far as I have myself been able to ascertain the facts of the case, I think, with many patriotic colonists, that the welfare of these North American provinces would on the whole, and in the long run, have been promoted by a less lavish cutting and exportation of the noble ship-timber which their woods formerly contained, and which has already become so scarce and dear. Home bounties have tempted them to cut down within a few years, and sell at a comparatively low price, what might for many years have afforded a handsome annual revenue, as well as an inexhaustible supply of material for the once flourishing colonial dockyard.

On the Restigouche, the traveller observed that the lumber trade, in difficulties elsewhere, was "as prosperous as ever." But "the mode of conducting it has been changed." Mercantile contracting in the old manner is giving way to a more characteristically industrial arrangement: the merchant himself becomes an industrial capitalist:

> Instead of making advances, as formerly, to persons who led out parties into the woods, and delivered the timber in spring to the merchant at a price, the merchant now engages his own gangs of cutters, places his foremen over them, provides their supplies, and the logs when they arrive are his own.

After 1856, the old square timber trade showed a continual decline in exports. But during Reciprocity the sawmill industry, particularly the enterprises situated at the mouths of the larger rivers, expanded, with the production of planks, boards, shingles and box shooks. By

1871 around 6,300 workers were employed in New Brunswick sawmills.

Manufacturing industry (outside of lumber and shipbuilding) developed with extreme slowness in the Maritimes. As late as 1865 A. G. Archibald could refer to rural self-sufficiency in such terms as these:

> The great body of the settlers in the country whose backs are covered with woollens of their own production—whose feet are shod from the hides of their own cattle—whose heads are covered with straw from their own fields—who sleep between blankets of their own wool and their own weaving—on feathers from their own farmyards.

The commercial economy based on colonial exploitation of fisheries and forests did not provide any substantial capital accumulation in the Maritimes themselves; and capital imports, whether from Britain or the United States, largely passed the Maritimes by in favor of the Province of Canada. The relatively slow Maritimes development is reflected in the population figures; while Montreal and Toronto doubled in population between 1851 and 1871, Halifax had increased only from 20,749 to 29,582, and Saint John from 22,745 to 28,805.

Small-scale individual capitalist enterprises were characteristic of Nova Scotia manufactures. The 1,144 sawmills on the average employed only two or three persons each at the time of the 1871 census. Capital accumulation by such individual small capitalists entails at best a slow rate of industrial development.

Only in mining and related areas were there signs of possibly significant growth (apart from the railway boom, which was to bring the two mainland provinces to the threshold of negotiations for union with Canada). The iron industry was represented solely by the Acadia Mining Company, established at Londonderry in 1850. In the same year the Kerosene Gas Light Company was established to light the streets and homes of Halifax, based on the invention of "the process of kerosene oil" by Dr. A. Gesner. His invention was sold to a New York firm, but Gesner is credited with laying the foundations for the use of petroleum for illuminating purposes on this continent. In 1861 gold was discovered in Halifax, Lunenburg and Guysborough counties and quartz mining boomed at various points near the coast. Many Americans took part in the short-lived Nova Scotia gold rush. But it was coal mining, which had been carried on sporadically for a century and a half, that came to life during the period of Reciprocity. Coal was exported to the United States during the 1860s to the value of around $1 million annually; only a relatively small amount was used for home consumption or sent to the other provinces.

Joseph Howe campaigned actively for the building of railways in the Maritimes as the chief means to develop the country and promote settlement. "If our Government," he said at one time, "had means sufficient to build railways, and carry the people free, we believe that this would be sound policy." He worked hard to get the necessary government support from Britain and the other provinces to build the Halifax & Quebec Railway through Nova Scotia and eastern New Brunswick to Lower Canada. The project bogged down because New Brunswick interests wished the road to go up the St. John valley while the British Government refused to contribute towards a railway so close to the United States border. Howe then, despite misgivings over the U.S. connection, lent his support to the European & North American Railway, a project to link up Halifax, Saint John and Portland, Maine. John A. Poor of Portland, Maine (also involved in promoting the Atlantic & St. Lawrence running up to Montreal), was one of the prime movers behind the European & North American: a scheme which included the project of a trans-Atlantic steamship line. The railway from Halifax to Windsor was expected to make the rich western counties of Nova Scotia tributary to Halifax, and it was hoped the line to Pictou would develop the coal mines there. Although Howe was opposed, the contract for the Nova Scotia lines was given to the British firm of railway contractors and promoters, Peto, Brassey, Jackson and Betts, who had built many railways in England and had strong ties with the Imperial Government. But in 1854 the contractors gave up the contract with nothing done and the Nova Scotia government took over the job. The triangle Halifax-Windsor-Truro was linked by rail in 1858; nine years later the railway was extended to Pictou.

The New Brunswick section of the European & North American was incorporated in 1851; the incorporators included the Speaker of the Provincial House, the Provincial Secretary, the Attorney-General, twenty-three members of the New Brunswick Legislature and the presidents of three of the province's banks. The act of incorporation granted such privileges as exemption from taxation of the railway's land, stock, personal property, etc. A month and a half later, the promoters voted themselves a land grant of five miles on each side of the railway along its entire route. The following year, a special session of the Legislature ratified the construction contract with Peto, Brassey, Jackson and Betts. The cost was estimated at £6,500 per mile, half to be provided by the provinces, while the contractors undertook to raise the remaining funds. Work started in 1853, but stopped the next year because of the financial condition of the contractors. They demanded further financial aid from the government, which refused it, and in 1856 took over the work and paid off the contractors.

The line from Saint John to Shediac on the Gulf of St. Lawrence was completed in 1860, another, from St. Andrews to Woodstock was not completed until 1868. Truro was also connected through Sackville to the Saint John-Shediac line. Thus the Maritimes by the time of Confederation possessed only 341 miles of railways, which were connected neither with Portland, Quebec, nor Montreal. Yet while the total mileage was not impressive the lines did link up the approaches to the seas on which the Maritime Provinces faced. This, however, meant that the coasting trade now suffered from railway competition. The cost of construction had been considerable; in the process Nova Scotia had accumulated a government railway debt of $6.1 millions and New Brunswick a debt of $4.5 millions.

Regional diversity and contradictory pressures marked the situation in the Atlantic provinces as a whole in the pre-Confederation years. A local bourgeoisie had achieved a measure of internal self-government, but in each case at a different phase of the slow transition from mercantile to industrial capitalism: the mainland provinces being the more advanced, the island provinces the most handicapped, by land monopoly in one case and mercantile colonial restrictions in the other. The seaward pull of the fishery, timber-trade and shipbuilding continued to be strong; the continental counter-pull of railways and western (i.e., Canadian) expansion was beginning to make itself felt in New Brunswick and Nova Scotia. The alternative choices of direction, complicated by a shifting international setting, posed a dilemma to the political leaders of the emergent business democracy. The debates over a possible Maritime Union, and then over union with the Canadas, expressed both the urge to a larger industrial development, and deep-seated reservations born of regional interest and regional identity.

11

U. S. Expansionists

The traditional pattern of colony and metropolis was modified in a peculiar way in the case of British North America.

Unlike most other colonial dependencies, the British provinces were linked with not just one metropolis but two. One was the official suzerain and distant centre of Empire, fount of authority and investment capital, source of the mainstream of immigrant manpower. The other, right next door, was any and all of a number of things: ancient military enemy, step-mother of Loyalists, home of slavery, shrine of revolutionary republicanism, triumphant rival in trade and settlement, a coming colossus of the new age of business. One stood as the dominant world power; the other was on the way to becoming its challenger. British North America could define itself only in relation to them both. Any effort at independent growth meant assertion of local interest and identity not only as against British Imperial ascendancy but as against United States expansionism also.

Attitudes towards the United States—then as later—tended to be as contradictory as the phenomena that evoked them. They ranged from envy and admiration of economic and technical achievement "south of the line" to resentment at domineering expansionism and economic penetration of the northern economy; from sentiments of fraternal solidarity (on the part of radical democrats) with the ideals of the American Revolution and currents such as Jacksonian democracy and the early movements of labor—to revulsion against Negro slavery, distaste for universal commercialism and its attendant political corrruption, and plain British, anti-Yankee loyalism. Examples of these conflicting views occur in the issues of *Le Canadien* of 1806, in the writings of W. L. Mackenzie, in the periodical press of the whole period under review, and are commented on by many of the travellers who recorded their impressions of British North America.

At this point, four areas of relations with the United States call for comment: economic penetration and "Manifest Destiny," Annexationism and "reciprocity."

Abraham Gesner, the Maritimes geologist who discovered the process for making coal-oil (kerosene), in 1849 published a survey, *The Industrial Resources of Nova Scotia*. In it he tells what happened to one of the early attempts at establishing an iron industry in the province. In 1826 at Moose River, N.S., the Annapolis Iron Mining Co. had started operations: the smelting, casting, and manufacture of iron were all in active and successful operation when

> the whole work was suddenly abandoned—the fires of the furnaces were extinguished—the trip hammers ceased to move, and the pretty village of Moose River was deserted by all its inhabitants, except such as were engaged in fishing and agriculture. The charge of the iron works was committed into the hands of persons belonging to the United States, the principal of whom was an iron-founder in Boston, who maintained the pig iron only should be made, that pig iron was to be sent to the United States, and there manufactured, and then returned to the British Provinces for sale, whereby the profits would fall into the hands of the American shareholders. Dissensions soon took

place. It has been publicly stated that the principal furnace was intentionally choked, and the enterprise was abandoned.

Gesner describes as follows the long-term result of this throttling of a colonial basic industry: "Implements of husbandry, stoves, culinary utensils, edge tools, and even the axes employed in felling the forest, are imported from the Americans. . . . The iron imported into Nova Scotia and New Brunswick amounts to £130,000 per an., still there is not a smelting furnace in any of the British North American Provinces, Canada only excepted . . ."

Mine the iron ore in the colonies to the north, ship it to the United States so as to have it "there manufactured, and then returned to the British Provinces for sale"— the pattern is not unfamiliar to us a century or so later.

But it was in timber rather than metal ores that large-scale incursions of U.S. enterprise first made themselves felt in the colonial provinces. In what Professor Lower has tactfully designated as the "North American" assault on the Canadian forest, U.S. capitalist interests moved in on the rich timber lands of New Brunswick and the Ottawa valley. By the mid-1830s capitalists from Boston and Maine had got possession of close to a million acres of the forest areas of New Brunswick and Quebec. The Montreal *Gazette* (Sept. 1835) made reference to "the great amount of American capital lately expended in timber lands, mill seats, etc." Collusion of colonial businessmen with the American operators drew the following sharp comment from the Montreal *Gazette's* correspondent at Kingston (August 7, 1836):

> It seems the valuable Lumber Trade of Upper Canada, its inexhaustless pine forests, its Canals, &c., have excited the greedy appetite of our southern neighbours who wishing to monopolize the New York timber trade, from their

> capital and commercial enterprise, have hit upon this scheme for effecting their purpose. The gentlemen of Kingston are made the cat's paw—they are to hold a knife to their own throats, to ruin a trade lucrative to themselves and children, while the Yankees are to reap the harvest.

The correspondent takes note of the argument that "Americans entering into the Province with their money, would give an impetus to business"; and states that "we should have no objection to the mere introduction of such capital"— but what is prejudicial is the Americans "buying up our lands, engrossing our trade, sending their profits to their own country . . . monopolizing a particular and highly important branch of trade. . . ."

As a result of lumbermen from Maine moving into New Brunswick to take timber, there had been riots on the Miramichi in the early 1820s. The State of Maine in 1825, despite the presence of long-established New Brunswick settlements at Aroostook and on the Madawaska, declared that the area was rightfully its own. In 1831 U.S. officials attempted to conduct an election in the territory, whereupon New Brunswick had them arrested. An endeavor to take a U.S. census of the inhabitants was likewise stopped. In 1838 Congress having authorized the calling out of the militia, and voted ten million dollars for any venture that might follow, the Governor of Maine ordered troops into the area, took forcible possession and proceeded to set up fortifications there. Nova Scotia thereupon rallied to support the New Brunswickers; a special session of its legislature voted funds to aid in the defense, and "amid scenes of great popular enthusiasm promised to place at the disposal of the junior province every dollar and every man in Nova Scotia, should war become an actuality."

At this point Washington ordered the U.S. troops withdrawn, and entered upon negotiations with the British government. The British negotiator, Alexander Baring, Lord Ashburton, was head of the banking house of Baring Brothers which handled large amounts of American securities in Britain. (He was on record as having stated at the close of the war of 1812 that he was in favor of giving Canada outright to the Americans.) Daniel Webster, the U.S. representative (he became Secretary of State in 1841), has been described by his biographer as "the hope and reliance of the moneyed and conservative classes, the merchants, manufacturers, capitalists and bankers." Since he represented U.S. banking and commercial concerns interested in selling stocks in Britain, his financial affinity with Ashburton augured well for understanding. Entrusted to such negotiators, it is hardly surprising that the interests of New Brunswick benefited least from the transaction. Seven-twelfths of the disputed territory, and four-fifths of the value at stake (according to Webster) went to the United States. Included were the right of navigation on the St. John River, and a drawing of the boundary that drove a deep enclave into Canadian territory, cutting off Saint John, N.B., from direct communication with Montreal. As if to round out the arrangement, further concessions were made to the U.S. in the Lake of the Woods area; and, the Americans having erected a fort on admittedly Canadian soil at Rouse's Point on Lake Champlain, they were presented with forty square miles here also.

There is a curious sidelight to the cession to the Americans of the disputed area of forest land that lies between New Brunswick and Quebec. The 1838 insurrection in Lower Canada and the Patriot border raids, widely supported from the United States, had put some strain on Anglo-American relations. Lord Durham had taken pains to ease the situation and secure the co-operation of the U.S. authorities. Now, with the negotiations arising from the "Aroostook War" in New Brunswick, Fox, the British ambassador to Washington, moved to secure an understanding that "until the acceptance or rejection by the British government of the *modus vivendi* was received, the United States would move no part of its regulars from the Canadian border where he considered them to be 'so usefully employed' . . . 'Considering the present state of things in Canada, I am sensible of the more than usual importance of maintaining peace if possible on the New Brunswick frontier'." (Letter of Feb. 23, 1839.)

It would seem that the surrender by the British of the New Brunswick enclave was not unconnected with an understanding with Washington for the exercise of joint military pressure to contain the revolutionary ferment in the Canadas.

After witnessing the acquisition by the United States of a great wedge of territory between New Brunswick and Quebec, it is instructive to turn to the argument advanced a couple of years later by a Washington official for annexing south-western Ontario. It was intolerable, he wrote, that there should be this "long slip of foreign territory obtruding itself between two states of the Union, and reaching down . . . into the very heart of the country." A straight line from Lake Huron to Lake Ontario "is the natural boundary of the United States." In the event of war with Britain, "no exertions on our part should be spared for the conquest of this part of Upper Canada . . . there is nothing to prevent us from conquering and annexing the 'State of Toronto'." (Matthew F. Maury, Superintendent of the U.S. Dept. of Charts and

Instruments, in the *National Intelligencer,* May 20, 1845.)

In 1831 the *North American Review* had urged on its readers the "desirableness of an extension of the United States to the north, to preserve a safe balance of its growth to the south." By the 1840s the expansionists were driving for Texas, California, "All Mexico!" —and Oregon.

The mainspring of U.S. expansionism was the phenomenal growth of capitalist industry. Production of iron trebled in the decades 1830-1850 (and trebled again in the two decades that followed). By 1852 the U.S. rail network had reached Chicago, and the westward surge of a population swelled by mass immigration steadily enlarged the confines of the domestic market for manufactured goods. Behind the assertion of "Manifest Destiny" was the self-expansion of capital.

In 1844 Vice-President Tyler had "subtly extended the Monroe Doctrine to Hawaii" and secured an unequal treaty with China that promised profitable markets to U.S. manufacturers; he now called for the take-over of the continental territories from Oregon to Mexico—in the name of "a wider and more extensive spread to the principles of civil and religious liberty." Professor W. A. Williams points out that this virtuous invocation went hand in hand with a turn on the part of the *laissez-faire* business interests from concern with overcoming internal mercantilist restrictions "to the expansion of the market place for the ostensible benefit of everyone." And, as Professor Frederick Merk has argued: "A boundless continent was expected to be attractive to the commercial and manufacturing classes. It would give them new markets."

After annexing Texas, the United States could choose fresh fields of conquest in any of several directions. The exuberant mood was affably expressed by John L. O'Sullivan: "Texas, we repeat, is secure; and so now, as the Razor Strop Man says, 'Who's the next customer?' Shall it be California or Canada?" (N.Y. *Morning News*, July 7, 1845)

It was O'Sullivan who coined the phrase that keynotes the period, when in reference to the U.S. demand for the whole Oregon Territory up to 54° 40′ he asserted that the claim "is by right of our manifest destiny to overspread to possess the whole of the continent . . ." (N.Y. *Morning News*, Dec. 27, 1845)

On the "Oregon Question," involving the expanse of territory along the Pacific coast between Russian America and California, the expansionism of the United States collided with the positions of Imperial Britain. Under the compromise of 1818 there had been agreement in fixing the international border along the line of 49° as far West as the Rocky Mountains, with the "Oregon Territory" left provisionally under the joint jurisdiction of the two powers. But the mountain and coastal area became a matter of contention that brought the powers to the brink of war. The reason for this was not only, or even mainly, the conflict of interest in terms of the expanding U.S. settlement south of the Columbia, and the barrier posed by the Hudson's Bay Company domain to the north. More vital to the dispute was *empire on the Pacific*: President Polk, with his campaign slogan of "54° 40′ or Fight!" was driving for U.S. Pacific coast ports that could become "the marts of an extensive and profitable commerce with China and the other countries of the East."

In the summer of 1845 the British and then the Americans sent their warships into Puget Sound or else to the mouth of the Columbia. In January 1846 the British government secured parliamentary backing for expenditures on military works in Canada. The defenses of Kingston were enlarged and strengthened. Troops were sent to Fort Garry, via Hudson Bay.

In England, a Militia Bill was brought forward. It was answered by a country-wide wave of great protest meetings, organized by the Chartists. "No Vote—No Musket!" was the slogan. Julian Harney wrote in the *Northern Star*: "When henceforth the masses—the impoverished, unrepresented masses, are called upon by their rulers to fight for 'their country' . . . they will answer . . . 'If you will monopolize all, fight for the country yourselves'." The revolutionary internationalist organization of the Fraternal Democrats issued an "Address to the Working Classes of Great Britain and the United States" on the Oregon question. At their place of meeting on Great Windmill-street "the subject of the threatened war between Great Britain and the United States" was brought under the consideration of "a very numerous meeting . . . the room being crowded with democrats belonging to most of the 'European States,' including (besides English,) French, German, Scandinavian, Swiss, &c., &c."

The address opened as follows:

> *"All men are brethren."*
>
> FRIENDS AND BROTHERS.—With extreme sorrow we have witnessed of late the attempts made by interested and ignorant parties, to foster enmity between the people of Britain and the United States; an enmity which, if not subdued and eradicated, threatens, at no distant day, to involve the two nations in war . . .

After emphasizing that "the working class is *our* class" and outlining the matters in dispute over Oregon, the Appeal protests against a resort to force and asks British workers: "What will *you* profit by a war? What have *you* gained by past wars?" Close to two million pounds wasted in a century and a quarter of dynastic wars: "on you has fallen *all* the cost, and the greater share of the *murder* occasioned by these wars . . . As regards this threatened war with America, you have no interest in 'The Oregon Territory.' The empire of Britain is already immense . . . The colonies are useful to your masters, because those colonies add to their wealth, power and magnificence; but to you they are barren acquisitions, or add but to your burdens . . . The privileged classes only can benefit by the acquisition of the Oregon: if there must be fighting, let them fight their own battles."

Then, turning to "our American brethren," the Fraternal Democrats point to the opposition of British working people to war; argue against "nationality-nonsense," and ask: "Do you desire an extensive national territory? You have it already; your republic is of almost illimitable extent . . . Suppose you take the Oregon, who will be its masters? Not you, the workingmen." Territorial expansion will mean moreover a permanent increase in navy and standing army, in "the continuance of 'war-establishments' in time of peace, to retain your force-won possessions. The result cannot fail to be the corruption of public morals, and the ultimate destruction of your Republican institutions." Lastly,

> There is one argument which the advocates of war address to the cupidity of the two nations—namely, "whichever nation shall command the ports of the Pacific, will ultimately command the trade with China." Suppose so; let the men who profit by "trade," and make fortunes by "trade," let them struggle for commercial supremacy if they will; but the victims of trade have no good reason for fighting for the ports of the Pacific, or any other ports. While in Britain manufacturers and merchants have gained princely fortunes, enabling them to out-rival the old territorial aristocracy, the working men, whose labour and skill have been so successfully employed by the "traders,"

have been reduced to the lowest state of social existence . . .
We have good reason to believe that a similar state of
things already exists in the United States. In the commercial and manufacturing portions of the Union, the tyranny
of capital is absolute, and the "slavery of wages" not less
galling than in Britain . . . What matters it, then, to the
working-men of either country who commands the China
trade? When the working-men of Europe and America
have the sense to insist upon a just distribution of the
products of their industry, and a fair exchange of their
superfluities, commercial ports will be of equal value, and
open to all nations; no one nation will have the monopoly
of them, and wars, for their acquisition, will be but a tale
of the past.*

This address of the Fraternal Democrats is noteworthy
on several grounds:

—As the earliest statement on British colonial policy in
North America by an organization with which Marx and
Engels were associated, and which was a forerunner of the
League of Communists (established the following year);
this agitation against a threat of Anglo-American war was
to be resumed on a vaster scale during the U.S. Civil War
crisis in the early 1860s;

—As presenting an argumentation on questions of imperialism and war which Thomas Macqueen was to reproduce and popularize in his writings in the Bathurst
Courier, and which thus became familiar to readers in
Canada;

—As an early working-class response to imperialist expansionism in the Pacific: the Oregon Dispute not being
unrelated to the developments that led to the Opium

---

*The Address of the Fraternal Democrats was printed in full in
The Northern Star of March 7, 1846, and also as a brochure. I am
indebted to Mr. R. S. Kenny for obtaining a copy of the text from
the Library of the British Museum.

War against China (1839-42)*, and such other expressions of incipient imperialism on the part of European powers as France's conquest of Algeria, 1830-40. (Today's danger zones and theatres of war in Asia and Africa thus were beginning to be "staked out" by the Powers in the second quarter of the 19th century . . .)

Military movements in the Canadas at the time of the Oregon crisis were a reminder that however distant the focal point of conflict, the simultaneous involvement of the colonial provinces in the imperial system and in the U.S. sphere of influence held implications for their own security and perhaps survival.

The Oregon dispute was resolved by a compromise: British concern over markets for their manufactures in the United States, and the large loans accorded to American capitalists, had a restraining effect; while U.S. expansionists' involvement in war with Mexico (May 1846) and their seizure of over a third of its territory led them to concentrate attention in the south-west. ("The balance is to be swallowed," wrote one U.S. senator who opposed the Mexican war, "when our anglo-saxon gastric juice shall clamor for another Cannibal breakfast.")

The compromise over Oregon provided for extension of the 49th parallel to the coast, with a deviation to the

---

*China's resistance to British imports of opium (from India and Turkey: the amount had increased in 1800 to 1838 from 2,000 to 40,000 chests) was answered by British military occupation of Canton, Shanghai and other ports; under the resulting Treaty of Nanking (1843) Britain annexed Hong Kong. Thereupon the U.S. extorted similar privileges for their commercial interests under the Treaty of Wanghsia (1844): refusal to negotiate, China was told by Caleb Cushing, U.S. plenipotentiary, would be regarded as "an act of national insult and a just cause for war." (I. Epstein, *From Opium War to Liberation* (1956), Ch. 2) Close on the heels of the Americans came the French; some time after securing "rights" in China they began their incursions (1858-1867) into Indo-China (Viet Nam).

south-west to leave Vancouver Island and some of the
Juan de Fuca islands in British hands. The U.S. thus secured its claim to the lower valley of the Columbia and
the harbors of Puget Sound.

While military-diplomatic confrontations between the
powers caused tremors at the periphery of British America, the upheaval in economic policy accompanying the
adoption of free trade produced crisis-shocks in the vital
centres of the Canadas. No sooner had the representatives
of the colonial bourgeoisie acceded to political power in
1848, than they were confronted with the question: Would
the young capitalist economy be able to stand on its own
feet in face of the pressures of the immensely more powerful industries of Britain and the United States? The question was the more urgent because the British adoption of
"free trade" (coinciding with the granting of 'responsible
government' to Canada) abruptly removed the protecting
shelter that Canadian exporters had hitherto enjoyed. In
November, 1848, Elgin reported to London that the adoption of free trade was "ruining at once the mill owners,
forwarders, and merchants, who saw their exports of
wheat and flour being diverted from Montreal to New
York." Faced with this blow a section of the bourgeoisie
became thoroughly defeatist about Canada's economic
prospects and called for outright annexation by the
United States.

The fact that British manufacturers were much more
interested in the U.S. market than in survival for the
colonial economy only added to the anger of Montreal
capitalists. As Elgin remarked: "What makes it more
serious is that all the prosperity of which Canada is thus
robbed is transplanted to the other side of the lines as if
to make the Canadians feel more bitterly how much

kinder England is to the children who desert her than to those who remain faithful . . ." He found that "the conviction that they would be better off if they were annexed is almost universal among the commercial classes at present. . . ."

The first outburst of mercantile exasperation occurred in connection with an issue in a quite different area: the Rebellion Losses Bill of 1849. This measure, designed to compensate those who had suffered loss in the Rebellion period (other than persons who had been convicted by the courts), had been under debate since 1840; the principle of compensation had been conceded in that year, for Upper Canada, at least; but the pressure of popular petitions and representations had been countered by Family Compact fanaticism, under the war-cry: "No pay for rebels!" When, in March 1849, the Assembly finally passed the Bill, the reactionaries demanded that Elgin withhold his signature. When over their protests he signed the Bill, thereby reaffirming the principle of responsible government, pandemonium broke loose. Tory-instigated riots raged for three days in Montreal. The mob stormed the Parliament buildings, dispersed the members, put the House to the torch. The Governor's carriage was stoned, and the Queen's representative pelted with rotten eggs. In Toronto, rioters attacked the homes of prominent Reform leaders.

Reaction, in its blind fury, had betrayed itself. The quality of its patriotism stood exposed. When MacNab raved against the French Canadians as "aliens and rebels" Edward Blake, the solicitor-general, answered him:

> I have no sympathy with the would-be loyalty of the honorable gentlemen opposite, which, while it at all times affects peculiar zeal for the prerogative of the Crown, is over ready to sacrifice the liberty of the subject. This . . .

is the spurious loyalty which at all periods of the world's history has lashed humanity into rebellion. . . . I tell the gentlemen on the other side that their public conduct has proved that they are the rebels to their constitution and country.

The 1849 rampage of the outraged Tory minority simply testified (in reverse, so to speak) to the democratic character of the people's movement that had compelled the yielding of both responsible government and some measure of recognition of French-Canadian national rights. The Tory mutiny was leading in quite another direction, however.

In September, 1849, a number of leading Montreal businessmen issued a manifesto that called for "a union upon equitable terms with the great North American confederacy of sovereign states." Their number included the Molsons and Torrances, Redpath, De Witt, Macpherson, Holton, Rose and Workman—the most prominent capitalists in the colony. The Manifesto literally invited U.S. capitalists to take over Canada, arguing as follows: "The proposed union would render Canada a field for American capital, into which it would enter as freely for the prosecution of public works and private enterprises as into any of the present states. . . . To Lower Canada especially, where water power and labor are cheap and abundant, it would attract manufacturing capital. . . ." The signatories offered inducements, as in an allusion to U.S. shipbuilders: "With them, the principal material in the construction of ships is rapidly diminishing, while we possess vast territories, covered with timber of excellent quality. . . ." Indeed, the Americans might help themselves to the entire St. Lawrence waterway as well: they were offered "the unrestricted use of the St. Lawrence, the natural highway from the Western States to the ocean."

The Annexationists rejected out of hand the arguments of the radical democrats in favor of an independent Canadian republic. As if to emphasize their complete lack of faith in the ability of the Canadian people to build a country of their own, the wealthy authors of the manifesto spelled out their defeatism: "The consolidation of . . . new institutions from elements hitherto so discordant—the formation of treaties with foreign powers—the acquirement of a name and character among the nations, would, we fear, prove an overmatch for the strength of the new republic."

Although they extended their campaign to Canada West, the Annexationists failed to enlist the support of the mass of the people in either section of the Province of Canada. The popular reaction was reflected in the jibe of a Kingston paper: "The Montreal Annexationists doubtless desire to retain their loyalty, but they flatly declare they can no longer afford the luxury." *Punch in Canada* published what it called "a business flourometer":

> "Flour, 33s. per barrel — loyalty up.
> Flour, 26s.   "   "   — cloudy.
> Flour, 22s.   "   "   — down to annexation."

The imperial authorities had conceded responsible government as a means of keeping Canada within the Empire. They emphasized the point afresh when the Annexation agitation got under way: Elgin was ordered "to resist, to the utmost of your power, any attempt which may be made to bring about the separation of Canada from the British dominions."*

---

*A point worth noting by those who have claimed that Britain in its "free trade" period wanted to rid herself of her colonial possessions.

As things turned out, strong measures were not required. Failure of the Annexationists to win any significant support among the people was followed in 1850 by an upturn in the trade cycle that restored the Montreal commercial interests' injured profit-balance (and the morale that rested thereon). Yet the basic problem of markets remained; and Elgin feared that unless a market was obtained for Canadian "natural products" in the United States, "there is nothing before us but violent agitation, ending in convulsion or annexation." Only if some sort of reciprocal trade arrangement could be worked out with Washington, was he prepared *"to assume the responsibility of keeping Canada quiet, with a much smaller garrison than we have now."*

The policy that came to be known—not altogether accurately—as "reciprocity" meant that U.S. importers would take over Canadian natural resources (particularly lumber) on a greatly increased scale.* But the colonies would be kept within the Empire; and British investors would benefit as well in a roundabout way, since their railway projects in Canada brought large orders for the manufacture of equipment in the U.S., in which British capital itself had an important interest. Moreover, as the Anglo-French imperialist conflict of interests with Russia in the Near East grew sharper (leading to the Crimean War, 1853-56), Britain was anxious to neutralize the United States. "Reciprocity" could contribute to this end.

Leading Montreal merchants who now foreswore Annexation, milling interests in Canada West and New Brunswick lumber and shipbuilding interests, all strongly supported the proposals for trade reciprocity with the

---

*Cf. Addendum; p. 243.

U.S. From the other side of the border American capitalists did not leave it to the spontaneous working of economic development to secure from Canada the policy they wanted. They had the U.S. government send up a special agent named Andrews to lobby officials, MPs, and newspaper editors. His expense-account showed payments of $5,000 each to an editor, a Deputy Inspector-General and an Attorney-General; a member of the New Brunswick Assembly got $15,000 for services of a "general and comprehensive character." Altogether, Andrews paid out more than $100,000 in "persuasion."

The Reciprocity Treaty of 1854, negotiated by Elgin on behalf of the British government and ratified by the Provincial Legislatures, provided for free trade in natural products, opened the Canadian waterways to U.S. shipping on equal terms with British, and gave the U.S. free access to the Maritime fisheries. Canada as supplier of raw materials to the United States and importer of its manufactured goods: this formula had now replaced "annexation."

Elgin's chief assistant in putting the policy through was Francis Hincks. One-time leading Reformer, author of the Railway Guarantee Act, he was the spokesman for those colonial capitalists who viewed Canada's long-term prospects of development strictly in the light of considerations of immediate profit. Speaking in Boston in 1851, Hincks issued the following invitation to American capitalists to move in on the Canadian market:

> We want to be able to furnish you with raw products, lumber, wheat, flour, grains, etc. We wish you to send us in exchange domestic manufactures. . . . We can give you an unlimited supply of our products and the whole trade gives employment to American shipping as well as to various classes of your operatives.

It has been claimed that Canada's position —"through-out most of its history . . . an economic satellite of other more advanced nations," supplying them with raw materials and foodstuffs in exchange for manufactured goods —is the result of a kind of geographic determinism: ". . . certain nations, because of their natural advantages in terms of resources and location, specialized in industrial production; other parts of the world specialized in supplying foodstuffs and materials to the industrial nations." Colonialism and imperialist policy vanish as causal factors in this argument; geography accounts for all. The retarding of Canadian industrialization was nobody's "fault" (certainly not that of the Canadian bourgeoisie): "This was not to any significant extent a matter of policy— of conscious decisions taken by some person or persons to encourage development in one direction and not in another; it was, rather, a matter of resources and technology." So argue Professors Easterbrook and Aitken. (*Canadian Economic History*, pp. 515-16.)

Yet the course advocated by Francis Hincks was surely a "matter of policy—of conscious decisions"; and so was the opposite course, urged before the decade ended, of working for industrialization. The hard facts of geography remained unaltered; but the *potentialities* in resources and technology came to be viewed in a somewhat different light, and to be grasped in a different manner. Even the modest industrialization brought by the railway boom of the '50s altered the colonial capitalists' "political economy"!

Professor Harold Innis, too, advanced the argument that "Because of lack of large coal and iron deposits in close proximity to each other . . . Canada has never become an industrial nation. . . . Absence of accessible industrial resources, combined with physical features which prevented growth of a dense population and the formation of a large domestic market, have forced Canadians to make a living by exploiting the natural resources which are available and exporting the resulting products to other countries. The Canadian economy has always been dependent on a few 'staple' industries. . . . Canada is still predominantly a staple producer, and there are cogent geographical reasons for expecting that her economic life will continue to be heavily dependent on a few primary industries." (*Economic Development in Canada*, H. A. Innis and J. H. Dales, 1946, pp. 169-70)

It is not to deny the crucial importance of coal, iron and geography to suggest that *political* institutions and *class* relations and policies were "also" present in the evolution of the colonial society; and an "economic determinism" that ignores them cannot but misrepresent the real processes of history. Galt's ringing declaration of 1859: "We deny the inferiority of our resources. We assert that a permanent injury is done by repressing every effort to act for ourselves . . ." expressed a political drive that was not without its effect on our history.

The years that saw the inauguration of "reciprocity" were also those of the peak of the railway construction boom. Francis Hincks, the champion of the "raw materials" trade policy, was likewise the negotiator of railway loans through Baring Bros., London. By virtue of his efforts the latter became the financial agents of the Government of Canada; Hincks' biographer sees his connection with the Barings as part and parcel of his effort to "suppress the annexation movement and to strengthen the bonds between colony and mother country."

In the long run, the railways furthered the industrialization of British North America—which was not at all the

object of Reciprocity. But their immediate effect was to
provide the means of speeding the extraction and export
of raw materials. U.S. capitalists were quick to seize on
this new, more effective means of capturing the traffic
flow to and from the opening west. As the *American Railroad Journal* had put it in 1850: "All of the great cities
of the United States have for years been prosecuting with
the most untiring perseverance works of immense magni-
tude and cost, for the purpose of draining from its natural channel the business of the vast region which the St.
Lawrence drains." By connecting up with Canadian railways and water lines at the border, and also by building
of railways within Canada, American businessmen could
tap the resources of the northern half of the continent.

This was particularly the case as regards the forest
wealth of the Canadas and New Brunswick. Penetration
by U.S. interests of the richest timber lands north of the
border was a major motive in the building not only of
the St. Lawrence & Atlantic Railway (Portland interests)
but also the Boston-financed Bytown & Prescott Railway
(1854). Both these roads speeded up the depredations of
American companies in the forests of the Ottawa Valley.
Meanwhile, running north from the shore of Lake Ontario,
the Cobourg & Peterborough Railway (built at huge cost
by a U.S. contractor) and the Port Hope & Lindsay Railway (both were built in 1854) brought down Canadian
lumber to lake ports for trans-shipment to the U.S. The
Northern Railway, from Toronto to Collingwood, was
also built by U.S. contractors; opened in 1855, it has been
said of it that "on its way north it literally sprouted
mills." Professor Lower in his study of *The North American Assault on the Canadian Forest* has given a vivid picture of the spoliation. What was referred to at the time as
"the American raid from New York across Canada to

Michigan" left in its wake, in place of rich timber lands, "desolated stump-filled regions" which "suggested an invading army." In a few years a lumber company with headquarters in Ithaca, New York, laid waste one of the largest and finest stands of pine in Canada, in the area between Lake Simcoe and Georgian Bay. (The profits from this raid are said to have provided the endowment for Cornell University.) Buffalo interests waxed rich on the pillage of the forests above Lake Erie, leaving most of the North Shore "often nothing but a breakwater, a few buildings and a waste of sand."

In the pillage of the Canadian forest, railway building and Reciprocity reinforced each other. One observer commented in 1862 on the effects of the latter: "As regards lumber—Canada lost millions by the Treaty . . . raw materials which would now be worth millions of dollars were it standing in the forests, never returned a farthing. . . . Labor expended in manufacturing it went to add to the wealth of our neighbors across the line, while their own timber was so far preserved for future use. They and they only were the gainers by reciprocity in lumber." In New Brunswick, the operations of the Treaty resulted in the final exhaustion of the once magnificent stands of hacmatac that had been used in shipbuilding.

Reciprocity not only facilitated the U.S. "assault on the Canadian forest"; it also gave the New Englanders free access to the northern fishery. The quarrel over fishing rights was of long standing. "The intrusion of American fishing vessels upon the fishing grounds of the Bay of Fundy is loudly complained of everywhere by the fishermen of the Bay," a committee of the New Brunswick Assembly had reported. A Charlottetown newspaper described the situation at the approaches to Prince Edward Island: "Our neighbors had so long trampled upon our privileges, that they imagined they had a perfect right to use our fishing grounds for their own benefit. . . . The complaints of the Colonists have been loud and long."

In response to colonial pressure the British Admiralty in 1852 sent a small squadron to patrol the fishing grounds. But war with Russia being imminent, London was most anxious to avoid any "unfortunate diversion in North America"— and thus was less inclined than ever to exert itself on behalf of the "colonials." The outcome of the Treaty was such that, in Edward Watkin's opinion, "As regards fishing rights, the U.S. appeared largely to have the advantage."

Spurred by Reciprocity, by the demands of railway-building and the Crimean War, trade between the Province of Canada and the United States nearly doubled in the period 1853-60. The exports from Canada were almost wholly raw materials and farm produce; while about 60% of the imports from the U.S. were manufactured goods. The American consul at Montreal noted with satisfaction that the Reciprocity Treaty was "quietly but effectually transforming these five provinces into States of the Union commercially speaking."

He was wrong, however. He reckoned without one thing: the fact that the burgeoning growth of manufacturing industries in British North America emboldened Canadian industrialists to take up the fight for an alternative course of development. W. H. Merritt's demand in 1855 for the imposition of protective tariffs on U.S. manufactured goods; Isaac Buchanan's launching, along with some 60 other businessmen, of the "Society for the Development of Canadian Industry"; and A. T. Galt's 1858 tariff for the protection of Canadian manufacturers: all bore witness not only to a rising resistance of Canadian industrialists to absorption by the United States, but to a new resolve to promote industrialization in face of British competition also.

What gave their resolution backbone was the speeding of industrial growth thanks to the great railway-building boom of the 1850s.

ADDENDUM

American industrialists had their own great expectations: "Although manufactures were excluded from the treaty, eastern manufacturers had been won over by the assurance that an increased sale of their products must inevitably follow an inrush of colonial produce into the United States".*

Andrews' report saw British North America as inevitably a component part of the commercial territory of the U.S.A.: "The trade with the colonies, if unrestricted, would partake of the character and advantages of a home trade". On the map that accompanied his submission, the St. Lawrence-Great-Lakes-Mississippi area appears as a geographic unit: "no national boundary lines are indicated", notes a study of the Andrews report.**

---

*D. C. Masters, *The Reciprocity Treaty of 1854*, p. 41.
**Irene W. D. Hecht: "Israel D. Andrews and the Reciprocity Treaty of 1854: a reappraisal", CHR, Dec. 1963, pp. 327-29.

12

"Make the Railroads First"!

It was entirely fitting that Sir Allan MacNab should be the one to sound the keynote for the new era with his memorable reply to a query about his politics: "Railways are my politics!" For the new confraternity of railway-promoter-politicians embraced a spectrum that ranged from such old-time colonial oligarchs as himself to prominent leaders of Reform such as Francis Hincks. The long-drawn gestation of MacNab's Great Western spanned the years from the heyday of Family Compact rule to the triumph of the Reformers: from 1834, when he and his friends first applied for a charter (under the name of the London & Gore Railroad Co.), to 1851 when work started on construction of the road. The kindly legislative measure under which the tax-paying public pledged itself to underwrite half of the bonded debt of private railway promoters—the railway Guarantee Act of 1849, a first-fruit of Responsible Government—was the work of financier and finance minister Francis Hincks.

After more than a decade of false starts and frustrations the railway boom got under way in the 1850s—once the constitutional struggle for self-government had been won (within limits that have been noted) and the crisis of "Annexation" had been overcome with the new upturn of the economic cycle. The men who chartered railroads were merchant-landowners, industrialists, speculator "mobilizers of capital": men like MacNab, Isaac Buchanan, W. Allan and Hincks from Canada West and Molson, Mc-

Gill and Galt from Canada East. The centres of promotion activity were the Toronto-Hamilton area and Montreal. The make-up of the railway crowd was almost wholly Anglo-Canadian: a few French Canadians, like J. Cauchon, A. N. Morin and G. E. Cartier, were drawn from the fields of law and politics to participate as auxiliaries (and as links with the great landowner of Lower Canada, the Church) in launching the new ventures.

The two rival constellations of promoters initiated conflicting projects designed to draw by different routes the trade of the West to ice-free ports in the United States. One was the St. Lawrence & Atlantic road, to join Montreal and Portland, Maine. A moving spirit in it was the New England railway magnate and promoter John Poor; associated with him, and representing ties with English as well as Canadian capital, were McGill, Moffatt, Molson and Torrance, of Montreal, and Alexander T. Galt of Sherbrooke, commissioner of the British-American Land Company.

In Toronto and Hamilton, meanwhile, MacNab pressed his scheme for a line to bridge the peninsula of South-Western Ontario and provide the shortest rail link between Buffalo and Detroit-Chicago: a venture that meant both a quickening of Toronto-Montreal rivalry and a strengthening of the former city's ties with U.S. investment capital. As the *Globe* wrote on March 19, 1850: "Let Toronto emulate Montreal and its St. Lawrence and Atlantic Railway. Let us in the west . . . sink our local and personal differences, and push through a western railroad, cheap or dear. Let us have the road!"

That year the Great Western promoters had their charter amended to allow for municipal stock subscriptions (as provided for by the 1849 Municipal Act). By this means the railway was able to obtain £25,000 each from the counties of Oxford and Middlesex and from the towns of Galt and London, and £100,000 from Hamilton. MacNab then turned to United States financiers who were eager for the speedy completion of a rail connection between the Niagara River and Detroit; 8,000 shares were promptly taken up by Erastus Corning of Albany, John M. Forbes of Boston and J. W. Brooks of Detroit, who thereupon joined the Great Western directorate as representatives of the interested U.S. railways.

In 1851 construction at last began, with the job let to contractors from the United States. In the years 1852-53 the company received £770,000 in government loans. By 1854 the Great Western was completed from Niagara Falls to Windsor; the Hamilton-Toronto line was finished the following year, and the bridge built over the Niagara Gorge. The Great Western now had direct connection with the New York group of ten separate railroads consolidated in 1853 under the name of the New York Central. It was on its way to fulfilling the promoters' original promise that it "would not only develop the internal trade of Canada, but would also form a connecting link between Boston and the Mississippi River." By thus helping to link the American West with Atlantic ports the Great Western threatened to short-circuit the Montreal promoters' operation, which was designed to draw the western trade via the St. Lawrence & Atlantic road to Portland, Maine.

The answer of the Montreal capitalists, in association with British investors, was the Grand Trunk Railway—a project to meet the threat of the Great Western by taking over and consolidating a number of local lines into a main or "trunk line." The Grand Trunk represented the combined forces of Montreal business (centred in the Bank of Montreal), their friends and agents in office, and in the background some of the most powerful British financial institutions. The list of Grand Trunk directors announced in a prospectus issued in London (1853) was calculated to impress investors: not least, by its disclosure of the extent to which railway promoters and government were intertwined in Canada. Together with heads of the big English private banking houses of Baring Brothers and Glyn, Mills and Company there appeared the names of John Ross, Solicitor-General (Canada West); Francis Hincks, Inspector-General of the Province of Canada; James Morris, Postmaster-General; Malcolm Cameron, President of the Executive Council; Peter McGill, member of the Executive Council, long-time President of the Bank of Montreal; E. P. Taché, Receiver-General; R. E. Caron, Speaker of the Legislative Council; Georges-E. Cartier, Chairman of the Parliamentary Committee on Railways and chief counsel for the Grank Trunk. Most of the Grand Trunk stock was held in England by ~~less~~ FEWER than six shareholders (individuals or concerns), the international banking firm of Rothschild's alone being credited with controlling one-eighth of the total capital.

From the outset it was Grand Trunk policy to take over other lines. It turned first to the west, securing the control of railways projected for the Montreal-Kingston and Kingston-Toronto route, incorporating into its structure the capitalists who controlled them—Galt, Holton, Macpherson—and overriding their plans for construction by a Canadian rather than by English contractors. However much of a test of strength there may have occurred at this point, as between Canadian and British capital, the latter clearly was henceforth to be dominant in the Grand Trunk.

With railway construction being paid for by the mile, the British contractors "scamped" the work. Employing the system of sub-contracting, they squeezed the sub-contractors; the latter in turn sweated their workers unmercifully and strikes were frequent. It was estimated that some 20,000 men were employed on railway construction by the summer of 1854. It is worthy of note that during this railway construction boom wages in Upper Canada were from 30 to 50 per cent higher than those paid in Lower Canada.

It was Francis Hincks himself who had arranged to have construction of the line east of Toronto done by the English firm of Peto, Brassey, Jackson & Betts (it was already engaged in the construction of the Quebec & Richmond Railway and of the European & North American in New Brunswick). For the Grand Trunk job they were being paid two-thirds in Grand Trunk bonds and stock plus large amounts of cash. For construction work west of Toronto (to Sarnia) most of the contracts went to Galt, Holton, and Macpherson in association with the engineer C. S. Gzowski. In 1854 it leaked out that Hincks had received a "gift" of £50,400 in Grand Trunk stock, and that he and some of his colleagues had taken advantage of their official posts to speculate in land, railway stocks and municipal railway bonds. The Legislative Council (many of whose members had railway interests of their own) appointed a commission of inquiry. Before it, George Brown charged that the £50,400 of Grand Trunk stock was a payment to Hincks by Peto, Brassey, Jackson & Betts for ensuring that they should get the contract. In reply to written questions from the commission to the English bankers, Glyn stated that the allotment of stock to Hincks and Ross was made by the Grand Trunk directors at the representation of Sir S. M. Peto. Baring's reply corroborated this.

Meanwhile to the east of Montreal the Grand Trunk

had taken over the St. Lawrence & Atlantic Railway (Montreal to the Maine border), controlled by A. T. Galt, A. N. Morin and John Young. In addition to this connection with Portland, the Grand Trunk took over the Quebec & Richmond Ry. and also obtained a charter for a line from Quebec to Trois Pistoles, the government providing a loan of £3,000 per mile (usual on Grand Trunk lines) with a land subsidy of 1,000,000 acres should the line be extended beyond Trois Pistoles.

No sooner had the work on the Grand Trunk got going than Jackson (of the contracting firm) wrote to Hincks seeking government financial aid for an extension of the line from Trois Pistoles to connect with the railways in New Brunswick and Nova Scotia. Soon further aid was demanded, and in 1855 the government loaned £900,000, then allowed the company to issue £2 millions of preferred bonds (to rank ahead of the government lien) and also agreed to meet the interest on bonds already outstanding for five years. Yet despite all this help, the contractors were not able to continue with construction and only the main line was opened for traffic.

While these profitable complexities were unfolding, a crucial struggle with MacNab's Great Western was being waged. At stake was control of communications from Toronto westward, and the lucrative tie-up with the N.Y. Central and Michigan Central: the "Canadian" segment of the most direct line from New York to Chicago. The Grand Trunk in its prospectus with serene self-confidence had alluded to the rival Great Western as "a continuation of the Trunk line, although under a different company." It likewise viewed the Hamilton-Toronto extension (projected by the Great Western) as a part of the main trunk. U.S. investors in the Great Western thought otherwise. In the Railway Committee of the Legislature MacNab (chairman of the committee) sought to secure for his Great Western a monopoly in the Ontario peninsula. But the Grand Trunk, having got control of the Toronto and Guelph Railway, now proposed its extension to Sarnia. The Great Western strongly protested at this planned invasion of "its" territory, but Hincks threw himself unreservedly on the side of the Grand Trunk (of which he was a director) and the Legislature granted the extension. In 1853 the Grand Trunk and the Great Western made an agreement to co-operate against "injurious competition" and together oppose competing schemes; but sharp competition between the two continued for several years.* Gradually, however, English capital got the upper hand in the Great Western; by 1857 its president was an Englishman, Robert Gill, and the U.S. railway interests began to look around for another line between Niagara and Detroit.

In the Canada Southern, itself a merger of the Woodstock & Lake Erie and the Amherstburg & St. Thomas railways, the Vanderbilts (who controlled both the New York Central and the Michigan Central) secured a direct line through Canada of their New York to Chicago network.

Over the antecedents of the Canada Southern there had been scandals to match those of the Grand Trunk. Isaac Buchanan, the Hamilton merchant-industrialist, was exposed by a parliamentary investigation in 1857 as having distributed some $100,000 in bribes in order to get control of the Woodstock and Lake Erie railway. Since he was also heavily involved in the Great Western it was never clear whether he was trying to protect the latter, as he claimed, or trying to hold it up by the threat of the Can-

---

*It was not until 1882 that the Grand Trunk at last bodily absorbed the Great Western.

ada Southern as a competing line (as the majority of Great Western directors implied). Of a number of other public figures implicated, the most notorious was Samuel Zimmerman, a Pennsylvania contractor involved in the construction of the Welland Canal, and a friend of Sir Francis Hincks.

Of him a contemporary, the prominent Canadian civil engineer T. C. Keefer, wrote as follows:

> One bold operator organized a system which virtually made him ruler of the province (of Canada) for several years. In person or by agents he kept "open house," where the choicest brands of champagne and cigars were free to all the people's representatives from the town councillor to the cabinet minister. . . . By extensive operations he held the prosperity of so many places, as well as the success of so many schemes and individuals, in his grasp, that he exercised a quasi-legitimate influence over many who could not be directly seduced. Companies about to build a railway or get a municipal loan or other grants were led to believe that if he were the contractor, he could get the sanction of the government to any extent.

For years this operator was "the power behind the scenes in the Canadian legislature." The English contractors for the Grand Trunk had to cut him in on their profits. When U.S. contractors on the Northern Railway needed a bill rushed through the Legislature to get the government guarantee that had been held up because they so blatantly scamped the construction work, Zimmerman looked after it for a "brokerage" of $100,000. When the Great Western wished to double track the line from Hamilton to London, Zimmerman had to be "fixed." His was the construction contract for the Cobourg & Peterborough Railway that cost the fabulous sum, for those days, of one million dollars. In the first winter of operation, the railway's bridge across Rice Lake gave way: investigation revealed that the work had been improperly done. One of Zimmerman's lobbying jobs was to get a waiver of the provisions of the Railway Act requiring trains to stop before crossing the bridge over the Desjardins Canal near Hamilton. Less than two years thereafter, a train which did not stop plunged through the open bridge; of some 60 victims one of the first bodies recovered was that of Zimmerman.

Although British capital was dominant in the emerging rail network that drew export produce eastward for shipment from the Atlantic ports, U.S. capital was already building railway "feeder lines" northward from the Grand Trunk to tap the lumber needed for the fast-growing towns and cities of Ohio, Illinois and beyond. Boston capitalists invested in the Bytown & Prescott Ry. (1854); American contractors built the Cobourg & Peterborough, the Port Hope & Lindsay; via the Northern Railway (Toronto-Collingwood), Georgian Bay lumber was shipped at first to New York State, later to Chicago. The Great Western of course embraced both British and large American interests. Thus from the start the railway network of the Canadas reflected the peculiar colonial relationship to both industrial powers, the trans-Atlantic and the continental.

By 1860 just over two thousand miles of railway had been built in British North America; there had been 66 miles laid when the decade opened. (Railway mileage in England and the U.S. in 1860: ten thousand and thirty-one thousand respectively.) Capital imports into Canada, according to Easterbrook and Aitken, had risen as follows:*

---

*These estimates include military expenditures; but, the authors note, cover only primary investments: "total capital formation must have been several times higher." (*Canadian Economic History*, p. 316)

1827 - 38	$25 million
1841 - 49	$35 million
1850 - 59	$100 million

For surplus capital seeking fields of investment, railway building in British North America held the promise of a profitable outlet. At the same time railways were to provide the means of stepping up the flow of raw materials and produce to the metropolis. There is least something of a parallel with the process that Marx described in relation to India, which the "English millocracy" had set out to endow with railways "with the exclusive view of extracting at diminished expense the cotton and other raw materials for their manufactures." If the parallel in this respect can be suggested only with reservations—the colonies of "white" settlement were not (except as regards the native peoples) of the same order as those of "white" occupation—it applies with considerable force to the other aspect of the process: the way imperial railway construction stimulated colonial industrialization, although this had by no means been its original intent. As Marx argued,

> You cannot maintain a net of railways over an immense country without introducing all those industrial processes necessary to meet the immediate and current wants of railway locomotion, and out of which there must grow the application of machinery to those branches of industry not immediately connected with the railways.

Marx saw in rail construction the "crowning work" of industrialization in the advanced countries (England, the U.S., France, etc.), because railways were "at last (together with steamships for oceanic intercourse and the telegraphs) the *means of communication* adequate to the modern means of production . . ." Moreover, as the start-

ing point for a veritable proliferation of joint stock companies, they gave an unprecedented impetus

> to the *concentration of capital,* and also to the accelerated
> and immensely *enlarged cosmopolitan activity of loanable
> capital,* thus embracing the whole world in a network of
> financial swindling and mutual indebtedness, the capitalist
> form of "international" brotherhood.
>
> On the other hand, the appearance of the railway sys-
> tem in the leading countries of capitalism allowed, and
> even forced, states where capitalism was confined to a
> few summits of society, to suddenly create and enlarge
> their capitalistic superstructure in dimensions altogether
> disproportionate to the bulk of the social body, carrying
> on the great work of production in the traditional modes.

In the case of the British North American colonies,
railway-building *preceded* large-scale factory industry, and
indeed gave much of the impetus to its establishment. The
"disproportionate dimensions" of the capitalistic super-
structure that was associated with railway ventures became a factor of crisis by the early 1860s. The early modes
of small-scale self-sufficient pioneer economy in colonial
English Canada gave way only slowly to the full-scale development of the market required by the exigencies of
industrialization. In French Canada railway building
"accelerated the social and political disintegration" of
the "traditional modes" of production. In both cases the
process was one of revolutionizing old patterns of relationships in order to make way for the basic capitalist
relation of capital and wage labor.

Here as in most other countries (England excepted) the
State acted as a lever in moving the economy into the
new stage of industrial growth: as Marx noted, "the government enriched and fostered the railway companies at
the expense of the Public Exchequer." As in the United
States, the railways received as a present "to their profit,

a great part of the public land . . . not only the land necessary for the construction of the lines but many miles of land along both sides of the lines, covered with forests . . ." (letter to Danielson, April 10, 1879).

This arrangement, as operated in the British provinces, has been described in detail by Gustavus Myers in his *History of Canadian Wealth*. Of "the inception of the railroad power" he wrote:

> High government officials and members of parliaments not only openly voted charters for themselves and associates, but in prospectuses, often issued for stock jobbing purposes, advertised their connection as a guarantee of the prominence and stability of these enterprises, and as the best assurance that could be given that the whole power of the state could be infallibly depended upon to pass whatever additional laws were necessary, and to give gratuities in loans, bonuses and land grants.*

The capitalists of colonial British America had a multiplicity of motives for pushing railway development: opening up of new territory, extension of the home market for agriculture and industry, aid to the export trade. They had already learned that big construction projects (like canals) were a contractors' and promoters' paradise. To the shipping and merchant group, the sweep and tempo of United States railway-building were making it evident that the barely-completed and costly Canadian canal system would surely fail them in their ambition of channeling the mid-west trade through the St. Lawrence route;

---

*H. A. Innis at one time considered that "It is scarcely necessary to dwell on the work of Gustavus Myers, . . . who has treated Canadian history as an evolution of the predatory culture." ("The Teaching of Economic History in Canada," 1929). The "culture" in question was of course capitalism, and Myers' well-documented description of its evolution is not to be so easily dismissed. For a "second thought" of Innis, see *Postscript* on interpretations.

so they now turned to the railways to do the job. In the Maritimes as in the Canadas there were groups who saw in the railway a means of linking up their interests with the far more rapidly expanding U.S. economy. Railway development offered the basis for a mutually profitable if doubly parasitic relationship: resources north of the border (especially those of the forests) were placed at the disposal of American businessmen, with whom Canadian capitalists acquired positions of minor partnership. Or, aligned with the other, earlier axis of investment-dependency, they strengthened their ties with the London banking houses and emphasized vocally the indispensability of the imperial connection.

Yet not all was sycophancy. Railroads, which stimulated local manufacturers, lent substance to the idea of a political unification that could enframe a merger of the colonial markets. Discussion of possibilities of an all-embracing legislative or federal union of the British provinces revived, following the winning of responsible government, with the "philosophy of railroads" as a new and heady ingredient. An example is the call of Joseph Howe of Nova Scotia, speaking at Quebec in 1850:

> We must make the railroads first before any combination is possible. To the advocate of legislative union I say, your scheme is impracticable without railroads. To the Federalist, my advice is, make the railroads first, and test your theory afterwards. To the people of the Maritime Provinces I say, make the railroads that you may behold the fertile and magnificent territory that lies behind you. To the Canadians I say, make the railroads, that you may come down upon the seaboard and witness its activity and appreciate the exhaustless treasures it contains.

If railway-promotion was the quintessence of business politics at the mid-century, it was because railways were seen as crucial to industrialization, growth of the economy, and perhaps autonomous statehood. The prophet-politicians were not far wrong. The capitalist industrialization for which railway building provided the backbone made it possible at least to envisage the creation of a transcontinental political state.

13

Prelude to an Industrial Revolution

Railways in British North America served both as an instrument of colonialism — extracting raw materials and semi-processed products required by the metropolis — and as engines of industrialization, stimulating the growth of local manufactures and of a home market. Their influence was exerted in manifold ways. In conjunction with the introduction of steam-power in the sawmills, the extension of rail lines hastened the transformation of the forest industries. In a number of urban centres, the requirements of railway equipment and rolling stock spurred the beginnings of a heavy manufacturing industry. To the economy as a whole, predominantly agricultural, the spreading rail network opened up new areas to settlement, and brought means of transport and communication to enlarge the market area and foster commercial interchange.

New railway lines probing northward into the bush country made it possible to multiply the number of sawmills just at a time when big changes were in progress in the industry. The change-over from the old squared-timber to the new sawn-lumber trade involved both a restructuring of the business and important changes in technique. The early British "timber factors" had worked under a colonial merchant-capitalist type of arrangement, buying timber and financing cutting operations through advances; the timber was squared by hand; and the profits were drained off for capital accumulation in Britain.

When sawn deals (three-inch planks) had been in demand on the British market, the timber merchants invested in sawmills, and a rudimentary industrial operation came into being at the river-mouth or other point of delivery for the great log-rafts brought down from the camps.

But the sawn-lumber trade called for a vast increase in volume of output, and required the large-scale machinery that goes with an industrial-capitalist type of undertaking. The introduction of the circular saw (1840) led to a series of innovations in the mills: the logging-chain, edging and butting saws, live rollers to clear lumber away from the saw. Steam-power was the prime mover in the changeover to large-scale production. The number of steam mills doubled in the decade 1851-61, from 158 to 325. By the mid-sixties, John Hamilton's steam-driven mills at Hawkesbury (on the Ottawa) were turning out 27 million board feet; a contemporary reports that they contained "92 vertical saws, 19 circular saws, 14 butting saws . . . and one hundred and sixty-five men and boys are employed in and about the mills. These are divided into day and night watches, alternately working for twelve hours each."

Whereas in 1851 it had taken all 1,618 sawmills in Upper Canada to produce 400 million feet of lumber, twenty years later a total output of 365 million feet was accounted for by six mills alone. Steam-driven machine production meant *concentration* of production and of capital, in this as in other sectors of capitalist industry. This general feature of industrialism was accompanied by a specific particularity: it was U.S. capitalists whose steam mill on the St. Maurice River (built in 1853) was the largest in the country at that time.

Becoming dominant in lumber, mechanization spread next to wood-working: factories using power-driven machinery turned out growing quantities of staves, shingles, doors and sashes, furniture, matches. Thus, in the village of Matilda in the Ottawa Valley (1861), ash and elm barrel-staves were produced by a "steam stave-cutting machine that cuts ten thousand staves per day, or from 60 to 70 per minute. . . . It is driven by a steam engine of 25 horse power . . . and gives employment to ten hands." In Hull, E. B. Eddy's mill by 1868 was "capable of turning out 100,000 feet of lumber per day" and 13,000 matches per minute.

The railway boom gave an impetus to industrialization generally, but its most direct and immediate effect was in the local manufacture of the railways' own equipment. As Montreal, Kingston, Toronto, Hamilton became centres for turning out engines, rolling stock, equipment, supplies, a heavy industry—until then largely lacking—was brought into being. In some cases an existing machine-shop was enlarged and converted to meet the new needs: thus it was that the workers in James Good's plow and stove works on Yonge Street, Toronto, in 1853 built the first locomotive in British North America for the Toronto, Simcoe & Huron (later the Northern) Railway. That same year the Scottish firm of Kinmond Bros. opened a plant in Montreal; their 170 to 180 workmen built nine locomotives in the first two years of operation. In Hamilton, D. C. Gunn's machine and farm-implement plant at the foot of Wellington St. turned out a number of locomotives for the Grand Trunk: they sported names both biblical and mythological—Shem, Ham, Japhet, and Achilles and Bacchus! At Kingston during the 1850s the Ontario Foundry Co. built 22 locomotives. The early Maritime railway locomotives were built by Fleming & Humber of Saint John, N.B. By the end of the decade, of 449 locomotives in service 78 had been built in Canada or the

Maritimes, 124 in Britain and 247 in the United States.

The Grand Trunk, the Great Western and Gzowski and Company, contractors, all established factories for rolling or re-rolling iron rails and repairing rolling stock. A plant in Kingston was turning out railway axles and wheels in 1855. In 1857 the rolling mill later known as the Montreal Rolling Mills Company was opened in Montreal. In 1866 the Steel, Iron and Railway Works of Toronto put into operation a patented process for manufacturing railway crossing points and putting steel ends on rails.

In Hamilton, Williams' and Cooper's carriage works on King St. West produced the first railway rolling stock built in Canada. It was Samuel Sharpe, the master mechanic on the Great Western, who developed the first railway sleeping car. In 1858 the Great Western's night trains were equipped with cars that permitted the space between the seats to be turned into beds—eight years before the first Pullman car made its initial run out of Washington.

By the 1860s products such as boilers, engines, springs, axles, mill gearing, piping and steam-fittings, tools, nails, rivets, bolts and nuts were all being made in Canada, many in sufficient volume to meet the growing needs of the country. The most impressive concentration of this metal work was at Montreal. Here the English traveller Samuel P. Day observed along the banks of the Lachine Canal "factories clustered together, from which the hum of industry constantly went forth." They included "the two puddling and rolling mills of Montreal . . . capable of supplying rails in sufficient number to meet the requirements of the entire Province" (of Canada).

Day describes his visit to a couple of plants:

> The first manufactory to which I wended my way was the Victoria Iron Works (the reader will observe how loyal the people are), where I noticed a rolling-mill for nail

plates in operation. . . . This mill turns out twelve tons per day, chiefly from Scotch pig iron, puddled at the works. One hundred and twenty hands are employed, and two thousand tons of plates were produced during the working months of 1862. The works were commenced as recently as 1859, and, I believe, were the first of the kind started in the Province. There is another rolling-mill in the suburbs of the city, and two nail and spike factories, in one of which I lost my hearing for some minutes, owing to the deafening clamour of the heavy cutting machines— fully a dozen of them being simultaneously in operation.

Mechanization was not limited to the iron and wood-working industries. Also alongside the Lachine Canal S. P. Day was able to observe with wonderment "three immense flour mills" using elevators for storage of grain, and considerable machinery. Concerning one of these mills, eight stories high, the visitor remarked that thanks to new devices "a wonderful economy of human labour is realised . . . By means of elevators a barge could be loaded or unloaded in an hour; a process that would otherwise occupy an entire day, even with the assistance of a large number of hands . . . The complicated and varied work of the Royal Mills is accomplished by the aid of twenty men and boys—an economisation of labour truly wonderful. The proprietors are Englishmen."*

Day went through Redpath's sugar refinery where "about seven eighths of the white sugar consumed in the Province are produced. . . ." He mentions also "the Steam Saw Mills, the Oil and Colour Works, the Chemical and India Rubber Works, and an immense establishment for the manufacture of doors, windows, frames, etc. by means of water power."

---

*Anglo-Canadians of Scots descent; W. W. Ogilvie, who had this mill built in the 1850s, was of the third generation of a family engaged in milling, first near Quebec (in 1801) then at Montreal.

What impressed him most in all this was the extent of mechanization: "One leading feature of these establishments is, that machinery is made to do what in the old country is accomplished by human hand. In Canada labour of this description is scarce. . . ."

Manufacturing industry in Toronto during the 1850s was expanding likewise, responding to increased consumer demand and to the needs of the railways. The *Globe* published a survey that included these examples:

—Jacques & Hay's, cabinet-making, furniture: 300 men employed at the peak of trade; annual output of 75,000 chairs, 10,000 bedsteads; £25,000 a year in wages.

—Phoenix Foundry, John McGee, prop.; the earliest such establishment in this part of the country; on Yonge St. between King and Adelaide; employs 100; annual consumption of pig-iron 700 tons; makes stoves & hollowware; "some of the finest flouring and saw mills have been furnished with machinery from this foundry."

—Also: Toronto Foundry & Machine Shop (65-70 men), City Foundry (30-40), Good's Toronto Engine Works (60), Toronto Iron Works (80) with a boiler shop, foundry and "shop with very heavy machinery for rolling and punching iron plates."

Iron puddling and rolling mills were started by several of the railways or capitalists associated with them. Gzowski and Macpherson (one an engineer, the other a railway promoter) established a rolling mill in Toronto in 1860; the Great Western did likewise four years later in Hamilton. By 1867 Montreal had "three Rolling Mills and Nail Works, employing about 600 men and boys." Until the mid-century Canada had depended for her supply of wrought-iron nails on Britain. In 1862 two hundred "hands" at the Victoria Iron Works (Montreal) were able

to turn out in six months some three thousand tons of
nail plate; this and another Montreal mill were "capable
of supplying nails in sufficient number to meet the requirements of the entire Province" (of Canada).

In a review of metal industries in the Montreal area in
1864 the *Gazette* listed sixteen establishments; their products included steam engines and boilers, agricultural
implements, mine machinery, mill gearing, piping and
steam-fittings, stoves and grates, spikes and nails. Iron
manufacturing was becoming the leading sector of the
city's industry. According to W. Kilbourn, investment in
manufacturing in Montreal rose during the 1860s from
just under one million dollars to more than ten million.

Railway-building, while dominant, was not the only
driving force in this early phase of industrialization. The
first steam-engines built in Canada had been ships' engines. The shipyards and machine-shops at Kingston built,
among many others, "the steel-plated steamer *Corinthian,*
one of the fastest and most elegant boats on the Lakes";
there were the foundry and boiler-shop linked with the
shipyard at Collingwood, and the shipbuilding works on
Sherman's Inlet, at Hamilton. The Canada Marine Works
at Montreal in the space of less than two decades built
and launched 111 vessels, "principally . . . for lake and
river navigation."

The transition from hand-work to mechanization, from
the early "manufactory" to the plant employing power-
driven machinery, was slow and uneven. Alongside the
introduction of machinery in many branches of industry,
production by hand persisted in others, due either to the
nature of the work process or the greater profitability of
employing hand labor. The glass manufactory at Montreal
is one example. Another is the numerous carriage works
in the larger towns; although here too mechanization was

appearing, as shown by the announcement of the Hamilton Steam Coach Factory (in 1856) that by a new steam process it was turning out "TWO CARRIAGES A DAY!"

While the flour mills that S. P. Day visited were introducing mechanization so as to increase production for export, boot and shoe manufacturers were doing likewise in order to capture the home market. H. B. Small, in his survey of "Products and Manufactures" (1868) spoke of how machinery "bids fair to revolutionize the old channels of trade; a boot now being stitched, fitted and pegged by machinery all in the space of two minutes." Another contemporary states: "The improvements in machinery, introduced into the principal factories, now enable the larger firms to produce nearly 200 different kinds of boots and shoes. . . . It is estimated that Montreal furnishes three-fourths of the whole quantity produced in . . . Ontario and Quebec. Some of the largest establishments make 1,000 to 1,500 pairs per day." The industry "employed about 5,000 hands; and total yearly production . . . was estimated at 2.4 million pairs" (Creighton).

Other consumer goods industries where machinery revolutionized the production process included: sugar refining—Redpath's refinery in Montreal, started in 1855, was able to supply the country's entire needs in less than a year's production; and tobacco—the McDonald firm (est. 1858) in the same city being mentioned by a contemporary as an example of "the inevitable tendency of all large and well-organized establishments to absorb the smaller and weaker ones."

Another area of industrial activity that must be noted was the production of farm machinery. The Canadian economy was still predominantly agrarian, with wheat and flour surpassing lumber in the 1850s as the chief item of export. With labor in strong demand for canal and railroad construction and in manufacturing, the incentive was strong to introduce labor-saving machinery on the farm. At Newcastle, Canada West, Daniel Massey turned his smithy into a farm implement factory: in 1852 his workmen produced the first mowing machine made in Canada. A couple of years later it was followed by a combined hand-rake, reaper and mower. At the Paris international exposition of 1855, where there was a considerable exhibit of Canadian manufactures, a steam plow invented by J. Romain of Peterborough was acclaimed by a French engineer: "I feel a high degree of satisfaction," he wrote, "that the problem of the application of steam to the plow has been solved by a Canadian mechanic who is proud of his French descent."

While British and Anglo-Canadian capitalists played the main part in this growth of consumer-goods industries, American capitalists had a hand in it also. They opened a carriage works in London (1845); at Guelph they established three companies (1859-60) in agricultural implements, sewing machines, flour milling. Massachusetts-born Hiram Walker had his distillery built at Walkerville in 1857.

It was natural that with railway-building and the growth of machine industry there should be further attempts to establish a basic iron industry in Canada. In 1854 the Van Norman Iron Works opened a blast furnace in Norfolk County. More ambitious was the Radnor Forges near Three Rivers, where 200 to 400 men were employed in a blast furnace, forge, rolling-mill and cast-iron railway-car wheel plant put into operation in 1857. That same year the Canadian Iron and Manufacturing Company of Montreal built a blast furnace at Hull, but it closed down two years later. A few other attempts were made, but the nature of the available ores, the absence of coal in central Canada, the more advanced technique of the iron and steel industry in Britain and the United States and the lower prices of the imported product all worked against the successful establishment of a basic iron and steel industry in Canada at this time.

The mineral deposits of the Precambrian Shield remained as yet practically untouched; but railway construction and the opening up of new areas in south-central Canada led to exploitation of such non-metallic minerals as gypsum for fertilizer, sandstone for glass, marble, clay for bricks and tiles. Indicative of a future pattern in mining developments was what happened with the discovery of oil in Lambton County. Here operations began in 1857, and U.S. capitalists moved in to take over.

The promise of "bringing to light the hidden wealth of Canadian rocks" acquired international prominence with the award to Sir William Logan, Canadian Provincial geologist, of the grand medal of honor of the Paris Exhibition of 1855: a triumph, noted a contemporary source, that "will do more in calling the attention of European capitalists to the vast mineral wealth of the country than the most elaborate description of its distribution and extent." It is of some interest to recall that Logan's listing of "principal Economic Minerals of Canada" included: "Magnetic Iron Ore . . . Titaniferous Iron . . . Copper . . . Nickel . . . Silver . . . Gold . . . Uranium; Chromium; Cobalt; Manganese . . ."

Professor Kilbourn designates as the likeliest date and birth-place of Canadian industry, "the banks of the Lachine Canal in 1846"—where, following completion of improvements on the canal, the government made available industrial sites and water-power rights to manufacturers: "Within two decades the factory had replaced the craftsman's shop and the small foundry as the typical industrial unit of Montreal." Certainly, the 50s and 60s marked the prelude, if not indeed the first actual stage, of the Industrial Revolution in this country.

Yet not a few authorities have tended to play down, or even ignore completely, this preliminary phase of industrialization. Whether this has been due to a sort of fixation on quantitative indices of the trade in staples (the predominance of whose volume in the colonial economy is undeniable); or to distinterest in the developments occurring in the process of industrial production (which have actually been the dynamic factor of change, as the outcome has shown)—judgments like the following have tended to become articles of faith:

> Generally speaking, before 1867, in fact before the 1880s, manufacturing was unimportant, for the chief interests of the country were in staples. (A. W. Currie: *Canadian Economic Development*, 1942, p. 152.)

The "chief interests" *were* in staples; but that is not where the mainspring of change, however small its proportions, was located. The change in man's relation to the forces of nature that accompanied the introduction of the steam engine, and the impact of that development on the basic pattern and structure of society, are not readily discernible in the statistics of external trade. But the fact is that along with the continuance of the quantitatively dominant role in the colonial economy of wheat and lumber exports, there was taking place a growth of the internal, home market; an increase in the number of factories, in the use of machinery and steam-power (particularly in the larger ones); the beginnings of a heavy industry. Together with a rise in the number engaged in "industrial employment" in the Province of Canada in the years 1851 to 1861 from 71,000 to 145,000, there was taking place at the top a consolidation of the new élite of railroad and factory-owners; the shaping of that ruling class of industrial capitalists who were to be the real (and not merely the titular) "fathers" of Confederation.

Industrial capitalism emerging at the mid-century leads to the crystallization of a new colonial ruling class. Gone are the days of the old Family Compact and Château Clique—oligarchies of landowner officialdom clustered about the colonial Governor. Thanks to the combined push of railway construction, mass immigration enlarging settlement, the beginnings of steam-driven machine production, and a measure of self-government, the groupings of colonial businessmen constitute themselves into an élite. Unlike its Family Compact predecessor it is able to rule in its own right; while a certain tone of servility and sycophancy in relation to the imperial power is not yet a thing of the past (nor will it be for a century), it is no longer the dominant one. A note of confident self-assertion increasingly is sounded—as in Alexander Galt's "declaration of economic independence" on the Canadian tariff in 1858. The new ruling class, undertaking to launch the industrial development of Canada, senses the historically progressive meaning of its mission. Capitalism, in that context, spells progress.

Whence came the capital that made possible the railway construction and manufacturing expansion of the mid-century? Not, assuredly, from the "hard work and thrift" of any individual entrepreneur. Useful as those virtues may have been to the aspiring small businessman (a few of whose breed did indeed emerge as "self-made" magnates), they could not possibly generate such masses of capital as were required to invest in the buildings, machinery, materials and wage-payments of large-scale industry. The men who could command such capital were those few whose families had already acquired fortunes either through mercantile piracy in an earlier era, or by getting into a position to control the financial resources of the community—through banking, insurance, or the public purse.

Financial power came to inherit the privileged positions of the Family Compact "colonial aristocracy." One result of the defeat of the 1837 revolution had been the ease with which the old élite (Allan MacNab, for one) evolved into or merged with the new. The new direct line of descent in the wealth of the McGill family, for instance, ran from fur trading and land monopoly to the Bank of Montreal and the Grand Trunk. Merchants' capital, accumulated in the fur-trade through profit extracted from the labor of Indian trappers and French-Canadian canoemen, merged with capital derived from land-company speculation, exploitation of settlers and the farming community; and thence to banking operations, railway speculation and profiteering, and the commandeering of the government apparatus and public exchequer. When to the foregoing process—which with one variant or another was characteristic of the rise of the new capitalist class—there is added the singularly lucrative connection with British capital, then the enrichment of the McGills, Molsons, Allans and others of the business oligarchy becomes understandable.

Bank and insurance companies (the latter dating from the 1830s) channeled the savings of the community into new capitalist undertakings. The 1850s witnessed a rash of chartering of banks in addition to the six already in operation, among which the Bank of Montreal (est. 1817) held the dominant position:

X PIRACY AND/OR PRIVATEERING; NEVER MIND "MERCANTILE".

—1855: the Eastern Township Bank, in which Galt and other government figures were interested: men with investments in the British-American Land Co., the cotton factory at Sherbrooke, the St. Lawrence & Atlantic Ry. (one of the first concerns to appeal for British capitalist backing);

—1855: Molson's Bank: brewery and foundry, steamship-line and financial ventures in a wider field, required a banking institution to serve both commercial and industrial needs;

—1855: the Niagara District Bank, whose directors included W. H. Merritt, canal and railway promoter, flour-milling magnate; James Morris, John Ross, J. Sandfield Macdonald, government figures and businessmen;

—1855: the Bank of Toronto, established by milling interests in Upper Canada;

1859 and 1865: La Banque Nationale and the Union Bank, both largely interested in the lumber trade;

—1864: the Merchants Bank, Hugh Allan, president, later to take over the Commercial Bank which failed due to over-extension in financing Great Western Railway projects;

—1865: the Bank of Montreal replaces the Bank of Upper Canada as fiscal agent for the government; the latter bank, the first chartered in Upper Canada, failed the year following.

The success of the Bank of Montreal and of the Merchants' Bank over rival banks in Upper Canada reflects the relation of forces as between Toronto and Montreal capitalist groupings at this time. The Hamilton *Times* in October 1867 stated: "We greatly fear the Bank of Montreal has the Government in its power and is disposed to play the tyrant."

Other financial institutions, such as insurance companies, were developed during this period, and they also provided a means of channelling the savings of individuals and smaller enterprises into investments in the new railways and industries. In 1849 the Canada Life Assurance

Company had been incorporated by Allan N. MacNab, Malcolm Cameron, John Young, etc., and in the same year the Ontario Marine and Fire Insurance Company (by substantially the same crowd). In 1850 John A. Macdonald, John Hamilton and others established the Kingston Fire and Marine Insurance Company. A Montreal group that included J. J. C. Abbott, George Moffatt and Hugh Allan in 1856 incorporated the Canada Marine Insurance Company.

Two features marked the growth of these instruments of financial control. First, was the heightened activity of Canadian capitalists in their development. In 1841 the Bank of British North America, representing British capital, was the largest. By 1867, the Canadian banks had grown up—one had paid-up capital of $6 million, one of $2 million, and three had capital of between $1 and $2 million.

Second, the banks learned to use the savings of the people to a much greater extent: for example, the ratio of deposits to capital had been only 37 per cent in 1841, whereas by 1867 it was over 100 per cent. (In other words, the banks had become much more adept at using other people's money for the source of funds for their loans, rather than their own capital.)

Of course, there were other ways in which the necessary capital was mobilized by individual capitalists or groups of capitalists for the development of industry. The operations of land speculators, particularly during the height of the railway boom in the mid-1850s, succeeded in transferring a considerable amount from the savings of large numbers of individuals into their own pockets and thence into industrial and other investments. The use of the joint-stock company technique, whereby the ownership of enterprises could be broken up into pieces for

THE SMITHS—Blair Bruce

Harrower's Distillery and Mills on the River Trois Saumons

BOUCHETTE

Cod Fishery

River Operations on the North Pacific

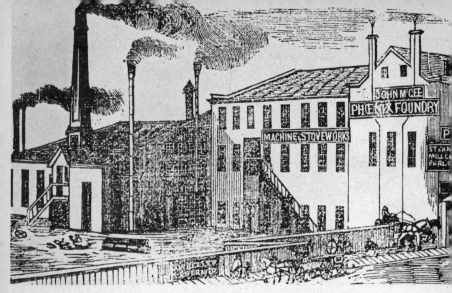

Phoenix Foundry, Toronto 1856

Brantford Foundry 1862

Moulding Shop, Montreal Foundry 1872

Allan Mills, Guelph 1872

Monsieur le Rédacteur,

Si les ouvriers de Québec ont élevé la voix à la dernière élection, ce n'était pas par le désir de supplanter les classes instruites ; mais par le motif qu'ils ont des droits à exercer comme elles. D'ailleurs, personne ne dira qu'il soit plus ridicule chez la classe industrielle qu'il ne l'est chez la branche mercantile de vouloir se faire représenter dans la législature. J'espère encore que le *marteau* et la *truelle* figureront dans les occasions publiques comme on les a vus hier sur le couronnement du superbe pain-béni offert par M. Joseph Larose dans l'église paroissiale de cette ville.

UN OUVRIER.

Letter *to* Le Canadien, *1848*

KARL MARX: *Portrait in the* Canadian Illustrated News, *Dec. 16, 1871*

"struck," as was probably foreseen; since the employers collected such help as they could find, and went on with their surplus work as they best could.

So far, we have the "old, old story"; but the next step forecasts a new order of things. Instead of idling for weeks or months, lounging around grog-shops, and cursing the tyranny of capital, the journeymen promptly formed a co-operative stone-cutting association, subscribed to its stock, elected officers, bought or leased a quarry, and resumed work on their own account; and we rode into Providence in company with their agent or treasurer, a good specimen of an intelligent, thrifty, wide-awake American artisan, who was taking down specimens of their workmanship, in the hope of obtaining orders that would enable them to keep their hammers going and their hearth-fires burning. And now, if anyone happens to be in want of granite, we venture to advise him to run over to Westerly, and confer with the proper officers of the Co-operative Stone-cutters' Association.

We should be glad to chronicle a similar outcome of any strike that may hereafter be resolved on. We hate wars of any kind; and strikes are simply declarations of industrial war. When a body of American workmen refuse the wages offered them and thereupon sink into idleness or stolid waiting for the bosses to give in, they seem to justify a low estimate of their general capacity. But when those who strike to-day contrive to set themselves at work to-morrow—no matter though they earn less than they were offered by their late bosses—we regard them with lively hope. Adam, expelled from Eden, did not sit down and starve because there was no one ready to hire him on his terms; on the contrary, he went to work; and we commend his inspiring example to all his decendants.—*N. Y. Tribune.*

THE WORKINGMEN'S VOICE ON THE NORMAL WORKING DAY.

To THE EMPLOYER :—The article I sold you—my own working power—differs from the other crowd of goods by *its use producing value,* and GREATER *value* than its own cost. For this reason you bought it. What appears on your side as a profitable investment of capital, that is on my side a surplus expenditure of working power. You and I, we both know in the market but one law, that of exchange, and the use (consumption) of the article does not belong to the seller offering it, but to the purchaser acquiring it. The use of my daily power of work therefore belongs to you, but by means of its daily selling price, I must be able to reproduce it daily, and so to sell it anew. Without regard to the natural process of wearing out by age, &c., I must be able to work to-hold forth to me the gospel of economy and continence. Very well. Like a rational, prudent husbandman, I shall economize my own WEALTH, *my power of work,* and I shall abstain from foolishly wasting it. I shall turn to use put in motion, convert into labor only so much of it daily, as is compatible with its normal durability and healthy development. By excessive prolongation of the working-day, you can consume a greater portion of my working power in one day than I can restore in three days. Thus your gain in labor is my loss of labor-substance. The *use* of my power of work and *robbing* me of it are two entirely different things. If the average period an average workingman may live, with a rational limitation of work, is 30 years, the value of my working power, you may pay me from day to day $\frac{1}{365 \times 30}$ or $\frac{1}{10950}$ of its total value. But you consume it within 10 years, you pay me only ⅓ of its value daily, and you defraud me daily of ⅔ of its value. You pay me *one* day power of work, then and whilst using *three* days' amount. That is against our agreement and against the law of exchange. Therefore I demand a working day of *normal* length, and I demand it without appealing to your feeling, because money matters are not matters of affection, and business is soulless. You may be a model citizen, perhaps a member of a society for the prevention of cruelty to animals, you may even have the scent of sanctity and piety, but no heart beats in the bosom of the *thing* you represent toward me. What seems to be pulsating therein is MY OWN HEART-BEAT. I demand the *normal working day,* because I demand the value of my article like every other dealer.—*From the "Kapital,"* Karl Marx.

THE NINE-HOUR MOVEMENT IN CANADA.

The Nine-hour movement is making considerable progress in the Canadian province notwithstanding the fact that it has met with the most determined opposition from the conservative element—the old fogy folk, who would fain keep the workingman of to-day in the same position which his great grandfather occupied years ago, ere steam and electric had leveled down and smoothed over the mighty barriers that obstructed the onward march of Progress. Toroughout the principal cities and towns of the Dominion the Nine hour movement is talked over and the prospects canvassed wherever the workmen congregate, and the question is discussed with a [zeal] which must lead to beneficial results. Despite the counter opposition on the part of the manufacturers, builders, &c., of Hamilton, organized workmen of that city have achieved an exemplary success, while Toronto is

Hamilton Procession of Nine-Hour Movement Men, June 1872

wider distribution, while leaving the control in the hands of a small group which worked closely together, was widespread, above all in the railway promotions of the period. Gustavus Myers cites a nice example of the method; a certain Timmins, secretary of the provisional committee of the Canada, New Brunswick & Nova Scotia Railway Company, wrote to Earl Grey in London, on January 7, 1850, reporting that on the strength of a letter of introduction from Archbishop Signy he had been canvassing the parishes along the proposed line of the railway to enroll stockholders. "In proof of the zeal shown by the clergy of Lower Canada, I have the pleasure to tell you that the name of every rector, vicar, and curé for the whole distance is entered in the Book of Enrollment [of stockholders] . . ." But, of course, the railways of the Canadas and the Maritimes were not built out of the voluntary (or directed) stock subscriptions of any number of parish priests or other "ordinary" people. The much more effective method was to use the government credit, loans, stock subscriptions and outright grants, all based on the power of levying taxes, to take the savings of the people, present and future, and channel them into private projects. In these more often than not high members of the government were quite indistinguishable from the private railway promoters: whence Allan MacNab's blunt declaration —in 1854, the year he became Prime Minister—that "railways are my politics."

As the identification of railway promoter and government official advanced, it was found to be a remarkably simple process to get laws enacted which in effect allowed the private capitalist to tax the whole people. Loans, most of them never to be repaid, outright grants of cash and land, bonuses from the public domain in the form of free appropriation of timber, stone and other construction

materials, all flowed into the hands of the railway promoters. Throughout this process the British capitalists
were adept at the technique of making junior partners
out of the Canadian capitalists, both in and out of government: a technique that American capitalists were to perfect only later, but on a vaster scale.

The same process of using the public taxing power to
develop private capitalist undertakings was also worked
through local government bodies. Besides direct loans and
stock subscriptions to the railway companies, the municipalities made extensive gifts of urban land for approaches,
terminals, and stations, and gave exemptions from local
taxes. The degree to which poor, small municipalities
were depleted of funds and cajoled (often by bribery of
local officials) into mortgaging future generations for the
benefit of the railway contractors and owners in the 1850s
is illustrated in Hind and Keefer's contemporary account,
Eighty Years of Progress in British North America: "From
the town of Port Hope with only about 3,000 population,
a loan of $740,000 was squeezed. The town of Niagara
with but 2,500 population, was influenced to give $280,-
000. Brockville, with a bare 4,000 population, yielded
$400,000" and so on. Such were the sources on which
"private initiative" levied tribute to acquire the capital
to build the railways!

Public debt on account of the railway system had been
piled up by the time of Confederation to the extent of
more than $33 million by the Province of Canada and
another $10.6 millions by Nova Scotia and New Bruns-
wick. In addition, the municipalities in the Province of
Canada had accumulated nearly $7 million in debt due
to railway assistance. In other words, a public debt of
about $15 for each man, woman and child in the new
Dominion had been contracted in order to bring the rail-

ways. Actually this was only about half the public debt which weighed down the Dominion at the start, for in addition to the specific railway debt there was that for the canals, for other public works that had been capitalized, and there were substantial outstanding capital commitments, some of which were also for the railways. The total debt, which Galt had reported equal to about $12 per capita in 1852, had grown to $30 per person by the time of Confederation.

While the national debt was thus employed in exerting a powerful leverage in the interest of private capital accumulation as well as of "public improvements," the relation of business to government had other sides to it. Municipal authorities that sought to tax private corporations encountered some resistance; and business worked out its own techniques for coping with the importunities of elected public bodies. A choice illustration of both these aspects of corporation policy is offered by an episode in the life of one of the land companies.

Messrs. Galt, McGill, Moffatt and their associates in the management of the British American Land Co. in the 1840s took a dim view of the establishment of municipal institutions. The attempt of the Sherbrooke District Council to tax unsettled lands at the rate of a penny an acre was a case in point: it would mean an impost on the Company of £2500. Galt lamented the fact that "the feeling of hostility to the proprietors of wild lands has extended from the lower classes to the Executive . . ." The conclusion he drew provides some insight into the politics of a business democracy:

> . . . the best security the Company could possess against injurious treatment either at the hands of the Provincial Legislature or of the Municipal Council was to obtain such

> an influence in these representative bodies as might render
> their opposition or support of importance. . . .

Galt assured the Governor of the Company: "It has always been our conviction that the interests of the British
American Land Co. were identified with British influence
in the colony." A few years later he rephrased the thought:
"I consider the interests of the Company and of the country to be identical. I ought perhaps to add that I am not
in the least likely to become a political partisan; my views
are all for objects of a material advantage." Just how such
broad-minded devotion to country and Company alike
would work in practice, is suggested when he later confided to the same correspondent: "It must be borne in
mind that the sales made of the Company's property have
been at a price enormously greater than their real cash
value."

Thus did "objects of a material advantage" patriotical-
ly translate themselves into accumulated capital.

The new ruling class of colonial capitalists comprised
a sort of patchwork of varigated interests; its chief components were:

—the successors (or vestigial remnants) of the old mercantile bourgeoisie; e.g., William Cawthra, the Toronto
millionaire whose fortune was said to be "mainly the result of compound interest"; or William Allan, president
of the Bank of Upper Canada, engaged in mercantile and
financial operations;

—industrial capitalists, such as the Gooderhams (dis-
tillers), the Molsons (brewers), Ogilvy (flour mills), the
Paxtons (Montreal Steam Cooperage, 1857), Warden King
iron founders (1852);

—railway and steamship-line promoters: of the former,

many have already been mentioned; of the latter, the Molsons, Hugh Allan and (in the Maritimes) Samuel Cunard were the most prominent;

—financial promoters, such as Hincks (insurance), John Rose (banking);

—representatives of the Church in Quebec, legal counsel serving its interesest on boards of directors and in government: G. E. Cartier, the outstanding example of the French-Canadian "junior partners" of Anglo-Canadian capital.

These men of the ascendant bourgeoisie set their imprint on the era of responsible government and Confederation. Not without reason has Professor Masters (in his study of the "Rise of Toronto") said that of developments in the period 1851-1866 "the most striking was the increasing prominence and activity of the rising capitalist class."

Its dominant group, embracing first and foremost the men of the Grand Trunk and of the Bank of Montreal, was centered in Montreal. In Toronto and Hamilton there was a second cluster, divided roughly into three subgroups, with somewhat divergent interests. One was connected with extractive industries (milling, lumbering and shipping) and its members had close ties with their opposite numbers or with markets in the United States. The up-and-coming manufacturing group, who were having to build up their own financial apparatus in opposition to the Montreal banks, were interested in government assistance in the form of protective tariffs against both the British and United States manufactures. A third group, not entirely distinct from the second, was part of the railway-government crowd, with interests both similar to and conflicting with those of the Montreal group, whose financial power they had good reason to respect.

In the Maritimes, the timber and shipping magnates
of Saint John and Halifax, the local manufacturers and
merchants, constituted groupings with interests and an
orientation that only remotely touched upon those of
their counterparts in the Canadas. Railway promoters
(some of whose first efforts had been directed southwest-
ward, towards the States) were the businessmen most likely to be receptive to schemes for a tie-up with Canada;
the project of the Intercolonial Railway, with its history
of long-drawn frustrations, expressed both the urge toward and the difficulties of such a connection.

The two thousand miles of railroad laid down in the
1850s, the accompanying spread of manufactures and
growth of the home market, all gave grounds for a turn
towards a new economic policy. Hence the demand for
abolition of the tariff barriers which the various provinces
had set up against each other's goods—and for the introduction of national tariffs to protect infant Canadian industries against competition from without. A letter from
Jacob de Witt, president of the People's Bank, to W. L.
Mackenzie in 1858 urged "a tariff so apportioned as to
give encouragements to the manufacturers of such articles
as we can produce or manufacture with advantage in our
country. . . . Why should we not work up our farm wool
into cloth, instead of sending money abroad?"

In 1859 Galt proposed that Canada appeal to the other
provinces for free trade among them and a common tariff.
In the same year, as Minister of Finance, he introduced
the duty on manufactured goods which brought a storm
of protest from English industrialists. His reply to the ensuing query from the authorities in London had something of the quality of a declaration of economic independence:

The Government of Canada cannot . . . in any manner

waive or diminish the right of the people of Canada to decide for themselves both as to the mode and extent to which taxation shall be imposed ... Self-government would be utterly annihilated if the views of the imperial government were to be preferred to those of the people of Canada. The Provincial Legislature . . . must necessarily claim and exercise the widest latitude as to the nature and extent of the burthens to be placed upon the industry of the people.

The British government pressed the point no further.

At Hamilton in 1860, Isaac Buchanan, founder of the "Association for the Promotion of Canadian Industry," presided over a meeting at which John A. Macdonald urged the need to encourage manufacturing industry. What was wanted was "to raise up a home market . . . Manufactories are springing up, east and west, and I hope this great commercial city will see the advantage of encouraging them. If you go to Montreal and look at the enormous factories at work near the canal basin, you will realize what a source of wealth to a city and country they are."

In 1862 an interprovincial conference at Quebec discussed the possibility of establishing free trade in manufactured goods; the participants failed to reach agreement on concrete measures, but they stressed the connection between the building of the long-awaited Intercolonial Railway and the need for "free interchange of goods, the growth, produce and manufacture of the Provinces, and uniformity of tariff." Two years later, at the time of the Quebec Confederation Conference a Mr. Joseph, president of the Board of Trade of that city, stated that "the merchants of Quebec . . . all heartily desired some change in their then position. They desired a thorough commercial union. They desired that the unequal and hostile tariffs of the several Provinces should disappear. They wanted one tariff instead of five."

In the Confederation debates in the Canadian Assembly the following winter, George Brown argued the need to overcome the obstacles to internal trade: "If a Canadian goes now to Nova Scotia or New Brunswick, or if a citizen of these provinces comes here, it is like going into a foreign country. The customs officer meets you on the frontier, and levies his imposts on your effects." And he contrasted with this situation the industrial expansion in the United States: "What has tended so much to the rapid advance for all branches of their industry, is the vast extent of their home market, creating an unlimited demand for all the commodities of daily use and stimulating the energy and ingenuity of producers."

Apprehensive of the likely effects of the threatened termination of the Reciprocity Treaty with the United States, the spokesmen of capitalism in the Canadas were concerned to expand and unify the home market for Canadian manufactures. Having started on the road to an industrial revolution, the new ruling class, the ascendant industrial bourgeoisie, were seeking the political structure that would both serve the needs of business—and at the same time, perhaps, "raise up a new country."

14

Lands and Learning: Reform and Reaction

The transition from an economy dominated by the old, mercantile-landowner, "Family Compact" ruling group to that of the new industrial-railroad oligarchy is the main content of the bourgeois revolution in British North America. It is a revolution effected "from above," the armed popular struggles having met defeat. (In this one respect it bears some distant similarity to the German experience of 1848-71.) But as the experience of the 1840s showed, mass popular pressure was needed to secure the main measures of reform: in the first place, "responsible government." Only after this was won did there take place the political regrouping that signalized the consolidation of power in the hands of the new business élite: first, in the Liberal-Conservative merger of 1854, and a decade later in the Macdonald-Brown coalition. The parallel crystallization of radical-liberalism in the Clear Grits and Parti Rouge provided the medium through which popular opposition movements could continue to exert pressure.

Land-reform and public education were two large areas of long-standing dispute in which the interplay of democratic demands and entrenched privilege eventually resulted in the achievement of remedial measures. Such were the enactments of 1854 on the clergy reserves and seigneurial tenure, and the school acts of the 1840s and 50s.

The clergy reserves issue involved both land-reform and education; from 1826 onward the Upper Canada

Assembly had been demanding that instead of subsidizing an Anglican state church these "reserved lands" should be used to finance a system of common schools. Ten thousand persons had petitioned in 1831 in support of the principle of separation of church and state. Refusal of the Executive and Family Compact to yield on the issue of the clergy reserves was considered by Durham to have been a prime cause of the outbreak of rebellion in the province. By the Act of 1854, the question of the reserves was finally settled. The Church of England leadership did all in its power to avert secularization—an "infidel" measure promoted by an "evil-minded and ungodly faction"— an act of "direct spoliation of the Church." The Act stated however, that "it is desirable to remove all semblance of connexion between Church and State." Proceeds from the sale of clergy reserve lands were to go to the municipalities—after deduction of life stipends for the then incumbent clergy: a sum capitalized at $1,662,678.* Opposition to this final subsidy was unavailing; and the funds turned over to the municipalities were wiped out in the 1857 depression.

The matter of "free schools" was a democratic and a class question. Its background included the absence of an effective, democratic educational system, the valiant efforts of settlers to set up their own schools, build school houses through cooperative effort, find teachers for the children. The patriot-reformers, from Gourlay and Bédard onward, had made the demand for free schools part of their fundamental program.

---

*"The principle of state endowments for religion was nominally repudiated and indirectly maintained through an elaborate system of actuarial compensations to existing incumbents . . ." (Alan Wilson, on the Clergy Reserves, CHR, Dec. 1961) Myers estimates at just over $4 millions the total in payments to the clergy from 1814 to the final settlement.

To community responsibility for public education the diehards in Upper Canada counterposed private schools for the élite (endowed, however, from the public purse), while common schools were supported directly by the parents.

During the preparation of the 1846 School Bill, Egerton Ryerson told Draper that he looked upon the *"rate bill* clause" (taxing all property-owners for school purposes, instead of parents only) "above all others to be the *poor man's* clause, and at the very foundation of a system of education . . ." It was objected to by certain of the wealthy whose children attended private schools; one of such, "a methodist—a magistrate . . . looks not beyond his own family. He says, I am told, 'he does not wish to be compelled to educate all the brats in the neighborhood.' Now to educate 'all the brats' in every neighborhood is the very object of this clause of the bill; and in order to do so it is proposed to compel selfish rich men to do what they ought to do, but what they will not do voluntarily."

The School Act of 1850 authorized municipalities to levy a property tax for purposes of education, but this arrangement, indispensable for free schooling, was not fully adopted until the Act of 1871. The kind of resistance offered to such a system is illustrated by the decision of the Township of York (it included the village of Yorkville) rejecting a proposal for a free school as reported in a letter to the *Globe* (January 31, 1852). The rejection was defended on the ground that for mechanics and laborers "there cannot be any such right, so wrongfully given them by the School Act, to educate their children at the expense of their more wealthy neighbors." The hope is voiced that the city of Toronto will follow Yorkville's example and "spurn the unrighteous counsel which is introducing communism in education, to the under-mining of property and society . . ."

The kind of "communism" that the advocates of free elementary schooling were striving for was simply the basic democratic demand that Ryerson formulated in these words: "That every child in the Land has a right to such an education as will make him a useful member of society, and that every inhabitant of the land is bound to con-tribute to that national object according to his property." Only thus would the prospect become realizable "of see-ing every child of my native land in the school going way . . . one comprehensive and unique system of educa-tion, from the a.b.c. of the child up to the matriculation of the youth into the Provincial University . . ."; or again: "Why should institutions be endowed for the education of lawyers, and none for the educating of farm-ers?" Enlisting the active participation of the people in the hundreds of school sections that he visited, the Superintendent of Education for Canada West laid a firm groundwork for free schools and elective bodies of trus-tees.

What was being undertaken was a response to both the industrial and the democratic revolutions: modern manu-facturing required, and the working people sought, uni-versal elementary education. "The knowledge required for the scientific pursuit of mechanics, agriculture and commerce must needs be provided to an extent corres-ponding with the demand and the exigencies of the country." This judgment of Ryerson's expressed recog-nition of the imperatives of national democratic develop-ment as well as of bourgeois industrialism.

In Canada East the struggle for democratic education was at once more arduous and more complex. Opposition to free popular schooling came not only from those men of wealth who saw in it a threat to privilege, but from a clerical hierarchy that distrusted secular aims. But these forces were able to take advantage of a further complicating factor: the tendency to deadlock as between the pressures for "anglifying" and "protestantizing" the Catholic French, and the counter-pressures of popular anxiety and national resistance. The refusal of the Legislative Council in 1836 to keep open the existing common schools had dramatized one aspect of the problem; Durham's advocacy of anglicization, another; while Bishop Lartigue's call in 1839 for religious schooling (at a time when 96 per cent of the teachers were laymen) heralded the long and ultimately successful offensive for outright clerical control.

In face of these multiple difficulties, the achievement of an effective school system was something of a triumph: the people in the communities, the school teachers, the Patriote and Reform forces all played their part. It is worth noting that the first manual of pedagogy published in the Canadas was Joseph François Perrault's *Cours d'Education élémentaire à l'usage de l'école gratuite établie dans la cité de Quebec en 1821*. Until the defeat of 1837 the people and the Assembly fought to establish common schools under democratic jurisdiction; but after the Union, the School Acts of 1841 and 1846 laid the groundwork for a confessional system, although full scale "clericalization" came only in the later 1860s. The democrats of the Parti rouge and the Institut Canadien campaigned for non-denominational schools. The Institut Canadien, founded in 1844, called for "secular and national education," such as would "make our country greater, fairer and more strong," and "raise up industry and commerce": "education of the popular classes has become the prime need of the age . . ." M. Papin, in a debate on the normal school bill of 1856 called for a universal, publicly financed system of free schools: "There cannot be a state religion," he argued, "and if this be so, the state cannot give money for the teaching of any religious faith. . . . We need a general system, applicable to all parts of the Province, which will cause the prejudices of Catholics and Protestants to disappear." The motion was defeated, rejecting what one orthodox contemporary characterized as "as system that would lead children into religious indifference, undermine the foundations of all religion, and have the most pernicious effects upon youth."

The opposition to clerical take-over was a hard-fought rear-guard action. An important element was the organization of the ill-paid school teachers themselves in 1845 to defend their interests, living standards and professional status. School superintendent Dr. J. B. Meilleur associated himself with this effort, in which the initiative however came from the teachers. The Montreal branch met in the hall of the Institut Canadien. André Labarrère-Paule in *Les Instituteurs Laiques au Canada francais* tells how, even as late as 1864, on the eve of the successful Ultramontane clerical offensive, the teachers founded a paper, *La Semaine*, to popularize their grievances and needs. "A veritable trade-union journal—in the modern sense—it neglects none of the teacher's problems: salaries, lack of social recognition, insecurity, housing. It is a fighting paper, respectfully insolent toward the Church."

The work of these pioneer democrats in the field of education contributed markedly to winning concessions in their own day; they also became part of a tradition that even the forces of reactionary Ultramontanism could not wholly snuff out.

Abolition of the system of seigneurial tenure in Lower Canada was a requirement of industrial capitalist development. Like every other aspect of the bourgeois revolution in the Canadas it involved national as well as class factors. The "Montrealers'" demand for capitalist modernization of landed property relationships carried unmistakable overtones of anglicization: English land-speculators trying to get their hands on the seigneuries could scarcely appear as protagonists of either democracy or progress to the French-Canadian farm population. Massive British immigration, combined with the simultaneous drain of emigrants from the habitant farmlands to New England, accentuated national tension.

Yet the conflict of interest between seigneurs and censitaires had been sharpening as the exactions of the former grew more onerous. The Patriote demand for abolition of feudal burdens had played its part in the rebellions, and the reform movements of the 1840s and 50s put forward the demand insistently.

In the process of piecemeal reform that led to eventual abolition of the tenure (the imperial Acts of 1822 and 1825, the Canadian measures of 1840 and 1854), conflicting forces with often widely divergent aims were at work. They included the following:

—The seigneurial interest, resisting the demand for abolition of their privileges, and then, as mounting pressures rendered change inescapable, holding out for maximum compensation. The Church, as the biggest landowner, was a major source of resistance; but opponents of change included also the seigneur of Montebello: L. J. Papineau, making his notorious statement that "I am a great reformer as regards political change, but a great conservative as regards the preservation of the sacred right of property."

—Some seigneurs, particularly the "new," English ones with strong merchant-capitalist ties, strove to have the tenure modified so as to turn what were originally feudal holdings-in-trust into the outright ownership of capitalist real-estate. Thus Ellice, seigneur of Beauharnois, inspired the Tenures Act of 1825 allowing the seigneurs to buy off the feudal rights of the Crown and become absolute owners of the ungranted part of their seigneuries. Few at the time took advantage of the measure but the aim of making the unconceded lands the outright property of the seigneurs became a central preoccupation a quarter-century later.*

—The Anglo-Canadian mercantile and industrial community urged abolition of the tenure (with "due compensation"), both in order to extend the scope of profitable land speculation and to remove impediments to industrial expansion.† The needs of modernization required the breaking down of social institutions and structures that stood in the way of mobility of capital investment and enlargement of the home market: the seigneuries being the stronghold of survivals of a self-sufficient, non-commercial, "natural" economy.

—The seigneuries also came to be identified, in the eyes of some, with the institutions and way of life of the French-Canadian community itself: hence a feeling that an essential condition of English capitalist progress was "putting down the French," and that abolishing the seigneurial tenure logically entailed the de-nationalizing

---

*In addition to Ellice, other English holders of seigneuries included Peter Pangman (Lachenaye), Simon McTavish (Terrebonne), Caldwell (Lauzon), Grant (Beauharnois): it is estimated that by the mid-19th century from a third to half of the seigneurs were English Canadian.

†The 1840 legislation provided for commutation into absolute property of the seigneurial holdings of the Sulpician Seminary on the Island of Montreal: these immensely valuable estates were thus transmuted into a modern business investment.

of the habitant. (Thus, Sewell, in 1801: "The Englishman detests the feudal tenure . . ."; Durham's Report, *passim*; Jacques Boucher, in 1964: ". . . maintenance of the seigneurial régime is one of the prime causes of the presence in Quebec today of more than four million French Canadians . . .")

—Despite the foregoing factor (to which seigneurial and clerical influences undoubtedly contributed) the strongest element was the French Canadians' opposition, expressed in the mass anti-seigneurial campaign of the censitaires and the middle-class radical democrats.*

From 1830 onward a "revolutionary wind" is rising, and anti-seigneurial agitation continues after the risings. Moses Hart refers in 1842 to "a great clamor . . . against the seigneurs"; the Institut Canadien, formed in 1844, gives leadership to a widespread campaign against the tenure. In response to its appeal, some 32,700 persons sign petitions calling for reform or abolition of the system. An "Anti-seigneurial convention" brings together 120 delegates from across the province to pursue the campaign of agitation. LaFontaine at this point comes out strongly in favor of full indemnity to the seigneurs; seeing in the popular movement a threat to the social order, he argues in the Assembly:

---

*The hitherto much-neglected role of the popular movement has been strongly brought out in Professor Georges Baillargeon's study, "La tenure seigneuriale a-t-elle ete abolie par suite des Plaintes des Censitaires?" (RHAF, juin 1967). He concludes that the Act of 1854 "was adopted as a result of the complaints and petitions of the people, which were provoked mainly by the exactions, considered abusive at the time, on the part of certain seigneurs, chiefly English-speaking and in the Montreal region . . . these exactions had raised a clamor such as no statesmen or government could resist . . ."

I am indebted to M. Baillargeon for providing me with the reference to Elgin's significant statement in London, cited below.

> Delay gives new occasion for the propagation of principles which tend to overturn society . . . as the seigneurs form the smallest number, they may expect to lose everything without compensation . . . I see the march of events: it is the struggle of the masses against the few. The masses are beginning to become indignant . . .

The demand that the censitaires should not have to bear the load of buying off rights that were largely a usurpation in any case, was seen by LaFontaine's biographer as a "pretension which verges on socialist and revolutionary aspirations, recalling Proudhon's famous maxim, 'property is theft'."

Lord Elgin also, as the agitation continued into the early 1850s, exerted pressure against any confiscatory move. In London with Hincks to negotiate a loan for the Grand Trunk, Elgin sought to reassure English investors that it was safe to invest in Canada: that having been granted responsible government the colonists would surely not throw away what they had won, by any "measure of spoliation" directed against seigneurial property . . .

Back in Canada, Elgin exerted pressure, first to delay, then to have drastically altered, a bill that would have restored to the Crown the ungranted part of seigneurial lands. The measure that finally passed in 1854, under the new tory-liberal coalition (precursor of the Macdonald-Cartier grouping), satisfied both the seigneurs and the London bankers. The unconceded lands became outright property of the seigneurs, who also were to receive some $10 million in compensation for loss of feudal privileges; while the censitaires were permitted to pay off the cens et rentes in a lump sum or over an extended period (the latter was the choice of most, and lasted until 1940.)

Settlement of the seigneurial tenure and clergy reserves

questions represented one kind of land reform. "Extinction of the Indian title" was quite another. In the former instances, generous compensation was paid for the surrender of feudal privileges, and the seigneurs acquired, scot-free, in outright ownership, the unceded lands they held in trust. The Indians, first occupants of these territories, were less fortunate. To loss of their lands through a colossal operation of fraud and legalized theft was added the disruption of their economy, livelihood and culture.*

Having been made wholly dependent on the fur trade during two centuries or more of European colonialism, the Indian peoples found themselves defenseless when the trade closed down in the east-central areas and settlement surged westward in the area of the Great Lakes and then the Prairie. In his study of Indian life in the upper Great Lakes G. I. Quimby notes that by the time of the British Conquest "every Indian in the region was in some way dependent upon the fur trade and thus in a sense was working for the white men." With the ending of the trade in the area, "The Indians were left without a livelihood. They no longer had the means of purchasing their supplies, and much of their old way of life was lost to them." Only in the northern marginal areas could the trap-line and the hunt continue to provide subsistence.

In the south, lands assigned by the British authorities to the Six Nations, the Mississauga, the Ojibway and others were rapidly reduced to a fraction of their initial area. The Grand River tract "shrank" from an initial 570,000 acres to less than 50,000. According to the testimony of the Indian Agent before an inquiry in 1839, the sale of land by the Six Nations took place under the most unfavorable conditions: "It is certain that the considera-

---

*Cf. "The Theft of Indian Lands," in *The Founding of Canada*, Ch. XXVII.

tion paid for it was for the most part merely of temporary benefit to them." As Ella Cork has pointed out, "the Six Nations lacked any corporate structure in which the ownership of land could be vested . . ." Deprived of the legal possibility of leasing their lands, and denied all sovereignty over them, the dwellers on the Grand Rivert Tract were placed at a permanent disadvantage, which contributed not a little to their impoverishment.

Bond Head envisaged a kind of *apartheid* policy aimed at expelling the Indians from all southern areas and isolating them in the north; for which purpose he acquired the whole of Manitoulin Island and the islands of Georgian Bay, "without spending one penny of compensation." This "transplanting" operation was not carried through, however, due to the Rebellion intervening and also to missionary protests. Later, the Lake Huron Ojibway under the Treaty of 1850 secured the payment of an annuity (maximum, £1 per person), in lieu of the traditional practice of giving "presents" as a means of securing their allegiance to the Crown.

Having been used to good advantage in the military operations of 1812-14, at Detroit, in the Niagara Peninsula and elsewhere, the Indians were rewarded in an odd manner; in the words of a contemporary, "their unlimited service is requited by depriving them of their possessions." The system of present-giving was gradually discontinued. When in 1846 the Canadian Assembly urged that the system be maintained in view of the solemn pledges made to the Indians by the British authorities, Earl Grey replied that there was no record of any pledge: "I can, therefore, only look upon this as a question of policy, and as such, I am constrained to state that neither on the ground of securing the defence of the province against external enemies, nor on the ground of the interest of the Indians themselves, can I regard it as desirable to depart from the intention of effecting a gradual reduction of these presents."

The assumption by the Canadian bourgeoisie of the powers of local self-government in this period included the taking over of administration of Indian Affairs. This was effected formally in 1860. Much earlier, however, the colonial ruling class had made its own the chauvinist Anglo-Saxon "superiority" attitudes that shaped the governing of the "native" peoples. Refusal of equality in individual civil rights went hand in hand with denial of respect for the ethnic identity of a community. When democratic pressures made themselves felt in this area, grudging concessions were made contingent on a renunciation of identity.

Peter Jones, the Ojibway missionary, had written in the 1830s of the Indians' desire "to be recognized as British subjects, and to be admitted to full participation in the rights and privileges of Britons"; and the Patriotes and Reformers had both taken their stand against discrimination and for equality and civil rights for Indians. But the colonial regime neither acceded to these demands nor recognized the claims to Indian sovereignty and self-government. In the year of "the first Indian Affairs legislation"—the 1839 *Act for the Protection of the Lands of the Crown* . . . —it had been stated bluntly by Chief Justice Macaulay "that the Indian had no claims to separate nationality."* The Act of 1857, while systematizing the

---

*Cf. the official declaration of a half-century later: "It is extremely inexpedient to deal with the Indian bands in the Dominion (except those inhabiting the territories acquired by the Hudson's Bay Co.) as being in any way separate nations . . . The great aim of our legislation has been to do away with the tribal system and assimilate the Indian people in all respects with the other inhabitants of the Dominion . . ." (Parliamentary Investigating Committee, 1887.)

tutelage in which the Indians were held, for the first time undertook to eliminate legal distinctions by offering an "enfranchisement" whose price was erasure of Indian identity: "any Indian so declared to be enfranchised . . . shall no longer be deemed an Indian . . ." This humiliating proviso was to remain for the succeeding century. Forcible assimilation, repudiation of identity, surrender of treaty rights—such was the "reward" for the Indian's accession to "equality." Little wonder that so few availed themselves of the offer. The resolve to maintain an identity as a people, to hold fast even to such slight security as the remnant of communal lands in the "reserve" provided, proved stronger than the "democratic" blandishment.

In a few cases in the east-central area, Indians resisted the despoilment of land-speculators and the despotic rule of the Indian Department. This happened on Manitoulin.

The Report of a special committee on Affairs of the Indians in Canada (1856) had noted that sometimes the Indians, "feeling the pressure of the tide of emigration, refuse to cede a part of their possessions for fear of being deprived of the whole." This unwillingness to surrender their territory "has been greatly increased by the losses they have suffered . . . they have ceded very large tracts of very valuable land without receiving one penny of compensation; and it will not be until these losses have been somewhat repaired, that we can expect them to give up voluntarily more of their reserves."

On Manitoulin Island in the summer of 1863 a demonstration of defiance on the part of some three hundred Indians confronted a police expedition sent from Toronto to impose a treaty for surrender of their lands. The force, whose mission was "to endeavor to arrest the aiders and abettors of the Indian revolt in these islands," came "armed with implements of death . . . to put in irons those opposed to surrender. The Indians were considered as rebels opposing the Government because they would not give up their land to be sold to white people!" After a brief resistance, "with billets of wood and staves, when attacked by men with revolvers," some of their leaders, including one Sawamackoo, were arrested. The resistance, however, led to a portion of the Island being left in Indian hands.

The dispossession of the Indian peoples in the Province of Canada was for the most part effected through fraud disguised as purchase, and coercion disguised as paternal solicitude. Sporadic and few were the efforts to halt the slow erosion. Only in the North West, in conjunction with the Métis, was there to be open resistance.

15

The Natural Sciences

It was the challenging task of traversing and taking inventory of an immense territory that gave the first impetus to science in the Canadas. Despite colonial restrictions that hampered growth, the pressure of an expanding capitalist industry combined with the stimulus of the great 19th century advances in science to overcome obstacles to progress.

First, in geography: the work of David Thompson, surveyor and map-maker, is the outstanding but not the sole example of the large contributions to scientific knowledge that were the by-product of the fur trade. In Arctic exploration Canadian fur-traders like Mackenzie and Rae were joined by British naval men like Franklin, Parry, Ross and McClintock, serving the imperial interest in the search for a Northwest Passage. With the forced retreat of the Hudson's Bay Company, Hind, Dawson, Palliser surveyed the western prairie.

As had been the case under the French regime, hand in hand with the mapping of terrain came early studies of its plant and animal life. Thus, in the course of his work with the overland expeditions led by Franklin, Dr. John Richardson collected materials on wild life in the Canadian far north (published as an appendix to Franklin's *Narrative*, 1832, and also under the title, *Fauna of N. America*).

In Upper Canada in the 1820s and '30s, Charles Fothergill of Port Hope compiled descriptions of over a hundred species of birds of the Lake Ontario region; and a paper by Dr. Anthony Gapper, who lived north of Toronto, appeared in the English Journal of Zoology (1830), containing data on mammals of the area—including the first published reports of the northern grey squirrel and the mole shrew.

In Lower Canada, the Natural History Society of Montreal had been founded in 1827. An active participant in its work was Philip Gosse, who in 1840 published *The Canadian Naturalist*, an illustrated work built around a month-by-month study of the changing climate, vegetation and wild-life of the area of the Eastern Townships.

Discoveries relating to the earth's magnetic properties drew attention to Canada at an early date. Sir James Ross, leading a naval expedition in the Arctic in 1831, located the north magnetic pole in Boothia Peninsula.* The Admiralty was considering the establishment of an observatory in Canada (there was none as yet in this hemisphere) when in 1836 the great German scientist Alexander von Humboldt advanced a proposal for a worldwide study of terrestrial magnetism. This project (in a sense a forerunner of the recent International Geophysical Year) was taken up by the British Royal Society; observation posts included St. Helena, Cape of Good Hope, Van Diemen's land (Tasmania) and Fort York (Toronto). This Canadian magnetic station later became the University of Toronto observatory. In the course of the survey J. H. Lefroy, a young English artilleryman, took magnetic observations as far north as Fort Good Hope on the Mackenzie River. He covered 6,000 miles, and during one entire

---

*The position of the magnetic pole is not constant: it is at present several degrees farther north and west on Prince of Wales Island.

six-month period, with the help of one assistant, register-
ed observations every hour.

While this work was proceeding on the earth's magnetic field, beginnings were also being made in study of
the rock-foundations and mineral deposits in the Canadas and the Maritimes. Dr. John Bigsby, former army
doctor who served on the Boundary Commission set up
by the Treaty of Ghent (1814), produced in 1820 a map
and "Notes on the Topography and Geological Structures
of the North West Portion of Lake Huron"— one of the
first geological maps of North America, and in fact
among the earliest made anywhere in the world. Other
surveys published a few years later by army engineers included studies of the geology of Lake Superior, Gaspé
Peninsula and south-eastern Labrador. This pioneer work
prepared the way for what was undoubtedly the outstanding achievement in science in pre-Confederation Canada:
the great geological survey by Logan and his assistants,
extending over the years 1842-69.

William Logan (1798-1875) was born in Montreal and
educated in Scotland; his early work in geology was done
in the Glamorganshire coal-fields of Wales. In 1842 he
was appointed geologist for the Province of Canada. The
task confronting him was immense: to chart the whole
rock-structure of the Province of Canada, only small portions of which had so far been examined. With wholly
inadequate funds (he frequently had to draw on his own
resources), with no provision by the government of
laboratory facilities or equipment, and with the help of
only one or two assistants, Logan surveyed some 100,000
square miles of rock-formations. Because of the deficiencies of early maps it was necessary, Logan wrote, "even in
surveyed parts, to count and register our paces over every
road and line we go, taking the bearings by prismatic

compass, and registering in its proper place every rock seen, with its dip and strike, and a short description of its character, and its economic and fossil contents, if it have any." In his earlier researches in Wales Logan had depended greatly on the help of the experienced coal miners; now in Canada he recorded a similar debt: "I am scarcely ever a day in the field in the settled parts of the country without getting a considerable amount of information from farmers and common laborers, particularly among such as are not haunted by the notion that all our researches have the precious metals for their object." Perseverance, single-minded devotion to his work, and concern for the advancement of his country were among Logan's chief characteristics.

It was he who discovered and made the initial maps of the ancient Canadian Shield, and named the Laurentian and Huronian systems of rock-formation. In 1863 he published the *Geology of Canada*, prepared jointly with his assistant Sterry Hunt, and in 1869 the large-scale geological map of Canada, which was one of the most complete and advanced of any such maps published anywhere. Logan's Geological Survey helped prepare the way for the big development in mining that came in the 20th century.

He himself conceived of his work as "economic researches, carried out in a scientific way"; and emphasized: *"The object of the Survey is to ascertain the mineral resources of the country . . ."* Logan approached his task as one of national development; he had no sympathy with stock-promoters and speculators obsessed with their own personal profit. The "vast stores of mineral materials" contained in Canada's subsoil, he wrote, "would hereafter become available for the support of native industry." And, of Canada: "It will become a great country hereafter." The English *Saturday Review* commented on the precision and perseverance which marked Logan's work, and went on to say: "No other Colonial Survey has ever yet assumed the same truly national character"— and surmised that should Canada one day "claim and obtain independence," the name of the Canadian William Logan would be honored by "the scientific public of a great nation, looking back upon the earlier dawnings of science in their land."

Next to that of Logan stands the name of the Nova Scotian, Dr. Abraham Gesner (1797-1864), surgeon, chemist, geologist. He made extensive studies of the geology and mineral resources of Nova Scotia, publishing a report on them in 1836. He was commissioned in 1838 to make a geological survey of New Brunswick, and in 1846 of Prince Edward Island. In 1849 he published a study with the ample title: "*The Industrial Resources of Nova Scotia*, comprehending the Physical Geography, Topography, Geology, Agriculture, Fisheries, Mines, Forests, Wild Lands, Lumbering, Manufactories, Navigation, Commerce, Emigration, Improvements, Industry, Contemplated Railways, Natural History and Resources of the Province." The Doctor was as good as his word. All of it is in the book—as well as an impassioned protest against colonial impediments to industrial development. "The manufactories of Nova Scotia," he wrote, "have been chiefly confined to the simple operations of sawing wood . . . No general effort has been made to encourage our own manufactures in preference to those of a foreign power . . ."*

Abraham Gesner is best remembered as the discoverer of kerosene (coal oil). He developed the process of dis-

---

*On his exposure of the crippling of the early Nova Scotian iron industry at the hands of U.S. interests, see above, ch. xi.

tilling this fuel oil from petroleum in 1852, and organized a company that supplied kerosene lighting for homes and streets in Halifax and Dartmouth. His work helped lay the foundation for the modern oil-refining industry. (His patents were acquired in 1874—by Standard Oil.)

Hand in hand with the industrial revolution there came what in fact amounted to a revolution in human thought: the founding of modern natural science. The needs of the textile and metalworking industries, of mining and engineering and agriculture, of transport and sanitation—all combined to call forth a series of scientific discoveries. Some of the most far-reaching in their effects were: the discovery of the *cell* as the unit of structure and growth in living beings (1839); the transformation of different forms of energy from one into another—mechanical, thermal, chemical, electrical (1842); and the origin and evolution of species (1859). As a result of these and other findings, "the main processes of nature were explained and referred to natural causes"; moreover, "natural science itself . . . was transformed . . . into a system of the materialist knowledge of nature." (Engels)

Colonial Canada was only on the outer fringes of this scientific upheaval, centred in Europe. But there were a few scattered points of contact that are of interest.

The idea that *nature has a history* was one of the most important ideas to come out of the revolution in science. And it was geology, the study of the structure of the earth and the records fossil-filed in successively superimposed strata of rock, that gave the strongest impetus to this new approach. Of Charles Lyell, the founder of modern geological science, Engels wrote that he "first

brought sense into geology by substituting for the sudden
revolutions due to the moods of the creator the gradual
effects of a slow transformation of the earth." (*Introduction, Dialectics of Nature*). Lyell visited Nova Scotia in
1842; in his *Manual of Geology* he noted: "One of the
finest examples in the world of a succession of fossil forests of the carboniferous period, laid open to view in a
natural section, is that seen in the lofty cliffs bordering
the Chignecto Channel, a branch of the Bay of Fundy."
(p. 321) *

Recognition of the fact that there had taken place a
"gradual transformation of the earth's surface and of all
conditions of life led directly to gradual transformation
of the organisms and their adaptation to the changing environment, to the mutability of species."† It was Darwin who supplied the proof that this in fact was what
took place. His *Origin of Species,* published Nov. 24,
1859, was a landmark in the history of science. On Dec. 12
Engels was writing to Marx: "Darwin, whom I am now
reading, is really splendid . . . Never before has so grand
an attempt been made to demonstrate historical development in nature, and with such success."

In February 1860 the *Origin of Species* was being advertised for sale in Montreal. The *Canadian Naturalist*
(vol. 5, p. 80) that month carried a notice, which stated
that the work "deals with questions of Natural History in

---

*In the same work Lyell paid tribute to Logan's earlier discovery
relating to the so-called underclays that accompany the coal seams:
"Mr. Logan first announced to the scientific world in 1841 that they
were regarded by the colliers in South Wales as an essential accompaniment of each of the one hundred seams met with in their coal-
field . . . All of them, as Mr. Logan pointed out, are characterized
by inclosing a peculiar species of fossil vegetable called *stigmaria*, to
the exclusion of other plants." (p. 310)

†*Dialectics of Nature*, p. 39

*Cf. Darwin's Black Box, Michael Behe, for a
refutation of Darwin's theory.*

a way most masterly and profound. That its views will meet with much opposition is to be expected. Few will be disposed to go to the sweeping lengths to which our author is disposed to go in the logical issue of his theory. It promises to create quite a furor in the minds of scientific enquirers." If the Montreal naturalists' journal showed signs of hedging, it was at least correct in its prediction of a "furor" of opposition. Soon outraged articles were appearing, penned by obscurantists of various hues, ranging from theologians to professors of science. William Dawson, principal of McGill, for instance, was "an uncompromising opponent of the more advanced school of scientific writers represented by such men as Darwin, Wallace, Huxley and Haeckel . . ."

Reactionary attitudes, however firmly entrenched, were unable to withstand the pressure for the inclusion of scientific subjects in school and university curricula. The needs of infant industry, the rise of manufacturing towns, the growth of medicine, the application of science to agriculture, all demanded it. Even that staunch upholder of Church control of education, Dr. Strachan, had secured the passage in Upper Canada of a measure—in 1806—for "the purchase of instruments for illustrating the principles of Natural Philosophy": to be used in a private school.

In 1833 the first Canadian text-book on chemistry was published in Montreal; it was by the French-Canadian educator J. B. Meilleur, and bore the title *Cours abrégè de Leçons de Chymie.* Two years later the Quebec Seminary decided that chemistry should be taught as a separate subject (distinct from philosophy). The first institution in the Maritimes to introduce science courses was the University of New Brunswick, in 1836. One of its professors (of chemistry, botany and biology) was James

Robb, M.C.; he actively promoted an interest in scientific agriculture, and conducted extension courses on it throughout the province. His outstanding published work was: *Agricultural Progress, an Outline of the Course of Improvement in Agriculture—with Special Reference to New Brunswick.*

In Upper Canada, the resistance of the Family Compact to secular education had held up for close to two decades the launching of the University of Toronto; science teaching started there only in 1843. Chemistry was one of the four original departments, and Henry H. Croft—recommended by the great English physicist, Faraday—was the first to head it. He not only inspired enthusiasm in his subject and in science generally; he also fought actively against the obscurantists who were still seeking to impose a clerical monopoly on higher education. A few years later, the celebrated Thomas Huxley applied for a post on the staff at Toronto: he was turned down. (The position went to a brother of the then Premier, Francis Hincks.) In the field of primary education, Egerton Ryerson's 1846 *Report on a System of Public Primary Elementary Instruction for Upper Canada* called for the inclusion in the curriculum of physiology, elements of chemistry and mechanics, and agriculture; and for the creation together with the school library, of a school museum.

By the early 1850s Laval University at Quebec was giving courses in "natural philosophy" (physics and chemistry) and "natural science" (botany and zoology). T. S. Hunt, who worked with Logan on the great geological survey, taught chemistry and mineralogy for ten years at Laval. (It was he, incidentally, who developed the green chromium-oxide ink for use on bank-notes— "green-backs.")

In 1856 the government of the United Province of Canada offered prizes for studies on "the weevil, Hessian fly midge and such other insects as have made ravages on the wheat crops in Canada, and on such diseases as the wheat crops have been subjected to, and on the best means of evading or guarding against them." The prize-winning essay was written by Henry Y. Hind, professor of chemistry and geology at Trinity College, Toronto. A few years later the first Entomological Society was organized.

Thus the 1840s and 50s witnessed the fairly active beginnings of education in the sciences. When one considers that Harvard established its school of science in 1849, and that it was two decades later that Oxford and Cambridge took similar action, it would seem that British North America, despite its colonial handicaps, was not doing badly. This early scientific interest and activity, spurred by the challenge of the vast expanse and rich resources of its territory, and pioneered by men like Logan, Gesner, Robb and others, laid the groundwork for solid achievement in the century that lay ahead.

It is no accident that the upsurge in the natural sciences occurred in the period of early industrialization. The beginnings of steam-power, machine industry and the harnessing of electricity meant a radically new extension of man's mastery of the natural environment, in production and communications. Both national communities were affected by what Léon Lortie has described as "the extraordinary climate of scientific curiosity that reigned in Montreal and Quebec during the period extending from about 1820 to 1850 . . ." The same writer refers to the "era of Confederation" as the time when "science managed to assert itself in the country." It was, of course, likewise the era in which a Canadian capitalist industry, asserting its presence, engendered a political state structure of its own.

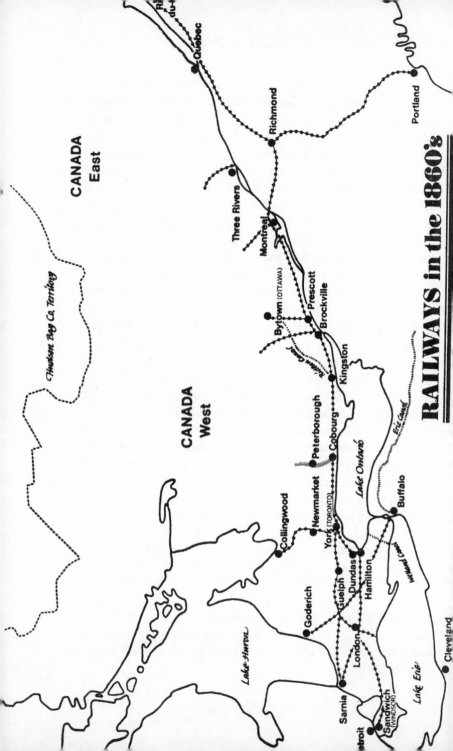

RAILWAYS in the 1860's

CANADA East

CANADA West

Hudson Bay Co. Territory

Quebec
Portland
Richmond
Three Rivers
Montreal
Bytown (OTTAWA)
Prescott
Brockville
Kingston
Peterborough
Cobourg
Lake Ontario
Collingwood
Newmarket
York (TORONTO)
Goderich
Guelph
Dundas
Hamilton
Buffalo
Erie Canal
Welland Canal
Sarnia
London
Sandwich (WINDSOR)
Detroit
Lake Huron
Lake Erie
Cleveland

PART THREE

COLONIAL UNIFICATION

16

"A Great Country May be Raised Up . . ."

Confederation of the British North American colonial provinces took place when it did because of two main pressures. One came from the growth of a native capitalist industry, with railway transport as its backbone, and expansion of the home market as the prime motive for creating a unified and autonomous state. The other sprang from an imperial strategy that required unification not only in order to preserve the colonies from United States absorption, but also to strengthen a link of Empire reaching to the Pacific and hence to the approaches to Asia.

The "problematic" of colonial union embraced three areas of difficulty: geographic, economic, ethnic. (After a century, they still bedevil the contemporary scene.) Let us look at each in turn:

First, a physical geography that was fostering an intense regionalism. Westward, between the Province of Canada and the trading posts on the Pacific, lay the all-but-unexplored wilderness of the rockbound Shield, the unsettled prairie and the peaks of the Cordillera—the closed domain of the Hudson's Bay Company. To the east, the great wedge of the Appalachian Highlands thrust between the St. Lawrence Valley and the Maritimes, while access to the sea from central Canada was blocked for close to half the year by ice in the river and Gulf of St. Lawrence.

An English visitor in the early 1860s cites a Canadian complaint about the Gulf: "Pity it's friz up so long. We

wouldn't envy the Yankees anything they've got to show
us if we had a port open all the year"— and the author
comments: "For the first time I began to feel sympathy
for a country that 'Can't get out' for five mortal months,
and that breathes through another man's nostrils and
mouth. No wonder the Canadians look longingly over at
that bit of land which Lord Ashburton yielded to the
United States and the State of Maine." The thirteen colonies had been neighboring communities strung out along
a common seacoast; the British provinces were isolated
pockets of population in the corners of a continent. Their
unification required at a minimum the kind of material
interconnection that railways alone could provide. (Yet
even these were barely to poke in the direction of the
great North, at a few rare spots; the last third of the 20th
century opened with the Arctic immensity almost untouched and the shores of our third ocean practically "another
country" to Canadians.)

Next, the relatively weak development of industrial
capitalism (as compared with the neighboring United
States): a side-effect of the condition of colonialism.
Hence the inadequate economic underpinning for the
huge railway construction projects, the chronic crises in
financing the Grand Trunk, the dependence on the London banking houses; and the corresponding political sub-
servience to (and frustration over) the fluctuations of policy at the Colonial Office. The Canadian bourgeoisie were
becoming just strong enough to assert their presence and
press for solutions in their own interest, but were too weak
still to call in question imperial dominance itself. Requir-
ing a state of their own, under their control, capable of
providing a favorable framework for the home market
and for securing advantageous terms for borrowing abroad,
they found it difficult to forge a unity of will and pur-

pose: geographic dispersal, uneven population growth, the inherited colonial state structure of the "United" Province of Canada and of the Atlantic provinces, all posed problems. But the largest one, and the one least consistently faced up to, was the "internal" national question.

Two historically constituted national communities—two nations—dwelt side by side in British North America, occupying distinct territories: the French Canadians, situated in a central position on the St. Lawrence, and flanked by separate, less homogeneous English-speaking populations living in Upper Canada, part of the Montreal and Eastern Townships area, and the Atlantic provinces. The striving of the French Canadians to maintain and strengthen their national identity demanded recognition, whatever the form of state to be considered. This striving in turn was countered by the efforts of those in English Canada (and in London) who could think in no other terms than those of "Anglo-Saxon" dominance over the "conquered" French. National cleavage was an overriding reality, and the course of the struggles that filled the century after 1763 had deepened rather than lessened the division. The fact that the colonial provinces were already "united" by imperial suzerainty (operating through the Colonial Office and the Governor-General), long before they were able to establish a unified state machinery of their own; and the further fact that the predominantly French-Canadian territory of "Canada East" being (under the Union of 1840) integrally part of the united Province of Canada, possessed neither real autonomy nor effective political identity—all this combined to deprive the French-Canadian nation of even the semblance of a footing of equality from which to negotiate the terms of any new union.

The idea of a union of the British colonial provinces in North America dates from the close of the American revolutionary war. It is important to note, however, that the proposals for union made at various times embodied widely different and even opposing strategic aims, ranging from reinforcement of imperial rule to its complete elimination and the achievement of independence.

Thus when William Smith, the Tory Loyalist Chief Justice of New York (and later of Quebec), proposed in 1783 "a general Government for the colonies" it was as a means of strengthening the imperial grip and staving off possible moves toward independence on the part of the Canadians. The Colonial Office at that time took a dim view of the idea of a general union. "Divide and rule" seemed a more prudent policy in the light of the recent revolutionary upheaval. J. H. Gray, a New Brunswick representative at the Confederation conferences, explained in these terms the view held by the imperial authorities in the late 18th century:

> The strength acquired by the union of the thirteen United States indicated . . . future dismemberment and severance of the remaining Colonies, should they be allowed to coalesce too much. New Brunswick was separated from Nova Scotia; the two Canadas were divided; Cape Breton was constitued a distinct government; Prince Edward Island . . . retained its old isolation, and Newfoundland was made a post captain's appointment. Separate governments, separate parliaments, different laws, and hostile tariffs fostered local prejudice and created divergent interests.

Although the policy of "divide and rule" prevailed for more than half a century, the alternative idea of a unified machinery designed to uphold the "British connection" cropped up intermittently: at times in answer to the threat of United States expansionism, at times as a means of securing English-Canadian dominance and the suppression of French-Canadian identity and rights.

In 1826 R. J. Uniacke, Attorney-General of Nova Scotia, submitted his "Observations on the British Colonies in North America, with a Proposal for the Confederation of the whole under one Government." This proposal (like a similar one made the year before by the Chief Justice, Brenton Haliburton) cited the danger of absorption by the United States, and the need to strengthen the Empire; but it made no reference to any distinct Canadian or Maritime interests or needs.

A different, if related, approach to the idea of union aimed at the suppression of French-Canadian rights and nationality. Inasmuch as the 1791 division of the old Quebec into Lower and Upper Canada, and the granting of Assemblies, had enabled the French Canadians to assert their national identity and press for equality of rights, the Montreal English merchants now sought to reimpose the relationships of conquest and the recognition of Anglo-Saxon dominance. The projects of Union put forward by Chief Justice Jonathan Sewell in 1810, and by Lord John Russell in the Union Bill of 1822, both aimed at stifling "French pretensions" and imposing "British ascendancy." Having been blocked by popular opposition in Lower Canada in 1822, the project was brought forward afresh in Russell's "coercion resolutions" in the summer of 1837. Then, once the Rebellions had been crushed, the reactionary imperial-mercantile aims found fulfilment in the Act of Union of 1840. Strengthening imperial rule, "putting down the French," curbing democracy, all were served by the Union; and all were challenged by the forces of Reform, self-government and national rights. Among the

national-democratic elements there was taking shape a
radically different approach to the idea of possible union:
one founded on the primacy of the interests and needs of
the colonists themselves. This approach envisioned the
sort of all-round development that had been suggested as
early as 1784 by Col. Robert Morse, reporting on a survey
of the defenses of Nova Scotia:

> My mind has been strongly impressed with the idea of
> uniting these provinces with Canada, to the advantage of
> both countries, and that by establishing the same laws,
> inducing a constant intercourse and mutual interest, a
> great country may yet be raised up in North America.

In 1824 W. L. Mackenzie in the *Colonial Advocate* put
forward the idea of a confederation of the two colonies,
as a step toward their achievement of an independent existence. In the same year he wrote to Canning at Westminster, proposing federation. He argued the theme in the
Colonial Advocate:

> There is only one way in which the home manufacture
> could be benefitted, and that is, by inducing people of
> capital to emigrate hither and to consider it their home
> when they are here, by giving the colonies a constitution
> of their own choosing. . . .
> A union of all the colonies, with a government suitably
> poised and modelled so as to have under its eye the
> resources of our whole territory and having the means in
> its power to administer impartial justice in all its bounds,
> to no one part at the expense of another, would require
> few boons from Britain.

Two years later Robert Gourlay wrote from an English
prison setting forth a scheme for confederation of the
provinces, "each to be as free within itself as any of the
United States and the whole to hold Congress at Quebec."

(He suggested as well that the confederacy be represented at Westminster, with voice but not with vote.)

The revolutionary democrats of 1837-38 sought the formation of a republic in each of the two Canadas, looking to a voluntary union that might embrace the Atlantic provinces as well. This vision of a Canadian people's republic was to remain a dream. The revolution having been defeated, a different and more tortuous path was taken. The industrial and railroad capitalists and their political spokesmen became the architects of a united Canadian state; its achievement was the work not of a people's uprising but of legislative deadlock and complicated negotiation; the result of the expansive power of capitalist industry, and a long-drawn struggle of conflicting forces within the provinces and on an international scale.

Lord Durham, exploring the possibilities of a British North American federation, had convened a meeting for consultation with officials from the Maritimes in 1838: but the matter was not pursued. The first gathering of representatives of the separate provinces to deal with practical measures was a conference on postal communications, held in Montreal in 1847. It presaged further moves toward a closer linking of the provinces. The 1849 convention of the conservative British American League (in which John A. Macdonald took part) unanimously adopted a resolution favoring a union of the provinces of British North America. The Montreal *Gazette* supported the idea: "A union of the provinces would give the colonists practical independence, so much desired, and remove the idea of annexation now existing among many influential persons."

In 1851 the leading Upper Canada merchant and industrialist, W. H. Merritt, moved a resolution in the Assembly calling for consideration of the question of a federal union. His resolution proposed that the Governor-General be authorized "to call a convention of delegates of the inhabitants of British North America to be composed of forty persons to be elected in proportion to population . . ." The resolution was defeated. Three years later Merritt wrote: "I have long since made up my mind that the inhabitants of Canada require a new constitution, one selected by delegates . . . from different parts of the Province, adapted for our peculiar situation, which the Imperial Government would readily sanction."

The call for a new constitution became insistent as population and economic activity increased while deadlock hardened in the legislature, with "Representation by Population" now a thorny issue. The 1851 census had shown the population of Canada West to comprise a majority in the Province of Canada, but the legislature was still constructed on the old principle of equal representation for the two sections of the province: an arrangement held to be wholly satisfactory so long as the English-speaking western section comprised a minority, but clearly insufferable now that the population balance was reversed! "Rep. by Pop." was clearly enough a democratic axiom, and with the winning of cabinet responsibility the pressures for democratization were enhanced rather than reduced. Yet equal rights for the two national communities that together had won responsible government was equally clearly a democratic principle. Moreover since 1848 it had been recognized in practice; in its operation the legislative union had subtly acquired a *de facto* federal character. Dual prime-ministerships, the principle of "double majority," and official maintenance of the distinction between "Canada East" and "Canada West," all showed this clearly. But with the shift in population whereby Canada West outnumbered its neighbor the "bi-national" and "federal" balance was subjected to un-manageable pressures. Canada West raised a larger part of the revenues, but these had to be divided equally between the two sections. Growing rivalry between the Toronto and Montreal capitalist groups aggravated the friction. George Brown's demand for "Rep. by Pop." meant submerging the French Canadians in an assembly where they would constitute a permanent minority, with no safeguards for their national identity or rights. Yet the existing set-up manifestly could not be maintained indefinitely.

To meet part way the demand of Brown and the Canada West Liberals, A. A. Dorion in 1856 countered with a proposal "to Substitute for the present Legislative union a Confederation of the two Canadas." (The Toronto Reform Convention, three years later, was to return to this proposal.)

In 1857 the conservative journalist J. C. Taché published a series of articles on "The North American Provinces and a Federal Union"; after appearing in *Le Courrier du Canada* they were published in book form. Having examined in detail the British and United States constitutions, the author urged the adoption of a "pact of Confederation"; this "federal pact would rest on the principle of perpetual and inevitable delegation to the general government of the powers of the separate governments of the provinces . . ."

Inherent in projects for the creation of a new British North American state was a growing sense of Canadian identity, and concern for the achievement of a political structure that would best embody national interests and aims. Although W. H. Merritt in 1851 had voiced regret that "we have not yet a sufficient growth of Canadian feeling to advocate any measure with no other motive than promoting the interest of Canada," changes of attitude were in the making. Symptomatic was a stirring lecture that Alexander Morris, a conservative lawyer, delivered in Montreal in 1858, on the future prospects of the Canadas. Nearly a decade before, at the age of 23, Morris had been one of the most ardent advocates of confederation in the British American League. He now painted a glowing picture of the rich resources and vast sweep of Canada. He urged his hearers to "boast a little of our country." He noted that the "instinct of nationality has been aroused. Already our people feel a patriotic pride in the growth of our infant country. It would be a wise policy to cherish and foster this feeling, to enlarge its bounds, to promote inter-colonial trade and other intercourse, to develop commerce and manufactures . . ." Morris spoke of the "formation of the national character"; he considered that the conditions for its emergence were "a widespread dissemination of a sound education—a steady maintenance of civil and religious liberty, and of freedom of speech and of thought, in the possession and enjoyment of all classes of the community. . . ." To the youth he declared:

> Here, you have a princely heritage before you. . . . Be true, then, to yourselves, and you cannot help rising with your country. Take a deeper interest in its affairs. . . . Cherish and promote by all means the spread of national sentiment. Familiarize yourself with all the interests of your country; and henceforth feel, if you have never felt before, that you have a country of which any people might be proud.

Alexander Morris envisioned a national-Canadian sense of identity that was already in the making. Was it, in fact, an *Anglo-Canadian* national spirit? *Le bonhomme s'exprima en anglais*: expressed in English, did this declaration of Canadian identity allow for national duality, for the presence of the "other" national community? The element of "Anglo-ambiguity" is not lessened by the title under which the Morris lecture was later published: *Nova Britannia; or Our New Canadian Dominion Foreshadowed* . . .

As against Dorion's proposal for a dual federal structure of the two Canadas, A. T. Galt in 1858 urged in the Assembly the creation of a wider federal union, to embrace Canada, the Maritimes and the Northwest Territories. He proposed "preserving to each province the . . . management of its peculiar institutions and . . . internal affairs," while promoting "that identity of feeling which pervades the possessions of the British crown in North America." Such a union "by the adoption of a uniform policy for the development of the vast and varied resources of these immense territories will greatly add to their national power and consideration." He emphasized both the opportunity, and the danger of losing it: "Such a thing has never occurred to any people as to have the offer of half a continent . . . the door should be opened to the young men of Canada to go into that country, otherwise the Americans would get there first."

Galt's resolutions did not even get put to a vote: they were sidetracked by the fall of one more of the precariously balanced ministries that were following each other down like ninepins. Shortly thereafter, however, Galt accepted office in the Cartier-Macdonald government on condition that it embody his federation proposals in its program. This was agreed to, and Cartier's statement of policy announced that the British government would be approached, and the other provinces invited to discuss "the principles upon which a bond of a federal character, uniting the provinces of North America, may perhaps . . . be practicable."

In line with this, Galt, Cartier, and John Ross were sent as a delegation to England to submit the proposals and urge the convening of a conference of all the provinces. Urging acceptance of the scheme, Galt told the Colonial Secretary, Lytton: "The question is simply one of Confederation . . . or of ultimate absorption in the United States." The imperial authorities, meeting the arguments of the Canadians with chilly indifference, declined to convene a conference.

Yet despite imperial indifference and domestic legislative deadlock, the expansive power of colonial industry continued to exert pressure on the cramped constitutional framework. The 1850s saw a marked growth of manufacturing, stimulated by the Crimean war and the attendant farm prosperity; but the backbone of the economic upsurge was the railway building boom. A workable, integrated economy in British North America linking the territory and population of the Canadas with the seaboard settlements and the ports of the Atlantic provinces would mean that the latter would acquire a hinterland and (it was hoped) an increased commerce; the former would be no longer, as E. P. Taché put it in the Confederation debate, "shut up in a prison, as it were, for five months of the year in fields of ice."

Galt in that debate pictured the mutual benefit that union would make possible: "One of the greatest . . . benefits to be derived from the union (of the provinces) will spring from the breaking down of these barriers, and the opening up of the markets of all provinces to the different industries of each. In this manner we may hope to supply Newfoundland and the great fishing districts of the Gulf with agricultural production of Western Canada, we may hope to obtain from Nova Scotia our supply of coal; and the manufacturing industry of Lower Canada may hope to find more extensive outlets in supplying many of these articles which are now purchased in foreign markets."

Galt voiced the general interests of capitalist development, albeit with the special overtones peculiar to the financial circles of Montreal. George Brown, chief spokesman for the Toronto element within the general capitalist interest, laid particular emphasis on the need to embrace the West in the new federation. Earlier, he had written in the *Globe*: "The opening up of the country belongs not to Great Britain, but to those who will benefit by it, to Canada." And again: "It is an empire we have in view, and its whole export and import trade will be concentrated in the hands of Canadian merchants and manufacturers if we strike for it now." The seriousness of the threat of U.S. expansion into the northwest was not disregarded: "If we let the West go to the United States, if the rest of the continent outside Canada and the Atlantic provinces acknowledges the sway of the Republic, we should be unable to contend with her. Our ultimate absorption would be inevitable."

For union to become a fact, not only had political obstacles to be overcome, but the material bond of railway communication had to be created—or at least firm decisions taken to that effect. Only the building of a railway between Halifax and Quebec would make union acceptable to the Maritimes; only the building of a transcontinental road would prevent the West from being swallowed by the United States. The overall requirements of capitalist industry and national development were brought into focus on this central need of an intercolonial and a Pacific railroad. To meet the need was beyond the capacity of the colonial capitalists alone. They turned once more to London. To the efforts of Galt and Macdonald, Cartier and Brown were now joined those of the imperial promoter, Edward Watkin.

Watkin was a colorful character who had come to the top in the fevered days of the "railway mania." In 1861 he had been sent to Canada as the representative of the English directors of the Grand Trunk. He reported that "the management of this railway is an organized mess—I will not say, a sink of iniquity." His solution to the Company's difficulties (wherein jobbery and corruption loomed large) was not retreat, but audacious advance —"the extension of railway communication to the Pacific." He noted that "the new gold fields on the Fraser River are attracting swarms of emigrants"; but his gaze extended far beyond the West coast, embracing a "China opened to British commerce; Japan . . . India, our Australian colonies—all our Eastern Empire." He visualized, crossing the continent, a "main through Railway, of which the first thousand miles belong to the Grand Trunk Company." "The result to this Empire would be beyond calculation: it would be something, in fact, to distinguish the age itself; and the doing of it would make the fortune of the Grand Trunk."

Watkin became the spokesman (and well-nigh the living embodiment) of a new merger of those financial and industrial interests in England which had a stake in imperial expansion, and the leading elements of the young Canadian capitalist class who, dependent on British capital, required imperial agreement in order to found a British North American state.

The nexus of this merger of interests was the Grand Trunk. Nine of its directors had been in the Canadian cabinet when the company was established in 1853. All three members of the government delegation to London in 1859 were Grand Trunk officials—Galt, Cartier and Ross (who combined in his person the offices of Solicitor-General of Canada and President of the Grand Trunk). Since 1840 the London banking houses of Glyn and Baring, now involved in promoting the Grand Trunk, had played a leading part in mobilizing British capital for investment in Canada; Baring's were the official financial agents of the Canadian Government in London.

In Canada Watkin lobbied, interviewed, pulled wires, organized junkets of Canadian MPs to the Maritimes; in London he helped set up a pressure group (originally initiated by Joseph Howe, when in England in 1862) to secure imperial backing to finance an inter-colonial railway. The group included, in addition to Glyn and the Barings, Samuel Cunard, M. Rothschild, officials of the Electric and International Telegraph Co., Lloyds, etc. Not even this imposing array sufficed to extract from the government the requested guarantee of several million pounds. Gladstone, Chancellor of the Exchequer, referred unkindly to "all these helps to other people who might help themselves" and displayed, says Watkin, "the expression of a man on his guard against a canvasser or a dun." (As well he might, considering the record of the Grand Trunk crowd.)

Balked in this crucial sector, the tireless Watkin launched a flanking movement. For a Pacific railway to materialize, not only was government backing needed, but a vast roadblock had still to be removed: the Hudson's Bay Company monopoly of the West. In the course of 1863 Watkin played a leading part in engineering the purchase by the Grand Trunk of a controlling interest in the Bay. The way was thus opened for arrangements which, for a "consideration," would result in the construction of a

"through road" to the West: the ancient company would
agree to be bought out, and the railway promoters would
be subsidized—provided only that the political obstacles
in the colonies and in London were overcome. Within a
year the turning-point was reached—thanks to initiatives
on the part of the Maritime and Canadian political leaders, and the pressure of international events.

For the Atlantic provinces the pressures from within
were less acute; but the long-term forces of industrial capitalist development were at work there also, pointing up
the need for rail communication, and indicating the advantages of union. Joseph Howe's interest in railway promotion has been referred to; in the Nova Scotia Assembly
the idea of federation was raised in 1854. In the next few
years, the idea of a Maritime Union began to gain support. Some business circles saw in it a step toward a larger union with Canada. Their spokesmen included Dr.
Charles Tupper in Nova Scotia, Leonard Tilley and Peter
Mitchell in New Brunswick. In November, 1860, Tupper
addressed the Mechanics' Institute of Saint John, N.B.,
on "The Political Condition of British North America."
He called for an assertion of colonial interests, as against
the "impotent position" held by the provinces. "Our
position is ever one of uncertainty. We have no constitution but the *dicta* of the ever-changing occupants of Downing Street." He called for the building of a "powerful
confederation" within the Empire. Tilley, a leading Saint
John business man and railway promoter, was present at
the lecture; he attended the 1862 conference at Quebec
on the Intercolonial Railway project; and two years later
took part, with Tupper, in convening the Charlottetown
Conference. Like Tilley, Mitchell was a prominent capitalist: "controlling large lumber and ship-building interests along the North Shore centering on Miramichi Bay,"

he had a direct stake in that particular route for the Intercolonial Railway.

Howe had worked actively to spread the idea of strengthened economic connections among the provinces, based in the first place on railway-building. In 1861 he moved a resolution in the Nova Scotia Assembly (Tupper seconded it) asking that the Colonial Secretary communicate with each of the provinces to urge consideration of "the subject of a union of the British North American Provinces, or of the maritime provinces." No action was taken on the resolution.

The Canadian proposal of 1858 for a discussion of federation had failed to win imperial endorsement, as had the request for a financial guarantee for the Intercolonial Railway. In 1862 the conference on intercolonial trade at Quebec favored in general "the adoption of a free trade policy between the British North American Provinces"; but it balked at coming to practical decisions, through reluctance "hastily, and without sufficient notice, to bring the larger and more advanced manufactures of Canada into competition with the limited and infant productions of the Maritime Provinces."

The colonial governors of Nova Scotia and New Brunswick, hewing to the traditional policy, at first discouraged proposals for maritime union; then they swung round to support them—as a means of blocking union with Canada. Thus Lieut.-Governor Sutton of New Brunswick in 1858 warned the Colonial Office: "All British North America is fermenting. And unless care is taken some bottles will burst, but I hope to keep the New Brunswick case in its right place." He was of the opinion that given a Maritime legislative union "there would be less danger that the People of this Province would, either now or hereafter, yield to Canadian influence, and express themselves in favor of a Federative Union . . ."

Yet despite official stalling and sectional cross-purposes, the change was not to be delayed much longer. In the spring of 1864 pressure in the Maritimes finally resulted in a decision to convene a conference at Charlottetown. The decision came at the very moment when the long log-jam in the Canadas was at last on the point of being broken.

17

Canada and the War Against Slavery

The framers of the 72 Confederation Resolutions worked in the ominous shadow of the Civil War in the United States. They were in session at Quebec when agents of the slave-holding Confederacy, operating from Canadian soil, perpetrated a military raid on St. Albans, Vermont. From start to finish, strands of the anti-slavery struggle were interwoven with Canadian locale and circumstance: here was the terminus of the "underground railway" that took escaping slaves to freedom; it was at Chatham, Canada West in May 1858, that John Brown's raid on Harper's Ferry was planned (the first blow struck for Emancipation); it was in Montreal that Confederate "Copperheads" plotted the murder of Lincoln . . .

Canadian democrats possessed an honorable tradition of opposition to slavery. The first session of the first parliament of Upper Canada in 1793 enacted a measure for extinguishing slave-ownership. When approached in 1826 in connection with the escape of slaves to Canada, the Canadian government, mindful of the sentiment in the colony, notified the U.S. authorities that it would be "utterly impossible for them to agree to a stipulation for the surrender of fugitive slaves." (The legal abolition of slavery by the British parliament came in 1833.) In Upper Canada in 1837 an Anti-Slavery Society was organized and W. L. Mackenzie, as Mayor of Toronto, presided at one of its meetings, held in the city hall. At this, as at other such meetings, resolutions were voted condemning slavery in the U.S. and calling for its abolition.

After the passing of the Fugitive Slave Act in 1851, sentiment was aroused even more strongly. George Brown at an anti-slavery demonstration in 1852 denounced the "despicable subserviency of the North," which then under the pro-slavery president Buchanan was carrying out the slaveholders' policies: "Free northerners are made man-catchers, northern judges are bribed to convict at five dollars a man, northern marshals are made slave-gaolers . . ." Further, he argued:

> The question is often put, What have we in Canada to do with American Slavery? We have everything to do with it. . . We have to do with it on the score of self-protection. The leprosy of the atrocious system affects all around it; it leavens the thoughts, the feelings, the institutions of the people who touch it. . . We are alongside of this great evil; our people mingle with it . . . it is our duty to raise our voices as free men against a system which brings so foul a blot on the cause of popular liberty.

To the Negro who could escape from the slave-plantation, the North star was a beacon on the path to freedom: the refrain of one song went:

> Farewell, old master,
>   Don't come after me.
> I'm on my way to Canada
>   Where colored men are free.

It was estimated that no less than forty thousand escaped slaves passed through Ohio alone via the "underground railway." Harriet Tubman, the courageous Negro abolitionist who made nineteen trips into the South organizing the deliverance of more than three hundred slaves, helped organize in St. Catharines, Canada West, a "Fugitives Aid Society," to provide legal aid for those who reached Canada and made their home here. At Sandwich (Windsor) Henry Bibb in 1851-2 published a newspaper for his people, *The Voice of the Fugitive*. It was followed in the years 1853-57 by *The Provincial Freeman* (printed first on King St. East, Toronto, and after 1855 in Chatham). Its editor was a young woman named Mary Shadd: "The first colored woman on the American Continent, to establish and edit a weekly newspaper."

In 1850 there were some 30,000 Negroes in the Province; by 1860 there were 60,000. Outstanding work on the "underground railway" was done by Dr. Alexander M. Ross, printer, surgeon, naturalist and author, a native of Belleville, Ont. In Richmond, Va., Nashville, Tenn., and New Orleans, he helped organize the escape and journey northward of dozens of slaves, both women and men. A reward was placed on his head, and in Columbus, Miss., he narrowly missed being lynched. From Mississippi he went on to work in Georgia, Alabama, and Kentucky. A friend of John Brown and of Lincoln, Dr. Ross during the Civil War served as surgeon in the Union Army and also worked to track down Confederate Copperhead operations in Canada. When the war ended, he offered his services to Benito Juarez in the struggle for Mexican freedom; but the French puppet Maximilian being overthrown in Mexico City in 1867, Ross returned to Toronto.

"Blessings upon him," wrote the poet Whittier in Tribute,

> For his steadfast strength and courage
>   In a dark and evil time,
> When the Golden Rule was treason
>   And to feed the hungry, crime.
> For the poor slave's hope and refuge,
>   When the hound was on his track . . .

The Civil War, the outcome of the irreconcilable conflict between the historically progressive industrial capitalism of the North and the reactionary Southern plantation system based on Negro slavery, was the "second American Revolution." In the South four million Negro slaves toiled on plantations for 325,000 white slave-owners. Among these, three or four thousand wealthy planters owned the largest estates and pocketed three-quarters of the profits. It has been estimated that a slave's upkeep cost $20 a year, while the profit on his labor amounted to over four times his "keep."

(A curiously revealing proposal for a "reform" of the slave system was advanced by Edward Watkin, president of the Grank Trunk, at the time of his visit to the U.S. about 1860. It was "to secure to the slave a personal right to some small portion of the day, and to the produce of his labor in that portion;—to say, in fact, that after a stipulated number of hours' labor for his master, the remainder of his time shall be his own. The effect of this would be to enable him legally to accumulate property." Mr. Watkin does not appear to have extended his analysis of the nature of the working day to the situation of his wage-slaves on the Grand Trunk . . .*)

With its base in the North, an expanding capitalist industry in the United States by 1860 was producing a million tons of iron annually, steampower was dominant in manufacturing, wage-workers numbered 1.3 million, the railway network of 30,000 miles was the largest in the world. The country ranked fourth as an industrial power. The plantation system, meanwhile, as the soil became exhausted, reached out to embrace ever larger territories

---

*Cf. Sir Charles Metcalfe's observations on slave labor and wage labor. (*Appendix*).

—Louisiana, Texas, Arkansas, Missouri—and challenged the northern capitalist class in contest for control of the West. The entrenched power of the plantation-owners at Washington had enabled them to enact the Fugitive Slave Law, thereby placing the federal machinery in the service of the slave states. The election of Abraham Lincoln in 1860 was the signal for Northern resistance to Southern encroachment. Secession of six of the slave states from the Union was followed by an attack of the rebel Confederacy on the federal garrison at Fort Sumter, South Carolina. What Marx, writing in the *N.Y. Daily Tribune* of Nov. 7, 1861, described as "the first grand war of contemporaneous history," had begun. "The people of Europe," he went on, "know that a fight for the continuance of the Union is a fight against the continuance of the slavocracy—that in this contest the highest form of popular self-government till now realized is giving battle to the meanest and most shameless form of man's enslaving recorded in the annals of history."

Capitalist industry, wage labor and the "free" market were incompatible with the spread of the slave economy. As Marx put it:

> The present struggle between the South and North is . . . nothing but a struggle between two social systems, between the system of slavery and the system of free labor. The struggle has broken out because the two systems can no longer live peacefully side by side on the North American continent. It can only be ended by the victory of one system or the other.

Since the South, with a population of 9 million (the North had 22 million) and a weak industrial base, was in no position to wage a long-drawn war, the slaveowners gambled on a speedy military offensive and the help of intervention from abroad. In the English governing class they found ready allies. Rivals of the U.S. industrial North, dependent on Southern cotton for their textile industry, the English bourgeoisie gave aid and encouragement to the Confederacy: they recognized it as a belligerent and enabled it to build and equip in English dockyards such sea-raiders as the *Alabama,* to prey on Northern shipping. In December, Palmerston "dispatched 3,000 men to Canada, an army ridiculous, if intended to cover a frontier of 1500 miles, but a clever sleight-of-hand if the rebellion was to be cheered, and the Union to be irritated." (Marx). When in November the North intercepted a British ship, the *Trent,* carrying two Confederate agents* to England, a furious uproar went up from the pro-war London press.

But the reactionary advocates of war were not to go unchallenged at home. Despite mass unemployment that brought terrible hardship, the cotton operatives of Lancashire stood solid against war with the United States. Solidarity with the Northern cause found widespread expression. In Manchester a meeting attended by 6,000 persons sent greetings to the North and urged the complete uprooting of slavery. (The Emancipation Proclamation was not issued until September, 1862.) When Lincoln was re-elected to the presidency in 1864, the International Workingmen's Association sent him an address, declaring that "The working classes of Europe understood at once, even before the fanatic partisanship of the upper classes for the Confederate gentry had given its dismal warning, that the slaveholders' rebellion was to sound the tocsin for a general holy crusade of property against labor, and that for the men of labor, with their hopes for the

---

*Mason and Slidell, leading sponsors of the Fugitive Slave Law; Marx describes Slidell as "the soul of the Southern Conspiratorial conclave;" Mason was later to settle at Niagara-on-the-Lake.

future, even their past conquests were at stake in that tremendous conflict on the other side of the Atlantic."

"It ought never to be forgotten in the United States," Marx wrote in the *N.Y. Tribune* of Feb. 1, 1862, "that at least the *working classes* of England, from the commencement to the termination of the difficulty, have never forsaken them. To them it was due that, despite the poisonous stimulants daily administered by a venal and reckless press, not one single public war meeting could be held in the United Kingdom during all the period that peace trembled in the balance."

In face of the gigantic upheaval to the south, where vast armies in collision were protagonists of a great social as well as political conflict, Canadian opinion was sharply divided. The mass of the people generally abhorred slavery, and hoped the North would win. D'Arcy McGee voiced their feelings when at London, C.W., he denounced the rule of "an oligarchy founded upon caste, the caste founded upon color . . . the monstrous doctrines of the innate diversity of the black and the hereditary mastery of the white." The *Globe* spoke for many when it wrote (July 23, 1861): "Every Canadian who desires to see his country prosperous should pray for the speedy success of the Northern arms and the prompt suppression of the slave power."

But the wealthy, like their English counterparts, sympathized with the rebel slavocracy. Montreal and Toronto "Society" wined and dined visiting Southern gentlemen, whose numbers multiplied as the war progressed. The Confederates established a large-scale base of operations in "neutral" Canada. From the fashionable Queen's Hotel in Toronto (where the Royal York now stands) and the St. Lawrence Hall Hotel on St. James St. in

Montreal, they hatched conspiracies, launched raids, and organized attacks on shipping, prisoner-of-war camps, and the civilian population of Northern cities. Confederate High Commissioners Thompson and Clay deposited huge sums (a million dollars, by one estimate) with the Bank of Montreal, with which they financed activities directed against the North. Valandigham, the leading Copperhead conspirator, worked in St. Catharines, Niagara Falls and Windsor. Confederate agents filtering through the North reached Canada via Detroit and Buffalo; some slipped through the blockade at sea to reach Halifax, where a headquarters of theirs operated from a hideout "on Barrington Street, over a confectionery store."

The Quebec Conference was in session when Confederates operating out of Montreal raided St. Albans, Vt., and got away with $170,000. Devlin, a prominent Montreal attorney, defended the bandits, and a Tory magistrate in defiance of international law hastened to set them free. In November, 1864, another Copperhead band carried out an arson raid on New York City, setting fire to shipping and to a dozen large hotels, in the hope of creating a panic in the Northern rear. On returning to their base in Toronto—having set the fires, but being foiled in their attempt at seizing control of the city—they decided to take certain precautions in case of prosecution. In his memoirs of "Confederate Operations in Canada and New York" Headley, one of the raiders, relates the following:

> At the suggestion of Col. Thompson (the chief Confederate Commissioner) it was deemed advisable that we retain Hon. John Macdonald as counsel in the event of a requisition, as he was friendly to our cause and was regarded as a very eminent lawyer. One evening after supper . . .

we rode in a sleigh to the residence of Mr. Macdonald in the suburbs of Toronto. He greeted us cordially and we discussed our case fully until a late hour. The arrangement was made and a retainer fee was paid the following day. But it happened that the time never arrived when his services were required.

There were no prosecutions. John A. Macdonald, after all, was Attorney-General for Canada West. It was not without significance that when speaking at a banquet in Halifax a few months earlier he had gone out of his way to laud "the gallant defence that is being made by the Southern Republic . . ."

Southern chivalry did not stop at attempts to burn down cities. The slaveowners' leaders in Canada had a fund of $200,000 set aside for subversion operations that ranged from germ warfare to presidential assassination. It was brought out later at state trials that in one effort aimed at "the introduction of pestilence" into the North, quantities of clothing infected with yellow fever were delivered to Washington in the hope (unrealized) of starting an epidemic that might lead to the death of the President and members of his cabinet . . .

Upper-class conservative sympathy with the South was an expression of class solidarity: the slaveowners' stand in defense of their property took on the aspect of a defense of the sacred right of property in general. Radical and working-class support for Lincoln and the North seemed only to confirm this position. Men of wealth in Canada, and the ardent upholders of British imperial policy, alike took the part of the Confederacy.

For a wider circle of Canadians, however, there were grounds for a certain mistrust of the North that stemmed from a quite different aspect of the situation. Whereas Lincoln was warmly admired and supported as the leader of the struggle to defeat the slave-power, his cabinet (and his cause) represented other interests as well. Expansionist Northern capital had an aggressive spokesman in Secretary of State William Seward. At the time of the presidential election of 1860 the British ambassador in Washington reported that Seward "publicly advocated . . . the annexation of Canada as a compensation for any loss, which might be occasioned by the disaffection of the South." The policy was rejected, however. "Mr. Lincoln was distinctly not interested." In December, 1861, A. T. Galt had an interview with the President, who assured him that

> he had implicit faith in the steady conduct of the American people even under the trying circumstances of the war, and though the existence of large armies had in other countries placed successful generals in positions of arbitrary power, he did not fear this result, but believed the people would quietly resume their peaceful avocations. . . . He pledged himself as a man of honor, that neither he nor his cabinet entertained the slightest aggressive designs upon Canada.

A year later a memorandum of the Canadian government of J. Sandfield Macdonald declared: "The people of Canada . . . feel that should war come, it will be produced by no act of theirs." The danger of war had its source, in the early stages of the civil conflict, in the provocative policy of the British imperialists under Palmerston; and later, in the ambitions of the expansionist wing of the rising U.S. bourgeoisie, curbed by Lincoln while he lived, but achieving dominance with his death and the conclusion of the war against the South.

On April 15, 1865, less than a week after Lee's surrender at Appomattox, and in the midst of the celebrations of victory, Abraham Lincoln was murdered. The assassin, John Wilkes Booth, wrote in his diary that "for six months we had worked . . . " at preparing the crime. It was just six months before that he had been in Montreal. From there he had gone to Maryland to recruit the murder gang. Later, attempts to prove a link between Booth and the Confederate Mission in Canada led nowhere. Col. Baker, head of the U.S. Secret Service, "would have been delighted" to prove a connection, writes a present-day admirer of the Copperheads, but "there was not a shred of evidence." It so happens, however, that there *was* evidence: a missing page, torn out of the register of the St. Lawrence Hall Hotel in Montreal, for the date of October 18, 1864, bearing the signature: *J. Wilkes Booth, Baltimore.* Undiscovered until a few years ago, it had been in the secret possession of Col. Baker—the North's chief intelligence officer.

A wave of anger and sorrow swept through Canada at the news of the assassination. Typical of many was one meeting attended by five hundred Canadians on April 19, 1865, which resolved "That this meeting of the inhabitants of the towns of Berlin and Waterloo, Province of Canada, assembled on the funeral day of Abraham Lincoln, late President of the United States, desires, with the deepest sincerity, to express its heartfelt indignation at the cowardly and wanton act by which the president and patriot, the ruler and friend of the Republic, has been lost to his country. . . . They regard the dastardly and barbarous murder of President Lincoln not only as an irreparable loss to the American nation in the present momentous transition crisis of their history—but as a common loss to humanity, liberty and the brotherhood of mankind all the world over." The meeting further "would desire most respectfully and tenderly to express their sympathy for Mrs. Lincoln . . ."

The Canadian working people shared in the grief felt by democratic and progressive people the world over. Of Abraham Lincoln, the message of condolence sent by the International Workingmen's Association declared:

> He was a man, neither to be browbeaten by adversity, nor intoxicated by success, inflexibly pressing on to his great goal, never compromising it by blind haste, slowly maturing his steps, never retracing them, carried away by no surge of popular favor, disheartened by no slackening of the popular pulse; tempering stern acts by the gleams of a kind heart, illuminating scenes dark with passion by the smile of humor, doing his titanic work as humbly and homely as heaven-born rulers do little things with the grandiloquence of pomp and state; in one word, one of the rare men who succeed in becoming great, without ceasing to be good. Such, indeed, was the modesty of this great and good man, that the world only discovered him a hero after he had fallen a martyr.

Following Lincoln's death, Northern reactionaries joined hands with the plantation owners to establish capitalist exploitation in the South and to prevent the democratic follow-through of Emancipation: land to the former slaves, equal citizenship for Negroes, etc. In foreign policy they took up once again the banner of Yankee expansion and "Manifest Destiny."

During the war, as tension rose in the relations between Britain and the North, the latter had given notice of termination of the 1817 Agreement on limiting naval forces on the Great Lakes; moves were made toward abrogating the Reciprocity Treaty with Canada; and sections of the press, notably the New York *Herald,* vociferously proclaimed the desirability of annexing Canada. While it was finally agreed that the Great Lakes naval agreement should be allowed to stand, the Reciprocity Treaty was abrogated. This move, the expansionists reckoned, would compel annexation. The *Chicago Tribune* (January 6, 1866) had no doubt of it: "The Canadians ... will stay out in the cold for a few years and try all sorts of expedients, but in the end will be constrained to knock for admission into the Great Republic." A fortnight later, this paper's appetite had grown, or its patience had shrunk; it assured its readers that Canada "will be snatched up by this Republic as quickly as a hawk would gobble up a quail."

Both in the East and the Northwest voices were raised in favor of taking over Canada. The Boston *Advertiser* quoted a state assemblyman as declaring that "the scheme ... would give New England a market for its manufactures." The Massachusetts legislature adopted a resolution favoring annexation. The Yankees viewed the Maritimes with an acquisitive eye. The official report of the U.S. Revenue Commissioners for 1866 put it bluntly: "If the Maritime Provinces would join us spontaneously today—sterile as they may be in the soil under a sky of steel—still with their hardy population, their harbors, fisheries and seamen, they would strengthen and improve our position, and aid us in our struggle for equality upon the ocean. If we would succeed upon the deep, we must either maintain our fisheries, or absorb the Provinces."

The greed of the expansionists was continental. On the West coast, where the memory of the Oregon Boundary struggle was still fresh, Edward Watkin had referred to indications in 1860 that "American commerce is anxious to extend itself, and . . . American cruisers in the Pacific wanted the coal of Vancouver."

In the Northwest, over seven million settlers had moved in with the new railways (the Northern Pacific built in 1864); and in 1865, W. Taylor, a special agent of the

U.S. Treasury Department for the Northwest, announced from Fort Garry: "The Americanization of the fertile belt is inevitable . . . Indeed, it is for the interest of the settlers here that annexation should take place at once." At Taylor's instigation, on July 2, 1866, Congressman Banks introduced "A Bill for the Admission of the States of Nova Scotia, New Brunswick, Canada East and Canada West, and for the organization of the Territories of Selkirk, Saskatchewan and Columbia . . . (the foregoing) are constituted and admitted as States and Territories of the United States of America." The Bill provided also that the U.S. should "aid the navigation of the St. Lawrence River" by constructing or enlarging canals — "Provided, that the expenditure under this article shall not exceed 50 millions of dollars."

The Bill did not pass; but neither did the machinations cease.

In April, 1867 the U.S. purchase of Alaska from Russia was openly referred to as a move to offset Canadian federation by securing the whole northwestern corner of the continent for the United States. Sen. Sumner announced: "The present treaty is a visible step in the occupation of the whole American continent. As such it will be recognized by the world and accepted by the American people."

Seward and other Washington politicians did not conceal their disapproval of Canadian moves toward union; they "were strongly opposed to Canadian federation." At the very time when the British North America Act was being dealt with by the House of Commons at Westminster, the U.S. House of Representatives adopted a resolution expressing "extreme solicitude" over the measure. A couple of years later, during the negotiations over the acquiring of Rupert's Land from the Hudson's

Bay Company, Brydges of the Grand Trunk wrote to Sir John A. Macdonald, following a conversation with the Governor of Vermont (who was also the president of the Northern Pacific) that an effort was under way "to prevent your getting control for Canada of the Hudson Bay Territory." Sir John replied: "It is quite evident to me, not only from this conversation, but from advices from Washington, that the U.S. government are resolved to do all they can, short of war, to get possession of the Western territory, and we must make immediate and vigorous steps to counteract them."

The new upsurge of U.S. expansionism, coming on the heels of the threat to Canadian security occasioned by the pro-Confederate policy of British and Canadian governing circles, acted as a strong spur to union in British and North America. The danger of a military collision with the U.S. loomed large in the thinking of Canadian and Maritime leaders. It proved decisive in bringing London around to agree to the Confederation proposals.

18

Engineering a Federal Union

What broke the log-jam in the summer of 1864 was the formation of a Canadian coalition government dedicated to finding a solution to the constitutional question in the direction of federation. In June, a parliamentary committee formed on Brown's initiative had reported "a strong feeling . . . in favor of changes in the direction of a federative system, applied either to Canada alone, or to the whole British North American provinces . . ." The following day the Taché-Macdonald government—the tenth in a decade—lost its precarious majority; and, through the intermediary of Alexander Morris (the lecturer on "Nova Britannia") and James Ferrier (of the Grand Trunk), negotiations between Brown and Macdonald, Galt and Cartier were started, leading to formation of the historic coalition.

It was George Brown's decision to offer to join forces with his ancient adversaries Macdonald and Cartier in an attempt to reach a solution in federation that made the new arrangement possible. It was Macdonald's canny mangement of the very mixed forces in the new coalition, and his leadership in the conferences with the Maritime delegates, that finally brought the Confederation project to fruition.

In the "Great Coalition" Macdonald, with Galt, represented the general interest of the leading English-Canadian business community, closely tied in with London and the

Grand Trunk, and having Montreal as its main head-quarters.

Brown spoke for the industrial and commercial leaders of Toronto, rivals of Montreal, and a large area of rural as well as urban Reform opinion in Canada West.

Cartier was the spokesman of the conservative wing of the French-Canadian bourgeoisie and of the Church, allied with Anglo-Canadian capital. Their adherence to the federation scheme had been secured since 1858, with Cartier's acceptance of it as the basis for his joining an administration led by Galt and Macdonald. The interests for whom Cartier spoke were secured by a twofold bond: association with the Grand Trunk and the Bank of Montreal; and a common abhorrence of the radical democracy of the *Parti rouge,* whose exclusion from the coalition was not the least of its attractions for them.

The radical democrats of Canada East combatted the Macdonald-Cartier proposals as being undemocratic on two main counts: their inadequate recognition of the rights of the French-Canadian nationality,* and an undue recognition of the rights of property. "The Grand Trunk people are at the bottom of it," Dorion charged, citing Edward Watkin's glowing assurances to the investors on "the enhanced value which will be given to their shares and bonds, by the adoption of the Confederation scheme and the construction of the Intercolonial . . ."

The new state structure was indeed designed to meet the economic and political requirements of the "dominant social groups" in the colonies and in the imperial metropolis. As Professor Alfred Dubuc points out:

---

*Cf. below: "French Canada and the Terms of Union." On this as on the role of the railway question, the criticism of the *Rouges* of a century ago is finding confirmation in the judgments of not a few of today's political scientists.

In economic terms Confederation was essentially an instrument of public finance whose object it was to make available to those responsible for effecting investment, the resources necessary for the unified economic development of the British colonies in North America.

Geared to an overall project of growth within the Empire, embracing farming and forest industries, protected manufactures and mass immigration, the approach "assumed that one economic sector could be nurtured for the benefit of all . . ."

The privileged sector was to be that of the railroads. It was precisely the interest of groups associated with the railroads which inspired Confederation.

On these economic foundations was to arise a state structure that would best serve the needs of the "rising capitalist class" whose new ascendancy is now being recognized as the crucial development of the mid-19th century (cf. D. C. Masters, above, p. 277). Alfred Dubuc continues:

The Canadian state was to be a bourgeois and capitalist state; through their lobbies the great financial institutions and the great industrial enterprises would dominate the political parties as much as the various ministries . . . Confederation, in the form it took, was made possible through the domination of the financial and commercial upper middle class over the lower middle class.

The "upper middle class" in question was actually the colonial ruling class: the financial-industrial bourgeoisie, than whom no other group stood higher in the social pyramid. Galt, Cartier, John Ross, at once Conservative cabinet members and Grand Trunk administrators, were the political protagonists of its Montreal wing.

While Canada West furnished the Conservatives with such prominent businessmen as John Ross and a number of railway promoters, an important grouping of Toronto capitalists supported the Liberals under George Brown's leadership. Toronto in 1863 was represented in the Canadian Assembly by "two wealthy Liberal business men;" J. Macdonald and A. M. Smith; W. P. Howland and Adam Wilson were among the leaders of "Toronto's Liberal commercial group."

By the time Confederation became a reality, the leading Toronto Liberals were men "well established in the city's business community . . . owners of leading city firms." John McMurrich, William McMaster, the Howlands, are among the names; the same ones, largely, recur in the list of directors of the newly-formed Bank of Commerce, "Toronto's latest answer to the Bank of Montreal," as Professor Careless calls it. George Brown was a substantial shareholder, McMaster the bank's first president. Not only were these men leading spokesmen of capitalist interests in the Province of Canada; they at the same time "were concerned with both political and economic control over the West. It was quite natural that the same men should be at the core of both the western Reform party and the big new western banking institution, each of which was dedicated to gaining power in the Dominion that was so soon to be established."

Herein lies the real significance of the alliance that Brown negotiated with Macdonald in the meetings at the Hotel St. Louis, Quebec, in June 1864. The resulting "great coalition" was a coalition of the two key sections of Anglo-Canadian business. Traditionally, historians in English Canada have hailed as decisive the Macdonald-Brown agreement to join forces in order to break the political deadlock and together solve the constitutional problem. Tribute to their statesmanship, however, has seemed to require a certain reticence about the class forces and class interests to which the Confederate leaders gave expression. Yet historically, it was just these forces that lent the alliance its decisive character.

Another related facet of the "great coalition" that is generally obscured should be mentioned, although dealt with more fully in a subsequent chapter. It is the relatively minor importance usually attached to Cartier's adherence to the coalition, as compared with Brown's decisive role in its formation. It is not only that Cartier had been committed to the scheme since 1858; it is the fact that the adherence of the clerical and French-Canadian business interests, while indispensable for British American union, quite definitely stood second in importance to the political consolidation of the English-speaking capitalist groupings for whom Brown and Macdonald spoke. The Canadian bourgeois state was to embody the political and economic hegemony of Anglo-Canadian business, the ruling interest in British North America.

If the formation of the Brown-Macdonald coalition government marked one decisive stage in the union process, negotiations with the Atlantic colonial provinces were another.

The new government, aware of the impending conference on Maritime Union, took advantage of the opportunity it offered. A communication went to the three provinces asking if they would agree to a delegation from Canada participating, "to ascertain whether the proposed Union may not be made to embrace the whole of the British North American Provinces." The response was favorable, but with the proviso that it be an informal participation.

Accordingly, at the end of August, eight Canadians embarked for Charlottetown: John A. Macdonald, George Brown, G. E. Cartier, A. T. Galt, T. D'Arcy McGee, H.

Langevin, William McDougall and Alex Campbell. On the morning of September 1 the Maritime delegates, gathered in the Colonial Building, decided to postpone discussion of a Maritime Union until the Canadians (whose ship was just then entering the harbor) had presented their point of view. Representing the Maritimes were, from Nova Scotia: Charles Tupper, W. A. Henry, R. B. Dickey, A. G. Archibald and J. McCully; New Brunswick: S. L. Tilley, W. H. Steeves, J. M. Johnson, E. D. Chandler, J. H. Gray; Prince Edward Island: John Hamilton Gray, G. Coles, W. H. Pope, E. Palmer, A. A. Macdonald.*

The Conference, under the chairmanship of Col. J. H. Gray, Premier of P.E.I., was largely taken up with addresses by the leading Canadian delegates on various phases of the confederation scheme. On Friday, September 2, Cartier and Brown each gave a general introduction, dealing with both the broad perspective and the specific question of provincial rights, about which their hearers were particularly concerned; Brown introducing the idea of combining representation based on population in the future federal lower house with equality of representation in the upper house for each of the three sections

---

*The foregoing, together with ten others who took part in the Quebec Conference a month later, comprise the "Fathers of Confederation." All 33 were at Quebec; the ten who were at Quebec and not at Charlottetown were: From Canada: E. P. Taché, Oliver Mowat, J. C. Chapais, J. Cockburn; New Brunswick: Peter Mitchell, C. Fisher; P.E.I.: T. H. Haviland, E. Whelan; Newfoundland: F. B. T. Carter, Ambrose Shea. At the Conference in London, in December, 1866, P.E.I. and Newfoundland were not represented, having withdrawn from the negotiations; and the Canadian delegation included one member who had not been at either Charlottetown or Quebec— W. H. Howland, a leading Toronto businessman.

(the two Canadas and the combined Maritimes). Macdonald, while not actually rejecting the federal principle, to which the Canadians were already committed, put great emphasis on the need for a strong central power. The argument is conveyed in a speech he made a few days later in Halifax (by agreement, no record was kept of the speeches in conference; this was also the procedure at Quebec). Pointing to the U.S. experience, where all power not specifically ceded to the central government had remained vested in the separate states, he observed: "The dangers that have arisen from this system we will avoid, if we can agree upon forming a strong central government, a great central legislature, a constitution for union which will have all the rights of sovereignty except those that are given to the local governments . . . I hope that we will be enabled to work out a constitution that will have a strong central government, able to offer a powerful resistance to any foe whatever, and at the same time will preserve for each Province its own identity, and will protect every local ambition: and if we cannot do this, we shall not be able to carry out the end we have in view."

This was indeed the problem; its solution required agreement on complicated financial as well as political questions, a basis for which was offered in Galt's speech on the Monday. But first, and above all, there had to be general agreement in principle with the idea as a whole. On each of the addresses there had been questions and discussion; there was one more day of general deliberation, concluding with an invitation by the Canadians to an official conference, to be held a month later at Quebec; and the day following the Maritime representatives met separately. It then became apparent that the project of a Maritime legislative union was unworkable, since Prince Edward Island would not give up its separate legislature, and insisted on Charlottetown as the capital of the union. The conference as a whole then adjourned to Halifax (D'Arcy McGee having meanwhile delivered a lecture in Charlottetown on Robert Burns), where agreement was reached on the Canadian proposal for a formal conference in Quebec, to open on October 10.

The idea of a larger federal union had won acceptance —in principle. At Quebec, the federal compact was embodied in 72 resolutions, which became the basis of the British North America Act of 1867. The first three resolutions read as follows:

> 1. The best interests and present and future prosperity of British North America will be promoted by a Federal Union under the Crown of Great Britain, provided such a Union can be effected on principles just to the several provinces.
>
> 2. In the Federation of the British North American Provinces the system of government best adapted under existing circumstances to protect the diversified interests of the several Provinces, and secure efficiency, harmony and permanency in the working of the Union, would be a General Government charged with matters of common interest to the whole country, and Local Governments for each of the Canadas, and for the Provinces of Nova Scotia, New Brunswick and Prince Edward Island, charged with the control of local matters in their respective sections; provision being made for the admission into the Union, on equitable terms, of Newfoundland, the North-West Territory, British Columbia and Vancouver.
>
> 3. In framing a Constitution for the General Government, the Conference, with a view to the perpetuation of our connections with the Mother country, and to the promotion of the best interests of the people of these Provinces, desire to follow the model of the British Constitution, so far as our circumstances will permit.

Thus was fashioned, in 1864, the cornerstone of the unified Canadian federal state.

The year and a half that intervened between the Quebec Conference and the proclamation of the British North America Act were marked by controversy, frustration and uncertainty. Debate waxed and waned in the Maritimes and Canada East: two of the three areas whose incorporation into the new Dominion presented thorny problems. The third—the Northwest—erupted later.

While the Legislative Assembly of the Province of Canada was debating the Quebec resolutions a swelling surge of anti-Confederation sentiment in the Maritimes threatened rejection of the scheme of union. This challenge called forth strenuous efforts by both railway-promoter-politicians and the Colonial Office to put through the project, which the needs of economic development and military security alike made imperative. As a strong reason for union with Canada, Tilley of New Brunswick pointed to the prospect of abrogation of Reciprocity. For his part Tupper of Nova Scotia had warned the Charlottetown Conference that the end of the Civil War might see the armies of the U.S. moving against the British provinces. Gray of P.E.I. "saw the issue squarely as a choice between federation and absorption by the United States."

Yet no sooner had the Canadian Assembly endorsed the Quebec Resolutions than the New Brunswick electors resoundingly repudiated them. Tilley's pro-confederation government was voted out of office at the end of March, 1865. In Nova Scotia a storm of opposition was brewing and Tupper, to avoid an upset, tacked hastily: he revived consideration of Maritime union, rather than steer head-on into the squall over Confederation. The governors of both provinces had intrigued and lobbied to defeat the project of a larger union. Both were firmly told by the Colonial Office that they were off course: the new imperial policy favored confederation. Prince Edward Island's legislature voted down the federation proposals. The Newfoundland government, after keeping the question in suspense for several years, moved toward agreement, then was repudiated at the polls.

Opposition to the confederation proposals in the Atlantic provinces in part reflected the concern of local commercial capitalist interests for their competitive position, in part the strong attachment of the people to their regional identity and autonomy. Some merchants in Saint John and Halifax were more interested in strengthening their ties with New England than with the Canadas. According to J. H. Gray of New Brunswick, the bankers of Saint John "dreaded the competition of Canadian banks coming here and the consequent destruction of (their) monopoly." Railway promoters in the same city wanted to put through an extension to Maine of their European & North American Railroad, so that "people . . . who had an eye to our resources" would be induced "to come in and develop them." Small manufacturers feared that larger Canadian producers would swamp their local market. There was anxiety lest Canada's burdens of debt be thrust on to Maritime taxpayers. Newfoundlanders feared that their interest in the fisheries would not be safeguarded in Canadian trade agreements with the United States; moreover they looked to London for support in resisting the encroachments of the French fishery. All four Atlantic colonies considered the financial arrangements worked out at Quebec to be unsatisfactory. As Joseph Howe put it: "All our revenues are to be taken by the general government, and we get back 80 cents per head, the price of a sheepskin."

The feeling of a regional—almost national—identity that had grown up among the inhabitants of the Maritimes found vehement expression. The method by which the federation scheme was being pursued, behind closed doors, and without popular consultation, strengthened the fear that democratic gains won in the 1830s and '40s might be sacrificed. Howe, while stating his readiness to agree to union on terms fair to the Maritimes, declared:

> The people of Nova Scotia for 108 years had their own Parliament, and responsible government for 25. I hold that to deprive them of these rights by an arbitrary act of Parliament, passed at the instigation of the Canadians, who have never invested a pound of capital in our country, would be an atrocious proceeding, out of which would grow undying hatreds and ultimate annexation.

To him, as to many, Nova Scotia was "our country." Howe's lieutenant, Annand, wrote: "We will not willingly allow ourselves to be brought into subjection to Canada or any other country." He demanded "exact equality" and not "the detestable confederation that has been attempted to be forced upon us . . . a union brought about by corrupt and arbitrary means." Another journalist warned that "Our nationality would be merged into that of Canada . . ."

In New Brunswick the anti-Confederation forces charged that the delegates to Charlottetown had "arrogated to themselves powers that did not legitimately belong to them, and undertook to alter the institutions of the country and surrender the independence we have so long enjoyed." Canada, a Fredericton editor declared, had "a pressing internal difficulty to overcome," and through union would gain "considerable material advantages."

New Brunswickers surely would regret "to see their roads, by-roads, bridges and schools going down, down, while they see Canada growing greatly partly by their money."

The rejection of the confederation proposal by the New Brunswick electors in March 1865 necessitated a combined operation to reverse the verdict. As a result of the exertions of the Colonial Office, the Governor General, the Lieutenant-Governor of New Brunswick, the Canadian Government, and the Grand Trunk, by the spring of 1866 the Smith government found itself obliged to appeal to the electorate. Tilley thereupon wired John A. (in code): "Will need $40 or $50 thousand." A few days later he followed up with a letter: "The election can be made certain if *the means* are used . . . It must be done with great caution and in such a way as not to awaken suspicion." The arrangements were to be worked through the intermediary of a wealthy Saint John ship-owner ("worth at least $100,000") who was to meet Brydges, the Grand Trunk manager, in Portland, Maine. Nor were the anti-Confederationists without cash backing. Together with assistance from U.S.-linked trading houses and railway speculators, they could count on "a certain enterprising lumber operator" who bolstered their campaign fund in exchange for 15,000 acres of the public domain.

For their part, the Colonial Office and Governor-General Monck exerted themselves as vigorously as the Canadian politicians and railway magnates in the cause of union. The Colonial Secretary penned a dispatch to the Maritimes stating as "the strong and deliberate opinion of Her Majesty's Government" that it was "an object much to be desired and that all the British North American colonies should agree to unite in one Government."

The "loyalty" cry was worked to the limit, with the Montreal *Gazette* admonishing the reluctant New Brunswick neighbors to the effect that "It is idle for them to conceal the fact from themselves—confederation or union of some sort is a condition of the continuance of the British connection"; it was up to them to show whether theirs was "mere lip loyalty." The alarms attendant on the Fenian raids of 1866 contributed a further element of leverage: a "war scare" hysteria was calculatingly kept up with the help of troop movements and parades, in Saint John especially. Tilley and the pro-confederation forces carried the election handily.

Tupper in Nova Scotia meanwhile managed to get around the difficulty of popular opposition to the confederation terms by having the Assembly pass a resolution in favor of "union" in general, to be negotiated with Britain and the provincial governments. In the fall of 1866 delegations from Nova Scotia and New Brunswick proceeded to London, to meet with representatives from Canada and the imperial authorities.

The Maritimers' concern for regional and local autonomy was reinforced by concern for democratic rights. In both respects their sentiments paralleled the attitude of the Canada East opposition. The leaders of the confederation movement did in fact betray a notable aversion to popular consultation. Union was to be effected "from above," in close and confidential association with key figures in the world of business and with the imperial authorities. Macdonald was quite explicit: "As it would be obviously absurd to submit the complicated details of such a measure to the people, it is not proposed to seek their sanction before asking the Imperial Government to introduce a Bill in the British Parliament." When the measure was in the early stages of preparation in London, in October 1866, Macdonald wrote to Tilley, who was already in England:

It appears to us to be important that the Bill should not be finally settled until just before the meeting of the British Parliament. The measure must be carried *per saltum* [in one leap], and no echo of it must reverberate through the British provinces till it becomes law . . . The Act once passed and beyond remedy the people would soon learn to be reconciled to it.

The character of the State that was in the making would be democratic only to a partial and limited degree. The popular liberties won in past struggles could not, assuredly, be effaced or altogether denied: yet they must be kept firmly within bounds! The bounds were set by property and class interest. After all, the men who shaped Confederation, the political spokesmen of the banking, trading and railway interests—the rising Canadian capitalist class—were themselves men of property, concerned with property. A spokesman for the seigneurs warned the Legislative Council against the possibility of local legislatures repudiating payment of the seigneurial debt (payment to the seigneurs guaranteed by the 1854 Act abolishing the tenure). "On this question," he said, "it will be easy to excite the passion of the people, prejudiced as they already are against the seigneurs. *Chiefly, and above all, we are bound to respect vested rights.*"

As his biographer Joseph Pope relates, Macdonald, until the last day of his life viewed universal suffrage "as one of the greatest evils that could befall a state . . . The idea that a man should vote simply because he breathed was ever repellant to Sir John Macdonald's conception of government." In 1861 he had argued that "unless property were protected, and made one of the principles upon which representation was based, we might perhaps have a people altogether equal, but we should cease to be a people altogether free." In the Confederation debate he reported that at Quebec "not a single one of the representatives of the Government or of the Opposition of any one of the Lower Provinces was in favor of universal suffrage. Everyone felt that in this respect the principle of the British constitution should be carried out, and that classes and property should be represented as well as numbers."

The radical democrats in both the Canadas, who saw in the bankers and railway financiers the principal opponents of a broader democracy, fought unsuccessfully for universal suffrage and the elective principal at all levels of government.

Despite the fact that in the Province of Canada popular pressure had secured an elective Legislative Council in 1856, the delegates at Quebec agreed readily to a non-elective upper chamber. A. A. Dorion denounced "the proposal to restrict the influence and control of the people over the Legislature of the country by substituting a Chamber nominated by the Crown for an Elective Legislative Council." The non-elective Senate was simply a rather more glaring instance of the manifold ways in which a business democracy saw to the safeguarding of the rights and privileges of those—the men of property—who comprise its permanent minority government. The prerogatives of the Crown were seen as a further reassurance.

The Act that enshrined at Westminster at once the interests of property and the deeper aspirations of those who sought "a new political nationality," was the joint product of colonial initiative and pressure and imperial strategy. The birth-certificate of the new transcontinental colonial state bore the imprint of this mixed parentage; the opening words of the British North American Act (1867) proclaim:

> Whereas the Provinces of Canada, Nova Scotia, and New Brunswick have expressed their desire to be federally united into one Dominion under the Crown of the United Kingdom of Great Britain and Ireland, with a constitution similar in principle to that of the United Kingdom: Be it therefore enacted and declared by the Queen's most Excellent Majesty . . . (that) the Provinces of Canada, Nova Scotia and New Brunswick shall form and be one Dominion under the name of Canada . . .

"Canada cannot remain as she is at present," John A. Macdonald had asserted at Quebec three years before. The imperatives of change were working their way toward a new political state, a semi-autonomous federation of colonial provinces, a "Dominion" under the aegis of an Empire which still retained the powers of decision in foreign relations and peace and war. The "dominion from sea to sea," in the text from which the term derived (72 Psalms, v. 8) referred to a fiefdom of the Deity. In practical terms, however, most British Americans took it to mean the domain of Empire that it was in fact. For some, in French Canada particularly, the dominion was exercised by the "other nation" — that of the heirs to the Conquest. First in Lower Canada, then among the Métis of the Northwest, that dominance was questioned.

19

French Canada and the Terms of Union

In the Confederation debate that has been going on for over a century now, diametrically opposed interpretations of what really happened in 1867 continue to multiply and flourish. They achieve their greatest luxuriance of growth and a kind of near-impenetrability on the matter of French-English relations, on the role and status of the "two founding races" (sic) in the Confederation settlement. It is here that we encounter the vexed question of the so-called Compact Theory: Was the British North America Act the product of a kind of treaty between the provinces, negotiated at Charlottetown and Quebec and London? Did it have the connotation of a solemn compact between the French and English speaking "cultural groups"? Or was it neither of these, but purely and simply an act of legislation of the imperial parliament? Or was it all of these together, a "compact-law" creating a new social and political institution?

It may help unravel some of the complexities if we distinguish in the Confederation process two interweaving strands. One is that of *industrial capitalist development,* the source of the drive to unify and expand the home market by uniting the colonial provinces in one state and extending its domain across the continent. (Regional diversities, whether in the Maritimes or Upper Canada or on the Pacific coast, are an argument for a composite or federated state structure; although the pressures of railways and manufacturing weigh on the side of centralization, for reasons of efficiency and control.)

The other strand is provided by the existence side by side of *two distinct national communities of people,* one French speaking, the other English speaking. These two societies had shared to some degree a common historical experience in the hard work of pioneering, in joint struggles against common oppressors, for self-government and popular liberties. But constantly offsetting the factor of community was the corroding, divisive influence of national inequality: the legacy of the Conquest, in Anglo-Canadian economic and political ascendancy, and French-Canadian national resentment.

An explanation that limited itself to only one of these two component strands would be inadequate. Both have to be taken into account, and their actual relationship established.

As we have seen, it was capitalist development in British North America, powered by railway building and an early stage of factory production, that provided the dynamic of change. The Anglo-Canadian bourgeoisie succeeded in unifying the colonies and bringing them under its leadership by means of a series of negotiated deals in five different areas:

1. The Brown-Macdonald alliance of June 1864, uniting the political representatives of Anglo-Canadian business in Toronto and Montreal.

2. Alliance of the foregoing with the leadership of the Roman Catholic Church and the small French Canadian business élite, with Cartier, Taché, Langevin, Chapais as their political spokesmen.

3. Agreement with the Maritime business and political leaders on colonial unification.

4. Negotiating the inclusion of the Hudson's Bay Co.

empire in the Northwest and of the Pacific coast settlements.

5. Getting authorization from the imperial authorities
(reluctant at first, then vigorously active) for the scheme
of British North American union.

Achievement of these agreements took seven years
(1864-71), nine if one includes the date of entry of Prince
Edward Island. (Saskatchewan and Alberta were constituted as provinces in 1905; Newfoundland entered in
1949; Yukon and the North West Territory have yet to
be given provincial status.)

The British North America Acts of 1867 and thereafter
inaugurated a state structure within which capitalist industrialization was able, albeit unevenly and spasmodic-
ally, to expand on an impressive scale the productive
plant of the Dominion. [In transforming the country from
an agrarian to a predominantly industrial one, capitalism
radically altered the social fabric—the urban-rural population ratio, the pattern of government expenditures at
all levels—and hence, rendered increasingly acute the
problems of dominion-provincial and municipal relations.]

In this whole area, the question of fact as to whether
Confederation was originally a compact or agreement
among provinces is perhaps of historical interest,* but
the argument appears somewhat academic in light of the
urgent imperatives of the present. Capitalist centralization of industry and finance posed questions that lay well

---

*Thus, D. G. Creighton: "The new Canada was not the result of
a compact or treaty between free and autonomous provinces; it was
the creation of the Imperial Parliament." Or, conversely, the recent
defense of the compact theory by the Conservative Attorney-General
of Ontario, Mr. Arthur Wishart. It is in relation to the manner of
amendment of the B.N.A. Act that the role and prerogatives of provinces involving a prior "compact" becomes a matter of judicial controversy.

beyond the ken of the most far-seeing of the Fathers. Their intentions (not always luminously clear or unambiguous, in any case) can hardly dictate solutions to problems that are wholly new.

When we turn to the "national question," however, history is relevant in a somewhat different way. For here experiences transmitted from the past are kept alive, embodied in conscious attitudes, patterns of thought and feeling. The inertia of remembrance is buttressed by continuance of conditions that re-enact, in however modified form, the initial trauma. The "actuality" of the British Conquest in French-Canadian experience is the classic example. For the Indian and Eskimo peoples, it has been the invasion by the "white" Europeans, with its ceaseless continuing reminder of conquest, expressed in the present relationship and conditions imposed by the rulers on the ruled. For the British-Canadians, the experience of having successfully and forcibly imposed their own ascendancy exacted its toll on the collective consciousness. "Superiority" can also have the effect of a trauma.

Was there in fact such a thing as a compact between the two "founding peoples"? What, if one did exist, were its terms? Or if there never was one, whence came the widespread and long-lived delusion? The fact is, of course, that somehow or other the two cultural-national communities did find themselves living, after 1867, within the political framework of one British North American state: Durham's "two nations warring in the bosom of a single state" had achieved some basis of cohabitation. The self-government attained by joint effort in 1848 had laid the groundwork for a possible new political relationship. For this, the prerequisite was some measure of recognition of the fact of French and English-Canadian duality, and therewith some acceptance of a concept of equality.

For the French Canadians, the population shift that since 1851 had placed them in the position of a minority made it imperative that they obtain a political structure responsive to the needs and subject to the decisions of their national community. The equality of representation provided in the old Province of Canada could no longer be preserved in face of the immigration-tide and the demand for "rep by pop." Hence the argument in favor of some sort of confederated structure that would include guarantees of national rights and a French Canadian member-state as one of its constituent parts. Herein lay the crucial importance of the "federal principle" in the Confederation controversies.

By the 1860s the Anglo-Canadian business and political leaders were apparently prepared to recognize the validity of Lower Canada's demand for a distinct status and guarantees of linguistic and religious rights. Because of this, they were ready to agree—reluctantly and under strong pressure—to the adoption of the federal principle. Their own preference was for a legislative union, but French-Canadian insistence on a federation was reinforced by similar pressures from Canada West and the Maritimes, none of which wanted to surrender their regional-provincial identities.

It was the acceptance of federalism as the basis of union and of the new state-structure that has given the strongest ground for entertaining the theory of a compact. Professor Donald Creighton, however, vehemently rejects such an interpretation. In his view not only was there no compact between provinces, but above all there was no compact between two peoples! Anything that suggests "cultural duality" or a union founded on recognition of it, is anathema: "The idea of a bicultural compact is a myth." The proof? The fact that the organization and course of discussions at Charlottetown and Quebec indicated only scant attention to "cultural matters":

> The Conferences were not organized on ethnic or cultural lines, and their purpose was not a bilateral cultural agreement . . . In comparison [with the major theme of federal structures] the discussion of ethnic and cultural questions occupied a very minor part of the proceedings. The resolutions adopted on cultural matters were important and essential; but they were few, very precise in their wording, and limited in scope. There was nothing that remotely approached a general declaration of principle that Canada was to be a bilingual or bicultural nation.

This description of the conferences by the most authoritative historian of Confederation is undoubtedly accurate—as far as it goes. But it is singularly incomplete. First, a key fact goes unmentioned. Second, a fact invoked (in the last sentence) is given a rather odd interpretation: a point to which I shall return.

The missing fact is that *prior to* the Charlottetown and Quebec conferences the Canadian leaders had *already* reached agreement on adoption of the federal principle and guarantees of language and religious rights in Lower Canada. What these amounted to, would be tempestuously fought over in French Canada later, once the terms of the Quebec resolution were made public; but at the conferences themselves, endorsation of the principle of federalism and special guarantees did not become an issue. Without that prior agreement among the Canadian representatives there might well not have been a conference at either Charlottetown or Quebec in 1864. Omission of this "detail" is surprising: the more so since Creighton himself, both in his classic biography of Macdonald and in his recent (and admirable) *Road to Confederation,* clearly documents the explicit recognition of Canadian dualism by the chief initiators of confederation. Thus in the Macdonald biography he cites the view, advanced by the Conservative chieftain in the 1850s, that "the Conservatives must learn to recognize and respect not only the multiple religious divisions of Canada West, but also the single basic cultural division between English-Speaking and French-Speaking Canada . . . [Macdonald] was prepared to accept the cultural duality of Canadian life, to recognize that what was in form a unitary province was in fact a half-acknowledged federal state. The union could only be preserved by series of compromises and conventions which sanctioned this cultural duality . . ."

In the later work on Confederation, Creighton writes:

> The acceptance of the "federal principle," against their own political traditions and wishes, was the great concession that the English speaking delegates at Quebec were prepared to make to French Canada; but they agreed to make it only on the clear understanding that the resulting British American union was to be a strongly centralized federation, a federation radically different from that which had helped to precipitate the American Civil War.

All of which sounds rather like an understanding . . . or even a compact. Macdonald himself was no less explicit. Explaining why he had agreed to forego a legislative union in favor of a federal one, despite his preference for a unitary state, Macdonald told the Canadian Assembly in 1865:

> I have again and again stated in the House, that, if practicable, I thought a Legislative Union would be preferable . . . But, on looking at the subject in the Conference, and discussing the matter as we did, most unreservedly, and with a desire to arrive at a satisfactory conclusion, we

found that such a system was impracticable. In the first place, it would not meet the assent of the people of Lower Canada, because they felt that in their peculiar position—being a minority with a different language, nationality and religion from the majority—in case of a junction with the other provinces, their institutions and their laws might be assailed, and their ancestral associations, on which they prided themselves, attacked and prejudiced; it was found that any proposition which involved the absorption of the individuality of Lower Canada—if I may use the expression—would not be received with favor by her people.

Clearly Macdonald had faced up to the necessity of recognition of "the individuality of Lower Canada," rooted in the "language, nationality and religion" of the French Canadians. This recognition was no small element in the Tory leader's statesmanship at this juncture. Without it, one may well doubt whether the union of the colonies could have been effected for many years to come. Acceptance, however limited, of French-English duality enabled the Macdonald-Cartier Government to overcome the deep-seated distrust of large numbers of French Canadians.

Opinion in French Canada was deeply divided. Some who supported the Confederation project saw in it a step toward greater Canadian independence, as a logical sequel to the 1848 achievement of ministerial responsibility. To the numerically small French-Canadian business élite the prospect of economic growth through expanding markets and railway construction (the Intercolonial was to traverse the counties of Rimouski and Temiscouata) was a compelling argument for union—even under Anglo-Canadian hegemony. For many, the establishment within the federation of a Province of Quebec meant a welcome return to the distinct identity possessed by the old province of Lower Canada; moreover the new legislative and political entity was to possess powers and a jurisdiction that held the promise of a significant measure of autonomy for the French-Canadian national community. Furthermore, the linguistic and religious educational provisions of the proposed union carried forward both the democratic gains of 1848 and the traditional safeguards of Church interests that were enshrined in the Quebec Act of 1774. On some or other of all these grounds, the leading businessmen, most of the higher clergy and an important segment of public opinion favored the Confederation agreement.

The overtone of a step toward Canadian independence evoked a sympathetic response on the part of those who thought of themselves as *Canadians,* for whom memories of the blow struck for independence a quarter-century before were vivid still; their past struggles for responsible government and national-democratic rights had scored gains that might now be extended. Moreover, to the memory of past striving was added the spur of present threat. What D'Arcy McGee spoke of as "the warning from without—the American warning" recurs repeatedly in the speeches of the French-Canadian advocates of union in the Canada Assembly debate of 1865. "If the opportunity which now presented itself," said the Prime Minister, E. P. Taché, "were allowed to pass by unimproved, whether we would or would not, we would be forced into the American Union by violence, and if not by violence, would be placed upon an inclined plane which would carry us there insensibly." Hector Langevin, Solicitor-General, posed the question: "What would be the fate of the French Canadians in the case of annexation to the United States? Let us profit by the example of the French race in the U.S., and enquire what has been the fate of the French in Louisiana? What has become of them? What has become of their language, their customs, their manners and their institutions? After the war, hardly a trace will remain to show that the French race has passed that way." Chartier de Lotbinière Harwood, member for Vaudreuil, warned that it would be folly to think that in the event of annexation "French Canadian nationality would long enjoy a separate existence."

Thus aspirations to independence and concern over U.S. expansionism alike offered some common ground with English Canada for agreement on terms of union. What those terms should be, what form the union might assume, and what kind of relationship between the two communities it should embody, became the theme of a hotly contested and long-drawn debate.

Once the substance of the Quebec resolutions became known, toward the close of 1864, a storm of controversy broke loose in Lower Canada. At issue in the dispute was not so much whether there should be established a new federal state, as the undemocratic manner of its proposed adoption and — even more vital — the adequacy or otherwise of the promised "guarantees" of French Canada's national survival.

Opposition both to procedure and to the actual terms of union found vigorous expression in a mass movement of protest headed by Antoine-Aimé Dorion and the *Parti Rouge*. Once again as in the 1830s and '40s petitions circulated and great public rallies were held, demanding popular consultation before federation should be enacted. Such meetings took place in the Montreal area and in the counties of Bagot, Berthier, Chambly, Drummond-Arthabaska, Iberville, Joliette, Maskinongé, Napierville, Richelieu, St. Hyacinthe, St. Jean, St. Maurice . . . The tone of the opposition campaign may be gathered from this excerpt from one of the petitions submitted to the Legislative Assembly and published in the radical democratic newspaper *Le Pays* in February 1865.

> . . . Your petitioners have learned with an astonishment as great as their anxiety, that consideration is being given to making extremely important changes in the Constitution, and this without the people having asked for them or being given any opportunity to express its opinion or its wishes, as to the opportuneness of changes however far-reaching may be the influence they may exert on its destinies . . .
>
> That the local legislature which under this project is to be given to Lower Canada, while the most essential objects of legislation will be beyond its reach, will not even be independent in its own sphere of jurisdiction, since its legislative powers will be permanently subject to interference by the federal government, the only one whose powers resemble those of sovereignty . . .
>
> . . . Your petitioners can see in the proposed Confederation nothing but the outcome and realization of plans hatched at various times by the adversaries of Lower Canada's institutions who, whenever they sought to attack and wipe out the influence of the majority, have urged as a means thereto just such changes as are now to be imposed on the people of Lower Canada . . .
>
> Since the changes proposed will affect both sections of the Province, they should only be adopted with the agreement of the majority of the inhabitants of each section.

Two charges are made here: one, that fundamental decision on constitutional change is being taken without a referral to the electorate; two, that the proposed "local legislature" will lack the status and powers that would be required to protect the rights of the French Canadians as a people.

The desire to evade any consultation with the electorate stemmed, as we have seen, from the acute anxiety of Macdonald and his associates over a possible rejection of their project. With all its intricately balanced commitments to the Grand Trunk directors, the Colonial Office and the governments of the Maritimes, it needed to be put through with an absolute minimum of popular involvement or debate. This flouting of the electorate until long after the union was a *fait accompli* (at which time endorsation was extorted with the help of peremptory admonitions to the voters from the Quebec bishops) is quite in the anti-democratic manner of colonialism. Exclusion from the Charlottetown and Quebec conferences of any representation from the Lower Canada opposition, in contrast with the contrary practice followed in the case of Upper Canadian and the Maritimes delegations, the fact that at the conferences, as one authority notes, "the deliberations were carried on exclusively in English" -- these all were part of a larger pattern. The presence of the "French fact" was to receive minimal recognition; and signs of opposition from that quarter in particular, were to be circumvented or ignored.

At the heart of the debate in Lower Canada were sharply divergent conceptions of what a federal union should be. As against Macdonald's strongly centralized version Dorion and the *Rouges* called for a confederacy of the two Canadas, with the major powers of decision vested in each of the two associated states. A decade earlier Dorion had urged "a Confederation of the two Canadas" based on full recognition of national differences, "giving the largest powers to the local governments and merely a delegated authority to the General Government." The present scheme, which "reserves for the local governments the smallest possible amount of freedom of action," he denounced as being nothing but a thinly disguised legislative union.

At stake here was not merely some minor shading of constitutional-juridical arrangement, but the issue of recognition of the French Canadians *as a nation*. They were being promised and denied that recognition both at once. There was promise in Macdonald's statements, quoted earlier, on "the single, basic cultural division," "cultural duality," and safeguards against "absorption of the individuality of Lower Canada" — an individuality based on "language, nationality and religion." He had clearly expressed his awareness of the implications of the French-Canadian national question in a letter (which the Creighton biography quotes) written in 1856 to a friend on the staff of the Montreal *Gazette*. Observing that in Canada East "More than half . . . of all offices of emolument are held by men not of French origin," an expression of the English "ascendancy . . . of political positions," Macdonald warned: "Take care the French don't find it out and make a counter-cry."

> The truth is, that you British Lower Canadians never can forget that you were once supreme—that Jean Baptiste was your hewer of wood and drawer of water. You struggle, like the Protestant Irish in Ireland, like the Norman invaders in England, not for equality, but ascendancy— the difference between you and those interesting and amiable people being that you have not the honesty to admit it.

And further:

> No man in his senses, can suppose that this country can for a century to come be governed by a totally unfrenchified government. If a Lower Canadian British desires to conquer he must "stoop to conquer." He must make friends with the French, without sacrificing the status of his race or language, he must respect their nationality. Treat them as a nation and they will act as a free people generally do

—generously. Call them a faction and they become factious.

"Treat them as a nation": there were not a few French Canadians who believed that the acceptance of the federal principle meant just that.

Were they being duped? Grounds for suspicion were not altogether lacking. Macdonald's unitary federalism showed disturbing signs of susceptibility to being turned into its opposite, a kind of unitary non-federalism. Galt, the man of Montreal business, told a Toronto audience that "at no far distant day, we may become willing to enter into a legislative union, instead of a federal union, as now proposed." Macdonald had confided to Malcolm Cameron in December 1864—a bare two months after the Quebec conference—a prophecy that revealed his real aim: "If the Confederation goes on, you, if spared the ordinary age of man, will see both local parliaments and governments absorbed in the federal power. This is as plain to me as if I saw it accomplished." There is an unconfirmed but plausible story to the effect that in London Macdonald right up to the last minute sought to have his scheme for a unitary state substituted for the federal union provided for in the Quebec agreement. In Cartier's words, Macdonald "would, but for me, have forced a legislative union upon us."

What emerged, in any case, was a design for federation, albeit a strongly centralized one. The designation "Confederation" was itself a curious misnomer:* was it derived from a politician's instinct to steal something from the Opposition (the *Rouges* were demanding the looser union of a confederacy) or from the well-known Tory sympathy with the Southern Confederacy?

*Cf. Reference Notes.

Was it accidental that recognition of the "French fact" was meager indeed, limited to the narrow clauses on linguistic and confessional rights? Donald Creighton is factually quite right in his insistence that in the B.N.A. Act, "there was nothing that remotely approached a general declaration of principle that Canada was to be a bilingual or bicultural nation." But to invoke this fact in order to suggest that there had been no understanding or compact between representatives of the two communities is to give history a peculiar twist, to say the least. It was precisely the lack, despite all earlier assurances, of any such declaration of principle that gave ground for angry suspicion in French Canada that the "federalism" was somehow strangely flawed.

What, in all this, was the role of the French-Canadian conservatives, the only spokesmen of their national community who were present at the Confederation conferences? Creighton makes much of the fact that at the Quebec conference the French-Canadian representatives "had very little to say." J. C. Bonenfant also notes that "Cartier himself seems to have been rather silent during the conference." As to the issue of minority language rights—to be protected for the English in Quebec but not for the French in New Brunswick or Ontario—Creighton states: "There is no evidence that the French speaking delegates at the Conference . . . were dissatisfied with these provisions . . ." "None of the delegates, moreover, either Canadians or Maritimers, showed much concern for ethnic or cultural values; they gave the French language and the French civil code comparatively little attention . . ." All that this proves, surely, is (a) that the English speaking majority assumed that the "French question" had already been fully resolved by the prior Macdonald-Cartier entente, and (b) that the French-Canadian representatives, being of the same opinion, saw no reason to agitate for better terms of union.

The historical reality of the "compact" is to be seen, not in any legal or political document, but in the fact that the creation of the Canadian state was the joint work of the dominant Anglo-Canadian bourgeoisie, its French-Canadian subordinates and the semi-feudal Church. The first step toward the compact was the "great coalition" of June 1864. The prime importance that English speaking historians have attached to Brown's alliance with Macdonald to institute a new state structure, is not without justification. The compact between Toronto and Montreal capitalists was a necessary pre-condition for a union in which hegemony was to belong to the English-Canadian bourgeoisie. The compact with the powerful Church and the weak French Canadian bourgeoisie, though indispensable, was secondary.

The role of Cartier and his associates in delivering French Canada to the Anglo-Canadian state builders is illuminated by some correspondence cited in the biography of George Brown by Professor J. M. S. Careless. Writing about the knighthood conferred on Macdonald alone, following Confederation*, Brown assured Cartier that "the great constitutional changes that have just been accomplished" owed much to him: ". . . without your aid they could not have been accomplished. Lower Canada was the difficulty in the way and you were the only man in Lower Canada, who when the crisis arrived, had the pluck and the influence to take the bull by the horns. You ran the risk of political death by the course you took, Mr. Macdonald ran no risk whatever."

Cartier's acceptance of the terms of federal union, involving as they did "both the loss of the entrenched

---

*Cartier and Galt were knighted later.

French position in the existing union and the establishment of rep by pop within a new federation" was, in the
words of Careless, "an act of highest political courage . . .
utterly essential." "Yet, by its very nature, Cartier's act
was fundamtally passive." The active driving force came
from English Canada: from Brown, in his biographer's
judgment: certainly, from the Anglo-Canadian business
community, of which he and Galt and Macdonald were
the dynamic political chieftains.

As representatives of the interests of the Church and of
the leading French-Canadian business group Cartier,
Taché and Langevin had insisted on a federal union as
the necessary means of safeguarding both those particular
interests and also (to the degree that they coincided) the
general interest of their national community. The "catch,"
however, lay in the limitedness of that convergence of
interests. Assuredly, protection of the confessional arrangements in the school system, and of landed and business
property rights under the Civil Code, were valid enough
priority claims of a society in which religion and the traditional order were dominant values; and they could be
largely safeguarded under the provincial-jurisdiction
clauses of the B.N.A. Act. A "provincial existence" was
sufficient for them. But was it enough to guarantee the
full right of the French-Canadian nation to *survivance*
and *épanouissement,* to survival and full flowering? Cartier apparently thought it was. His argument, unwit-
tingly, revealed the fatal flaw in the whole clerical-conservative conception—a flaw which has since been devoutly
taken over by the most fervent apologists of official Libe-
ralism. In the 1865 Canada Assembly debate Cartier assured his compatriots:

Under the Federation system, granting to the control of

the General Government these large questions of general interest in which the differences of race and religion had no place, it could not be pretended that the rights of either race or religion could be invaded at all. We were to have a General Parliament to deal with the matters of defence, tariff, excise, public works, and these matters absorbed all individual interest. Now, he would ask those self-styled nationalists who accused him of bartering fifty-eight counties in Lower Canada to John Bull . . . under what supposition could they think it possible for any injustice to be done to the French Canadians by the General Government?

Only, perhaps, under the supposition that national equality involved more than "cultural matters" alone; that these could not be severed from the areas of economic and political decision and assigned to the "local" government, while the other, basic powers were left to the central authority; and that this arrangement constituted something less than an "equal partnership" of peoples.*

To appreciate the implications of Cartier's approach it is sufficient to recall the terms in which Macdonald visualized the relationship between the central and "local" (or provincial) governments. His analogy is striking:

The General Government assumes towards the local governments precisely the same position as the Imperial Government holds with respect to each of the colonies now.

What it all adds up to is this: on the one hand the French-Canadian nation is "given to understand" that it is entering into a partnership based on the principle of

*CF. Donald V. Smiley: "Those French speaking leaders influential in the contriving of the Confederation settlement saw no challenge to their cultural community in the dominance of the federal authorities in economic matters." (*The Canadian Political Nationality*, p. 8.)

equality. On the other, it is accorded a state structure which embodies no such relationship. The much-vaunted "federalism" is not that of a bi-national state; it is something else again. The optical illusion may persist, but the reality is different. The deceptive ambiguity has been well characterized by M. Francois-Albert Angers:

> At bottom what was evil in the Canadian "confederation" derived from the ambiguity of a federative system which juridically only associated territorial units, at the very time that it had engendered the hope, through the statements of the constitutional conferences, that two peoples (not identified in the constitutional structure) were to be associated on an equal footing to create a great country.
>
> (LE DEVOIR, 30 juin, 1967)

What was wrong with the 1867 conception of British North American federalism was not that its authors failed to foresee the changes in allocation of governmental responsibilities that urbanization and modern industrialism would later make necessary. *It was that they evaded the binational reality.* Their effort to reduce the nation to a matter of limited religious and linguistic peculiarity, their denial of the nation as an organic entity whose cultural component cannot be arbitrarily detached from the rest of its socio-economic being, all this relieved them of having to conceive of a genuinely binational federation based on equal rights of full self-determination for each of its components. Such a conception in any case would have seemed to them a fantasy of democracy, if not of Red republicanism.

Cartier shared with Macdonald and the rest of their colleagues an abhorrence of the tenets of democracy: universal suffrage, he argued, meant "mob rule" (hence the Civil War in the U.S.!) :

> We were not now discussing the great problem presented
> to our consideration, in order to propagate democratic
> principles. Our attempt was for the purpose of forming a
> Federation with a view of perpetuating the monarchical
> element . . . In our Federation the monarchical principle
> would form the leading feature, while on the other side
> of the lines . . . the ruling power was the will of the mob,
> the rule of the populace.

Wedded to the Grand Trunk and Bank of Montreal
interests, the clerical-conservative mind in its addiction to
cultivation of the "monarchical element" was logically
colonialist and anti-democratic. It excluded in advance a
democratic stand on the national question. With British
and Anglo-Canadian control of the economy of Lower
Canada, Anglo-Canadian dominance in the federal state
power, reinforced by all the panoply and military might
of Westminster—what more was needed to ensure the ascendancy of the Anglo-Canadians in the new Dominion?

More, in any event, was forthcoming. In particular, the
unabashed intervention of the bishops in the elections of
October 1867, after the new Constitution had been proclaimed and set in operation. Bishop Laroque of St. Hyacinthe reminded the electorate that their liberty of choice
did not extend to the right of "rejecting a constitutionally
and legitimately accomplished fact." Opposition to the
Government, warned Bishop Baillargeon of Quebec,
would be equivalent to "taking the path of anarchy,
treason and revolt." Hector Langevin's brother, the Bishop
of Rimouski, indicated in terms that did not exactly
invite dissent, the true and awesome origin of the British
North America Act:

> You will respect this new constitution that is given you,
> as the expression of the supreme will of the legislator, of
> the legitimate authority, and consequently that of God
> Himself.

That the Quebec electorate should thereupon have returned twenty opposition members (as against some forty government supporters) is a tribute to the independence of spirit of no inconsiderable number of voters.

In the years 1864 to 1867 mass popular opposition, led by the *Parti rouge* combined with the pressure of some more conservative forces, had defeated the effort to impose a unitary state. The federal character of the new state structure embodied at least a partial recognition of the "French fact" in Canada. But full recognition was withheld. The collusion of the bourgeois-clerical French-Canadian leadership with Anglo-Canadian big business and the imperial power constituted a more potent force than the small middle-class, national-democratic and radical movement. Yet the declaration of Antoine-Aimé Dorion on the indestructibility of the demand for recognition of the French-Canadian nation embodied a kernel of fundamental truth regarding democracy and the nation that has retained its cogency for a century. To those who would deny national equality it states a challenge that is vital still:

> The people of Lower Canada are attached to their institutions in a manner that defies any attempt to change them in that way. They will not change their religious institutions, their laws and their language, for any consideration whatever. A million of inhabitants may seem a small thing to the mind of a philosopher who sits down to write out a constitution. He may think it would be better that there should be one religion, one language and one system of laws . . . but the history of every country goes to show that not even by the power of the sword can such changes be accomplished.

20

A People's Rising in the Northwest

> *The Métis have as their paternal ancestors the former employees of the Hudson's Bay and Northwest companies; and as their maternal ancestors Indian women belonging to different tribes.*
>
> *The French word "Métis" is derived from the latin participle* mixtus, *meaning mixed; it renders well the idea it is meant to convey.*
>
> *Appropriate as the corresponding English expression "Half breed" was for the first generation of mixture of blood, now that European and Indian blood is mingled in all degrees, it is no longer adequate.*
>
> *The French word Métis expresses the idea of this mixing as satisfactorily as possible.*

With these words Louis Riel began the last memorandum written before his death. Before proceeding to a description of the background of the struggles of 1869-70 and 1885, he made "a small observation, *en passant* and not to hurt anyone's feelings." Sometimes, he notes, a quite kind and polite person will say to one of his people, "You don't look Métis at all. Surely you haven't much Indian blood. Anyone would take you for white." Disconcerted, the Métis, who is proud of his origin on both sides, casts about for an answer. What he is thinking to himself is: "True, our Indian origin is humble, but it is right that we should honor our mothers as well as our fathers. Why should we be concerned about the proportion of our European or Indian blood? Since we have some of each, gratitude and filial love command us to say: *We are Métis."*

These were the people who made up the majority of the population in the Red River settlement. Buffalo-hunters, boatmen, carters, small farmers, they were kinsmen of the Cree and Sarcee, the Saulteaux and Blackfoot. Of some 30,000 Indian warriors in the Northwest, Riel estimated that a third were of the Métis. It was these part-Indian plainsmen who struck a blow against arbitrary rule imposed from Ottawa, and won self-government for the people of the Prairies in the people's rising of 1869-70 and again in 1885. In these movements of armed resistance to a peculiar variant of colonialism, the Indian and his kindred, from being objects became the active subjects of the historical process: the fact that the Métis risings were the only instance of effective intervention "from below", by the masses, in the Confederation settlement, has not been emphasized by Canadian historians. Their reticence is not without significance.

> "He is an Indian" is a statement that carries with it a connotation of *belonging to a certain social stratum or class* . . . Indian "race" is a vague biological notion, but a perfectly clear social one: the "Indian race" is the great mass of people, indigenous or of mixed origin, which in its majority from Mexico to the south of the continent, continues to live in a wretched economic, physical and cultural state . . . in spite of the existence of railroads, automobiles and aeroplanes.

In these words Dr. Alejandro Lipschutz, the eminent Chilean anthropologist and authority on race and *métissage,* exposes the roots of a hypocrisy that resorts to race prejudice in order to justify social oppression. "This discrimination that is called *racial* is nothing but a powerful instrument of *social* discrimination, in defense of social privileges acquired by conquest . . ." The myth of white racial "superiority" is the *post factum* attempt at justification of the conditions created by European enslavement of other peoples in Africa, Asia, the Americas. The myth is of ancient lineage:

> Racial discrimination between different human ethnic groups, the notion that some human races are *predestined* to rule and others to obey, has antecedents thousands of years old. This concept of a *social* predestination deriving from a *biological* and racial one, European thought acquired from Aristotle* . . . So tranquilizing is the concept of biological predestination that we forget any other concept of the origin of social stratification among men. We hardly know the names of those pre-Aristotelian historians who insisted that the division into masters and slaves is not the result of *physis,* or differentiated nature, but of *nomos,* of law imposed by human malevolence, dictated by the interest of one group, and facilitated by brute force.

By the provisions of the B.N.A. Act Indian affairs came under the federal jurisdiction. In view of the prospective takeover of the West, Ottawa had Crown Lands Inspector A. J. Russell conduct an inquiry into resources and legal title in the new territories. Reporting in 1868 on the vast wealth and expanse of the H.B. Co. domain, Russell expressed the view that while the Company held lawful hunting and fishing rights in the territories ceded to it under the Charter of 1670, it had no outright claim to ownership, this belonging rightfully from time immemorial to the original occupants—the Indian peoples. As Russell pointed out:

*The "Nature" (physis) of every man is given "right from the moment of birth"; and this nature determines that some are made to command, and others to obey. (Aristotle, *Politics,* p. 18)

> In Canada, Britain recognized the rights of the Indians by purchasing their lands and paying annually stipulated amounts . . .
>
> Today this annual payment is made by the Government of Canada. In face of these facts, after having paid for all the lands purchased on our behalf (by Britain) and for those which we ourselves bought from the Indians, are we to be compelled to recognize the rights of the Hudson's Bay Company to lands which it has never bought or paid for? And is it in conformity with justice to the Indians, so loudly proclaimed in Britain, that in taking possession of their lands, instead of paying them full value for it, we should make a gift of the greater part of this sum to the H.B. Co., which never acquired from the true proprietors the slightest right to these territories?

If not in conformity with justice, the arrangement was wholly consonant with the class interests and outlook of the businessmen-politicans who were negotiating with the London bankers and Hudson's Bay shareholders. Because in the eyes of Victorian imperialists the Indians and Métis of the Northwest were not worthy of notice, the transfer of Rupert's Land was being effected with total disregard for the inhabitants. In the words of W. L. Morton, "One of the greatest transfers of territory and sovereignty in history was conducted as a mere transaction in real estate."

A contemporary who himself participated in the military expedition against the Métis had this to say of the handling of the transfer:

> In these negotiations between the Hudson's Bay Company and the Imperial and Dominion Governments, it does not appear that the feelings of the little colony at Red River were taken into account at all . . . Though there can be no doubt that they would have been fairly and justly treated by Canada, yet it cannot be a matter of wonder to any impartial person that they did not take quite the

same view of the matter, but objected to be transformed from a Crown colony to a "colony of a colony," and handed over to the Dominion, *bon gré mal gré,* like so many head of cattle.

Such was the opinion of Captain G. L. Huyshe, author of *The Red River Expedition (1871).*

For the people of the Red River and Assiniboine country, the coming change loomed as a threat from the unknown. Descendants of the Scots settlement "planted" by Lord Selkirk in 1813, survivors of the war of extermination waged by the Nor'westers and the Bay, pioneers who had withstood the scourges of drought and flood and locusts, they held their land, laid out in narrow river-lots like those on the St. Lawrence, under the suzerainty of the merchant-feudal monopoly of the Bay.* Takeover by the new Dominion would affect in different ways the nomadic Indians and the settled Métis; but for both the prospect of large-scale immigration from the East, railway-construction and a new urban commercialism loomed as a threatening upheaval.

The merchant-capitalism of the Bay had been based on a semi-feudal exploitation of its own "servants," and of the labor of the hunting tribes of Cree, Assiniboine and Blackfoot. The Indian labor force was the main foundation of the trade in furs; it was "paid" in cheap trade-goods (over-priced) at the Company store—a swindle of colossal proportions that had been worked for two hundred years, and had built the wealth and power of the private proprietors of half a continent.

The Company was now, seemingly, to be bought off. Having held these vast territories in feudal trust, with

---

*Population of the Red River settlement in 1831: 2,417; 1840: 4,369. In 1871 it was made up of: 5,720 French Métis; 4,080 English-speaking Métis; 1,600 Canadians, Scots and others.

accompanying rights to carry on hunting and an enormously profitable trade, it was now to be paid for the land as though it were its outright property (which it was not), and still left with its rights of trade and its main northern posts.

The Indians, the original occupants, were to be driven ever further west, and "relieved" of their hunting-grounds by a series of bargain-treaties (the first, in 1872), the rich beneficiaries of which were regularly the new purchaser-occupants. As for the Métis of the settlements, their answer to this "annexation without consultation" was a movement of democratic mass resistance that stopped the Ottawa take-over in its tracks, struck a blow for national equality and won a modicum of self-government for the people of the Northwest.

Months before the December 1, 1869 date set for transfer of the territory, survey parties arrived from Canada and began laying out township and section lines that cut across the long, narrow river lots of the settlers. In response to what looked like a threat of eviction, the Métis began to organize resistance. A party of eighteen horsemen rode up to the farm of André Nault and compelled the surveyors to abandon their task: without the permission of the people, the Métis spokesman asserted, the Canadian authorities had no right to conduct surveys in the territory. The spokesman was Louis Riel, 25 year old son of the miller who had led the protest movement in 1849.

From this first challenge to the arbitrary incursion from Canada the militant Métis went on to establish a disciplined organization and central leadership, in the traditional style of the buffalo hunt. The "Comité national des Métis" was formed on October 16, 1869, with John Bruce as chairman, Louis Riel as secretary, representing the united effort of English and French-speaking Métis. Their counsellor, at whose house they had met, was Abbé Ritchot, who represented the interest of the Church in maintaining its foothold in the West against encroachment from Orange Protestant Ontario: clerical influence that would persist in the Métis resistance movement.

Ottawa, having in August sent surveyors, in September dispatched its Lieutenant-Governor-designate William McDougall to take over at Fort Garry. He got no farther than Pembina, south of the border. The Métis Committee, now with some five hundred armed horsemen under its command, had a barricade put up at St. Norbert on the road from the U.S. border and sent McDougall a peremptory order denying him admittance to the territory except by permission of the Committee. So at Pembina McDougall remained, ignominiously camped on the doorstep.

On November 2 the Committee took possession of Fort Garry itself, the key position at Red River. The Hudson's Bay Company authorities were powerless to resist. A fortnight later, representatives of the Red River parishes assembled in Convention. Riel urged them "to give thought to the formation of a provisional government, both to provide protection and to deal with Canada and compel it to accord us a form of responsible government."

On learning of the stand taken by the Métis, Ottawa postponed the date of the takeover and appealed to London for assistance. So long as the actual transfer of ownership from the H.B. Co. had not occurred, responsibility could conveniently be placed on the Imperial authority, despite the fact that it was the premature initiatives on the part of Canada that had provoked the popular resistance. Uninformed of the postponement, McDougall crossed the border, issued a proclamation "taking possession" of the Territory of Assiniboia in the Queen's name, and prudently withdrew once more to Pembina. Meanwhile he sent in military agents to assist the handful of Orange Ontario annexationists, led by the aggressive John Schultz, in organizing the overthrow of the Métis Committee. This movement of subversion, through its organ *The Nor'Wester*, asserted that the "indolent and careless" Métis and Indian peoples were fated to "fall back before the march of a superior intelligence" (of Anglo-Saxondom). Its repeated attempts at violent overthrow of the popularly-constituted regime were to create constant tension and later compelled Riel to resort to measures of retribution.

On December 8 the Convention replied to McDougall with a "Declaration of the People of Rupert's Land and the North West." "A people," it said, "when it has no government, is free to adopt one form of government in preference to another . . ." Two days later a provisional government was formed. The "responsible government" that Riel had advocated as against the appointive council provided for in McDougall's instructions was now a reality—established by the essentially revolutionary action of the popular majority.

As had been the case in 1837, the militant base of the popular resistance movement was made up of workers; while the "men of property" were those who vacillated in the name of "moderation," or stood aside entirely from the struggle. Those who were "restless" and "listened to Riel," Morton notes, were "The tripmen and the hunters, . . . particularly the turbulent Saskatchewan boatmen of the Portage la Loche brigades" — all of whom formed the core of the Métis military force. On the other hand, "The wealthy plains traders and the well-to-do traders" held back, undermining Métis unity — "a factor of prime importance throughout the insurrection."

Ottawa's response to the affirmation of a new, people's power was twofold. It combined partial recognition with preparations for repression. As though to rub salt into the wounded pride of its discomfited "plenipotentiary" at Pembina, Macdonald informed him that "It is quite open by the Law of Nations for the inhabitants to form a Government *ex necessitate* [from necessity] for the protection of life and property, and such a Government has certain sovereign rights by the *jus gentium* [law of nations] . . ." Commissioners were sent to Red River from Ottawa to sound out the Provisional Government: first, two French Canadians, then a powerful figure in the Hudson Bay Co., Donald Smith (with £500 for bribery where such might seem judicious).

Ottawa trod gently at this juncture: the danger of intervention at Red River by U.S. agents was apparent; the majority of the Métis were Catholic, and the Church was a power there; an armed clash might lead to an Indian war (on the plains across the border the Sioux had been fighting desperately to stem American encroachment); above all, there was *no armed force available and in reach*, with which to impose annexation.

So Donald Smith intrigued, spent £500 bribing whom he could, and on Jan. 18-19 spoke, together with Riel, to a two-day mass meeting of the settlers, held outdoors in 20° below weather. A new committee was elected, of twenty French and twenty English-speaking settlers, to draw up terms of negotiation with Canada. Smith invited them to send delegates to Ottawa.

Instead of undermining the Provisional Government, Smith's visit actually had the effect of consolidating it and sanctioning its authority. The terms of negotiation were drafted as a "List of Rights" for presentation to Ottawa. After lengthy discussions and some revisions, the List finally included the demand that "the country shall be governed, as regards its local affairs, as the provinces of Ontario and Quebec are now governed, by a Legislature elected by the people, and a Ministry responsible to it, under a Lieutenant-Governor appointed by the Governor-General of Canada . . . That the English and French languages be common in the Legislature and Courts, and that all public documents and acts of the Legislature be published in both languages. That the judge of the Supreme Court speak the French and English languages. That treaties be concluded between the Dominion and the several Indian tribes of the country as soon as possible . . . That all properties, rights and privileges, as hitherto enjoyed by us, be respected; and the recognition and arrangement of local custom, usages, and privileges, be made under the control of the Local Legislature. That the Local Legislature of this Territory have full control of all the public land inside a circumference having Fort Garry as the centre, and that the radii of this circumference be the number of miles that the American line is distant from Fort Garry." A delegation of three, including Abbé Ritchot, was elected to convey the List of Rights to Ottawa.

During the whole period of the visit of commissioners to Red River, the preliminary negotiation and the journey to Ottawa of delegates from the Provisional Government, a line of policy with quite different implications was being set in train by Macdonald and his cabinet. By December they had applied to London for the use of Imperial troops; in a private letter that referred to Smith's being sent west "to carry the olive branch," Macdonald wrote: "Should these miserable half-breeds not disband, they must be put down." And in another letter: "These impulsive half-breeds have got spoiled by this *émeute* [disturbance], and must be kept down by a strong hand until they are swamped by the influx of settlers."

Like Durham before him, Macdonald took it for granted that representative institutions were admissible for a British majority only; and until a satisfactory ethnic composition was obtained, the majority must be "kept down." (This same colonialist principle was to be adhered to in our own day in the North West Territories, with their "non-white" aboriginal majority.)

While negotiating with the Provisional Government, Ottawa was secretly arranging to have it crushed by military force. On January 3 Macdonald referred to a projected "exhibition of force next Spring"; early that month orders were given to have a military road prepared west of the Lakehead. On January 26 he wrote to the Colonial Secretary urging that the Imperial Government "co-operate liberally with us in the way of a Regular Force." In addition to putting down the Métis, the provision of such a force, he argued, "will convince the U.S. Government and people that Her Majesty's Government have no intention of abandoning this continent." On February 23 word came that the British Government had agreed on participation in the punitive expedition.

Relations with the United States being what they were, there was no prospect of Ottawa's getting permission to send an armed force to Red River via Chicago and St. Paul. It would have to go by way of the Great Lakes and then overland, clearing a road as it went; and that could not be done until Spring.

The hot-heads of Schultz's "Canadian party," however, were not prepared to wait. Towards the end of February at Portage la Prairie they raised the banner of revolt and a detachment marched on Fort Garry. Once again, as with that of two months earlier, the attempt failed for lack of support among the settlers. Forty-eight men with their leader, a Major Boulton, were taken prisoner. One of the prisoners, an Orangeman named Thomas Scott, attacked the guards and threatened Riel's life: he was court-martialed and, on March 4, executed. This measure, intended as a warning to would-be subverters of the Provisional Government, apparently had the desired effect at Red River; but in Ontario it was seized upon by the jingoist backers of Schultz, who launched a frenzied campaign to "avenge the murder of Scott!" With French Canada strongly sympathizing with Riel, the Ontario agitation seriously strained relations within the newly-formed Confederation. But the issue of Scott's execution gave Macdonald a political justification for the planned military expedition which it had hitherto lacked. So much so, in fact, that the impression was allowed to grow up that the "Scott case" was the *cause* of the expedition: a fallacy that the dates and correspondence cited above emphatically refute.

On April 11 the delegates of the Provisional Government, led by Abbé Ritchot, arrived in Ottawa. Macdonald, Cartier and other members of the cabinet negotiated with them on the basis of the "List of Rights" drawn up at Red River. Out of these negotiations came the draft of the Manitoba* Act. Passed on May 12, 1870, it established a new province, as the people of the Northwest had demanded. True, the province was limited in size to what is now the southern part of Manitoba: the rest of the territory was still to be administered by Ottawa. The equal right to use of the French language was upheld. An appointive legislative council was provided; but by and large, the demand of the people of Red River for

---

*The name is from the Cree, "Spirit Strait."

recognition and representative government had been met.

Yet simultaneously with the negotiations and drafting of the Act, preparations quietly went on for what Macdonald referred to as the "military matter." So far as Ottawa was concerned, a corollary of the passing of the Manitoba Act was the requirement that the people's power set up at Fort Garry must be put down. If parliamentary institutions were to be granted—and they could not, clearly, be withheld with safety—then they must be installed "from above," by the Anglo-Canadian bourgeois state, controlled by businessmen and backed by bayonets.

In May, a combined force of British regular troops and Canadian volunteer militia, commanded by Col. Wolseley, took ship at Collingwood; from the Lakehead, it made a laborious trek overland, reaching Red River in August.

At Fort Garry, meanwhile, Riel and the Provisional Government and Legislative Assembly (formed in April) had agreed to the proposed terms of the Manitoba Act. Both Abbé Ritchot and Bishop Taché assured Riel that Ottawa stood pledged to grant a full amnesty. The military force then heading westward was, in the words of its commander, engaged upon a "mission of peace." Riel, anticipating a peaceful transfer of office, disbanded his garrison. Only at the last moment did he realize that the force advancing in assault formation intended to storm the fort and take himself and other members of his government prisoner . . . or lynch them: the volunteers from Ontario were sworn to "hang Riel!" There was no alternative but flight; the Provisional Government dispersed, its leaders going into hiding. Macdonald's policy of coercion-with-conciliation had worked.

The issue of amnesty was not finally resolved for another seven years. The courts denied that the Provisional

Government had possessed a legal character; executive power, under British law, derives only from the Crown. The people, however, had nonetheless asserted their claim to sovereignty; the existence of Manitoba as a province was the proof of it. As though to underline the point, they twice elected Louis Riel, when in hiding and in banishment, to the House of Commons. He might not take his seat (though once he appeared, to sign the register of the House, then vanished); but the people of Red River had spoken out, and their voice could not be wholly silenced.

By a curious irony, when a threat of Fenian incursions took shape in 1871, it was to the fugitive Louis Riel that the Provincial authorities turned for help. He organized a detachment of Métis horsemen; then, when the threat passed, withdrew once more into obscurity.

Responsible government, which was withheld in the first years of the new provisional administration, was conceded by 1874. By then a new era of settlement was under way. The Métis, many of them, withdrew westward to the Saskatchewan; their trials—and their struggles—were not ended yet.

Manitoba was thus the product of a complex of forces: the momentum of the Confederation movement, combining Canadian political and economic aims with an imperial strategy of continental unification of the colonial settlements; an Ontario-based western expansionism leading to agricultural settlement on the Prairies and a new regional capitalist development; relinquishment by the Bay of its rule in the southern areas, the effort of the Roman Catholic Church to establish its position in the West, and of French Canada to assert its claim to equal rights and recognition as a participant in an all-Canadian

development;* the dispossession and driving further westward of the Indians of the Plains; the national-democratic
resistance of the Métis winning, through mass action and
the creation of a short-lived people's power, a larger
measure of self-government sooner than was intended by
Ottawa, and leaving a heritage of militant democracy that
became one of the vital components of Western radicalism.

It is noteworthy that in the organization of the Métis
convention and formation of the Provisional Government
the principle of French-English binational equality was
observed. The people's movement in the Northwest not
only embodied a first attempt to realize a French-Canadian presence in the new territories; it exemplified the
principle of equal rights on which alone a joint partnership of the two national communities could be successfully
built. The Anglo-Canadian rejection of that approach in
the years that followed has left a breach that is part of
the contemporary Confederation crisis.

---

*For Morton, "the fundamental issue of the troubles, (was) the
relation of French and English in Canada and in Manitoba": and
what began in the later 1870s was "the modification of the constitution of 1870 and of the principle of duality"—a process marked by
"the growing weight of Ontario settlers in the electorate . . ."

21

Self-Government on the Pacific Coast

When the Nor'westers pushed their trading outposts beyond the Rockies to the mouth of the Columbia, they blazed the trail for a future transcontinental British North America with its commercial headquarters on the St. Lawrence. But the prospect was drastically altered by the defeat of the North West Company in 1821 at the hands of the Hudson's Bay Company. Montreal's link with the Pacific coast was thereby severed, and the English monopoly, with its head office in Fenchurch Street (between St. Paul's and the Tower of London), suddenly came into possession of a vast new domain on the Pacific. To the overlords of the Bay, the change meant simply an enlargement in prospects of profit, bearing no relation to Canadian interests or possibilities. Settlement and agriculture were repugnant to the interests of fur-pillage; the Company would tolerate them only insofar as distance and economy demanded the build-up of local bases of supply.

Yet settlement was needed if the ill-defined expanse of empire on the Coast was to be kept in British hands. The North Pacific was witnessing a sharp and growing struggle among Russian, American and British traders, behind whom stood the merchant-imperial capitalist powers, reaching out for the markets of Asia. The sea-otter and beaver pelts promised a handsome profit; sold in Canton or North China, they were a means of obtaining tea, silks and other luxury goods, for shipment to London or Boston or St. Petersburg.

In this broad setting, the north-west fur trade established new and wider connections with the rapidly growing world market. Based on the exploitation of the Indian and Aleut tribes in one of the last "unsettled" areas of the continent, the traders of three mercantile powers waged ruthless, cut-throat competition among themselves. What united them, however, was their readiness to join hands at the slightest sign of resistance on the part of the native peoples.

Thus, when Dr. John McLoughlin, chief factor of the H.B. Co. at Fort Vancouver (on the Columbia) learned that some American fur-traders were being worsted by an Indian war party he promptly went to their rescue. He informed those Indians who were in the employ of his Company that "if they injured one American, it would be just the same offense as if they injured one of his servants, and they would be treated equally as enemies." In 1847 the H.B. Co. provided $1800 worth of provisions to American traders warring against the Cayuse Indians in Oregon. The policy of a united front against "natives" had been laid down by the London Committee of the Company, which told McLoughlin: ". . . You will on all occasions render any protection in your power to Americans, Russians, or any other strangers . . . against the treachery or violence of the natives." Even though the strangers might be "competitors in trade," the letter went on, "all feelings of self interest must be laid aside when we can relieve or assist our fellow creatures." With such Christian sentiments did the Company sanctify the dispossession of the Indians (who evidently were something less than "fellow creatures").

As imperial expansion, impelled by the industrial

revolution in Britain and the U.S.A., led to sharpening contest for control of the Pacific northwest, the rival powers drew boundary lines across the continent, corresponding more or less closely to their power to enforce them. Thus, in 1818 Britain and the U.S.A. had fixed the frontiers of British North America at the 49th parallel, westward from Lake of the Woods to the Rockies. Beyond the mountains, no agreement as to the border could be arrived at; so a ten-year joint occupancy was proclaimed (it was renewed in 1828). In 1819 Spain and the U.S. set their California border at the 42nd parallel. From here northward was the disputed expanse of "Old Oregon," embracing what are now the states of Oregon, Washington, Idaho, parts of Montana and British Columbia.

In 1824 the H.B. Co. established its headquarters at Fort Vancouver, on the Columbia River: the fort on the site of Astoria (on the south shore of the river mouth) was given up in the expectation that that side of the Columbia would become U.S. territory. This same consideration led the Hudson's Bay men to set about exterminating the beaver throughout the entire area. Less successful was the Company's attempt to break into the market at Canton. Here, since the monopoly rights of the East India Company barred the way to the monopolists of the Bay, the latter had to arrange to have their furs sold in China by an American firm: this subterfuge worked for a time, but did not suffice to compel the East India Co. to allow its London rival access to Canton.

The Hudson's Bay Co. operated in the districts of Columbia and New Caledonia (in the interior country). To the north was Russian America (Alaska), which by the mid-century numbered some 45 Russian settlements with a population of around 10,000 people, more than three times as many as the H.B. Co.'s employees on the Coast. Russian trading operations were not confined to Alaska: in 1811 they had established Fort Ross, in Bodega Bay, California, as a provisioning base (it was sold to the Americans in 1839). The actual southern boundary of Russian America, however, was fixed by agreement with Britain and the U.S. in 1825, at 54° 40′ (now the southern tip of the Alaska "Panhandle").

The British and Russian fur-traders, although competing for control of the Indian tribes of the northern interior, tended to unite in opposition to the expanding trade of the Americans. Thus in 1839 the H.B. Co. and the Russian-American Fur Co. reached an agreement on the sale of provisions to the latter: the H.B. Co. set up a subsidiary, the "Puget Sound Agricultural Co.," to develop farming, for this purpose as well as for its own needs, on the mainland near Nisqually. For its part, the Russian company leased the Alaska "Panhandle" to the H.B. Co. under an agreement that was renewed every ten years, for as long as Alaska remained Russian territory. At the time of the Crimean War, the two companies mutually maintained a benevolent neutrality.

Protected on its northern flank by this arrangement, the Hudson's Bay Co. could now face with more assurance the threat developing to the south. American settlement had started moving westward from the Mississippi during the 1830s; by the early '40s it had reached the valleys of the Willamette and the Columbia. In 1841 the U.S. government drew on its secret service funds to finance the sending of a group of Methodist missionaries to help establish claims of ownership of the Oregon country. In 1843-44 two thousand settlers reached Oregon. In the midwest, a noisy agitation got under way, supporting the demand for "the whole of Oregon" and for the ousting of the British from the northwest.

The expansionist drive was not confined to agrarian land-speculators: New England commercial interests looked on Oregon as a potential base for shipping in their growing trade with the Orient. As one of their spokesmen put it: "The great present value of this Territory has relation to the commerce and navigation of the Pacific Ocean . . ." J. C. Calhoun, the U.S. Secretary of State, agreed with him; said he: "The whole of that portion of Asia, containing nearly half·the population and wealth of the globe, will be thrown open to the commerce of the world . . ." Already the U.S., which had gained forcible entry to the China market in the wake of the odious Opium War waged by the British in 1842, saw itself as the banner-bearer of "world commerce . . ."

As yet no treaty recognized the U.S. claim to a coastline on the Pacific. But President Polk was elected in 1844 on a program of aggressive expansionism. "Fifty-four forty or fight!" — the demand for the whole coast as far up as the Panhandle — became the slogan of northern conquest. In the negotiations that ensued, the British proposed the line of the lower Columbia as the border. The Americans refused to accept it. To them, more important than land for settlement was the requirement of a navigable port on the northwest coast. The mouth of the Columbia, with its hazardous sandbars, was useless for this purpose; but Juan de Fuca Strait and Puget Sound possessed excellent potential harbors.

In the face of U.S. insistence the British representatives retreated to the proposal of a boundary at the 49th parallel, extended westward from the Rockies to the coast. The 58,000 square miles between that line and the lower Columbia seemed of slight importance as viewed from

Westminster: "a few miles of pine swamp," one spokesman called it.

By the Treaty of Washington of 1846, the line was fixed at the 49th parallel, with Britain retaining Vancouver Island (which dips south of it). Three years later the Island was ceded to the Hudson's Bay Co. for a yearly "rent" of — seven shillings. The Company tried to get outright possession of the whole of the mainland territory as well; but was only granted monopoly rights to trade with the Indians. In practice, however, it applied its exclusive trading privileges to all operations on the mainland for the ensuing decade.

The period 1849-58 was marked by Company-colonial rule and the beginnings of successful popular resistance to it.

Vancouver Island was constituted a Crown Colony with Richard Blanshard, a barrister, as governor. At the same time the Hudson's Bay Co. held proprietory rights to the Island (on condition of establishing settlement); and its chief factor, James Douglas—an old fur-trader and able administrator, with strong authoritarian views—was the real power in the colony. (After two years, he replaced Blanshard as colonial governor). The Company headquarters had been moved from the Columbia to Fort Victoria (established on Vancouver Island in 1843); from here it administered its eight posts on the mainland and its other enterprises. Victoria was also made the capital of the island colony.

To maintain its fur-trading operations and economize on the import of food supplies, the Company developed farming around Victoria and in the Puget Sound area of the mainland. It did as little as possible to further settlement; yet even the limited growth of agriculture created a category of "servant-settlers" who, on starting to build a community life of their own, were soon chafing under Company rule. It is recorded that the farm laborers of the H.B. Co.'s subsidiary, the Puget Sound Agricultural Company, received wages "much lower than those paid in American settlements on the other side of Puget Sound." Also, that they founded a "scientific institute" at which the better-read members gave weekly talks on natural science, history and other topics. Their interest in and demand for education secured them the establishment of a schoolhouse (now the oldest still standing in the province). The farm-laborers later became an active force in the demand for democratic rights and an end to Company rule in the colony.

If farming stimulated the beginnings of a popular opposition, the exploitation of mineral resources by the Company brought into being a still more challenging force: a detachment of miners with a background of militant struggle in the "Old Country." Coal seams had been found at Fort Rupert (Alert Bay) at the north end of the Island. In 1849 the Company brought out eight Scottish miners. All of them — John Muir, his four sons and a nephew, and John McGregor and John Smith — "went on strike when they were ordered to do laborers' work. Two of them, Andrew Muir and John McGregor, were put in irons for six days." When Governor Blanshard visited Fort Rupert "he reported that the miners were extremely discontented, their discontent at times amounting to open revolt at the conditions under which they were obliged to work." Six of the eight took the first chance to stow away on a collier bound for California.

On learning from the Indians that there was coal at Nanaimo, the Company brought out another party of miners in 1854, this time from Staffordshire. Within a year they too were on strike. "Twelve hours a day, six

days a week, for little more than three shillings a day"
— such were the conditions they sought to better. With
the help of a strikebreaker, and by evicting the miners'
families from their homes, the Company forced the men
to give in. Their wages were cut instead of raised. The
strikebreaker's name was Dunsmuir; he was rewarded
with help in setting up as an independent operator; it
was his start on the road to a fortune built on greed and
ruthlessness: the future Dunsmuir coal empire. The
miners struck again, in 1861, in 1870 . . . The tradition
of militant struggle was born on the West Coast from
the founding days of the Vancouver Island colony.

The Crimean War (1853-6) raised apprehensions as to
possible moves against the colony from the adjoining
territory of Russian America. A proposal was even mooted
of arming the Indians as well as the British settlers, to
defend Vancouver Island against attack. It was dropped,
however, "for fear the Native Indians might use the
arms against the British colonialists" instead.

Although a naval base was established at Esquimalt,
the British warship stationed there made no move against
the Russian colonies. This, together with the fact that the
profitable trade between the Hudson's Bay and Russian-
American companies continued undisturbed throughout
the war, pointed to the existence of a secret agreement
between the two governments not to extend hostilities
to the North Pacific. It was noted, however, that "The
presence of the Royal Navy in British Columbian waters
had a marked influence on the people of the colony."

The people, indeed, were in need of "influencing" — as
the colonial authorities viewed it. All during the war,
agitation for self-government continued to mount. At the
time of Governor Blanshard's removal in 1851 — he had

shown some alarming signs of sympathy with the settlers' grievances — a petition had been circulated asking relief from Company rule. In 1853 some 450 settlers petitioned the Crown, putting forward a like demand.

The strongest opponent of all proposals for self-government or democracy in any form was the Company's chief factor and Colonial Governor James Douglas. But popular pressure overbore his resistance. In 1856 the Colonial Office instructed him to convene an elective assembly. This victory of the democratic forces in the colony was hedged about with as many restrictions as Douglas and the Colonial Office could devise. The franchise was limited to owners of 20 acres of land — thereby excluding nearly all the inhabitants of Victoria and the Company employees: forty land-owners thus became the electorate! (Douglas, in any event, was "utterly averse to universal franchise.") Ownership of property worth £300 was a requirement of membership in the Assembly. Seven members were elected — all with past or present Company connections. A contemporary described the set-up as being no better than a "semblance of free representative government."

The winning of an Assembly — even one of so limited a character — was a first victory in the settlers' struggle. Their next objective was to end the outright domination of the Colony by the Company. They attained it two years later, thanks largely to two developments that decisively reinforced the popular pressure for change. One was the strong growth in free-trade, anti-monopoly sentiment in England, reflected in the 1857 parliamentary hearings on the Hudson's Bay Company.* The other was

---

* In that same year, on the other side of the world, the impact of the Indian Mutiny compelled the revoking of the monopoly privileges of the East India Co.

the rising tide of the gold rush of 1858, which cracked the last barriers to free trade in the colony.

Even Douglas recognized that the Company's trade monopoly was doomed: he advised the directors in London "to make a virtue of necessity, and to surrender with a good grace, a right which is no longer tenable." For giving up its Vancouver Island grant (for which it had been paying seven shillings rent) the H.B. Co. was paid £57,500; it retained its fort at Victoria, valuable town-lots, and thousands of acres outside the town limits. On the Mainland, the Company's license of exclusive trade was cancelled.

In surrendering its monopoly privileges on the Pacific Coast, the Company allowed its lease of the Alaska Panhandle from the Russian-American Fur Company to lapse. Here, if ever, was an opportunity to obtain possession for the colony of this vital strip of coastal territory; but the British government made no effort to do so. Tsarist Russia for its part, weakened by the strain of the Crimean war, showed scant interest in maintaining its hold on northwestern America: a few years later (in 1867) it sold Alaska, including the Panhandle, to the United States for $7 million.

In the spring of 1858 word had reached the outside world that gold had been discovered on the Fraser River. Small deposits had been found at Lake Okanagan as early as 1833 by the botanist David Douglas; and later, others in the Queen Charlotte Islands. But the news of gold on the Fraser came in the wake of the great gold rushes to California (1848) and Australia (1851): feverish migrations of fortune-seekers, whose "finds" in the aggregate mounted to millions, and provided a powerful stimulant to capitalist expansion.

As shipload after shipload of gold-seekers entered Victoria harbor, the population of the colony swelled from a thousand or so "white" settlers to close to thirty thousand. As Griffin tells it:

> The quiet harbor at Victoria woke to a feverish life as one boat followed another after the *Commodore* docked on April 5, 1858 and still more miners streamed ashore to pitch their tents or build their rough shelters in the fields. Few paused longer than to buy supplies and then push on across the Gulf of Georgia by steamboat, rowboat or canoe, whatever craft they could get to take them up the Fraser River to Fort Hope and Fort Yale where the sand bars were being stripped and other cities were springing up along the banks. And fast as they streamed out in the first hectic months others arrived to take their place in the city burgeoning around Fort Victoria, among them the craftsmen and mechanics who would remain to build a city when the gold rush had spent its fever, and a few who would seize the resources of a virgin land, not gold but coal and timber, to build private fortunes for themselves.

In addition to Englishmen and Americans, the newcomers included (as one official noted): "Frenchmen, very numerous, Germans in abundance, Italians, several Hungarians, Poles, Danes, Swedes, Spaniards, Mexicans, and Chinese." Douglas observed "a strong American feeling among them" and concluded that "They will require constant watching, until the English element preponderates in the country."

The increase in population brought by the gold rush heightened the pressure for representative government. An Act of the British Parliament in 1858 established a separate colony on the Mainland, named British Columbia; but instead of there being an elective assembly (such as had been granted to Vancouver Island two years earlier) absolute power was vested in a governor. The reason was stated unashamedly: the mixed national composition of the mainland population. Representative institutions "were only applicable to colonists of the English race"(!).

The gold miners had their own views on this, however; and in the absence of any constituted local authority, they set up an elementary self-government of their own: elective bodies, to deal with disputes over claims and to maintain order. As a result of this initiative Douglas, Governor of the Mainland colony as well as of the Island, was compelled to authorize the establishment of local elective mining boards. In the Colony as a whole, however, he continued to rule as "a virtual dictator." He imposed a 21 shillings-a-month license fee on the miners, in spite of a warning reminder from the Colonial Office that in Australia just such a measure had led to the Ballarat Riot — the Eureka Stockade — and the great miners' battles for their rights in the colony across the Pacific.

On the Mainland, Douglas with London's assent blocked the establishment of an elective assembly; on the Island, he thwarted the growing demand for ministerial responsibility to the Assembly. In so doing, he acted as the spokesman of a minority of well-to-do English landowners and officials: "the Family-Company-Compact" was the name the newly-founded weekly *British Colonist* gave them. Its editor was Amor de Cosmos (originally W. A. Smith), who soon became the tribune of the people of both colonies on the Coast.

Born in Windsor, Nova Scotia, in 1825, de Cosmos was a devoted admirer of the Reform leader Joseph Howe. He came to Victoria from California (where he had his name changed to that of "Love of the Universe") at the time of the Gold Rush. Tall, black-bearded, with keen, piercing eyes, he was a striking figure in the frontier settlement. The first issue of his paper appeared in December 1858; it was printed in the small plant where, some time before, the first newspaper in what is now B.C. had been produced: the short-lived French-language *Courrier de la Nouvelle Calédonie,* published by the Catholic bishop De Mers.

From the start, the *British Colonist* aimed its blows at the "toadyism, consanguinity and incompetence" of the ruling clique; and demanded the granting of responsible government. Within a few months, Douglas tried to suppress the paper, ordering de Cosmos to post bond of £800 or suspend publication forthwith. A public meeting of protest promptly raised the amount, denounced the "rascality that was done under the guise of government" — and saved the *Colonist.* The Governor's next move was to have the Assembly charge the editor with libel — for publishing accounts of its proceedings. De Cosmos was taken into custody and an apology was extracted from him; but next day the *Colonist* declared defiantly that "attempts to stop the freedom of speech have only resulted in enlarging the area of freedom." Moreover, "it is vain, puffed-up, tyrannical, corrupt, short-witted, conceited mummies and numbskulls that fear the press and strive to gag it."

The struggle for freedom of the press and representative government on the West Coast went on for a decade. Starting with opposition to the restrictive rule of the "Family-Company-Compact" minority, the popular-democratic movement went on to demand the union of the two colonies of British Columbia and Vancouver Island, then union with Canada.

In these measures it saw the best chance of securing a political framework favorable to economic expansion. The industries that had started as minor offshoots of Hudson's Bay Co. trading operations were by the 1860s taking on the character of independent capitalist enterprises. By 1865 it was reported that the Nanaimo coal mines "even at their present early stage, give steady employment to several hundred men."

Along with coal, there was lumber. A visitor to Cowichan Lake enthused: "The spars and lumber alone, with their capabilities of being floated to the sea, would prove a certain fortune to any man with capital enough to buy an axe and a grindstone." But it was men with capital enough to erect saw-mills who were to obtain the "certain fortune." The same writer noted that at the head of Barclay Sound (Port Alberni), "two or three hundred hands are employed in connection with a large sawmill company, engaged in the export of spars and sawn lumber."

Industrial growth gave new weight to the demand of the emerging West Coast business community for political reform and responsible government; their economic influence was combined with the insistent pressure of a broad popular demand. In 1863 a grudging concession was made with the granting to the Mainland of a partly-elective legislative council (five elective members, eight appointive); and in the same year the detachment of Royal Engineers was recalled to Britain. In 1866 popular pressure secured the union of Vancouver Island and the Mainland under one government; but the new colony, named British Columbia, was also saddled with a legislative council in which members appointed by the Crown were in the majority.

The moves towards a federal union of Canada and the eastern Maritime provinces in 1864-7 gave a strong impetus to the demand that British Columbia be included in the new transcontinental dominion. There were several reasons why the democratic movement became a pro-Confederation movement. For one thing, union with Canada seemed to offer escape from the status of a Crown Colony; and it was the rule of the "Crown Colony clique" that stood as the obstacle to responsible government. In Canada the battle for responsible government had been fought and won; and Canadians were in the forefront of the people's movement on the Coast—men like de Cosmos, pupil of Howe, and John Robson, born in Perth, Upper Canada, and now the editor of the New Westminster *British Columbian.*

The opponents of democratic reform, by their snobbery and imperialist chauvinism, helped swell the pro-Canadian sentiment. Governor Douglas told the Colonial Office that the agitation of "New Westminster radicals" was caused by his not "cultivating the Canadian, in preference to the sound sterling English element in the Colony." Some years later Governor Musgrave reported: "The more prominent Agitators for Confederation are a small knot of Canadians who hope . . . to make fuller representative institutions and Responsible Government part of the new arrangements, and that they may so place themselves in positions of influence and emolument."

While the English officialdom, landowners and investors sought to keep the Coast a Crown Colony, United States expansionists promoted an annexationist movement among Victoria merchants possessing close financial ties with San Francisco. Particularly after the close of the Civil War did annexationism become vocal. Its spokesmen were not only Congressmen and Senators. The Bishop of California joined in the chorus: "May we not," he asked, "by getting British Columbia, extend our territory in an unbroken line from Mexico to the Arctic Sea? How natural when one has four volumes of a work, to desire the fifth!" As late as November, 1869, a petition addressed to President Ulysses S. Grant was circulating in Victoria, warning against B.C. union with Canada as a measure that would be ruinous to commerce.

American pretensions to control of the whole Pacific Coast, by adding cogency to the arguments of the pro-Confederationists, speeded adoption by Downing Street of a stand favoring transcontinental union. In British Columbia the U.S.-annexationist agitation was drowned out by the rising popular movement for responsible government and union with Canada.

De Cosmos, who after two unsuccessful attempts had won election to the Legislative Council in 1863, in 1866 introduced a resolution calling for Confederation. It was finally adopted in March, 1867; but the government did not act on it. In December the miners of the Cariboo district held a mass meeting to call for action; a rally in Victoria echoed the demand. In an effort to dampen down the agitation the predominantly non-elective Legislative Council in April 1868 reversed its stand of a year before by voting down concrete proposals put forward by De Cosmos for terms of negotiation with Ottawa.

In response, De Cosmos and John Robson launched the Confederation League, and set about calling meetings throughout the colony to elect delegates to a people's convention. On July 1, 1868, a great open-air rally of the Cariboo miners at Barkerville demanded an end to official obstruction at Victoria, declaring that "the conduct of the government of British Columbia is contrary both to the policy of the imperial government and the declared wishes of the people of this colony." The series of mass meetings held throughout the summer culminated in the holding of the Convention on September 14 at Yale, B.C. There 26 delegates from sixteen localities called for union with Canada and democratic reform. The Convention represented a coalition of varied social forces: small industrialists, professionals, farmers, "free miners" and wage-earners. The most militant were the miners of the Interior, who set their imprint on the resolutions that were adopted. "All governments," the Convention declared, "should exist by the free and just consent of the governed. . . . The government of British Columbia does not exist by the free and just consent of the governed and is, therefore, a despotism." Another resolution demanded "that, whether admission into the Dominion of Canada shall occur or not, representative institutions and responsible government shall be inaugurated forthwith in British Columbia."

The Yale Convention, the high point of the active intervention of the people in settling British Columbia's future, was a landmark in the history of representative government in Canada. Said De Cosmos afterwards: "The people . . . took the matter into their own hands, which they had a perfect right to do."

The action of the working people having broken the political log-jam, things began to move. In 1869 Ottawa secured the appointment by the Colonial Office of a pro-Confederation governor for B.C. Action on union had to wait, however, until Canada could acquire ownership of the vast intervening territory of Rupert's Land. Moreover, although the new governor, Musgrave, was in favor of Confederation he was opposed to a simultaneous grant of responsible government. The fight on this issue had to be pressed right into the final stage of the forthcoming negotiations. Finally in March, 1870, the B.C. Legislative Council voted for Confederation, and appointed a delegation to negotiate with the Canadian government. Included in it were representatives of Canadian investors and of British capital: but not De Cosmos and Robson, spokesmen of the people's movement. Yet the pressure of the movement they had led unmistakably made itself felt: responsible government was conceded in the terms of agreement for Confederation. Provided also, along with financial assistance to overcome the colony's indebtedness, was the promise, not just of a wagonroad (as originally requested), but of a railroad, to span the mountains and join the West Coast and the East. Thereby could Confederation take on flesh and blood, in terms of intercommunication and economic unity.

22

Nation and Class: Aftermath and Projection

With the entry of British Columbia into the federation the transcontinental Canadian Dominion was a reality at last. Characteristically, the pledge to build a railway was written into the Act of 1871: like the Intercolonial in the east, a Pacific railway to the west was the condition of viable union. And as with the East, so in the case of the West the capitalist-business element dominated the operation. The "Pacific Scandal" of profiteering promoter and venal politician gave its flavor to the era.

Yet there was something else. The vision of "a new nationality," the project of creating a new country, was present in the minds of the business-politicians. Their grand design transcended their class limitations. As for the working people on the land and in the towns and cities, the sense of a new identity merged with the pride in accomplishment of builders, producers, craftsmen. At the same time, for some of those who were hired "hands" the status of labor in the business society, its exploitation at the hands of the masters, its hardship and conditions of existence, gave rise to questioning.

For French Canadians, the new political State had mixed connotations. Having regained, with the Province of Quebec, an area of limited but distinct autonomy, some sensed a new beginning. Yet having had to accept a British-colonialist state structure as the larger framework for a provincial existence, they experienced foreboding.

It is significant, surely, that the aftermath of Confederation witnessed the simultaneous emergence of the "Canada First" movement, of the *Parti national*, and the appearance of the pioneering labor newspaper *The Ontario Workman*. One expressed that national Canadian feeling which British colonialism had overshadowed and retarded in English-speaking Canada. One gave voice to the national identity and national demands of French Canada. One bore witness to an emergent proletarian class consciousness.

In 1871 the young barrister W. A. Foster published at Toronto a brochure entitled, *Canada First; or, Our New Nationality*. It contained an eloquent rejoinder to certain remarks made by a visiting Englishman to the effect that "to the Canadian it is of small concern what you think of his country. He has little of patriotic pride in it himself. Whatever pride of country a Canadian has, its object, for the most part, is outside of Canada." Foster called for "some cement more binding than geographical contact, some bond more uniting than a shiftless expediency; some lodestar more potent than a mere community of profit . . . Unless we intend to be mere hewers of wood and drawers of water until the end, we should in right earnest set about strengthening the foundations of our identity . . ."

Foster struck out at colonialism, whether emanating from overseas or from the south. He discerned the retarding factor in the cramping of national sentiment:

> The citizen of the United States has a flag of his own and a nationality of his own—the Canadian has ever had to look abroad for his. For years British policy isolated the Provinces, to prevent their absorption in the neighboring Republic, and in so doing stunted the growth of a native national sentiment.

After invoking the record of early Canadian struggles and the role of the land in forming a sense of identity, the author continued:

> We have been alternately flattered and threatened, yet neither wile nor threat has mortgaged our country with dishonour, or caused us to sacrifice our identity. So if we take pride in the past there is some excuse for us; if we hope for the future, we have, at least, some justification, Thanks to Dr. Ryerson, our school children have now the means of acquiring a knowledge of Canadian geography without first searching through every State in the American Union to find the country they live in, and can now learn something of Canadian history without first pumping dry the reservoir of Yankee buncombe.

Some years later, in an Introduction to the writings of Foster, Goldwin Smith analyzed the movement in these terms:

> The aim of Canada First was never very clearly defined. Some of the group, borne on by the tide of the time, aspired more or less consciously, more or less openly, to an independent nationality. Others aspired to a nationality which they deemed possible without independence, and desired only to complete the measure of Canadian self-government, make the interest of Canada paramount in our policy, and fill all offices with men who, whether natives or not, were thoroughly Canadian in spirit. Some, perhaps, as the program presently to be quoted indicates, had partly in view commercial legislation on the line since designated as the National Policy. To some probably Canada First was rather a vague sentiment than a distinct opinion or idea. All however united in striving to cultivate Canadian patriotism, to raise Canada above the rank of a mere dependency, and to give her the first place in Canadian hearts.

Foster himself was at pains to emphasize that "when we

say Canada First we don't mean Canadians first. We are not such fools as to suppose that a Canadian is better than anybody else, or is entitled as such to a preference over anybody else. But at the same time many of us think a Canadian is no worse than other people, and we would have all who have made Canada their home, feel or try to feel that there is no disgrace attached to the name Canadian, and that to be known as such, either here or abroad, involves no social or political obstruction. The great lesson to be learned after all is, as D'Arcy McGee taught, to learn to respect ourselves, to have a modest but firm confidence in our own strength, and an equally certain hope in our future."

"Canada First" gave expression to the crystallizing consciousness of a Canadian nation. This nation had English as its language. Its historic memories, culture, tradition, stemmed mainly from the British Isles; but it included descendants of many peoples (such as the German and Dutch among the settlers after 1786). It sought to assert an identity, a national individuality in the face of both American pressures and British imperial dominance. It was Canadian—but "English," or Anglo-Canadian. The effort to affirm and unfold the creative potential and collective energies of these Canadians as a nation was gradually to enlist the adherence of the far-flung, heterogeneous community "from sea to sea" whose common tongue was English.

Yet this English-speaking Canadian nation was imbued with a bias inherited from the Conquest and revived by the events on the Red River. It was able neither to exorcise the spectre of a "threatening" French minority-nation (both "alien" and oppressed), nor to propose to this "other nation" a relationship of dual-national equality.

The unassimilated, seemingly unassimilable "other

nation" was that of the French Canadians based on their national territory of Quebec. Disguised as a province, it was nonetheless, to the extent permitted, the state of a nation. Incomplete, unavowed, dependent, colonized: but still the homeland-state of French Canada.

If Canada First was a protest against persistent colonialism and a call for a spirit of independent Canadianism, the *Parti national* was a protest against denial of full recognition of the national character of French Canada. On the issue of Canadian independence they had some common ground: Honoré Mercier spoke out for it in the House of Commons in 1873, and his *Parti national* was "independentist" in spirit. The main emphasis, however, was on Quebec's identity and status, on resistance to a centralizing Anglo-Canadian-dominated Ottawa, on the demand for a national status. As one of his supporters put it later, rejecting the official doctrine of Macdonald and of English-Canadian authority: "Our province does not occupy in relation to Canada the position that the latter holds in relation to Great Britain. We are neither a colony nor a dependency of Confederation . . . The source of powers, it cannot be repeated too often, goes not from Canada to the provinces but from the provinces to Canada . . ."

Canada First and *Parti national* both originate with small groups of professionals, writers, intellectuals. While giving expression to a sentiment that is fairly widespread in their respective communities, they are able to become an effective political force only in association with one or another of the social classes that occupy a determining position. Thus Canada First fades out as a distinct political current, its idea of Independence being carried forward (and in a sense swallowed up) by the National Policy of the manufacturing bourgeoisie. This is less than

Independence, but more tangible than an ideal: it is capitalist-industrial progress towards political autonomy within the Empire.

So also with the *Parti national*: after a brief flicker it fades, reviving some fifteen years later (once again stirred by Riel). But it achieves political substance and durability only by merging with a clerical conservatism that embodies the combined interests of the Quebec Church hierarchy and French-Canadian business.

The 19th century Anglo-Canadian bourgeoisie was not able to create an effective consciousness of Canadian political nationhood. For one thing, the new ruling class clung to a British-colonialist mentality: British investment in the new Dominion was, it could be said, political as well as financial. The attitude derived in part from inherent weakness and dependency; more particularly, from the need for a buttressing counterweight to United States expansionist pressures. Equally operative was the role of the idea of "British ascendancy" as an instrument of rule over French Canada. The Anglo-Canadian nation, then still in process of formation, was not so solidly or consciously constituted as to impose its will unaided: the link of Empire was required to lend authority for a posture of superiority.* The British Crown weighed helpfully on the side of English-Canadian dominance.

At the same time, the relationship of political and eco-

---

*How tenuous was the Anglo-Canadian identity then, and how problematic even today, is suggested by Donald Smiley's argument in *Le Devoir*, June 30, 1967: ". . . what is missing in the equation of the two nations is the other nation, that is, the Anglo-Canadian nation. Such a nation, in the cultural sense, may have existed in the period preceding ours, when most English-speaking Canadians, at least those of Anglo-Saxon origin, identified themselves more or less fully with an empire that had worldwide ramifications. This 'nation' ceased to exist with the decline of British imperial power. . . . The dominant

Postscript: Polemical

Our inquiry into the origins of Confederation has indicated the presence of certain decisive driving forces and relationships. Capitalist industrialization within the framework of a colonial empire; the emergence of a class of businessmen and their gradual acquisition of power ("Le règne des hommes d'affaires . . . était commencé"—as LaFontaine's biographer observed); the formation of a class of wage-workers and, through their struggle with capital, the beginnings of organization, and of political consciousness: all these are elements of an evolving *class structure,* socio-economic and political.

Interwoven and interacting with this social structure is the presence side by side of two distinct national communities, one of them enjoying a dominant position, thanks to its special ties with the leading world Empire. The dominance operated when English Canadians were a minority; it was reinforced when they gained a numerical majority; it was not diminished when in our day British power yielded its sceptre of hegemony to the United States.

It was within that by no means simple context of colonial power, capitalist development and cohabitation of "two nations in a single state" that individuals worked, made choices and decisions, strove to influence conditions and events. To recognize the existence and study the evolution of that class and national context is not to deny the role of individuals, but to make it explicable. Our acts have meaning only to the degree that they transcend our persons. The terms of that possible transcendence are "given" by the stage of development of the productive forces (man's relation to nature) and social relationships that each generation finds to hand on its arrival. As Marx put it, men act in a certain social setting, and "these material relations are only the necessary forms in which their material and individual activity is realized."

There is hardly need to point out that this approach to history

nomic inequality as between French and English impaired the prospect of a common emerging sense of Canadian-
ness, of any strong feeling of dual-national identity. The
ruling social forces in Quebec, while collaborating for
their own private reasons with Anglo-Canadian capital
and imperial authority, were not averse to the growth of
a narrow, clerical-traditionalist variety of nationalism that
crusaded against the *Rouges*, and shunned democracy.

What made it an unequal union was not so much a
plot by English-speaking Canadians to repress the French
—although impulses in that direction were not unknown.
Nor was it a stubborn refusal of French Canadians to
compete on equal terms with Anglo-Canadian business.
(The latter argument has been advanced by Fernand Ouellet, the former by Gerard Filteau and others.) The
sources of inequality were multiple and complex; the
chief ones were:

—Uneven capitalist development: the priority in time
of the English bourgeois revolution of the 17th century
and of the Industrial Revolution in England in the 18th
meant that when England defeated France in the Seven
Years War, and annexed Canada, a certain imbalance was
built into the colony's development, economic as well as
political.

—When to the structure (emanating from the Conquest)
of British-colonial political rule over a population of
Canadian French there was added a mass influx of
English-speaking settlers, there resulted a dualism of national communities; one of which, quite apart from its
own volition, was from the outset closely and advan-

---

nationalism of English-speaking Canadians—and the strength of that
nationalism must not be underestimated — is political in character
rather than racial or cultural." (Cf. also the same author's *The Canadian Political Nationality.*)

tageously associated with the imperial power and English investment capital; while the other not only suffered the direct consequences and side-effects of the defeat of the French metropolis, but labored under the handicap of that semi-feudal underdevelopment which was the heritage of the French *ancien régime.*

—Against this background, the unfolding of early capitalist industrialization and of the related class-political struggles for self-government, against colonialism, followed a tortuous and contradictory course: one marked both by joint efforts of national and class groupings to win colonial autonomy (1837, 1848, and more narrowly, 1867) and by deep cleavage between the national communities resulting from inequality and oppression. As against Downing Street (much later, it would be United States domination) it was possible to achieve a measure of unity. As between the two nations within Canada, only an uneasy compromise was ever reached, charged with the tension of persisting inequality.

—The centralized, unitary federalism of 1867 bore the imprint of this inequality in several respects: the British-monarchical configuration of the colonial dominion proclaimed a British (and Anglo-Canadian) ascendancy; the demographic pattern (since 1850) of an English-speaking majority and a permanent minority position for the French Canadians was reflected in limited linguistic-religious concessions to the latter as a "cultural minority" and denial of political recognition as a national entity; while the economic thrust of expansion through railway-building and manufactures, which the unitary state structure was to subserve,* tied the society in its growth to the English and United States capital markets—with both of

---

*Cf. Alfred Dubuc's analysis, above, pp. 343-4.

which English Canadians possessed the kindred connections that French-Canadian business lacked. The "business democracy" of 1867 was weighted in favor of the Anglo-Canadian capitalist class that was its architect.

The ruling bloc of social forces of the Canada of 1867, the inheritor and continuator of that of 1774, while capable of promoting capitalist enterprise, proved inadequate as a creator of national values or of democratic solidarity. The positive, creative forces in the two Canadas were to be found elsewhere, in the mass of those who toiled and built, from whose work sprang the roads and farms, canals and factories, the mines and lumber camps and homes and schools, the substance and material underpinnings of a modern community.

Just at the time when Canada First and the *Parti national* were seeking ways to express a sense of identity in each of the Canadas, a movement of quite a different kind was getting under way. Not national but social, class consciousness was taking form in the Nine Hours Movement for the shorter working day. The working men who in 1871 established the Toronto Trades Assembly and nine-hour leagues in Hamilton and other industrial centres; who in 1872 conducted the Toronto printers' strike and the mass demonstrations in support of it, and founded the *Ontario Workman*—they were asserting, in the face of the masters, the class identity and solidarity of "the men," of the wage-earning working class.

In pursuit of profit and to hold down wages the masters combined their forces: Master Printers, Master Cabinet-Makers, etc.—"Master Carriage Makers! Men that could not make a decent wheelbarrow," wrote an indignant "Woodworker" in a letter to the editor of the *Workman* —voicing the proud contempt of the producer for a parasitic owner-class . . .

cf.

cf.

The *Globe*—the focal point of employer resistance to the Typographical Union—was at some pains to refute the idea that there existed in Canada such a thing as classes or class conflict: "When you speak of the working-men of Canada you speak of everybody. We all work. We all began with nothing. There is no such class as those styled capitalists in other countries. The whole people are the capitalists of Canada." This pleasant fiction was no doubt then as now more readily concurred in by the well-to-do than by operatives working at machinery and in factories owned by the employing class. But it took only the challenge of workers' organization in their plants for the owners to manifest the most vehement class senti-ments, as voiced by the 160 employers in Toronto who united under George Brown's leadership to denounce the formation of "Trades Unions and Labour Leagues for purposes antagonistic to the interests of their employers and the public at large." They proclaimed the sacredness of the rights of capital, rejecting the nine-hour demand or "any attempts on the part of our employees to dictate to us by what rules we shall govern our business." If the typographical workers were organized in their own de-fense, "It is in obedience to foreign agents who have nothing to lose as the result of their mischievous counsels that the printers of this city have succumbed." The ten thousand who demonstrated in Queen's Park in support of the nine hours demand offered a fitting rejoinder to this charge. The struggle that established the modern trade-union movement was at once indigenous and strong with solidarity. At the root of its common action was awareness of common interests and aims.

It is worthy of note that in the first issue of the *Ontario Workman*, April 18, 1872, there appears an excerpt from a work that was yet to be published in English translation:

the first volume of *Capital*, by Karl Marx. It is a passage from the chapter on "The Working Day."

The concept of the nation held by the men of property who had founded the new Dominion was colored by their preoccupation with the "cash nexus." Nation-building was a huge transaction in real-estate and railway company shares, an investors' challenge. Such an approach might unite the business classes of the two national communities; it would with difficulty inspire the great mass of working men and women who did the work of production, who by their labor built the new country. Still less could it offer an answer to the deep-seated inequality between the two national communities. It would take an approach that transcended the exploitive individualism of a private-business society, to encompass the radical democratization on which alone national equality would be achieved. The motto at the masthead of *The Ontario Workman*, for all its note of utopian-socialist simplicity, pointed towards the answer of a new order, recalling now at a new stage the dream of Toon O'Maxwell. It read: "The Equalization of All the Elements of Society in the Social Scale Should be the True Aim of Civilization."

Such a social equality, realistically understood, could only mean the overcoming of class rule: ending the class cleavage based on private, minority ownership of the modern large-scale tools of labor. The processes now working for such a social transformation in contemporary Canada are interwoven and interact with the struggle for national equality and self-determination. The dictum: No people that oppresses another people can itself be free, has social as well as national implications. *"Maîtres chez nous!"* means mastering alien monopolies as well as achieving state sovereignty. While distinct, the political and the social-economic struggles are convergent. The peoples of the Canadas, facing the need to rectify the "unequal union" of a colonialist Confederation, begin to sense the need to call in question something else as well: the social system of corporate-business rule, the *unequal society* of "masters and men."

Postscript: Polemical

Our inquiry into the origins of Confederation has indicated the presence of certain decisive driving forces and relationships. Capitalist industrialization within the framework of a colonial empire; the emergence of a class of businessmen and their gradual acquisition of power ("Le règne des hommes d'affaires . . . était commencé"—as LaFontaine's biographer observed); the formation of a class of wage-workers and, through their struggle with capital, the beginnings of organization, and of political consciousness: all these are elements of an evolving *class structure,* socio-economic and political.

Interwoven and interacting with this social structure is the presence side by side of two distinct national communities, one of them enjoying a dominant position, thanks to its special ties with the leading world Empire. The dominance operated when English Canadians were a minority; it was reinforced when they gained a numerical majority; it was not diminished when in our day British power yielded its sceptre of hegemony to the United States.

It was within that by no means simple context of colonial power, capitalist development and cohabitation of "two nations in a single state" that individuals worked, made choices and decisions, strove to influence conditions and events. To recognize the existence and study the evolution of that class and national context is not to deny the role of individuals, but to make it explicable. Our acts have meaning only to the degree that they transcend our persons. The terms of that possible transcendence are "given" by the stage of development of the productive forces (man's relation to nature) and social relationships that each generation finds to hand on its arrival. As Marx put it, men act in a certain social setting, and "these material relations are only the necessary forms in which their material and individual activity is realized."

There is hardly need to point out that this approach to history is anathema to our business society (not least, by reason of the disconcerting insight that is shed on its inner workings). The Marxist historical-materialist interpretation finds pitted against it an opposing view, that of metaphysical idealism. Where once theology reigned in historical interpretation, there took over the idealist metaphysic of the disembodied Idea as prime mover of events. Thus the "idea of unity" becomes the "cause of Confederation": assuredly, without the idea it could not have happened; but *what engendered the idea?* That approach, which tends to give special privilege to the *political* Idea, dominated the long era of constitutionalist historiography in this country. Its thought pattern comes out clearly in Rosa Langstone's listing of "the three fundamental factors which had always determined the course of Canadian history, namely, opinion in England, the personality of the governor, and political conditions in Canada,"

A striking illustration of the idealist metaphysic in history is Professor W. L. Morton's thesis that "the moral core of Canadian nationhood is found in the fact that Canada is a monarchy and in the nature of monarchical allegiance . . Allegiance means that the law and the state . . . do not rest on contemporary assent . . . In Canada, a country of economic hazard, external dependence, and plural culture, only the objective reality of a monarchy could form the centre and pivot of unity." Professor Morton is one of our most eminent historians. Those who cling to the belief that history is solely "accumulation of facts" and who decry all interpretation as an intrusion of inadmissible bias, might ask themselves whether their objection may not itself be biased—against one interpretive theory in particular . . .

A counter-current that set in early in this century began to take into account the role of economic development in social change. Its partial recognition by historians whose basic approach is still historical-idealist results in a kind of miscellaneous eclectic assembling of factors, no one of which is seen as causally determinant. Thus Professor Lower, in *Canada One Hundred: 1867-1967* (p. 17) enumerates a dozen or so "factors in Confederation," singling out two as especially important:

> There were two major predisposing forces towards union. One of these was common allegiance: the British North American provinces were *British* . . .

The other major predisposing factor was the extension of communication . . .

There can be no doubt as to the importance of each of these. But not much is explained until "allegiance" (read: the British imperial system) and "extension of communication" (read: capitalist industrialization) are shown in their real, developing interrelationship. And for that, one has to situate them in the evolution of a specific socio-economic "formation" or social system: capitalism. But for Professor Lower, capitalism barely exists, or if it does, it is only as an "attitude," not a social structure: it is one of the "old-world attitudes of exploitation"; "capitalism is simply a pagan attitude towards power and pelf."

A decisive advance toward a scientific historiography was the massive pioneering work of Harold A. Innis. He exhaustively examined the main areas of activity on which the economy of Canada has been founded. Intensely interested in the evolution of techniques, their relationship with geographic environment and their influence on economic change, he evolved a "theory of staples"—fish, fur, lumber and wheat—as the determinants in this country's development.

Undoubtedly, geography and technique were of crucial importance for economic development. But they operated within a framework of *socio-political relationships;* those of merchant's capital and then of nascent industrial capital, under the conditions of colonialism. It is just these socio-economic and political relationships—class and property relationships—that Innis in effect ignored. C. B. Macpherson has argued that Innis's approach was one of "taking for granted the profit and power dynamics of capitalist enterprise"—while finding the driving force of economic growth in "the application of changing technologies to abundant natural resources." But one *cannot* simply "take for granted" the dynamics of capitalism and still explain the driving forces of economic development. Marx commented that Proudhon had "grasped the fact that men produce cloth, linen, silks . . . What he had not grasped is that these men, according to their powers, also produced the *social relations* amid which they prepare cloth and linen." A mechanist, one-sided fixation on the "role" of a single product or of one element in technology (from wood-pulp as a staple, to media of communication, as in the Innis-to-McLuhan trajectory)—abstracted from *social structure,* leads to a new idealist metaphysic.

At present, studies in depth in the field of economic history are being advanced in such significant contemporary work as that of Fernand Ouellet (*Histoire économique et sociale du Québec: 1760-1850*) and H. C. Pentland (papers in learned journals, and his unpublished doctoral thesis, "Labor and the Development of Industrial Capitalism in Canada").

Professor Ouellet's* vast survey of long-range factors adds greatly, particularly in quantifying terms, to our knowledge of the actual process of economic evolution in Lower Canada. But on the crucial question of the relationship between class forces and national movements he stands history on its head, in my opinion. Like Donald Creighton, he sees the Patriote movement as a retrograde, reactionary force and the English Montreal merchant oligarchy as the bearers of enlightenment and progress. In this view, two vital ingredients are made to vanish—imperial domination of the colony, in which *merchant's* capital eagerly collaborated; and the democratic interest in self-determination (expressing the needs of local *industrial* capital) for which Patriotes and Reformers fought in solidarity in the two Canadas.

There are two problems of theory at issue here. One has to do with forms of capital in the early stages of the system; the other with the role of nation and nationalism in social development.

I have referred elsewhere to the significance, in the early period of New France, that attached to the differing and conflicting roles of merchant's and industrial capital.† The former

---

*The following discussion is drawn from my review of M. Ouellet's book, in HORIZONS: *The Marxist Quarterly*, no. 25. An English version of M. Ouellet's argument appears in Cornell, Hamelin, Ouellet, Trudel: *Canada: Unity in Diversity* (1967), ch. 16, esp. pp. 176-80; and 216-24: ". . . the *Patriote* party . . . was dominated by a nationalistic ideology, and thought it could attain its reactionary objectives by means of democratic institutions" (224).

†*Founding of Canada*: "The merchants who achieved the 'primitive accumulation' of capital, through extracting fabulous profits from 'trade' with the Indians, had little interest in the small (and as yet relatively less profitable) hemp-works or tanneries or other forms of early capitalist production, such as Talon had tried to foster." (p. 149)

allied itself with feudal landownership and accommodated itself
to colonial subordination, while the nascent industrial bourgeoisie
tended to challenge both—for good, practical reasons, since they
thwarted indigenous industrialization.

In his chapter on "Historical Facts about Merchant's Capital"
(in Vol. III of *Capital*) Marx notes that "In modern English
history, the commercial estate proper and the merchant town
are also politically reactionary and in league with the landed
interest and moneyed interest against industrial capital . . . The
complete rule of industrial capital was not acknowledged by
English merchant's capital and moneyed interest until after the
abolition of the corn tax, etc."

What has given rise to "wholly erroneous conceptions," Marx
argues, is a confusion between two phases: one, involving the
role of merchant's capital in the revolution in commerce that
accompanied the era of geographic discovery and the instituting
of colonialism; the other, its radically altered position once the
Industrial Revolution began. "The independent development of
merchant's capital . . . stands in inverse proportion to the general
economic development of society."

Ouellet, by equating the Montreal merchants with "the capitalist classes," overlooks the differentiation within the strata of
the colonial bourgeoisie, the ties of one section with mercantile
imperialism, those of the other with "native manufactures"—
industrial capitalism. The latter section, referred to as "the
liberal professions," are simply (and erroneously) identified with
the *ancien régime.*

On the basis of this approach, Sydenham and Metcalfe, the
representatives of the imperial metropolis, the patrons of the
merchant oligarchy, appear as the "constructive" statesmen, while
the forces of the colonial bourgeoisie and the nationalist movement are "obstructionist." (E.g.: "le caractère constructif de
l'expérience Metcalfe," p. 533; also pp. 532, 535.) What Ouellet
refers to as the "temporary reinforcement of the authority of the
Crown" under the Metcalfe administration (p. 533) was "temporary," *not* because of benevolent imperial foresight (the Queen
in 1847 called for its indefinite continuance) but because mass
popular struggle forced the discontinuance of the Governor's
assumption of decisive executive power in internal affairs. The
Union, Ouellet argues, "had been conceived with the aim of

putting into effect, while breaking the oppositions of the past, this program of reforms which in a few years was to become reality. All the clauses of the Act of Union tended toward these priority economic and institutional aims. Political unification itself was destined both to consecrate the economic solidarity of east and west and to make possible the financing of public works. The other clauses on representation and the relations between Executive and Legislature sought to prevent the French Canadians from obstructing, through their deputies, indispensable reforms." As for such a "less realistic" aim as Durham's cultural assimilation policy—the "product of a sort of desperation in business circles, (it) was purely a function of the success of the desired program of reforms. . ." (p. 443) While the Union "doubtless expressed a will to cultural assimilation, it corresponded to more fundamental preoccupations. The promoters of this forcible solution, advocated for over twenty years by the merchants, wished above all to prevent the French Canadians from continuing to obstruct an ensemble of economic, juridical and institutional reforms that had long been necessary but retarded by political anarchy. It was a matter, not of punishing the French group, but of obliging it, in the absence of a willing acceptance of evolution, to agree to certain compromises. That was the essential" (p. 593).

As to the role of nations and national movements in the historical process, it clearly depends on the aims pursued by the social, class forces that lead them.* The struggles of the Patriote

*The nation, as an enduring, historically-formed community of people dwelling together and speaking a common tongue, is a phenomenon that transcends specific forms of economic and political organization. If in the "West" it tended to reach maturity in the era of capitalism, its roots are earlier, and its vitality is not (as yet) diminished in socialist society. Underestimation of this phenomenon, and consequent oversimplified approaches to it, have long bedevilled dogmatic "Marxism." Signs of a fresh approach, in current discussions of European Marxists—the recent debates in the pages of the Soviet journal *Questions of History,* and studies such as those of J. Chesneaux, cited earlier, and of Horace B. Davis: *Nationalism and Socialism* (1967)—hold out some promise of the overcoming of dogmatic fixations. (On the debate, cf. articles of Chesneaux and I. P. Averkieva in HORIZONS: *The Marxist Quarterly,* Nos. 25 and 26, 1968.)

and Reform forces in the 1830s and '40s were directed to the winning of independence and political power for the Canadian bourgeoisie; the French-Canadian national liberation movement was a major force in the bourgeois-democratic revolution. That its outcome, following military defeat, was a precarious compromise, does not alter the progressive character of the national and democratic movements whose aim was independence.

But if one's view is, that all national movements are inherently reactionary, it is not too difficult to identify with their opponents (who may well "happen" to be the holders of power). A rather widespread tendency, among ideologues of some dominant nations, is to proclaim that nationalism is "obsolete": world order, and disappearance of the "tribal" nation-state are the rational, "functionalist" answer to present strife. Enlightened as this prospect is, its immediate usefulness is impaired by failure of its proponents to face up to existing national inequality and oppression. To reprove the victims of these for being so "narrow-minded" as to resist, is itself a form of nationalism. Some such "nihilism" on the national question seems to enter into Ouellet's interpretation. Over-reacting to a traditional French-Canadian rightist clerical-nationalist approach, his argument unfortunately leads him to embrace a rightist Anglo-Canadian one.

The most articulate exponent of the Anglo-Canadian conservative view is the research director of the Canadian Labor Congress, Dr. Eugene Forsey.* His 1962 presidential address to the Canadian Political Science Association posed the question: "Canada: Two Nations or One?" Was it "really necessary" to ask the question? He replied:

> I'm afraid it is, for two reasons. The first is the rise of separatism in Quebec. The second, and to my mind much more serious

---

*Cf. the present writer's "Eugene Forsey, P. E. Trudeau and the Question: 'What Is A Nation?'" in the Crisis of Confederation issue of The Marxist Quarterly, no. 7, Autumn 1963.

Following up an earlier paper on national and social consciousness in Quel Avenir Attend l'Homme? (Paris, 1962) and a communication on "The Formation of Two National Communities (in Canada)" read to the VII International Congress of Anthropology and Ethnography (1964), I propose to pursue this question in a future study on nationalism and social structure.

reason, is the rise of the theory of "two nations in a bi-national state" . . .

(Why the latter consideration appears "much more serious" will become apparent shortly.)

Conceding that the word "nation" is in fact employed in two senses (referring either to "an ethnic, cultural, sociological entity" or to "a legal, constitutional, juristic entity") Forsey is not content with asserting his preference for the latter of the two. From his private preference he derives a public fiat. Since "nation" is to mean only "sovereign state" and not "a people," and since the French Canadians do not possess an independent state, *ergo* they do not constitute a nation! Q.E.D. Dissolution of the two national communities is proclaimed, and proponents of the "two-nations" concept are excommunicated. (To say nothing of the advocates of national self-determination.)

Such are the heady benefits of legalistic fetishism. Recognition of the obvious fact that there exists a unified Canadian *state* becomes an argument against recognition of its bi-national character. Deny the existence of the French-Canadian nation, and you eliminate the need for any recognition of its right of self-determination (a right that includes the right of secession).

With the help of quotations from the Fathers of Confederation, who offer a distinguished precedent for his terminological confusion, Dr. Forsey brings us safely back to bi-culturalism. This country "has two basic traditions, French and British"; this dualism must be accepted, and "each group has got to learn to respect the culture of the other." Fine! Yet . . . there remains a doubtless unconscious but nonetheless hugely patronizing superiority attitude:

> Finally, I think we English Canadians must get to work on what I am inclined to call nationalizing, or, if you prefer, biculturalizing, the Dominion government and all its departments and emanations . . . We could help by making French Canadians feel more at home in Ottawa.

Merci, milord! Whose "home" you think it is, is only too admirably evident. A thinly disguised imperial Anglo-Saxon chauvinism is a corollary of stubborn attachment to the Victorian constitutional status quo.

According to Professor Michel Brunet, there are two kinds of "anti-nationalists":

> The first is made up of those who see in the nationalism of other nations an obstacle to the expansion and hegemony of their own nation. They themselves are ardent nationalists, protecting their nation-state against the ambitions of other national collectives.

Such an "anti-nationalist" is Dr. Forsey.

A second kind are those whom Brunet calls the Utopians: according to them, "nationalism is responsible for all the evils of our epoch . . . a sin, an aberration of which humanity must rid itself as quickly as possible . . . They call on all men to recognize their solidarity and fraternity."

Like the not altogether disinterested "anti-nationalists" of the first category, these liberal-humanitarian souls preach an "end to nationalism" . . . to *oppressed* nations, and "renunciation of sovereignty" to those from whom sovereignty has been filched, or by whom it is yet to be achieved. (And for whom, without such achievement, all talk of "equality" is humbug.) The end result is a sort of Olympian but deceptive "nihilism" on the subject of nations.

A notable proponent of just such pseudo-nihilism on the national question is the author of a recent study of federalism. M. Pierre-Elliott Trudeau sees the arrangement of 1867 as the "rational compromise"; if it has since drifted into a condition of imbalance, the fault lies with nationalism. (A "lasting consensus" could not be achieved because, on the one hand, "an emotional sop," made up of Anglo-Canadian nationalism, "calmly assumed away the existence of one-third of the nation"; hence, on the other hand, counter-movements in Quebec "which quite logically argued that if Canada was to be the nation-state of the English-speaking Canadians, Quebec should be the nation-state of the French-Canadians.")

But far from all this being some sort of "lapse," it was in fact inherent in the "rational compromise" of 1867 itself. No amount of sentimental invocation of the rule of reason, no dosage of "rational functionalism," can exorcise the hard facts of dual-national existence, and of resentments engendered by national inequality.

In defiance of the Canadian bi-national reality, the Trudeau conjuring-trick would cause the national fact of French Canada to vanish: just as Quebec becomes "une province comme les autres," so does the French-Canadian community become a regionalism like any other. At most, there is a "factor of culture and language," conveniently reducible to a matter of individual rights. By no means is there a matter of national identity that might raise a question of political sovereignty!

M. Trudeau's difficulty derives from his "idealistic" condemnation of nations and nation-states as dangerous anachronisms. He rejects "The absurd and retrograde idea of national sovereignty." For him, *"Le concept de nation . . . est un concept qui pourrit tout."* ("The concept of nation . . . is one that turns everything rotten.") He continues:

> The very idea of Nation-State is absurd . . . The principle of nationalities has brought the world two centuries of wars and revolutions, but not a single definite solution.

The fallacy is rooted in an *abstract metaphysic.* Not "the principle of nationalities," but *capitalist development* and the rise of the bourgeoisie are the reason for the wars and revolutions of the post-feudal era; while the twentieth century emergence of monopoly-capitalist imperialism has brought with it a dual process: nationalism being exploited by the ultra-right and fascism, and tidal counter-movements of national-colonial revolt and socialist revolution. So long as imperialism engenders national oppression, the "principle of nationality" will have the validity of an assertion of democratic, community rights. Certainly, the ideal of a world community is fundamentally progressive. Mankind will of necessity achieve it, or will perish. But its achievement will require the prior disappearance of a social system in which billion-dollar war contracts for private corporations are as "functional" and "normal" to its operation as is the exploitation of hired "hands" at home or of subject peoples abroad. The world without frontiers and sovereignties, governed by pure reason, awaits the triumph of reason in the social realm.

To pretend as Trudeau does that in "advanced societies" that day is already come, is sophisticated self-deception.

M. Trudeau's metaphysical negativism on the national question owes not a little to the theories set forth in Elie Kedourie's *Nationalism*. A mood common to both appears to be one of abhorrence of disturbance. This emotional conservatism pervades Kedourie's pages: he is aghast at "turbulence," "the European system disrupted" (p. 92); "nationalism tends to disrupt . . . equilibrium . . . to reopen settled questions and to renew strife" (p. 115); for Kedourie, national problems are the fruit of "nationalist doctrine" (p. 116) . . . In similar vein, Trudeau in a recent study of federalism makes disapproving reference to the fact that in past centuries "self-determination . . . proposed to challenge the legitimacy and the very existence of the territorial states"; it "was bound to dissolve whatever order and balance existed in the society of states." In certain cases even the use of the word nation "is disruptive of political stability."

Metaphysical functionalism makes a fetish of stability. One does not have to be addicted to disorder, to distrust such fervent immobilism: one only has to be in favor of change.

A change, in the direction of national equality, through a restructuring of the Canadian state (not excluding even the possibility of what Marx envisaged in the case of Ireland, in 1867 —separation, "although after the separation there may come federation") will require, if it is to effected peaceably, the concurrence of English-speaking Canada based on recognition of its own real national interest. It is worth recalling the moments of binational unity of action touched on in this book. They were times when both peoples took their stand for *independence* from imperial domination. Anglo-Canadian strivings for nationhood, from the 1830s onward, expressed the basic interests of the Canadian nation whose common tongue was English: a nation then still in process of formation, already embodying such minority groups as the 200,000 German-Canadians (6 per cent of the 1871 population); a nation that could find in the movement for self-government a *common denominator* with its sister-nation of French Canada.

Such a common denominator still exists. It is to be found, in the changed conditions of today's world, in the unfinished business of independence. As against the U.S. neo-colonialist take-over, there can and must be a united effort of the Canadas. One impediment to its realization, however, is an attitude that invokes the threat of U.S. domination in order to justify an acceptance by French Canada of the inequitable status quo, and capitulation in its demand for national equality and sovereignty. Such blackmail will not work. Indeed, it undermines the possibility of a new, democratic relationship based on equality and common interests.

The defeat of the rising of 1837-38 was the defeat of a combined attempt to establish "from below" the independent union of the Canadas. The twin Republics were still-born. Colonialism, triumphing over the *indépendantistes,* reimposed the unequal union of the Conquest.

The Confederation of 1867 was the establishment "from above" of a centralized-federal colonial union. It opened the way to industrial growth and, within a half-century, the autonomy of the Dominion. It made possible the slow emergence of a Canadian identity. Flawed by the equivocal "recognition" accorded the national fact of French Canada, and perpetuating national inequality, it has provided no solid bulwark against the expansionist pressures of big business American neo-colonialism.

Whether a new and equal union can be fashioned now, hangs on the decision of the "double majority": of the peoples of the Canadas.

Appendix

I

"WHAT SHALL WE DO WITH CANADA?"

(P. 65)

An 8-page pamphlet with this title was reprinted from the Leeds *Mercury* in 1838. Its author was Henry Vincent, the Chartist leader. (A year later, during the South Wales Chartist rising he was the object of an attempted rescue from Monmouth prison: Gwyn Thomas has done a fine portrayal of the Welsh ironworkers' part in this struggle, in his novel, *All Things Betray Thee.*)

Vincent notes that the demand for an elective Legislative Council—the main demand, at one stage, of the Patriotes— "was a disguised demand of *independence.*" Lord John Russell's resolutions approving the illegal seizure by the Executive of public revenues had "led the people of Lower Canada to take up arms, and to fight openly for independence, as the only safeguard of their liberties . . ." Therefore, "the question is put fairly and broadly before the British Parliament and people— *Shall Great Britain consent to the independence of Canada?* To this question we are not prepared to give a negative."

The pamphlet closes with a condemnation of wars in which "a color of justice [is given] to acts of oppression":

> War, except when it is *just* and *necessary,* is the *greatest of crimes.* It involves an amount of horror and misery never imagined by men who have not trodden the battlefield, and witnessed the storming of cities. *Has England a just cause for inflicting these horrors on Canada?* Has she so clear a right to hold a nation on the other side of the Atlantic in subjection? — Has her colonial administration been so incorrupt and excellent? Is it so unreasonable that the Canadians should seek independence? . . . Our answer is, NO! . . . our interest, beyond question, is that Canada shall be independent.
>
> [*The Vincent pamphlet is in the Toronto Public Library.*]

II
THE PATRIOTES TRANSPORTED TO AUSTRALIA
(P. 80)

For the following material on 58 *Patriote* deportees I am indebted to Professor George Rudé of the University of Adelaide, Australia, who very kindly made available his file on Canadians transported to New South Wales and Van Diemen's Land: and also obtained for me a copy of an unpublished thesis by Mary Gordon Milne (University of Tasmania) on the North American Political Prisoners.

58 French Canadians transported to New South Wales on the "Buffalo" (arrived in Sydney, 25.2.1840)

> Notes against each name refer to:
> 1. Age at time of arrival in colony.
> 2. R—can read; W—can write; RW—can read and write; Nil—can neither read nor write.
> 3. M(arried) or S(ingle).
> 4. Children.
> 5. Occupation.

ALLARY, Michel—38. Nil. M. 1 boy. Joiner.

BECHARD, Théodore—49. Nil. M. 2 boys, 8 girls. Farmer and Veterinarian.

BERGEVIN, Charles—53. Nil. M. 7 boys. Farmer.
(dit Langevin, Charles the Elder)

BIGONESSE, François—49. Nil. M. 3 boys, 4 girls. Farmer.
(dit BEAUCAIRE)

BOUC, Guillaume Charles—48. RW. M. 2 boys, 5 girls. Clerk.

BOURBONNAIS, Désiré—20. Nil. S. Blacksmith.

BOURDON, Louis—23. RW. M. 1 boy, 1 girl. Farmer and merchant's clerk.

BOUSQUET, J. B.—44. RW. S. Farmer and miller.

BUISSON, Constant—30. RW. M 3 girls. Blacksmith.

CHEVREFILS, Gabriel—43. Nil. M. 1 boy, 5 girls. Farmer.

COUPAL, Antoine—50. Nil. M. 2 boys, 10 girls. Farmer.
(dit la REINE)

DEFAILLETTE, Louis—48. Nil. M. 4 boys, 4 girls. Farmer.

DUCHARME, Léon—23. RW. S. Merchant's clerk.

DUMOUCHELLE, Joseph—47. Nil. M. 3 boys, 1 girl. Farmer.

DUMOUCHELLE, Louis—42. Nil. 2 boys, 4 girls. Farmer.

DUS(S)AULT, Louis Guérin—37. RW. M. 3 boys, 1 girl. Merchant.
(dit Blanc Dusault)

GAGNON, David—29. Nil. M. 2 girls. Joiner & Carpenter.
GOYETTE, Jacques—49. Nil. M. 2 boys, 1 girl. Mason & Farmer.
GOYETTE, Joseph—29. RW. M. 2 boys, 1 girl. Carpenter.
GUERTIN, François—44. RW. S. Carpenter & Joiner.
GUIMOND, Joseph—48. Nil. M. 1 boy, 2 girls. Carpenter & Farmer.
HEBERT, Joseph-David—49. Nil. M. 3 boys, 2 girls. Farmer.
HEBERT, Joseph Jacques—42. Nil. S. Farmer.
HUOT, Charles—53. RW. S. Notary Public.
LABERGE, Jean—36. Nil. M. 4 boys, 2 girls. Farmer.
LANCTOT, Hyppolite—23. RW. M. 2 boys. Notary Public.
LANGLOIS, Etienne—26. Nil. S. Farmer.
LANGUEDOC, Etienne—22. Nil. S. Farmer.
LAVOIE, Pierre—49. Nil. M. 8 boys, 1 girl. Farmer.
LEBLANC, David Drossin—36. RW. M. 5 boys, 1 girl. Farmer.
LEBLANC, Hubert Drossin—32. RW. M. 2 boys, 2 girls. Farmer.
LEPAILLEURE, François Macervie—33, RW. M. 2 boys. House
    Painter.
LONGTIN, Jacques—59. Nil. M. 4 boys, 8 girls. Farmer.
LONGTIN, Moyse or Jacques fils—21. Nil. S. Farmer.
MARCEAU, Joseph—34. RW. M. 2 boys, 1 girl. Farmer & Weaver.
    (dit Petit Jacques)
MORIN, Achille—25. RW. S. Clerk.
MORIN, Pierre Hector—54. RW. M. 3 boys. Mariner.
MOTT, Benjamin—43. RW. M. 2 boys, 3 girls. Farmer.
NEWCOMBE, Samuel—65. RW. M. 3 boys, 2 girls. Surgeon.
PAPINEAU, André—40. Nil. M. 3 boys, 4 girls. Blacksmith.
    (dit Montiguy)
PARE, Joseph—48. RW. M. Farmer.
PINSONNAULT, Louis—40. Nil. M. 2 girls. Farmer.
PINSONNAULT, Paschal—27. Nil. S. Farmer.
PINSONNAULT, René—48. Nil. M. 3 boys, 4 girls. Farmer.
PREVOST, François-Xavier—30. RW. M. 2 boys, 1 girl. Innkeeper.
PRIEUR, François-Xavier—24. RW. S. Merchant.
ROBERT, Théophile—25. Nil. M. Farmer.
ROCHON, Jérémie—36. RW. M. 5 girls. Wheelwright.
ROCHON, Edouard Pascal—39. RW. M. 1 boy. Carriage-maker and
    Painter.
ROCHON, Toussaint—30. RW. M. 2 girls. Carriage-maker and
    Painter.
ROY, Basile—42. Nil. M. 6 boys. Farmer.
ROY, Charles—52. Nil. M. 5 boys, 3 girls. Farmer.
    (dit La pensée the Elder)
ROY, Joseph—24. Nil. M. 1 girl. Laborer.
    (dit La pensée fils de Louis)

THIBERT, Jean-Louis—52. Nil. M. 2 boys, 1 girl. Farm laborer.

THIBERT, Jean-Marie—38, Nil. M. 2 boys, 2 girls. Farm laborer.

TOUCHETTE, François-Xavier—32. RW. M. 1 boy, 3 girls. Black-smith and Farmer.

TRUDELLE, Jean Baptiste—34. Nil. M. 4 boys, 1 girl. Farmer and Joiner.

TURCOT, Louis—36. RW. M. 5 boys, 1 girl. Farmer.

Of the foregoing, all but two are listed as Roman Catholic (and one Methodist, one, no religion given). All were charged with "treason" and sentenced to transportation for life.

The Mary G. Milne thesis provides the following further data on the prisoners from three transport ships:

	Average Age	Range
Anglo-Canadians	34	18-65
Americans	28	19-57
French Canadians	38.1	20-54

Occupations:

Sample from Anglo-Canadians and Americans on the *Canton* and *Marquis of Hastings:*

> 3 Plowmen-farmers; 2 wheelwrights; 1 law student; 1 circular-sawyer-laborer; 1 carpenter millwright; 1 merchant-clerk; 1 house carpenter; 1 gardener.

Sample from French-Canadians on H.M.S. *Buffalo:*

> 30 yeomen (farmers); 2 joiners; 1 baker; 2 "gentlemen"; 2 blacksmiths; 6 laborers; 1 miller; 1 wheelwright; 3 bailiffs; 1 merchant; 1 carriage-maker; 1 clerk; 2 inn-keepers; 1 notary; 2 carpenters; 1 medical practitioner. One of the 30 yeomen also doubled as a "Veterinary Surgeon."

Offenses for which convicted:

Americans:	Piratical invasion of U.C.:	79
	High Treason:	7
Anglo-Canadians:	Murder	3
	High Treason:	7
	Desertion:	46
	Highway Robbery:	1
French-Canadians:	High Treason:	56
	Highway Robbery:	2

(M. G. Milne, *Appendices,* pp. vi-ix)

Campaigns for the release of the transportees resulted in pardons being granted in 1844. Most of those from U.C. and the U.S., and all but four of the 58 from Lower Canada, managed after many hardships to reach their native land.

III
HINCKS ON INDUSTRIALIZATION
(P. 238)

In 1846 Hincks deprecated the effort to develop "infant and embryo manufactures" . . . "We hope it will not encourage the absurd idea that it would be at this time advantageous to the country to attempt to manufacture our own broadcloths and the finer fabrics . . . The supposition that we might jump all at once from an agricultural people just emerging from the forest to the perfection of European manufactures is preposterous in the extreme, and can only find a place in the wildest imagination."

(Address to Provincial Agricultural Association: Middleton: *History of Ontario,* i, 634-5.)

IV
A BANQUET FOR LORD ELGIN
(P. 290)

On the matter of compensation to the seigneurs, whose right to such reward for a long-overdue surrender of feudal benefits was being hotly contested, *La Minerve* (5 janvier, 1854) cited a British view, from *Wilmer and Smith's Times:* "It is a most embarrassing matter, and is made doubly so by the attitude taken by the habitants, who will not hear of a compromise. Nothing will satisfy them except the entire destruction of the existing system of tenure: a step which, however advantageous it be to themselves, would cause a serious injury to the landowners, whose privileges, whatever one may think of them morally, are at least legally guaranteed . . ." The paper voices regret that the issue was not settled in Durham's time; but now that Responsible Government has been granted them, the moral onus is on the colonists to resolve the issue, "without the intervention of the Imperial Authorities."

This scarcely veiled threat sounded a note that was to be taken up afresh a few months later, by none other than Lord Elgin himself. *La Minerve* (25 avril) reports on a

"BANQUET AT THE 'LONDON TAVERN' IN HONOR OF LORD ELGIN, GOVERNOR-GENERAL OF CANADA"

The guest of honor, in his speech, noted the presence of an array of dignitaries (Earl Grey, Gladstone, the Duke of Newcastle, Lord John Russell in the chair) and of "so many distinguished merchants of the City of London" having connections in Canada. After praising Russell's "sage and beneficent administration of colonial affairs," Elgin went on:

> It has been said that the new system of Responsible Government which has happily replaced the former system, assures the ascendancy of extreme views; but I am led to believe the opposite; and if the new system remains in force, there will reign among colonial politicians a greater moderation than hitherto . . . (I have given my Canadian friends to) understand that, were they not to display toward the rights of property the scrupulous respect displayed in England, they would bring ruin upon their country . . .

The warning was not misunderstood. In Montreal the radical *Le Pays* is quoted to the effect that the banquet was a "demonstration" got up by "enemies of Canada" and as revealing "the cupidity of English capitalists who are creditors of Canada."

Elgin, acting for the men of property, saw to it that efforts to block payment of compensation to the seigneurs were set at naught; and in the Speech from the Throne the following September, he reminded the Assembly that in dealing with the seigneurial tenure they should not forget that "security of property is an indispensable condition of material progress," and that they should therefore be mindful of "those who invest their capital in the country."

[*The foregoing quotations are re-translated from the French: in* La Minerve, *5 jan., 25 avr., 9 sept., 1854. I am indebted for these references to Professor Georges Baillargeon, who kindly made them available to me following the presentation of his paper on the role of popular pressure in abolishing seigneurial tenure, at the Institut d'Histoire de l'Amérique française, annual meeting, May, 1967, in Montreal.*]

V
LORD METCALFE ON WAGE-LABOR
(P. 330 fn.)

The Earl of Metcalfe, on the social implications of the freeing of the slaves in Jamaica in 1833:

". . . New relations (were) thus established between the proprietary and the working classes . . .

"So many thousands of machines had suddenly been converted into men . . . they who yesterday had been only property, today became . . . proprietors of their own labor, free agents to work or not to work.

"Where before there was only one party to the cultivation of the land—the slave-owning proprietors," there now were two: "one party with labor to sell, and another party with labor to buy. A great question then arose regarding the terms on which henceforth this free labor should be bought and sold in the colony.

"Then the great struggle commenced.

"The General Assembly, or Parliament of the island, being mainly composed of planters, or their agents, was necessarily more inclined to regard the rights of property than the rights of labor."

> J. W. Kaye: *Life and Correspondence of Lord Metcalfe* (1858), i, 243, 250.

VI
CONFEDERACY AND FEDERATION
(P. 371)

According to common usage, a *Confederacy* is a league or union of states in which the constituent bodies delegate certain powers to a central government of limited sovereignty. In a federal state, the central government is fully sovereign, while the component bodies possess limited or at most co-ordinate authority in certain fields. Cf. W. P. M. Kennedy: *The Constitution of Canada* (1922), pp. 400-5. Kennedy suggests that in the 1865 Confederation debates the terms " 'federation' and 'confederation' seem to have been deliberately used to confuse the issue. It is clear that there was a certain amount of camouflage. . . . It is not without significance that in the title of the official debates the word 'confederation' appears. The object was to carry the proposals" (pp. 403-4).

VII
POPULATION, 1871
OCCUPATIONS; ORIGINS
(Pp. 268, 420)

Of the 3,371,000 people in British North America at the time of Confederation, four-fifths were classified as rural, with only 12 per cent of the total living in urban centres with a population of 5,000 or more. The proportional division by occupations (1871) was as follows:

Farming, lumbering and fishing	51%
Manufacturing and handicrafts	13%
Construction and unskilled work	18%
Trade, transportation, government, education, finance, professions, personal and all other services	18%
	100%

The majority of Canadians still made their living from the extractive industries. But a dynamic factor of economic growth was evident in the increase in those listed as the "industrial class," whose percentage of the "gainfully occupied" rose from 16 to 21, between 1851 and 1871, and numerically as follows:

1851	71,222	(excl. Maritimes)
1861	144,736	" "
1871	212,808	

An appreciation of the stage reached by modern factory production necessitates some reclassification of the census figures and the elimination as far as possible of the older local industry and handicraft elements. This is shown here in summary form:

		No. of employed	Per cent
Shop crafts and local services		23,200	12
Initial processing of raw materials (mainly flour and saw milling)		83,300	43
Other (mainly modern) manufactures:			
boots and shoes	18,719		
clothing	17,123		
metal working	13,598		
carriage making	4,849		
wool textiles	4,464		
furniture	4,366		
saddle & harness making	2,667		
tobacco working	2,216		
all others	18,998	87,000	45
Total manufacturing:		193,500	100

In Upper Canada and in Montreal particularly, manufacturing had developed considerably beyond the simple flour, lumber, woollen mill and distillery stage.

While the number of gainfully occupied as a whole increased 1.7 times, the number of foundry-workers increased over four times, the number of machinists 5.6 times. On the other hand, the proportion listed as "laborers" diminished from 31.6% to 12.5% of the gainfully occupied. These changes reflect the changeover from a stage where the largest number of workers were employed at canal and railroad-building, to one at which factory industry was coming to occupy a significant place in the economy and politics of the country.

(Sources: *Census of 1871*, vol. v; *Report*, Royal Commission on Dominion-Provincial Relations, 1940, Book I, p. 22, and Appendix ii, pp. 20-27; and F. A. Angers and Patrick Allen: "Evolution de la Structure des Emplois au Canada," *Actualité Economique*, xxix, p. 80.)

National origins of the population of the four original provinces of Canada are given as follows in the 1871 census:

British:	2,110,502
English	706,369
Irish	846,414
Scottish	549,946
Other	7,773
French	1,082,940
European:	
German	202,991
Italian	1,035
Jewish	125
Netherlands	29,662
Russian	607
Scandinavian	1,623
Other	3,791
Indian & Eskimo	23,037
Negro	21,496
Not stated	7,561
Total	3,485,761

(Urquhart and Buckley: *Historical Statistics of Canada* (1965), pp. 6, 18.)

Note: Until quite recently the Canadian Census designated as "racial origins" what are in fact national origins. The totally unscientific use of the term "race" (as in the "founding races" of the terms of reference of the Commission on Bilingualism and Biculturalism) fosters chauvinism. Respectable Anglo-Canadian historians even today persist in this misuse of the term; a related practice being to rebut advocacy of the right of national self-determination by qualifying it as "racial nationalism."

VIII
AN EARLY SUPPORTER
OF MARX IN CANADA
(P. 421)

It is remarkable that the *Ontario Workman* of 1872 should publish an excerpt from *Das Kapital,* the first English translation of which appeared only in 1886. Pending further research, my surmise is that the person responsible for the excerpt appearing was Mark Szalatnay, secretary of the Toronto cigarmakers' local union.

In his booklet, *We are Canadians* (pp. 57-61), the late Istvan Szoke, drawing on research by the Hungarian historian Dezso Lang, provided the following information about this remarkable man:

A revolutionary student in Budapest in the 1830s, Szalatnay was imprisoned for four years by the Hapsburg authorities. During the 1848-49 Revolution he served under Kossuth as a second lieutenant. Following the defeat he went to England, made contact with the Chartists, and was for six years the secretary of the miners' union of South Wales, participating in some thirty strikes and suffering numerous arrests. After an unsuccessful effort to win trade union endorsation of the *Communist Manifesto* he was deported from England in 1855. Coming to the United States, he joined the cigarmakers' union in Baltimore, which was led by his comrade-in-arms of 1848, Tasszilo Mariassy. Wounded in an anti-slavery protest demonstration, Szalatnay moved to Montreal with Mariassy and a group of cigarmakers in 1864. They helped organize a union local there, and another in Toronto in 1869. Following a strike in Toronto (reported in the *Ontario Workman,* Oct. 10, 1872), Szalatnay was sentenced to four months' imprisonment and later deported to the U.S. In 1875 Mark Szalatnay was shot and killed by the Los Angeles police during a bakery workers' strike. In 1855 he had married Mary Fergusson, a leading fighter for women's rights, who for twenty years shared with him a life of struggle for workers' rights and socialism.

Reference Notes

Abbreviations:

BALPQ: Bibliothèque de l'Assemblée Législative de la Province
     de Québec
BRH: *Bulletin de Recherches Historiques*
CHA: Canadian Historical Association
CHR: *Canadian Historical Review*
CJEPS: *Canadian Journal of Economics and Political Science*
NYDT: *New York Daily Tribune* (1850s)
OHS: Ontario Historical Society
PAC: Public Archives of Canada
RAPQ: *Rapport de l'Archiviste de la Province de Québec*
RHAF: *Revue d'Histoire de l'Amérique française*
RSC: Royal Society of Canada

Page Line

PROLOGUE

13 24 *Documents Relating to the Constitutional History of Canada* 1719-1818, ed. A. G. Doughty and D. A. McArthur (1914), 323-5.

16 3 "fragment" theory of Louis Hartz: *The Founding of New Societies* (1964). Defining the colonial "fragment" of an Old World nation as "the partial embodiment of the European ideological complex" Hartz presents a subjective idealist "theory of the development of new societies"; his approach, in his own words, celebrates "the ultimate experience of the American liberal tradition" (3-4).

16 19 Joseph Sansom: *Sketches of Lower Canada* (1817), ix.

17 27 *The Harvesters.* Sickle in hand, in Fortune's field,/ We see them race, the Englishman and the Canadian;/ Active both, and with a common ardor, to acquire what we call wealth;/ But as the Englishman's place is out in front he alone, lucky reaper, can harvest,/ The other humbly following in his footsteps/ Works just as much, yet does no more than glean.

22 27 G. Boyer: *Globe and Mail*, Sept. 14, 1967.

24 34 Jean Chesneaux: "Le Processus de Formation des Nations en Afrique et en Asie." *La Pensée*, No. 119, février 1965, 75-6.

26 8 Bruce Hutchison: *The Struggle for the Border* (1955), ix.

26 K. Marx and F. Engels: *The Holy Family* (1844), 107, 115, 125.

ROOTS OF CONFLICT IN LOWER CANADA

30 13 *Lord Durham's Report on the Affairs of British North America.* Ed. C. P. Lucas. Vol. ii, 24.

22 Ibid., 35-6.

31 2 R. Christie: *History of Lower Canada* (1866), iii, 413.

15 Ibid., iv, 13.

22 Durham, ii, 183, 199. (The latter reference is to Prince Edward Island, but the condition was general.)

28 *Le Canadien*, 11 juillet 1832. cit. E. Dubois: *Le Feu de la Rivière-du-Chêne* (1937), 44-5.

32 6 Christie, iv, 338.

33 in Klaus E. Knorr: *British Colonial Theories 1570-1850* (1944), 271n.

33 7 Brougham, cit. Knorr, 233.

9 Ibid., 305.

14 Ibid., 279.

29 The expression is Charles Buller's.

34 18 E. G. Wakefield: *England and America* (1833), ii, 17ff., 191-2; cit. K. Marx, *Capital*, i, ch. xxxiii, "The Modern Theory of Colonization."

24 Christie, iii, 409-10.

35 11 H. Merivale; cf. Marx, loc. cit.

36 1 Christie, iii, 377.

29 Malte-Brun, *Universal Geography* (1827), iii, 193.

37 23 Joseph Bouchette: *The British Dominions in North America* (1832), i, 199.

29 Ibid., i, 263.

38 3 in G. P. de T. Glazebrook: *A History of Transportation in Canada* (1964), i, 67; and Innis and Lower: *Select Documents in Canadian Economic History* (1783-1885), 140.

22 N. Bosworth: *Hochelaga Depicta* (1839), 179.

39 7 W. J. A. Donald: *The Canadian Iron and Steel Industry* (1915), 44-6.

40 3 in J. B. A. Allaire: *Histoire de la Paroisse de Saint-Denis Sur Richelieu* (1905), 341n, 345-7.

fn. R. L. Séguin: *Le Mouvement insurrectionnel dans la Presqu'ile de Vaudreuil, 1837 - 1838* (1955), 42.

41 10 F. Ouellet: *Histoire économique et sociale du Québec: 1760-1850* (1966), 29.

fn. Ibid., 13.

DEMOCRACY AND SELF-DETERMINATION

42 19 Sir John Simcoe: cit. Aileen Dunham: *Political Unrest in Upper Canada* (1927), 162.

43 1 L. Groulx: *Histoire du Canada français* (1952), iii, 155.

18 Dunham, 41.

21 *Durham's Report*, ii, 79.

44 19 Groulx, 158.

45 22 *Constitutional Documents* (1791-1818), 392.
46 19 Speech to l'Institut Canadien.
47 16 Christie, iii, 174-5.
48 5 Christie, iii, 414.
16 Ibid., 437.
32 Excerpts from the 92 Resolutions: cf. G. Filteau, *Histoire des Patriotes* (1938), i, 160-71; and D. Vaugeois: *L'Union des Deux Canadas: Nouvelle Conquête?* (1962), 225-34.
50 15 *Le Canadien,* 9 Nov. 1832: in E. Dubois: *Le Feu de la Rivière du Chêne,* 42-3.
25 Christie, iii, 337.
30 Filteau, i, 169.
51 28 M. Gibbon: *The Canadian Mosaic* (1938), 399-400.
52 24 Dubois, 72.
53 15 Filteau, i, 192.
54 8 Ibid., 177-8.
55 9 Dubois, 100-1.
21 Christie, iv, 397.
56 25 Dubois, 261-3.
58 16 O. D. Skelton: *Life and Times of A. T. Galt,* 121.
27 L. Groulx: *Histoire…* iii, 211.
60 15 *The Vindicator,* May 26, 1837.
fn. F. Létourneau: *Histoire de l'Agriculture* (1950), 106.
61 fn. A richly-documented study of early working-class economic and political action is C. Lipton: *Trade Union Movement of Canada: 1827-1959,* (1967), ch. i-ii.
62 12 Filteau, ii, 85.
29 L. Groulx: *L'Indépendance du Canada* (1949), 28.
63 4 Filteau, ii, 85.
13 Ibid., 86.
63 23 W. Lovett: *Life and Struggles* (1920), 109ff.
64 18 *Vindicator,* May 16, 1837: cit. C. Vance, *The Marxist Quarterly,* no. 12, pp. 34-5.
21 Ibid., *Vindicator,* May 26, 1837.
65 3 Ibid.
9 Christie, v, 59-66.
26 Dubois, 258-9.
66 18 Ibid., 311-7.
67 3 cit. T. S. Hudon, s.j. in *Le Devoir,* 1937.
68 10 Filteau, ii, 182.
31 Despatch of August 9, 1838: in *Report,* Vol. iii, 323.

A NATIONAL-DEMOCRATIC REVOLUTION

69-84 The account in the main follows that given in my *1837,* the chief sources being:
F.-X. Garneau: *Histoire du Canada* (5e édition, 1920), livre xvi, ch. ii.
L. J. Papineau: *Histoire de l'Insurrection* (1839).
L. O. David: *Les Patriotes de 1837-1838* (1884), pp. 11-71.
Christie, op. cit., vols. iii-iv, ch. xxxix-xl.
M. Globenski: *La Rébellion . . . à St. Eustache* (1883).
A. Fauteux: *Patriotes de 1837-1838* (1950).
G. Filteau, op. cit., t. iii.
E. Dubois, op. cit.

W. Nelson: *Wolfred Nelson et son Temps* (1946).
R.-L. Séguin, op. cit.
Catharine Vance: articles in *The Marxist Quarterly*, nos. 3 and 12.
Newspapers: *Le Canadien, La Minerve, Vindicator*.

83 19 C. Gagnon: "Les Classes sociales au Québec et l'Insurrection de 1837-38"; also Gilles Bourque et Luc Racine: "Histoire et Idéologie": *Parti pris*, vol. 4, nos. 9-12, 5-6.

LAND, LIBERTY — AND CAPITAL

85 17 G. Myers: *History of Canadian Wealth* (1914), 84-5.

86 1 F. Landon: *Western Ontario and The American Frontier* (1941), 155.
   6 G. Myers, 82n.
  20 Report of a House of Commons Select Committee: cit. Durham, ii, 204n, 220.
  31 W. R. Riddell: *Robert (Fleming) Gourlay* (1916), 79.

87 3 Ibid., 10-11.
  12 R. Gourlay: *Statistical Account of Upper Canada* (1822), i, 274.
  20 Ibid., 280, 334, 362.
88 20 Riddell, 24.
90 3 O. D. Skelton, *A. T. Galt*, 20, 27-8.
  20 *Seventh Report from the Committee of Grievances* (1835) Appendix, 27; cf. W. Kilbourn: *The Firebrand* (1956), 135.

91 3 *Colonial Advocate*.
  24 C. Lindsey: *Life and Times of W. L. Mackenzie* (1862), i, 40-1.
92 21 G. Myers, 69-70.
  25 Durham, ii, 148.
93 1 W. L. Mackenzie: *Sketches . . .* (1833), 408-9.
  20 E. C. Guillet: *The Lives and Times of the Patriots* (1938), 8.
  26 Ibid.
94 20 *Loyalist Narratives from Upper Canada* (Champlain Society), 125.
95 11 Innis and Lower, 46, 49.
  21 A. Haydon: *Pioneer Sketches in The District of Bathurst* (1925), 92.
96 6 Ibid., 104.
  26 W. L. Mackenzie, *Sketches . . .* : in H. Scadding: *Toronto of Old* (1873), 242.
96 31 K. Marx: *Capital*, i, ch. xiv: "Division of Labor and Manufacture."
97 13 *Colonial Advocate*, June 3, 1824.
  22 Ibid.
98 5 *Colonial Advocate*, Dec. 22, 1825.
  16 Scadding, 204.
  33 M. Q. Innis: *Economic History of Canada* (1935), 161; Innis & Lower, 60, 296-7.
99 8 Lindsey, ii, 55.
  17 W. Riddell in OHS, xxiv, 475.
  28 Sydney Smith on the day of the Peterloo Massacre (1819): in C. R. Fay: *Life and Labour in the 19th Century* (1920), 26.
100 1 Haydon, 84.

6   Ibid., 10.
30   Ibid., 132.
101 18   Durham, ii, 243-4.
102 16   Haydon, 118-9.
103 17   Rev. J. Morrison (Sarnia): "The Toon O'Maxwell — an Owen Settlement in Lambton Cty., Ont." OHS Papers & Records xvii (1914).
27   Rev. Peter Jones: *Life and Journals of Kah-ke-wa-que-na-by* (1860), 200.
104 8   *Canada and Its Provinces*, ix, 292-3.
24   E. C. Guillet: *Cobourg: 1798-1948*, 173.
106 1   Christie, i, 31.
15   Ibid.
33   *Colonial Advocate*, May 28, 1824.
107 16   Lindsey, ii, 364.
27   Landon, 198.
35   Lindsey, ii, 366.

"SOME CHANGE IN OUR CIRCUMSTANCES"

110 1   Landon, 147; Scadding, 107.
14   Lindsey, ii, 346.
111 8   Margaret Fairley: *Selected Writings of W. L. Mackenzie: 1824 - 1837* (1960), 64-89; also, in *New Frontiers*, Spring issue, 1953.
112 16   J. S. Moir: *Church and State in Canada* (1967), 180-1.
113 28   *Colonial Advocate*, vol. i, no. 4.
114 26   J. C. Dent: *The Story of the Upper Canadian Rebellion* (1885), i, 268ff, 280.
115 20   *Colonial Advocate*, May 22, 1834.

26   *Christian Guardian*, June 4, 1834; in G. W. Brown: *Canada in the Making* (1953), 59.
116 5   Lindsey, i, 319.
27   *Seventh Report on Grievances*.
30   Ibid.
117 11   Guillet, 6.
27   Ibid., 270: Lindsey Papers.
31   *Report*, ii, 161.
119 1   Lindsey, ii, 15ff; 334-44.
11   Ibid., 341-2.
30   Ibid., 19.
120 3   Ibid., fn.
26   Ibid., 23-4.

THE RISING IN
UPPER CANADA

121-33   The account of the rising is based on Mackenzie's *Narrative* and those of Lindsey, Dent, Christie; with some reference to the recent studies by E. C. Guillet, S. D. Clark, W. Kilbourn and G. Craig.
121 15   F. Bond Head: *Narrative*, 329.
122 1   Mackenzie's *Narrative*.
123 7   G. H. Needler: *Colonel Anthony Van Egmond* (1956), 43.
127 7   Dent, i, 278.
23   Lindsey papers: Guillet, 270.
128 18   Mary Holmes: in *New Frontiers*, Summer 1954; from *Pontiac Herald*, June 12, 1838: in Lindsey Papers, Ontario Provincial Archives.
32   Letter of John Ryerson, in C. B. Sissons: *Egerton Ryerson*, i, 448.
130 34   Guillet, 250-6; Lindsey,

373-400. The figures given are those of Guillet, p. 251.

131 15 F. Landon, 171, 167.
132 fn Dent, ii, 295.

SELF-GOVERNMENT AND NATIONAL RIGHTS

139 19 Russell's argument is contained in his despatch of Oct. 15, 1839; H. E. Egerton and W. L. Grant: *Canadian Constitutional Development*, 267.

28 Lewis: in R. Langstone, *Responsible Government* (1927), 109n.

35 J. W. Kaye: *Life and Correspondence of Lord Metcalfe* (1858), ii. 236.

141 22 *Documents of the Canadian Constitution*: ed. W. Houston (1891), 162-3.

142 5 J. L. Morison: *British Supremacy and Canadian Self-Government* (1919), 100.

8 Letter of Nov. 20, 1839: in Egerton & Grant, 277-8.

20 Morison, 20-1.

34 Dec. 12, 1839; Egerton & Grant, 279-80.

143 22 Turcotte: *Le Canada Sous l'Union* (1871), i, 106.

28 A. Gérin-Lajoie: *Dix Ans au Canada* (1888), 87.

144 10 S. Leacock: *Baldwin, Lafontaine, Hincks* (1907), 70.

13 A. Gérin-Lajoie, 60.

28 R. Longley: *Sir Francis Hincks* (1943), 48.

145 28 Leacock, 230, 240.

146 5 *Canada and Its Provinces*, x, 524.

18 Chester Martin: *Foundations of Canadian Nationhood* (1955), 165.

147 7 Leacock, 71.

17 Martin, 162.

21 M. Wade: *The French Canadians* (1955), 229.

25 L. Groulx: *L'Indépendance du Canada* (1949), 111; *Histoire du Canada français* (1952), iii, 290.

148 16 Gérin-Lajoie, 77.

24 Morison, 102, 121-3.

149 26 Longley, 221-2; W. P. M. Kennedy: *The Constitution of Canada* (1931), 202-3.

150 5 Leacock, 108.

28 Ibid., 140-1.

151 1 Longley, 135.

ACHIEVEMENT IN 1848

153 13 Kaye: *Metcalfe*, ii, 315.

17 Ibid., 370-1.

27 Despatch of May 12, 1943: in Leacock, 163.

30 Kaye, 333.

34 Ibid., 371n.

154 25 Leacock, 238.

32 Ibid., 245.

155 10 Kaye, 337.

25 Ibid., 390-1.

156 6 Ibid., 477.

19 Ibid., 373-4.

21 Letter of May 13, 1845: Gérin-Lajoie, 298-9.

157 18 Gérin-Lajoie, 371.

22 Ibid., 549.

32 Ibid., 297-8.

159 16 Speech in 1848: Gérin-Lajoie, 536.

160 1 Ibid., 330, 334.

13 Ibid., 528.

21 Kaye, 337n.

26 Gérin-Lajoie, 444ff.
162 25 Egerton & Grant, 311.
163 18 F. Engels: Preface to Eng. edition, *Condition of the Working Class in England.*
27 Langstone, 155n.
165 3 April 14, 1848: *Elgin-Grey Papers,* i, 138.
7 March 27, 1848: Ibid., 139.
17 Ibid.
166 9 Elgin to Grey, Dec. 18, 1854; Langstone, 165.
11 Ibid., 157.
19 Egerton & Grant, 297.
27 Ibid., 300-1.
167 3 Martin, 197.
32 Langstone, 165.
168 2 Ibid., 166.
9 Ibid., 165.
15 T. Walrond: *Elgin, Letters and Journals,* 38; Langstone, 165n.
29 Langstone, 166.

MASTERS AND MEN

170 1 *Le Fantasque,* Dec. 10, 1840. Public Archives of Canada.
171 26 F. Ouellet: *Histoire . . .,* 501.
173 22 *Canada and Its Provinces,* ix, 524.
174 13 *Poverty of Philosophy* (1963 ed.), 109.
176 20 *Le Canadien,* 3 avril, 1844. Bibliothèque de l'Assemblée Législative, Québec.
177 1 Ibid.
9 Innis & Lower, 299-300.
28 Ibid., 304.
178 12 Ibid., 302-3.
180 15 Marx, NYDT March 22, 1853; in *Marx & Engels on Britain,* 372.
28 In H. I. Cowan: *British Emigration to British North America* (1961), 211.
181 7 Haydon: *Pioneer Sketches,* 250.
15 Ibid., 246-7.
25 H. C. Pentland: "The Lachine Strike," CHR, Sept. 1948; the account which follows is based on this paper, and on supplementary material in H. C. Pentland: "Labor and the Development of Industrial Capital in Canada" (U. of T. Ph.D. Thesis, 1960) pp. 407ff.
181 31 Ibid., 409-10.
184 3 Pentland, 433.
32 D. Héroux: *Le Travailleur Québecois et le Syndicalisme* (Cahiers de Sainte-Marie), 9.
185 17 *Le Fantasque,* 1840: PAC.
23 *People's Magazine and Workingman's Guardian:* PAC.
29 Letter to Ermatinger: PAC.
187 1 E. Parent: in *La Littérature canadienne* (1863), pp. 37-75.
9 Ibid., 41, 50.
24 Ibid., 123-5.
188 17 *Le Canadien,* 1848: in BASLQ.
190 30 Ibid. See text on illustrations, between pp. 272 and 273.

MARITIME IDENTITY AND DEMOCRACY

192 22 T. Raddall: *Halifax, Warden of the North,* 62.
26 Ibid., 91.

193 5 B. Murdoch: *History of Nova Scotia*, iii, 289.

20 I am indebted to Mr. J. K. Bell, of Halifax, for obtaining the text of the Act of 1816.

194 13 MacNutt, 192.

23 CHR, xix: J. Martell, "The Press of the Maritime Provinces in the 1830s."

27 J. A. Roy: *Joseph Howe*, 49.

195 19 Editorial, "My Country": *The Acadian*, March 16, 1827.

28 J. A. Chisholm: *The Speeches and Public Letters of Joseph Howe* (1909), i, 8-9, 12.

196 18 Ibid., 72.

197 9 Ibid., 17-8.

198 12 C. Martin: *Foundations . . .*, 131.

23 *Nova Scotian*, 22 April, 1830.

199 3 Roy, 58.

8 Chisholm, 65.

14 Ibid., 66.

21 Ibid.

33 J. H. Roy: *Joseph Howe* (1935), 118.

200 10 *Nova Scotian*, Dec. 21, 1837.

23 Chisholm, 84.

201 7 Ibid., 85.

18 Ibid., 609.

30 Egerton & Grant, 301.

202 10 W. S. MacNutt: *The Atlantic Provinces* (1965), 188.

203 19 Ibid., 210-11.

25 Ibid.

30 Ibid., 231.

204 7 Ibid., 211.

28 F. W. Bolger: *Prince Edward Island and Confederation 1863-1873* (1964), 8-9.

205 1 Ibid., 199, 203.

13 Ibid., 215.

30 R. Bonnycastle: *Newfoundland*, (1842) ii, 9-10.

206 3 Ibid.

12 MacNutt, 74.

28 D. W. Prowse: *History of Newfoundland* (1895), 418-9.

207 7 Ibid., 401.

31 Ibid., 405.

208 3 Ibid.

12 H. A. Innis: *The Cod Fishery* (1954), 388, 389.

29 Bonnycastle, ii, 161-2.

209 5 Ibid., 167.

13 Ibid., 166-7.

210 21 Prowse, 398-9.

211 6 MacNutt, 206.

15 Prowse, 428.

30 Ibid., 456-7.

212 4 H. A. Innis: *Essays in Canadian Economic History* (1956), 38.

213 4 MacNutt, 218.

6 D. G. Creighton: *British North America at Confederation* (1940), 25. (Appendix 2 of Report of Royal Commission on Dominion Provincial Relations.)

18 MacNutt, 216.

26 J. F. W. Johnston: *Notes on N. America*, i, 35-6.

214 19 Ibid., 408.

215 7 Creighton, 27.

21 Ibid.

24 Ibid., 24.

216 1 C. J. S. Warrington and R. V. Nichols: *A History of Chemistry in Canada* (1949), 27.

4 Ibid., 134.

20 S. J. McLean in *Canada and Its Provinces*, x, 388.

216-18 The account of railway promotion is based on G. Myers, op. cit., 163-4; and the chapter cited above, by S. J. McLean, "National Highways Overland."

U.S. EXPANSIONISTS

221 23 Abraham Gesner: *The Industrial Resources of Nova Scotia* (1849), 255-7.

222 25 A. R. M. Lower: *The North American Assault on the Canadian Forest* (1938), 99, 101.

30 Innis & Lower, 253-4.

8 Ibid., 254.

223 31 H. Keenleyside: *Canada and the United States* (1927), 180.

224 10 C. A. & M. Beard: *Rise of American Civilization* (1936), i, 556.

225 5 A. B. Corey: *Crisis of 1830-42 in Canadian-American Relations* (1941), 115.

24 F. Merk: *Manifest Destiny and Mission in American History* (1963), 69-70.

226 4 Corey, 16.

16 W. A. Williams: *The Contours of American History* (1966), 272.

29 Merck, 52.

227 1 Ibid., 50

8 Ibid., 32.

228 5 A. R. Schoyen: *The Chartist Challenge* (1958), 138-9.

15 *Northern Star*, March 7, 1846.

231 18 N. A. Graebner: *Empire on the Pacific* (1955), 224.

232 20 C. D. Allin & G. M. Jones: *Annexation, Preferential Trade and Reciprocity*, 269.

30 Elgin - Grey Papers, i, 256.

233 31 Leacock: *Baldwin, Lafontaine, Hincks*, 315.

234 15 Allin & Jones, 109-15.

235 19 Ibid., 131.

28 L. B. Shippee: *Canadian-American Relations 1849-74* (1939), 21.

236 9 Ibid., 12.

237 9 Ibid., 76.

20 Longley: *Hincks*, 262.

238 20 Hincks: cf. *Appendix*.

239 30 Longley, 441.

240 6 *Canada and Its Provinces*, ix, 374.

34 Lower, op. cit., 139.

241 1 Ibid., and 119-21.

14 Ibid., 146.

28 Shippee, 42.

34 Ibid., 48.

242 11 E. Watkin: *Canada and the States*, 375.

20 D. C. Masters: *The Reciprocity Treaty of 1854* (1937), 106.

"MAKE THE RAILROADS FIRST!"

Work on this and the following chapter was a project of members of the economics group of the Marxist Study Centre, to whom I am indebted for their assistance.

Main sources for this chapter have been:

Myers: *History of Canadian Wealth*, ch. x, xi

(pp. 150-217); Skelton: *The Railway Builders* (1920); Glazebrook: *History of Transportation in Canada* (1938); W. J. Wilgus: *Railway Interrelations of the U.S. and Canada* (1937), S. J. McLean in *Canada and Its Provinces*, x.

245 27 D. C. Masters: *The Rise of Toronto* (1947), 16.

246 20 J. S. McLean, op. cit., 392.

251 9 H. Y. Hind & T. C. Keefer: *Eighty Years Progress in British North America (The Dominion of Canada)* (1868), 222-3.

22 Myers, 183-6.

253 11 Marx: in N.Y. *Daily Tribune*, Aug. 8, 1853; in *K. Marx and F. Engels On Britain* (1955), 389.

28 Marx-Engels: *Selected Correspondence* (1936), 358-9.

254 3 Ibid.

32 Ibid., 359.

255 9 Myers, 166.

fn. Innis: *Essays in Canadian Economic History* (1956), 12.

256 23 *Speeches and Letters of Joseph Howe*, ii, 199.

PRELUDE TO AN
INDUSTRIAL REVOLUTION

258 20 A. R. M. Lower: *North American Assault on the Canadian Forest*, 43, 99. About 1840 or '50 "... the forest industries began to assume a capitalistic form . . .": 76. The timber and lumber trade "responded to demands of British urbanization in the first half of the 19th century, U.S. in the second, and domestic market and Pacific countries in the 20th." (Ibid.: H. A. Innis, Editor's Preface, xvi.)

259 9 Ibid., 46-7.

17 H. B. Small: *Products and Manufactures of the New Dominion* (1868), 50-1.

22 D. G. Creighton: *British N. America at Confederation* (1940), 15. This Appendix to the Rowell-Sirois Report is the outstanding work on the economic background of Confederation.

260 2 J. Croil: *Dundas* (1861), 244.

7 Small, 129; Lower, 112: The "second period of immigration of American capital began with migration to Bytown" (1851).

18 Scadding: *Toronto of Old,* 391.

25 Hamilton *Spectator*: Saga of a City (1938), 123.

32 *Railway & Locomotive Historical Society,* Bulletin no. 51, p. 43n.

261 5 W. J. A. Donald: *Canadian Iron and Steel Industry* (1915), 61.

25 S. P. Day: *English America* (1864), 180.

262 14 Ibid., 186.

26 Ibid., 191.

263 2 Ibid., 179.

10 "Rise, Progress & Pres-

ent Position of Toronto" *Globe*, Dec. 13, 1856.
29 Small, 148.
264 2 Day, i, 180-1.
11 W. Kilbourn: *The Elements Combined* (1960) 21-2.
24 Day, Ibid., 187.
256 1 C. M. Johnston: *Head of the Lake* (1958), 202, 323.
9 Small, 149.
18 Creighton, 19.
27 Small, 146.
266 3 Innis & Lower, 596; J. Spelt: *Urban Development in South Central Ontario* (1955), 117; Small, 139.
11 Middleton, J. E., and Landon, F.: *The Province of Ontario* (1927), i, 639.
18 H. Marshall & others: *Canadian-American Industry* (1936), 11.
31 After an attempt to mine iron ore near Hull in 1857, a new works was started by "local capitalists" in 1866; ore was "shipped to Cleveland . . . Some of the iron so produced was purchased by the Car & Wheel Co. of Toronto." *Canadian Illustrated News*, Jan. 20, 1872.
267 13 Creighton, 18.
20 *Emigration to Canada . . . Geographical Position, etc.* (1861), 11.
24 *Canada at the Universal Exhibition of 1855* (J. C. Taché, 1856), 449-50.
29 Kilbourn, 9-10.
269 1 Cf. *Appendix*.
271 30 Masters, *Toronto*, 117.

273 11 **Myers, 166-7.**
274 18 Hind & Keefer, 216-7.
29 Cf. Note to p. 218.
275 26 Skelton, *Galt*, 132-3.
276 3 Ibid., 137, 143.
13 Ibid., 52.
24 Masters, 153.
277 15 Ibid., 73.
278 21 Letter of Jacob DeWitt, president of the Banque du Peuple, to W. L. Mackenzie, July 26, 1858: "Home Manufactures the True Policy for Canada," in Isaac Buchanan: *Industry of Canada*, ed. H. J. Morgan (1864), 299 ff.
33 Skelton, *Galt*, 330.
279 14 J. Pope: *Memoirs of J. A. Macdonald*, 221.
26 R. G. Trotter: *Canadian Federation* (1924), 196.
30 J. H. Gray: *Confederation* (1872), 83.
280 3 *Confederation Debates* (1865), 99.

LANDS AND LEARNING

282 4 Cf. Ref. Note to p. 112.
11 Myers, 105.
20 J. S. Moir: *Church and State in Canada*, 244-5.
283 7 C. B. Sissons: *Egerton Ryerson*, ii, 101.
30 J. H. Putnam: *Egerton Ryerson and Education in Upper Canada* (1912), 167-8.
284 6 Sissons, ii, 188.
10 Robin S. Harris: "Egerton Ryerson": in R. L. McDougall, ed. *Our Living Tradition* (1959), 260.
15 Putnam, 112, 161; Harris, 266.
25 Putnam, 112.

285 10 A. Labarrère-Paule: *Les Instituteurs Laiques au Canada français, 1836-1900* (1965), 7.
19 Ibid., 84.
286 1 Turcotte: *L'Union des Canadas* (1871), ii, 279.
21 Labarrère-Paule, 457.
287 29 A. DeCelles: *LaFontaine et son Temps* (1907), 154.
288 6 Georges Baillargeon: "La Tenure seigneuriale a-t-elle été abolie par suite des Plaintes des Censitaires?" R H A F, juin 1967, 65-6; Jacques Boucher: "Aspects économiques de la Tenure seigneuriale" in P. Salomon, *Recherches d'Histoire économique* (1964), 177.
289 1 Boucher, 179.
3 Ibid.
fn. Baillargeon, 80.
290 1 T. Chapais: *Cours d'Histoire*, vi, 169-70.
10 DeCelles, 153.
15 Cf. *Appendix*.
291 17 G. I. Quimby: *Indian Life in the Upper Great Lakes* (1960), 147, 157.
31 Ella Cork: *The Worst of the Bargain* (1962), 98.
292 2 Ibid., 96, 95.
13 Ibid., 112.
31 Report of Committee of 1856; in Enemikeese: *The Indian Chief* (1867).
293 17 Peter Jones, op. cit.
24 Cork, 119.
27 Duncan Campbell Scott: "Indian Affairs": *Canada and Its Provinces*, v, 351.

fn. Cork, 92-3.
294 4 Ibid., 121.
22 Enemikeese, 110.
295 1 Ibid.; *The Globe*, July 30, 1863.

THE NATURAL SCIENCES

296 27 H. N. Tory: *History of Science in Canada* (1939), 43.
297 2 Ibid.
10 Ibid.
15 G. F. Stanley: *Introduction* to Lefroy, *Search for the Magnetic Pole*, xiii, xiv, xxii-iv.
29 Ibid.
298 9 Tory, 9.
20 B. J. Harrington: *Life of Sir Wm. Logan* (1883).
32 Ibid., 287.
299 6 Ibid., 288.
18 Tory, 13.
24 Ibid., 15, 16.
28 Logan, 398, 321.
33 Ibid., 235.
300 2 Ibid., 351-2.
24 Gesner, op. cit., 210, 212.
30 Warrington & Nicholls: *History of Chemistry in Canada*, 133-4.
301 6 F. Engels: *Anti-Dühring*, ch. vi-viii, xii-xiii; *Ludwig Feuerbach*, parts ii & iv.
J. D. Bernal: *Science in History* (1957), ch. viii.
302 5 C. Lyell, op. cit., 321.
19 Marx-Engels: *Briefwechsel*, ii, 547.
303 11 *Canada and Its Provinces*, xxv, 526.
23 Hind: *Eighty Years' Progress*, 383.
28 Warrington & Nicholls, 413.

304 4 Ibid., 424.
    12 Ibid., 434.
    18 Tory, 46-7.
    21 Sissons, ii, 96-7.
    27 In 1862 Abbé Léon Provancher published *La Flore canadienne* (2 vols.)—the first Canadian botany text; in 1868 he founded *Le Naturaliste canadien*. G. F. Stanley, ed.: *Pioneers of Canadian Science* (RSC: 1966), 48-9.
    33 Tory, 25.
305 2 Ibid., 48.

"A GREAT COUNTRY . . ."

309 26 W. H. Russell: *Canada: Its Defences, Condition and Resources* (1865), 72.
312 20 J. H. Gray: *Confederation*.
313 6 W. M. Whitelaw: *The Maritimes and Canada Before Confederation* (1934), 75.
314 8 R. G. Trotter: *Canadian Federation* (1924), 5.
    19 *Colonial Advocate*, July 1, 1824; also, May 28; and cf. M. Fairley, op. cit., 291.
    32 Trotter, 8.
315 28 Ibid., 21-2.
316 3 J. P. Merritt: *Biography of W. H. Merritt* (1875), 395.
    7 Ibid., 410.
317 15 *Confederation Debates*, 246.
    34 Shippee, 8.
318 10 A. Morris: *Nova Britania* (1884), 4, 42, 49-51.
319 11 Skelton, *Galt*, 220-1.

320 7 Ibid.
    25 *Confederation Debates*, 6.
    28 Ibid., 64.
321 12 F. Underhill: "Some Aspects of Upper Canadian Radical Opinion . . .": CHA *Report*, 1927.
322 9 Edward W. Watkin: *Canada & the States* (1887), 519.
    14 Ibid., 12, 14ff.: letter of Nov., 1860.
323 21 Ibid., 80ff.
324 21 Trotter, 38.
    33 Whitelaw, 233.
325 17 Trotter, 196.
    29 Whitelaw, 134-5.
    33 Ibid., 133-4.

CANADA AND THE WAR AGAINST SLAVERY

327 21 B. Quarles: *The Negro in the Civil War*, 151.
328 6 A. Mackenzie: *Life & Speeches of George Brown* (1882), 254, 260.
    24 Landon, *Western Ontario . . .* 204.
329 7 A. L. Murray, in *Journal of Negro History*, Apr. 1959.
    12 F. Landon, in *Michigan History Magazine*, V (1921), 364-74.
    24 Ibid.
330 12 Watkin, op. cit., 344.
331 12 Marx-Engels: *The Civil War in the United States* (1937), 24.
    24 Ibid., 81.
332 7 Ibid., 45-6.
    26 Ibid., 280-1.
333 3 Ibid., 47-8.
    18 J. Phelan: *The Ardent Exile*, 193.

23 Shippee, 114.

334 12 J. Horan: *Confederate Agent* (1954), 115.

30 J. Headley: *Confederate Operations in Canada and New York* (1906), 282-3.

335 11 *Globe,* Sept. 21, 1864: Creighton: *John A. Macdonald—the Young Politician* (1952), 369.

17 Horan, 104.

336 6 Shippee, 115.

9 J. P. Smith: "American Republican Leadership and the Movement for the Annexation of Canada in the 1860s": CHA Report (1935), 67.

13 Skelton, *Galt,* 315.

23 Ibid., 349.

337 1 Clinton Gray: *The Montreal Story* (1949), 46-8.

7 Horan, 264-7.

20 Waterloo Historical Society, xxxi, 43-5.

338 5 Marx-Engels, *Civil War . . .,* 284.

339 2 Watkin, 425.

8 Shippee, 192.

12 Ibid., 211.

18 Watkin, 415.

29 Ibid., 425.

340 2 C. Martin, "The United States and Canadian Nationality," CHR Vol. 18, (1937), 6.

6 Watkin, 228-32.

22 C. Sumner: *Works,* xi, 222, in A. K. Weinberg: *Manifest Destiny* (1935), 240-1. Cf. also D. F. Warner: *The Idea of Continental Union* (1960), ch. iii.

28 Landon, RSC Proceedings, 1927, p. 61.

32 Trotter, 138.

341 4 J. Pope: *Correspondence of Sir John Macdonald* (1921), 124-5. Of the "steps to counteract them," Sir John emphasized that one of the first was "to show unmistakably our resolve to build the Pacific Railway . . . It must be taken up by a body of capitalists, and not constructed by the Government directly."

ENGINEERING A FEDERAL UNION

342 5 *Journals of the Legislative Assembly* (1864), 384; Trotter, 64.

343 21 *Confederation Debates,* 251.

344 1 A. Dubuc: "The Decline of Confederation and the New Nationalism," in Peter Russell, ed. *Nationalism in Canada* (1966), 114, 119.

345 4 J. S. Careless: *Brown of the Globe* (1963), ii, 96.

9 P. G. Cornell: *Alignment of Political Groups in Canada 1841-1867* (1962), 50.

18 Careless, op. cit., ii, 244.

346 17 Trotter, 88.

348 10 Gray: *Confederation,* 44-5.

349 12 Ibid., 66.

350 23 Glazebrook: *Short History of Canada* (1950), 97.

351 16 Gray, 382.

3 2 M. O. Hammond: *Confederation and Its Leaders* (1917), 277.

352 9 Chisholm, *Letters &
Speeches,* ii, 463-4.
17 Hammond, 68, 290, 292.
353 12 Tilley to Macdonald,
April 14, 17, 20; cf.
Creighton, *Road to Con-
federation,* 373.
29 Trotter, 130, 139.
355 1 Pope, *Memoirs . . .,*
326-7.
21 J. O. Bureau; in *Con-
federation Debates,* 191.
26 Pope, 242, 616.
30 Ibid., 242.
356 1 Ibid., 294.
17 *Confederation Debates,*
245.

FRENCH CANADA AND THE
TERMS OF UNION

358 7 Terms of reference of
Royal Commission on Bi-
lingualism and Bicultur-
alism (1963).
17 in R. Arès: *Dossier sur
le Pacte fédératif de 1867*
(1967), 135.
360 fn. D. G. Creighton: *Dominion of the North*
(1957), 307.
363 1 Creighton, *Saturday
Night,* Sept. 1966.
22 Cf. pp. 343, 346 above.
364 5 Creighton, *John A. Macdonald,* i, 182-3.
16 *Road to Confederation*
(1964), 145.
30 *Confederation Debates,*
29.
365 29 C. Bonenfant: *The
French Canadians and
the Birth of Confedera-
tion* (CHA, 1966), 12.
366 2 *Confederation Debates,*
6.
31 Ibid., 366.
367 7 Ibid., 837.
368 4 *Le Pays,* 15 fév. 1865; in

Collection Gagnon, Bi-
bliothèque municipale
de Montréal.
369 15 Bonenfant, 4.
26 *Confederation Debates,*
246.
370 14 Creighton, *John A. Macdonald,* 226-7.
19 Ibid.
371 11 Cit. Dorion in Confederation Debates, 263.
15 Creighton, *Road to Confederation,* 165.
372 5 *Saturday Night,* Sept.
1966.
19 Ibid.
20 Bonenfant, 4.
25 Creighton, loc. cit.
373 24 *Brown of the Globe,* ii,
263.
34 Ibid., 145-6.
374 4 Ibid., 146.
33 *Confederation Debates,*
60-1.
375 24 Ibid., 42.
376 33 *Confederation Debates,*
59.
377 23 L. O. David: *Le Canada
sous l'Union,* 294.
27 Ibid., 302.
31 Ibid., 298.
378 2 Bonenfant, 8: "The
French-Canadian voters
of Lower Canada could
not express their views
on the project of Con-
federation before it was
adopted, but the fact re-
mains that a large num-
ber of their representa-
tives in both houses were
opposed to it."
22 *Confederation Debates,*
263-4.

A PEOPLE'S RISING IN
THE NORTH WEST

379 1 "Dernier Mémoire de
         Louis Riel": in Adolphe
         Ouimet: *La Vérité sur
         la Question métisse au
         Nord-Ouest* (1889),
         77-8.
     19 Ibid.
380 21 Dr. Alejandro Lipschutz:
         *El Problema racial en la
         Conquista de America y
         el Mestizaje* (Santiago
         de Chile 1963), 295.
         (Translation of excerpts
         is mine: SBR.) This re-
         markable study of the
         Indian and Métis (or
         Mestizo) question is
         shortly to be published
         in French—and, it is to
         be hoped, eventually in
         English also.
381 7 Ibid., 305.
     fn. Ibid., 34.
382 1 Ouimet, op. cit., 14.
     24 *Manitoba: A History*
         (1967), 117.
     30 Huyshe, op. cit., 3-4.
385 21 G. F. Stanley: *The Birth
         of Western Canada*
         (1960), 73, 418, n.23.
386 7 *Canada and Its Prov-
         inces*, ix, 67.
     15 Ibid., 84.
     27 Morton, *Manitoba*, 119,
         121, 124-5.
387 5 Macdonald to McDou-
         gall, Nov. 27, 1869; in
         Pope, *Memoirs*, 410.
388 1 Huyshe, *Red River Ex-
         pedition*, 242-3.
     31 Pope, *Correspondence*,
         112-3. Letter of Dec. 13.
         Macdonald follows refer-
         ence to an "olive branch"
         with: "We must not
         make any indications of

even thinking of a mili-
tary force until peace-
able means have been
exhausted."
     32 Letter of Feb. 23, 1870.
         Ibid., 128.
389 13 Ibid., 119.
     16 Stanley, 129.
     21 Pope, 128.
390 fn. Morton, *Manitoba*, 141.
391 4 Creighton, *Macdonald*,
         ii, 66.
393 fn. Morton, 148-9.

SELF-GOVERNMENT ON
THE PACIFIC COAST

395 17 F. W. Howay, W. N.
         Sage and H. F. Angus:
         *British Columbia and
         the United States* (1942),
         73.
     24 Ibid., 76.
398 7 N. A. Graebner: *Empire
         on the Pacific* (1955),
         38.
     10 Ibid., 28.
400 4 Margaret Ormsby: *Bri-
         tish Columbia: a History*
         (1958), 127, 115.
     22 Harold Griffin: *British
         Columbia: the People's
         Early Story* (1958), 7,
         19, 44.
     34 Ibid., 45.
401 19 Ibid., 15.
     28 Howay, 183.
402 16 Griffin, 21.
     21 M. Macfie: *Vancouver
         Island and British Co-
         lumbia* (1865), 63.
404 5 Griffin, 24-5.
     25 Ormsby, 170, 160.
405 3 Ibid., 151.
     12 Howay, 6.
     15 Griffin, 27.
     29 Roland Wild: *Amor de
         Cosmos* (1958).
406 8 Ibid., 30.

20 Ibid., 52, 54.
407 3 Macfie, 48.
7 Ibid., 47, 51.
408 16 Wild, 116.
18 Ormsby, 242.
31 Howay, 200-1.
409 28 Griffin, 39.
410 6 Griffin, 40; Wild, 120-1.
18 Wild, 121.

NATION AND CLASS: AFTERMATH AND PROJECTION

413 15 W. A. Foster: *Canada First* (1890), 41.
19 Ibid., 39.
29 Ibid., 37.
414 4 Ibid., 27.
18 Ibid., 3.
35 Ibid., 79.
416 13 Lionel Groulx: *Histoire du Canada français*, iv, 145.
420 24 B. Ratz: "United Front in Toronto—1872": *New Frontier*, I, iii, June, 1936, p. 18.
32 Ibid.
421 10 Ibid., 19.
17 Ibid. Cf. also C. Lipton, *Trade Union Movement . . .*, "The Nine-Hour Movement. 1872," 28-34.
30 See Illustration facing p. 273. Cf. *Appendix*.

POSTSCRIPT—POLEMICAL

424 5 DeCelles, LaFontaine, 161.
26 Marx to P. V. Annenkov, Dec. 28, 1846; in *Selected Correspondence*, 7-8.
425 13 R. Langstone, *Responsible Government*, 125.
17 W. L. Morton: *The Canadian Identity* (1964), 85, 11.
426 11 A. R. M. Lower: *Colony to Nation*, xii, 552.
28 C. B. Macpherson: "The Social Sciences": in Julian Park, ed. *The Culture of Contemporary Canada* (1957), 201.
34 Marx, op. cit., 14.
428 6 Marx, *Capital*, iii (1959), 312. The whole chapter is extremely pertinent to this discussion.
430 28 CJEPS, Nov. 1962, p. 486ff.
432 5 M. Brunet: *La Présence anglaise et les Canadiens*, 233.
25 *Future of Canadian Federalism*, ed. C. B. Macpherson (1965), 27-9, 32-4.
433 14 *Cité Libre*, avril, 1962.
434 5 E. Kedourie: *Nationalism* (1961).
13 Trudeau, in *Future . . . Federalism*, 18-21.
25 Marx to Engels, Nov. 2, 1867: *Selected Correspondence*, 128. Also, in a resolution drafted by Marx in 1869 and adopted by the International Workingmen's Association: ". . . *the essential preliminary condition of the emancipation of the English working class* is the turning of the present *compulsory union*, that is slavery, of Ireland with England, into an *equal and free union*, if that is possible, or *into full separation*, if this is inevitable." In Emile Burns: *Handbook of Marxism* (1935), 197.

Index of Authors

General Index

ADDENDA TO REFERENCE NOTES

Page	Line		
57	29	*La Minerve.* 4 déc. 1834.	Should follow line 30 in col. 1, p. *449*.
140	34 (last line)	*Melbourne Papers*, 444.	Should follow line 20 in col. 2, p. *452*.